T5-DID-018

GOD AND GOVERNMENT IN AN 'AGE OF REASON'

By the same author

John Henry Newman: Reason, Rhetoric and Romanticism
co-editor
(Bristol Press, 1991)

Deity and Domination:
Images of God and the State in the 19th and 20th Centuries
(Routledge, 1989, 1994)

Haiti in Caribbean Context: Ethnicity, Economy & Revolt
(Macmillan, 1985)

From Dessalines to Duvalier:
Race, Colour and National Independence in Haiti
(Cambridge University Press, 1979;
2nd edn Macmillan, 1988; 3rd edn Macmillan, 1995)

The Pluralist State
(Macmillan, 1975; 2nd edn, 1994)

Three Varieties of Pluralism
(Macmillan, 1974)

Church and State in Britain Since 1820
editor
(Routledge, 1967)

GOD AND GOVERNMENT IN AN 'AGE OF REASON'

David Nicholls

London and New York

BR
115
.P7
N39
1995

First published 1995
by Routledge
11 New Fetter Lane, London EC4P 4EE

Simultaneously published in the USA and Canada
by Routledge
29 West 35th Street, New York, NY 10001

©1995 David Nicholls
The moral right of the author has been asserted

Typeset in Palatino by
Michael Mepham, Frome, Somerset
Printed and bound in Great Britain by
TJ Press (Padstow) Ltd, Padstow, Cornwall

All rights reserved. No part of this book may be reprinted
or reproduced or utilized in any form or by any electronic,
mechanical, or other means, now known or hereafter
invented, including photocopying and recording, or in any
information storage or retrieval system, without permission
in writing from the publishers.

British Library Cataloguing in Publication Data
Nicholls, David
God and Government in an 'Age of Reason'
I. Title
261.709033

Library of Congress Cataloguing in Publication Data
A catalogue record for this book has been requested

ISBN 0–415–01173–6

For Percy Coleman and Cosmo Pouncey

CONTENTS

CONTENTS

PREFACE

God's relationship to the universe has often been viewed as a model for a government's relationship to its people. This volume – together with *Deity and Domination: Images of God and the State in the Nineteenth and Twentieth Centuries* (Routledge, 1989 and 1994), and a work which is to follow dealing with the seventeenth century – form three parts of a triptych. Their unity is constituted by their being focused on a very specific analogy: that between human government and divine government. They represent a much-expanded version of the Hulsean Lectures given at Cambridge University in 1985–6.

God is frequently thought of as *governing* the universe. When this language is used, how do people conceive of God's government, and how does it relate to what they believe about human government? Here I suggest an interaction between religious and political discourse – a mutual borrowing of concepts and images – with sometimes the divine and sometimes the political playing the more constructive or dynamic role.

Transformations in language and imagery are connected to changes in economic and political conditions as experienced by given cultural communities. The religious experience of particular groups (charismatic or apocalyptic minorities, for example) will affect the way they envisage God and possibly – by analogy – civil government too. Such groups may then propose (and indeed fight for) modifications in political structures. To represent Milton, Baxter and the puritans of the seventeenth century, or Clarkson, Wilberforce and the abolitionists of the early nineteenth century, as *merely* defending particular class interests is absurd. Few would today deny the importance of their vision of God and his relationship to the world as relevant factors in understanding their respective political crusades.

To speak of a *causal* relationship between religious and political discourse would be to misconceive the situation. It would be a mistake on the one hand to think that if only we will change our religious images this will necessarily result in specifiable changes in political discourse and thereby in political practice. This is sometimes asserted by over-enthusiastic theologians, carried away with the importance and supposed autonomy of their chosen discipline. On the other hand certain sociologists indulge in a reductionism which sees religious language and practice as merely reflections of changes in social and political structures and in the discourse that such changes promote. The relationship is more subtle and at times quite difficult to discern.

Powerful images are frequently borrowed from other disciplines and applied to divine and human government. Images taken from family or social relationships, like 'father', 'bride' or 'shepherd', assume a key role in religious and political discourse. In the eighteenth century mechanical analogies became particularly salient in both political and religious rhetoric; they were in turn used to promote and legitimate favoured political and economic policies and to justify specific ways of conceptualising God's relationship to the universe.

The analogy between divine and civil authority becomes more explicit as we go back in history. In the nineteenth and twentieth centuries we must be prepared to dig below the surface of the current discourse to discover the analogy at work. By the beginning of the eighteenth century, for example in the Leibniz–Clarke correspondence, appeals to the analogy are openly made. I shall argue in the final part of this triptych that many of the political heresies of the modern world may be traced to the theologies of Thomas Hobbes on the one hand and Baruch Spinoza on the other. In one we find a doctrine of God's transcendence without immanence, in the other immanence without transcendence. One tends towards a divine autocracy, the other towards a divine totalitarianism. Both were transposed by their authors into the political realm.

I would like to thank the following for help and advice during the preparation of this volume: John Walsh, Richard Griffiths and Martin Hall, D. O. Thomas and John Stephens, David Lovejoy and Jack Pole, Jennifer Loach, John Maddicott and Paul Slack, John Bramble, Paul Williamson, Philip Wheatley, Bernard Crick, Charles Vereker. Special thanks are due to David Price who read through the complete manuscript and gave me much helpful advice.

Spelling, punctuation, etc., of seventeenth- and eighteenth-century texts have generally been modernised, except in the case of poetry and of book titles. In references to books in the notes to each chapter, abbreviated titles are used. Titles which recur frequently in a chapter are usually abbreviated in accordance with a note at the head of each chapter's endnotes. Publication details of books quoted are in the bibliography, which lists the edition used in the text.

Parts of chapter 9 have appeared as separate articles: 'Addressing God as Ruler', in *The British Journal of Sociology*, lxiv, March 1993, pp. 125ff; 'Trinity and Conflict', in *Theology*, xcvi, no. 769, 1993, pp. 19ff. Also, a version of chapter 2, 'Primates, prelates and prophets' will be appearing in

The Anglican Theological Review 77: 3, 1995. I am grateful to the editors and publishers for permission to include this material.

David Nicholls
Littlemore Vicarage, Oxford
Epiphany 1995

1

INTRODUCTION

'I have often wondered', mused Professor Leonard Hodgson in his remarkable series of lectures on *The Doctrine of the Trinity*, 'whether the *political* experience of the Jews in exile did not influence their theological development more than is commonly recognised'.[1] He went on to point out that the parallel between the idea of the Babylonian monarch, as autocratic and remote, and the idea of Jehovah in later Jewish theology 'is remarkably close'.[2] Unfortunately he resumed the course of his lectures untroubled by this disturbing reflection and made little attempt to relate the development of Trinitarian doctrine to the political context in which it developed. His political 'innocence' has characterised the work of most Anglican theologians of the past century.

Much of the language used about God in the history of religion (Christian and non-Christian) has, in fact, been political in its primary reference. Terms such as might, majesty, dominion and power are ascribed to God, who is said to *rule* the universe, as a monarch; or in the eighteenth century to 'govern' or 'manage' the cosmos as a complex machine. In the first part of this triptych, I examined the relationship between religion and politics by focusing on the analogy between divine and civil government in the nineteenth and twentieth centuries. The analogy has not always been explicitly drawn, particularly in more recent times. As Boyd Hilton has remarked, 'Links between economic and theological thought mostly took place below the surface of consciousness, and usually have to be adduced, with caution, from linguistic parallels'.[3] Here I shall conduct a similar enquiry into the images and concepts used of God and the state in the period from the Glorious Revolution of 1688 to the Reform Bill of 1832, beginning with certain British writers of the late eighteenth and early nineteenth centuries who examined the relationship between economic thinking and Christian theology.

I have continued the method of my earlier book *Deity and Domination* by working 'backwards'. I have, in general, begun with the more recent movements, going on to look at the earlier, showing some of the roots of the former in the latter. I would not wish to argue that this is invariably the best way to deal with the past, or to deny that it has certain disadvantages. If, however, it be argued that we cannot properly expound later movements without having first expounded the earlier, then modern history would never be written. Where would we begin?

Most writers who deal with the relationship between religion and politics are concerned either with the role that religious movements actually do play in national and world politics, or with ethical questions about the role that Christians or adherents of other faiths should play in the politics of their respective contexts. The link between doctrine and political policy is usually ethics. Doctrine prescribes ethical values and principles, which in turn determine how believers ought to behave in politics. The structure is deductive. It assumes that doctrine is given in some holy book, or in a sacred tradition, and develops (if it does develop at all) in a kind of religious vacuum. Yet doctrine is never simply given. Even those who believe in divine revelation (as Christians do) must recognise that revelation, as a communication between God and humanity, is not only given but received; it involves a two-way relationship.

The reception and recording of revelation is, and cannot help being, in categories, concepts and images that are socially conditioned. These 'earthly vessels' within which revelation is imparted and grasped carry with them many connotations. They often have a primary reference in spheres of human experience other than religion: the natural world (God as rock), social relationships (God as father), and political experience (God as king). These images inevitably carry with them connotations and memories from their use in their primary, secular, field of discourse. Our political experience and commitments affect our apprehension of doctrine. The deductive model is thus unsatisfactory, as there is an interplay between doctrine and human experience, in particular (from the standpoint of this work) political experience.

In any case it is important to recognise that social and political ethics should be seen not as the application of general principles to the particular case, because Christian moral judgment is made in the particular case. Principles are to be seen as abstractions from particular judgments. The judgment that I have acted wrongly in a particular case is prior to my belief that all similar actions are evil. 'It is', W. G. Ward maintained, 'with indefinitely more keenness manifest to me that my past act was base, than those general propositions are true'.[4] Thus universal principles are secondary deductions based on judgments about the moral status of particular actions, and the logic of resolving ethical disputes should ultimately be downwards to the moral status of particular actions, rather than upwards to the validity of general principles. The adequacy of such principles must be tested by the moral status of the consequences they entail.[5]

God is frequently spoken of in non-political terms, sometimes in inanimate images (rock or fortress, for example) sometimes in social – though not directly political – language (father, shepherd, bride). Yet even these social terms have often acquired political connotations, due to their appropriation by civil rulers. Royalist writers of the seventeenth century insisted that the king was *pater patriae*,[6] for 'the whole world is nothing but a great state; a state no other than a great family, and a family is no other than a great body'.[7] King James 1 of England told Parliament in 1604 'I am the husband, and all the whole isle is my lawful wife, I am the head and it is my body; I am the shepherd and it is my flock'.[8] In a different era and another country, many rulers of Haiti have rejoiced in the title 'Papa', the most recent being 'Papa Doc', François Duvalier.[9] In most periods of history, however, the directly political analogy has predominated.

THE EIGHTEENTH CENTURY

While monarchical images of God predominated in seventeenth-century England, there was a significant change in the eighteenth. As the Hanoverian kings began to play a less obvious role in government, real political power seemed to be wielded by their ministers and advisers. God, in turn, was increasingly portrayed as an administrator, or manager, of a system or machine, which generally runs according to pre-established laws. After 1688 the monarch did indeed retain important powers, but the exercise of prerogative was restricted. Laws came to be seen more as rational decisions of a legislature operating within a constitutional system than as arbitrary commands of an absolute sovereign.

Increasing stability

English history beginning in 1688 is characterised by a growing social and political stability. Although it is easy to overemphasise this, there is a striking contrast with the turbulent decades which preceded the Glorious Revolution. The English, as one writer put it, 'were becoming used to the idea of reading about their domestic politics, rather than fighting about them.'[10] As late as 1700, however, there was no certainty that stability would triumph.[11] There was in the early years, a fear of Jacobite counter-revolution, with an extensive system of spies reporting on suspicious groups; but by the middle of the eighteenth century a relative tranquillity pervaded the social and political life of the country. *The New Whole Duty of Man*, first published in 1747, contrasted the contemporary situation in the country with the 'unhappy times of strife and confusion' when the old *Whole Duty* was published, during the Commonwealth period.[12]

The British saw the government of church and state as taking place in the context of a constitution inherited from the distant past which gave some assurance of government according to law with a considerable measure of freedom for the subject. One writer lamented the decline of the old gothic halls and their replacement by the Italianate villas; he saw an analogy between the gothic halls and the gothic constitution: 'Our old gothic constitution had a noble strength and simplicity in it, which was well enough represented by the bold arches, and the solid pillars of the edifices of those days.'[13] Jacob Viner notes how this stability also characterised the economic institutions of the time:

> An outstanding aspect of literate and articulate England for the century from 1660 to 1760 was its contentment with its existing economic institutions and its absence of desire for significant change . . . no single statute can be cited in this entire century as marking an important change in the economic institutions of England, whether by way of destruction, repair or innovation.[14]

In the context of the French Revolution the idea of a constitution also became central, as it did in the American colonies. God rules according to general laws which derive from 'the constitution of the universe'; in a similar manner, earthly rule should be characterised by the same predictability and rationality. Some American writers denied indeed that the ramshackle collection of laws and customs according to which British government proceeded could properly be called a constitution at all. Late eighteenth-century France, by contrast, lacked the stability to which the British had become accustomed. This is reflected in the insistence by radical groups, like the Jacobins and some of the Paris sections, that although constitutional government was the ideal, it may be superseded by dictatorship in times of political crisis. A similar positivism emerged in the writings of those reactionaries who condemned the French Revolution and all its works. Maistre, Bonald and the so-called 'Ultras' developed a theory of sovereignty remarkably similar to that of Hobbes.[15]

Monarchical images of God by no means disappeared in the years following 1688; they continue especially in hymns, prayers and sermons. Issac Watts, who based many of his hymns on the Hebrew psalms, referred frequently to God as king, and wrote more revealingly of Christ (and elsewhere the Holy Spirit) as God's 'prime minister', reflecting the crucial role played by Sir Robert Walpole at the time.[16] Most of our eighteenth-century thinkers were, however, careful not to attack earthly monarchy as such. Deists, like John Toland, actually celebrated the Hanoverians as defenders of liberty and toleration. Some supporters of 'free thought' in religion, though, were denounced for 'undermining monarchy on earth by denying that it existed in heaven'.[17]

Theology and trade

An increasing political stability provided a structure within which significant economic expansion could take place. An increasingly complex pattern of trade and commerce required a stable political and social context within which to develop. Trade, wrote Daniel Defoe in 1705, is 'the life of the nation the soul of its felicity, the spring of its wealth, the support of its greatness, and the staff on which both king and people lean'.[18] Critics of Walpole, like Bolingbroke, Pope and Swift, attacked precisely this commercialisation of social life, which brought with it the domination of newly acquired wealth. 'Growing prosperity in a wider economic context', as J. H. Plumb, has observed, 'was creating in so many towns a nucleus of rich men, deeply rooted locally but with nation-wide economic links'.[19] This was accompanied by improved technology and a rapid growth in population. As a result of the Seven Years War (1756–63) Britain gained new colonies, giving a further boost to trade. Transport became more rapid and domestic life more comfortable. It was a time of great private initiative and enterprise. Fire services, madhouses and even prisons were privately owned and run for profit. 'There was never from the earliest ages', wrote Samuel Johnson, 'a time in which trade so much engaged the attention of mankind'.[20] England was swiftly becoming a nation of shopkeepers. Even bishops asked: 'Is not the creation of wants the likeliest way to produce industry in a people?'[21] And deans demanded: 'Whether the artificial wants of mankind . . . are not the great master-spring of the machine of commerce?'[22] Of Josiah Tucker, dean of Bristol, it was said that religion was his trade, and trade was his religion.

The image used here by Dean Tucker is central and was taken up by Robert Malthus. The economic and social structure of the country was pictured as a machine, and it was the object of social theorists to discern the laws according to which it works – to perceive the order which undergirds the apparent confusion – just as Isaac Newton had discovered the rational system which underlies the overtly haphazard behaviour of the natural world. 'Adam Smith's efforts to discover the general laws of economics', it has recently been argued, 'were directly inspired and shaped by the example of Newton's success in discovering the natural laws of motion.'[23] The social machine was an integrated system in which even what appears to be a defect may serve some useful purpose. It was, of course, Bernard Mandeville who gained notoriety by vividly expressing this sentiment in *The Fable of the Bees*. He actually maintained that vices, such as a love of extravagance and luxury, were the very stimulant needed for general prosperity. Private vices may become public benefits:

> Every part was full of vice
> Yet the whole mass a paradise
> Such were the blessings of that state;
> Their crimes conspired to make them great.[24]

Yet even with Mandeville it was not a purely natural harmony. 'Private vices', he wrote, '*by the dextrous management of a skilful politician* may be turned into public benefits.'[25]

The order manifest in the cosmos was seen as the work of a divine architect and engineer, who had designed and set in motion this great machine. Furthermore most eighteenth-century thinkers insisted that God continues to move and manage the course of things in the physical world, occasionally intervening to set things right. This was, of course, the view of Isaac Newton himself, and he was criticised by Leibniz on this ground. Although particular divine actions were admitted, God's providence was generally to be seen in the regular order of the universe. He was, as William James put it in a memorable phrase, 'a God who does a wholesale not a retail business'.[26] The order of grace and revelation, when admitted, was believed to perfect and complete rather to challenge or contradict the natural order of things; this was in certain respects a return to some basic medieval assumptions.

As in the natural world, so in the economic and social order, could be discerned

> the mighty Hand
> That, ever busy, wheels the silent spheres.[27]

Economists taught that there is a general harmony and that 'the self-love and self-interest of each individual will prompt him to seek ways of gain, trades and occupations of life, as by serving himself, will promote the public welfare at the same time'.[28] The divine, almighty but invisible hand is a familiar image of the time. It appears in the celebrated hymn of Joseph Addison:

> The spacious firmament on high
> With all the blue ethereal sky,
> And spangled heavens, a shining frame,
> Their great Original proclaim.
> The unwearied sun from day to day
> Does his Creator's power display,
> And publishes to every land
> The works of an Almighty hand.

The same image may be found in Joseph Priestley, and makes its most distinguished appearance in Adam Smith's *Wealth of Nations*, where it is transposed into the social and economic order.

WELFARE STATE OR MARKET ECONOMY?

Deity and Domination began with a consideration of the rise of the welfare state, and the relationship between welfare images of God and of the state. The introduction of welfare legislation in early twentieth-century Britain was calculated to preserve capitalism by state action to mitigate some of the worst features of the system. It was motivated also by moral considerations, which in turn were often closely related to liberal Christianity – 'the fatherhood of God and the brotherhood of man'. It was generally believed by the Balliol liberals that the state would act in a benevolent and efficient manner, and that welfare would no longer be dependent on the vagaries of locally organised charities and friendly societies.[29] In the 1970s the general consensus favourable to the welfare state was increasingly called into question, and a rival model of social organisation was proposed. A system where goods, including such things as health and education, were distributed according to the workings of the market was said to be more efficient in achieving those ends which even defenders of the welfare state desired. True, it would lead to greater inequalities, but the total wealth would increase so that even the worst-off would be better-off. The proponents of such a system were less manifestly propelled by moral considerations; nevertheless such values as individual freedom of choice and personal responsibility were stressed.

It was not only the welfare role of the state that came under scrutiny in the 1970s, but even more the workings of nationalised industries and public utilities. These were said to be bureaucratic, over-staffed and unresponsive to consumer demands. The 1980s witnessed a determined effort by the Thatcher regime to change the economic structure of the country, by privatising industries and utilities and attempting to introduce competition into those public utilities which remained under government ownership by establishing a so-called 'internal market' and competitive tendering for ancillary services. This discrediting of the state in Britain was reinforced in the late 1980s and early 1990s by the collapse of the Soviet Union and its East European satellites. In the 1980s the British experienced the most radical and ideologically motivated government since the Attlee administration of 1945–50 or perhaps even since the Asquith government of the pre-First World War period.

Spokespersons of the Thatcher government claimed that the privatising of industries and utilities, and the reforms in education, local government and the health service, constitute a cutting-back of the state. In certain ways this has been so, but in other ways central government is much more powerful today than it was fifteen years ago. County and city governments, elected by the people, have lost many of their powers and responsibilities.

These changes, while they are most obvious in the administrative and economic spheres, derive inspiration from cultural and moral ideals. Shirley Robin Letwin has argued convincingly that 'Thatcherism' should be seen not primarily in economic terms, but as a moral crusade to re-establish the 'vigorous virtues' of self-reliance, enterprise and hard work, in the face of excessive dependence, caring and concern which were said to be encouraged by the welfare mentality. Extensive provision of social benefits by the state was also said to discourage private benevolence and corporate charity, depriving people of the opportunity to exercise their moral responsibilities.

Though they insisted on the idea of a free market, Thatcherites acknowledged the need for some kind of limits to free competition. For one thing a market needs to be regulated and protected to prevent 'justling', as Adam Smith put it. Thatcherites have also recognised the danger of unleashing human covetousness and have advocated a kind of 'civic religion' which, combined with an individualistic pietism, would support moral restraints to unlimited acquisitive tendencies. Thatcher herself claimed to return in certain respects to a late eighteenth-century liberalism, associated particularly with the name of Adam Smith, combined in some unspecified way with what she has called 'Victorian values'.[30] But there is another anticipation of Thatcherism, which may appear at first sight surprising. Remarkable similarities exist between the political vision of Thatcherism and the ideas and ideals of the leading French Jacobin, Maximilien Robespierre, with respect to both God and the state.

THE NEW JACOBINS?

The eighteenth-century Jacobins combined a belief in individual liberty (particularly in the economic sphere) with an insistence on a strong state, allowing little room for any significant intermediate groups, with the possible exception of the family. This suspicion of groups was inherited from Jean-Jacques Rousseau, whose ideas exercised a major influence over Robespierre and over his younger colleague and collaborator Saint-Just.[31] Laws would create and maintain a framework within which economic activity could proceed, without inhibiting market forces by protective legislation. Saint-Just was particularly concerned to defend a policy of free trade and *laissez-faire*. The Jacobins sometimes *spoke* of the dangers of a centralised state and the benefits of subsidiary groups but, as in Thatcherism, practical policies tended to undermine the power of such groups and to enhance that of central government.

A property-owning democracy

Jacobins believed that the rights of private property are 'sacred' and that as many citizens as possible should be proprietors. Their ideal was indeed a property-owning democracy presided over by strong central government. Though Robespierre himself was no radical egalitarian, he did believe in sweeping away the old system of aristocratic privilege which prevented social mobility; he accepted the ideal of equality of opportunity. Georges Lefebvre summarised Robespierre's ideal as 'a society of small producers, each possessing some land, a small *atelier* and a *boutique*'.[32] Thatcher also professed a particular affection for small businesses, and her early years in

8

office saw a rapid growth in their number. (In later years to be sure, almost unprecedented numbers went bankrupt.) Governments are to provide and regulate a structure within which private enterprise may flourish. Policies, such as the sale of council houses and the privatisation of state-owned industry by the sale of shares to the general public, were defended on the grounds of encouraging a widespread ownership of land and capital. Individual responsibility must be encouraged.

The rhetoric of populism is a feature shared by Jacobins and Thatcherites. Appeals to 'the people' were frequently made by Robespierre and Saint-Just. Yet, as politicians, they were selective in putting these appeals into concrete form. They opposed a referendum on the fate of the king and later saw the Convention and the Committee of Public Safety as reflecting the real opinions and true interests of the masses better than a referendum would; they were also prepared to appeal to the people over the heads of the legislators when it suited them. So Thatcherism claimed to speak for the ordinary man and woman in the street. Thatcher's November 1991 speech in Parliament calling for a referendum on Britain's relations with the European Community is a clear echo of Jacobin populism: 'Let the people speak.' On other occasions (in particular when discussing proportional representation) it is argued that the British system of government is founded on institutions which represent the settled views and long-term interests of the people.

Civil religion and moral values

Yet such an ideology of populism and free enterprise was only one aspect of the Thatcherite vision. The state also exists to protect and forward certain 'values'. Through education in particular (backed up by the penal system) the state is able to maintain civic virtues. These are not derived from the state itself, but from the church, which is seen as its partner. The notions of a national church allied to the state and of a civic religion are thus integral to the Thatcherite dream, supplying not only values but also historical roots which bind the nation together. Furthermore they give legitimacy to a belief that the pursuit of self-interest, within an ordered framework, will in general forward the common good.

Robespierre retained throughout his life a deep conviction that a supreme all-powerful being, who is good and just, watches over human affairs and 'presides over the destiny of empires'. In this early letter, he urged the king to 're-forge the immortal chain that must bind man to God and to his fellow-men'.[33] He went on to insist that this idea of God has too often been employed to legitimate the power of governments; it should be seen also as providing a foundation for individual rights. Belief in a supreme being gives legitimacy to moral and civil laws, supplementing the insufficiency of human authority by imprinting in the soul the belief in a

9

sanction given to moral precepts by 'a power superior to man'.[34] We are reminded of Douglas Hurd's call for church and state to 'work together... to rebuild the moral standards and values which should form the sure foundation of a cohesive and united nation'.[35]

Thatcherite, like Jacobin, 'theology' was deeply tainted with Pelagianism.[36] Individual moral effort was preached. Virtue should be rewarded. This is why scandals in the City like the Guinness affair caused so much embarrassment to the government. Tied to this moralistic individualism was a peculiar pietism. We may recall the 'Prayer of St Francis' read from the steps of 10 Downing Street. The all-powerful divine despot of deism was allied to the rather sentimental recognition of a father-figure; morality touched with emotion, as Matthew Arnold put it. Robespierre, for his part, saw God as a consolation for those in trouble and 'our only hope on earth'.[37]

Providence and patriotism

In a debate at the Jacobins in March 1792, Robespierre referred to the death of the Austrian emperor as due to a 'Providence, which always watches over us better that our own wisdom'. One member objected that this idea of providence would undo the revolutionary work of liberation and bring the people back under the yoke of superstition. Robespierre denied that using the name of the deity implies superstition. Despite commotion in the meeting he defended belief in a particular providence personally watching over the course of the French Revolution.[38]

Robespierre's religion was, thus, different from the cold rationalism of much eighteenth-century deism. Thatcher too sometimes embarrassed her more sceptical cabinet colleagues by a similar emphasis upon religion (in her case a form of Christianity). Hers was, she claimed, a Christian government. Closely related to this was her patriotic stance. She quoted the hymn 'I vow to thee my country' as expressing her religious nationalism. Robespierre's speeches likewise contained outbursts of patriotic fervour in which he invoked a divine providence. The foundation of the French Republic could not be seen as a matter of chance, but was the work of a guiding providence, the same power and wisdom as presided over the creation of the universe.[39]

It may be said that my argument can simply be reduced to the observation that the social ideals of Robespierre were rather typical of late eighteenth-century deism, and not therefore very far removed from those of Adam Smith, whose example Thatcherites are happy to follow and to acknowledge. Clearly this contains some truth, but there is an important distinguishing feature which Thatcher and Robespierre share. Their style is characterised – as Smith's is not – by a lack of humour and a crusading determination to transform the social order. Robespierre was, to be sure, somewhat more optimistic about the creation of a new humanity, while

Thatcher sees an essentially sinful human nature as prescribing limits to this vision; though with the mobilisation of the church, the education system and the legal apparatus much could be achieved.

Governments, Smith had cynically remarked, exist to protect the rich against the poor.[40] Both Thatcher and Robespierre saw possibilities for a dynamic government, strengthened by civic religion, transforming the social order and establishing virtue and a new or reborn people. In his speech already quoted, Douglas Hurd has indeed claimed that, as a result of Thatcherite policies, 'the nation has pulled itself out of the cycle of defeatism. Confidence has returned. Individual citizens are regaining power over their own lives.' Robespierre, for his part, believed that education and social reform would create 'a new people . . . a renewed race, strong, laborious, disciplined.'[41]

The idea of individual autonomy is clearly seen, by many of its advocates, as the principal moral justification of the market economy. It is stressed particularly by John Gray and is a point of agreement with Lord (Raymond) Plant, a Labour peer and spokesman of democratic socialism.[42]

AN AGE OF REASON?

There are certain respects in which it might be proper to refer to the eighteenth century as an age of reason. Most theologians claimed that the particular brand of religious belief they adopted could be justified, or at least defended, by reason. Some deists went so far as to claim that all legitimate religion can be derived from reason and nature. The law of nature, so it was claimed, was sufficient to live and die by; revelation and supernatural religion were only a hindrance. This radical position was, however, taken by a very small minority. Even deists like Toland claimed (at times) to accept the validity of revelation.

Yet there was among eighteenth-century intellectuals a deep suspicion of rationalism. By the end of the seventeenth century the philosophical systems of Descartes and Leibniz were rejected by most English writers in favour of the empirical philosophy of Bacon, Newton and Locke, which suggested a rather pragmatic approach to both religion and politics. The social order, like the cosmic order, was pictured as a system or machine, whose workings were to be understood not by deductive reason, but by generalisations from careful observation. The question to be asked is not 'what God might have done', but rather 'what he has in fact done'. This latter question is answered by reference to the natural world, rather than by deductions from his supposed nature. Voltaire carried the message to France, where Leibnizian philosophy was still influential. Translations of Pope's works were immensely popular in France during the late 1730s, and writers like Condillac and D'Alembert responded positively to the new empiricism, which they associated with the British system of limited government and religious toleration. This anglophile attitude was adopted also by Quesnay and the physiocrats: their God was also a constitutional monarch.[43]

The rejection of Cartesian rationalism, according to one writer, provided a climate within which analogical reasoning might flourish. 'A system of analogical thought', writes Earl Wasserman, 'is indigenous to the skeptical, empirical, and anti-metaphysical climate of the eighteenth century.'[44] One eighteenth-century Irishman wrote:

> The Deity has stamped the face of nature with a great seal, from whose impression resulted all those analogies and relations we find diffused throughout the universe. There is, especially, a general analogy between natural and moral things, by which they resemble, and reflect a mutual light upon each other.[45]

There was seen to be an order and coherence which derives from the creative purpose of a divine architect or musician. When we hear today the term 'concert' we think of a musical performance on a narrow stage before an audience of observers. Originally it was 'a song in praise of God, uttered by a mightily-ordered nature, and by the human community serving as an echo'.[46]

2

GOD AND THE MARKET

The early decades of the nineteenth century witnessed the flourishing of a
school of ecclesiastical economists, whose writings – while being mostly
apologetic in purpose – contributed to the development of political economy in Britain.[1] Thomas Chalmers, John Bird Sumner, Edward Copleston
and Richard Whately all owed much, in differing degrees, to the population
theories of 'Parson Malthus', to the theology of Paley and, of course, to
Adam Smith's pioneering work in the field of political economy. It is
sometimes said that the economic theories of these men, so far from being
derived from their religious beliefs, merely reflected current secular opinions.[2] The relationship between religion and politics in these writers is
rather more complex.

The law-governed universe constitutes, in their view, a system that
requires only occasional intervention from a supreme governor. This system they saw replicated at the social and economic level, where the market
generally supplies the needs of citizens, with only very limited intervention
by the government. As God maintains the machine of the universe in being
and occasionally interposes to set things right, so the civil government
ensures the conditions necessary for a free and fair market, intervening now
and then to remedy defects. The general harmony found in the physical
universe is mirrored in a general harmony between individual interests and
the common good. In both cases the harmony is general but not invariable,
hence the need for occasional direct action by governments.

PRIMATES, PRELATES AND PROPHETS

The four ecclesiastics whom we are considering in the first part of this
chapter each reached a position of eminence in his respective church.
Richard Whately (1787–1863) and Edward Copleston (1776–1849) had been
Fellows of Oriel College, Oxford, in the great days of the 'Noetics', a group
of intellectuals well known for their Whig politics and liberal but rather
'high church' theology. In 1831 the former became archbishop of Dublin
only a year or so after accepting the Drummond Chair of Political Economy

13

at Oxford. Whately's principal contribution to the study of economics was his *Introductory Lectures on Political Economy*, delivered at Oxford in 1830. There he attempted to establish the theological respectability and scientific nature of economics. He later used his influence to promote the study of economics in Dublin.[3] Copleston became provost of Oriel in 1814 and later a bishop. His ideas on economic theory are to be found in his two open letters to Robert Peel, where he discussed the problem of poverty, ascribing many of the ills of the country to inflation resulting from the use of paper money.

John Bird Sumner (1780–1862) was educated at Cambridge, where he came under the influence of the celebrated evangelical Charles Simeon. He became bishop of Chester in 1828, and archbishop of Canterbury twenty years later. In 1816 he had published a two-volume work entitled *A Treatise on the Records of Creation; with Particular Reference to Jewish History, and the Consistency of the Principle of Population with the Wisdom and Goodness of the Deity*. The work was recommended by Malthus as 'containing a masterly development and completion' of his own views as set forth in the *Essay on Population*.[4] On hearing of Sumner's decision to quit writing on economics, David Ricardo wrote to a friend: 'I very much regret that the science will no longer be assisted by his distinguished talents.'[5] These three Anglican writers made acute if fairly scanty contributions to the study of economics.

By contrast, the contentious Scottish Presbyterian Thomas Chalmers (1780–1847) published over 150 separate books and pamphlets.[6] He was, in his day, perhaps the most influential of these ecclesiastical political economists. 'I consider you my ablest and best ally', Malthus told him in 1822.[7] In his early years Chalmers adopted a liberal form of Christianity – being one of the 'Moderates' in the Scottish church – but underwent an evangelical conversion between 1809 and 1811, while working in the parish of Kilmany. From being an ambitious but rather slack parish minister he became an impassioned evangelical preacher, with a generally Calvinist theology.[8] In 1814 Chalmers moved to a parish in Glasgow and later became professor of Moral Philosophy at his old university of St Andrews in 1823. He played a leading role in Scottish church controversies, which culminated in the Disruption of 1843.

Chalmers's occasional lectures in London during the 1830s were attended by the highest in the land. Nassau Senior praised his work and, writing from London in 1832, added: 'Your political economy is creating a great sensation here.'[9] Economists rarely agree, and a month later his fellow Scotsman J. R. McCulloch – receiving a review copy of *On Political Economy, in Connexion with the Moral State and Moral Prospects of Society* – told the editor of the *Edinburgh Review*: 'A more thorough piece of quackery never came into my hands.'[10]

Whether Chalmers himself generated controversy and conflict, or whether he was ineluctably drawn into situations of strife, is not clear; but

14

there is certainly something of the ecclesiastical warrior about him. When he died in 1847, 2000 mourners followed his coffin, and an estimated 100,000 people lined the route. As the procession reached the cemetery, the appearance, recalled an observer, 'was that of an army'![11]

Chalmers on God and social harmony

Thomas Chalmers saw God as a heavenly monarch presiding over a universe which he has created and guides by his providence. Whereas the Newtonians had seen arguments for the existence of God from the stars, and Paley had pointed to the contrivance and design manifested in the biological world, it was principally to the social order that Chalmers looked for evidence of God's existence, though an early book had been devoted to astronomy. Chalmers saw a remarkable harmony of interests manifested in the workings of the market economy, but was never uncritical in his assessment of commercial life. He defined political economy as the science of 'the laws by which the increase and distribution of wealth are regulated', and defended the discipline against its critics. It was, he insisted, in no way responsible for the errors of its practitioners.[12]

Following Adam Smith, he believed that there is a general harmony so that the common good will normally be served by each person pursuing his or her own interest. In his celebrated Bridgewater Treatise, published in 1833, he stated that 'the greatest economic good is rendered to the community by each man being left to consult and to labour for his own particular good', and he celebrated the 'spontaneous play and busy competition of many thousand wills,' preferring that to 'the anxious superintendence of a government vainly attempting to medicate the fancied imperfections of nature'.[13] As each strives to better his own condition, we see 'the cheapening and multiplying to the uttermost all the articles of human enjoyment, and establishing a thousand reciprocities of mutual interest in the world'. This for him was evidence for the 'benevolence and comprehensive wisdom of God'.[14] The action of a corn merchant in raising the price of corn during an acute shortage, decreases consumption, thereby conserving supplies and helping to prevent famine. He is the unwitting cause of a general benefit. 'It is', pronounced Chalmers, 'the doing of a higher hand, of him who ordaineth both the laws of nature and the laws of human society . . . who can make even the selfishness of individuals work out a country's salvation'.[15] Like Mandeville, he saw this egoism as holding together the mercantile world. 'Would not the world of trade,' he demanded,

> sustain as violent a derangement on this mighty hold being cut asunder, as the world of nature would on the suspending of the law

of gravitation? Would not the whole system, in fact, fall to pieces and be dissolved?[16]

Chalmers's conversion, in the words of his recent biographer, 'fundamentally changed the way he conceived of God and the world'.[17] He became acutely aware of human sinfulness and the need for redemption. This conviction was strengthened and legitimated by his economic theories. While it was the duty of Christians to do the right for its own sake, most people obey the laws of a country out of fear and self-interest.[18] Even in the case of sincere Christians, he was conscious that the selfish motive is present in the best of human actions and that 'all our righteousnesses are as filthy rags' (Isaiah 64:6). So he was able to state in a memorable dictum that 'society is held together, only because the grace of God can turn to account the worthless propensities of the individuals who compose it'.[19] His Calvinist belief in total depravity led him to recognise not only flagrant acts of evil in the world, but to discern 'amid the blandness of social courtesies, a moral violence that carries as grievous and substantial iniquity in its train.'[20]

At times, therefore, Chalmers saw the harmony between individual selfishness and the common good as part of a theodicy – an argument for the existence of a benign and powerful creator. God has not left social order and the general good to depend on individual altruism. It is when 'each man is left to seek, with concentrated and exclusive aim, his own individual benefit' that markets are best supplied and economic progress takes place. Such a result, which no one intends, 'strongly bespeaks of a higher agent, by whose transcendental wisdom it is, that all is made to conspire so harmoniously and to terminate so beneficially'.[21] God is indeed 'the Supreme Contriver'.[22]

God: artist and righteous governor

As with Mandeville, the recognition that vice and selfishness hold the economic and commercial system together does not mean that Chalmers gave unambiguous approval to these institutions or to the individual motives that support them. In fact his conversion had led him to appreciate the value of co-operation and community, which he began to experience among the young evangelicals with whom he associated. There is in his social ideas a strong communitarian emphasis which sits uneasily with his economic theories. Like the people of ancient Israel, Chalmers saw a harmony between the moral virtue of a nation and economic prosperity, between goodness and happiness:

If anything can demonstrate the hand of a righteous Deity in the nature and workings of what may well be termed a mechanism, the very peculiar mechanism of trade; it is the healthful impulse given to all its movements wherever there is a reigning principle of sobriety and virtue in the land – so as to ensure an inseparable connection between the moral worth and the economic comfort of a people.[23]

Chalmers rejected the ethical positivism often associated with Calvinism, arguing that 'virtue is not the creation of the Divine will, but has had everlasting residence in the nature of the Godhead'.[24] Following Bishop Joseph Butler, he saw conscience as both the instrument for discovering what is right and the rightful 'governor' of human action.[25] It is in the laws and lessons of human conscience that we are able to know something of the nature of God, 'just as we should study the views and dispositions of a monarch, in the instructions given by him to the viceroy of one of his provinces'.[26]

God is pictured as 'designer' and 'moral architect', as 'a real and living artist, whose fingers did frame the economy of actual things, and who hath so marvellously suited all that is around us to our senses and our powers of gratification'.[27] For Chalmers, however, God was not a detached designer, on the deist model: 'Thou at once superintendest the government of this immense universe, and exercisest the most perfect vigilence and care over the meanest portions of it.'[28] We find a belief, then, not only in God's general providence, but in his detailed supervision of earthly affairs. 'The same God who framed and who organized our great mundane system', he proclaimed, ' has never so left it to the play and the impulses of its own mechanism, as to have resigned even for one moment that mastery over it which belongs to Him'.[29]

Though God is conceived of as a benevolent governor, human happiness is not his only concern. Chalmers echoed Butler's belief that the justice of God cannot be reduced to benevolence, attacking those who would

resolve the whole character of the Deity into but one attribute – that of a placid undistinguishing tenderness; and . . . would despoil Him of all sovereignty and of all sacredness – holding Him forth as but the indulgent Father, and not also the righteous Governor of men.[30]

He saw the determination of liberal theologians to remove 'everything like jurisprudence from the relation in which God stands to man' as undermining any adequate idea of the Atonement and subverting attempts to formulate a satisfactory theodicy.[31] Rejecting the idea of God as 'a universal parent, throned in soft and smiling radiance', he was, by analogy, equally critical of state paternalism.

Government, community and famine

If God superintends the universe in such detail, it might be thought that civil government is superfluous. Not so, declared the preacher: 'The doc-

17

trine of a celestial influence does not supersede, but rather calls for, a terrestrial mechanism, to guide and to extend the distribution of it.'[32] Though he admitted the possibility of constructive collective action, he insisted that a government must respect 'the beautiful arrangements of nature', not meddling 'with the operations of a previous and better mechanism than its own'.[33] Even the most mighty despot must respect the human nature of his subjects, or 'they would hurl him from his throne'.[34] The care of the poor, for example, is best left to the affections which nature has planted in individuals and families, rather than being organised by the state or imposed by law.

In true Lockean style Chalmers insisted that the principal role of the state is to protect the rights of citizens to life, liberty and estate.[35] He saw the state both as an instrument of God in the world and also as a terrestrial analogue to the system of divine rule in the universe. Both must operate according to laws, leaving their subjects scope to make responsible decisions, which have generally predictable consequences. He advocated a basically *laissez-faire* approach to government, leaving social action to individuals and voluntary groups. Chalmers favoured the development of savings banks and popular education, which would lead to an 'enlightened peasantry'.[36] This he contrasted with the current poor law arrangements, which had resulted in a dependent class of paupers. Savings banks would give labourers 'a far more effective control over the labour market, than men in a condition of helpless dependency . . . could possibly realize'.[37] Furthermore, in 1824 he supported the repeal of the Combination Acts of 1799 and 1800, which had effectively outlawed strikes and prevented the formation of trade unions.[38] 'We should like to see,' he declared,

> a great stable independent property in the hands of the labouring classes, and their interests elevated to one of the high co-ordinate interests of the state . . . In this competition between capitalists and workmen, we profess ourselves to be on the side of the latter.[39]

Towards the end of his life Chalmers witnessed the horrors of the Irish potato famines of 1845 and 1846. He led the efforts in his church to raise money for the starving, but soon came to the conclusion that voluntary action by individuals and groups was insufficient; the state must act. Already, in 1844, he had limited the scope of the *laissez-faire* principle to the exchange of commodities, advocating positive action by 'a righteous government' in matters of health and morals.[40] He began advocating, in 1846, a huge programme of government aid for Ireland, financed by taxing the luxuries of the wealthy. Chalmers distinguished between a concentrated disaster as was occurring in Ireland and a more evenly spread and less serious shortage, as had been experienced in 1795 and 1800, arguing for special steps to be taken by the government in the former case.

In an article on the Irish famine Chalmers criticised the idea that free trade is a panacea for all ills. In cases where there is a near monopoly in the supply of basic goods like corn, government may properly intervene. He recommended the transfer of public funds to the Irish poor to purchase food. This would indeed raise the price of corn but would encourage merchants to import. 'It is thus that the urgent demand of Ireland for food would, in the language of the economists, have become an effective demand.' He furthermore argued for massive government aid to 'put Ireland into a right economic condition' and to transform her into 'a prosperous and smiling land'.[41]

Stewart Brown sees this proposed positive state action as a retreat from a *laissez-faire* position.[42] Boyd Hilton, however, maintains that Chalmers's 'response to the Famine was less of a departure from evangelical economics than might be supposed'. He goes on to state quixotically that Chalmers's advocacy of state aid for Ireland, financed by direct taxation,

> is not an abandonment of the principle of voluntary benevolence in favour of state aid, as Brown avers, but a call for the British state to exercise, in an hour of special providence, a voluntary benevolence towards Ireland.[43]

Chalmers further modified his *laissez-faire* position in the hesitant support he gave in 1846 to Oastler's agitation for a ten hours factory bill.[44]

Chalmers had never been a straightforward individualist liberal. In an early treatise, written before his conversion experience, he had been critical of the commercial spirit – of the rush for economic growth and increasing international trade – preferring a more stable and humble form of community life for the country.[45] After his conversion he looked back to the ideal of a godly commonwealth composed of parish communities, sustained by the idea of a covenant and guided by an established church. His co-operative ideas even encouraged the socialist Robert Owen in the 1820s to think of him as a potential ally. While both men were, in a sense, millenarians, Owen had renounced Christianity, and adopted a kind of moral or humanist vision of the millennium. Chalmers, on the other hand, saw the conversion of individuals as the precondition of social reform and the coming millennium.[46]

In the 1820s and 1830s Chalmers appears, however, to have adopted ideas of a harmony between individual self-interest and the general commercial good – ideas associated with what today we would call a free market economy. But even in this period he was careful not to give unambiguous approval to the *laissez-faire* principle. In his later work he became increasingly critical of a pure market economy and restricted the legitimate scope of the commercial spirit. 'Everything now', he declared, in words which might have been written in the post-Thatcher era of purchasers and providers and grant-maintained schools, 'is made a question of finance; and science, with all which can grace or dignify a nation is vulgarised and brought down to a common standard – the standard of the market and of the counting house'.[47] He reiterated his belief that although the operations of a free market can best cope in general with the commercial life of the country, such matters as education and public health must be dealt with in a more direct and deliberate manner. There were, for him, 'other and far greater interests' than wealth.[48]

Self-interest and the free market

The motto on the cover of Edward Copleston's *Letter to the Rt Hon Robert Peel* of 1819, *'Laissez nous faire'*, reflects the general attitude of the ecclesiastical political economists to the question of state intervention in the economic life of a country. They believed that there is in human affairs a 'principle of self-correction which the analogy of nature teaches us is the universal law of her constitution'.[49] As God, in his government of the universe, generally respects the laws of the cosmic constitution which he has created, so human governments should normally limit their actions to removing obstacles to the free operation of the market. We here see how political policy may be legitimated by an appeal to 'nature', which is in fact an appeal to theology. The analogy of nature becomes thereby one of several arguments for governmental activity (or inactivity).

J. B. Sumner insisted that when industry is circumscribed, things cannot prosper, 'and are then only in a healthy state, when every avenue to personal advantage is open to every talent'.[50] The 'vast and complicated machine of human society', he continued, is kept going by each individual desiring to better his own condition:

> That natural and spirit-stirring desire is the nourishment of the body politic; it is the fertilizing source which supplies the juices to the tree; and though the stem may for a while show signs of life, and even continue to put forth shoots after the nourishment is dried up, it soon becomes a barren trunk, the decaying monument of former strength and vigour.[51]

He asserted that the growth of civilisation depends upon this stimulus and that decline will set in when 'the hope of improving fortune, and of accumulating property, is removed'.[52]

Citing Robertson and von Humboldt, Sumner contrasted the communal ownership of property and the caste system found among the Incas of Peru – leading to a lack of refinement and of military enterprise – with the situation in Mexico, where 'markets were held, and whatever could supply any want or desire of man was an object of commerce'.[53] Taking up a theme found in the writings of Adam Smith, these ecclesiastical economists pointed out that God has not left the future of the race and the development of civilisation in the hands of human reason and virtuous intentions. This would indeed be a fragile basis upon which to build. As Richard Whately insisted, 'not making the public good dependent on pure public spirit' is an indication of the benevolent wisdom of divine providence; the general tendency 'toward the advancement of national wealth' does not rest primarily on human wisdom or virtue.[54] Whately joined Chalmers in seeing this general harmony of interests as a version of the argument from design, and in his fourth lecture considered the progress of 'society' as a branch of natural theology.[55]

Those then who pursue their own interests 'in the crowded scene of civilization' are able to attain their end only 'by promoting colaterally the happiness of their neighbours'.[56] As Smith had maintained, the poor benefit from the extravagant expenditure of the rich. The future archbishop illustrated vividly what has since been called the 'trickle-down effect':

> The labour of the lowest class, which feeds the superfluities of the highest, like the vapour which has been drawn from the earth, descends again in a thousand channels, and fertilizes the soil into which it falls.[57]

Despite their recognition of the fact of human egoism, which is seen as a necessary condition for the operation of the market, there is also a condemnation of selfishness from the standpoint of Christian morality. Certainly the reckless pursuit of self-interest to the detriment of others may undermine the social fabric. Sumner even acknowledged that this selfishness may in part be *ascribed* to the social structure of the day. 'A spirit of selfishness', he declared from the pulpit,

> is apt to be generated by the state of society in which we live, which is a great hindrance to the active love of our neighbour. We consider the different ranks of men as unalterably fixed by the circumstances of their birth and education; and this belief, which is no doubt just in the main, tends to withhold the attention of one class from the wants or difficulties of the other. Nothing can be more contrary to the merciful spirit of the gospel.[58]

Inequality and the poor

Sumner was much exercised by the question of social and economic inequality, which appeared to be a consequence of the theories he was defending. The importance of saving and of owning property, together with the right of inheritance, are clearly incompatible with strict equality. Progress demands 'industrious emulation', and inequality is a precondition of virtue – giving an opportunity for the exercise of benevolence among the rich, and contentment among the lower ranks. Inequality seems indeed to be built into the very constitution of human nature.[59] The advocates of

21

equality have a vision of humans as self-sufficient and independent, which they can never be. Rather, thought Sumner, there is an interdependence which is closely related to inequalities in the human condition.[60] This position is somewhat out of line with a general belief among these political economists that independence is a virtue to be cultivated. There is an almost Coleridgian ring to this idea of social interdependence.

Yet, with Malthus, Sumner warned against huge inequalities, believing that the most healthy social condition demands many different grades in the ownership of wealth.[61] Furthermore, he distinguished between indigence and poverty. The former is a wretched state which 'is pitiable and is usually contemptible'. Poverty, by contrast, is 'often both honourable and comfortable'. Indigence is commonly the result of intemperance and a lack of prudent foresight, and is, he asserted, 'the punishment which the moral government of God inflicts in this world upon thoughtlessness and guilty extravagance'.[62]

Malthus had denied any natural universal right of the poor to subsistence. Yet Copleston drew a distinction between an alleged right to a particular level of support and the right to self-preservation. Following classic Christian teaching – found, for example, in Aquinas – he asserted that this latter right may even 'render a violation of property excusable'. 'If we deny to any human being the means of support ourselves', declared the Oxford don, in a potentially revolutionary statement, 'we have no right to deprive him of the chance he may have of finding it elsewhere.'[63] These men favoured the growth of savings banks and friendly societies among the responsible poor, and like Malthus were critical of the pre-1834 Poor Law arrangements. Copleston told Robert Peel that 'all endeavours to embody benevolence into law, and thus impiously as it were to effect by human laws what the Author of the system of nature has not effected by his laws, must be abortive'.[64] So to act would be to deprive the rich of occasions for the exercise of virtue, which by its essential nature must be voluntary.

God's purpose and human destiny

Sumner maintained that this present life is to be seen as a state of discipline and preparation – a situation in which human character is developed by virtuous actions, as though God 'had it not in contemplation to create a perfect character, but to discipline an imperfect one'.[65] God's government is contrasted with civil government insofar as the former works more by gratification than by punishment, by carrot rather than stick. 'We are not tormented into a course of action conformable to the divine plan of government, but allured to obey it, by the prospect of some attainable satisfaction.'[66] The divine system of punishment and reward operates differently from the human system because the end is different. The principal purpose of human punishment is to prevent or deter crime. Therefore punishment should whenever possible follow the offence swiftly and visibly. In the case of divine government the case is different: 'If the divine interference descended immediately upon good or evil actions, little room would be left for moral probation . . . the exercise of faith would be precluded; servile fear alone would deter from vice and selfish expectation become the leading motive to virtue'.[67]

God, like human government, normally acts according to law. It is this that makes a rational and moral life possible. There are, nevertheless, certain exceptional circumstances when direct intervention, divine and civil, is called for. Chalmers, as we have seen, believed that the Irish famine of 1845–6 was one such occasion when the state should intervene directly; Malthus thought that any major slump justified such direct government action. *Laissez-faire*, as a general principle, with only occasional direct interventions, was applied to divine government by Whately, who instructed the Almighty:

> Such knowledge, and such knowledge only should be imparted to Man *supernaturally*, as he could not *otherwise* have attained; and that whatever he is capable of discovering by the exercise of his natural faculties . . . he should be left so to discover for himself: – in short, that no further miraculous interference should take place, than is absolutely indispensable.[68]

These ecclesiastical economists acknowledged a major debt to Robert Malthus, to whom the origins of many of their ideas can be traced.

POPULATION AND PROCESS: 'PARSON MALTHUS'

The *Essay on the Principle of Population* first appeared anonymously in 1798. Its author was a priest of the Church of England, the Reverend Thomas Robert Malthus (1766–1834). It was a polemical tract designed to demolish the utopian ideas of William Godwin, the marquis de Condorcet and other radical humanists of the time. While it must be seen in the context of the British reaction to the French Revolution, its influence among intellectuals continued well into the nineteenth century. Not only did it affect the development of economic theory and demography, but it contributed in a major way to the ideas of progress through struggle and challenge, manifested classically in the thought of Herbert Spencer, Charles Darwin and the 'Social Darwinists'.[69] Ronald Meek, a bitterly critical Marxist economist, recognised the importance of 'the principle of population'. 'There was probably no other idea,' he wrote,

> which exercised so great an influence on economic theory and practice during the first half of the nineteenth century, and certainly no other

which aroused such impassioned attacks and defences. And it was destined to exercise considerable influence even outside the strictly economic sphere.[70]

Many who had initially responded sympathetically to the Revolution gradually became disillusioned as its dynamic revealed itself. They were alarmed at the Jacobin terror and the subsequent move towards Napoleonic dictatorship. Enlightenment beliefs in the basic goodness of human beings and in the idea that all evil stems from corrupt institutions were blamed for the way things had gone. Social institutions like the family, the social hierarchy, the church and the penal system were seen as necessary barriers to social unrest and disaffection. While utopian radicals, like Thomas Paine, had lost much of their sway, William Godwin remained influential.[71] Malthus's purpose was to destroy his political and social theory. The proposed abolition of family and property, so far from leading to a peaceful, just and happy society, would result in disaster. Human nature, he asserted, if left to itself, liberated from institutional safeguards, would sink into sloth and barbarism. It is the challenge and stimulus of pain and hunger that alone promotes constructive action, leading to the development of mind and of civilisation.

In chapters 18 and 19 of his *Essay*, Malthus proposed an understanding of God which would vindicate his goodness in the face of the pain and evil generally manifest in the world, of which his own population principle was a startling exemplification. Malthus argued that, unchecked, there is a tendency for population to grow faster than food supplies and that the potential checks to this growth are invariably of a painful or vicious nature. He rejected the generally accepted idea that this life is a time of testing and probation for a future life and put forward a notion of God's relationship to the universe strikingly similar to later 'process' ideas of A. N. Whitehead and his followers.

The 'partial evil' in the world – which includes the population principle – was seen by Malthus as the necessary condition of a greater good, the development of mind. Though omnipotent, God could not have created, ready-made, minds tempered in the furnace of moral conflict, for this tempering necessarily takes 'time', even for God. The idea of human moral development, and the social and economic progress inseparably associated with it in the thinking of Malthus, is at the centre of what he graphically called 'man's commerce with the skies'.[72] His understanding of human nature and of social reality is closely related to his religious beliefs and assumptions. In particular there is a striking analogy between his idea of God's relationship to the natural world and the role which, in his view, ought to be played by civil government in the social and economic sphere. Both act in accordance with general laws which – though resulting in some pain and evil – have consequences which contain a balance of good. Hence it is rather misleading to suggest that 'his career exemplified the separation of religious from nonreligious into discrete elements'.[73]

The theory of population

Malthus showed an early interest in political economy.[74] He wrote, in 1796, a tract defending poor relief in cases of real need, though generally stressing the value of independence.[75] His *Essay on the Principle of Population* immediately created a stir. He appeared to be following in the scandalous footsteps of Bernard Mandeville by maintaining that misery and vice are in some way providentially designed to be a necessary means to the public benefits of social progress and a balanced population. The author was later denounced by Marx as a 'shameless sycophant of the ruling classes'.[76] The principle that population has a tendency, if unchecked, to outstrip the means for its survival, was not original. Malthus's originality rests in the way he used the principle to attack utopian theories and to defend the goodness of God.

In 1803 a radically revised and more systematic edition was published, giving statistical support to his theory. It is characterised by a somewhat more optimistic spirit. Malthus acknowledged the real possibility of moral restraint, through the postponement of marriage and a consequent lowering of the birth-rate; also he explicitly recognised the possible avoidance of the worst kinds of check (misery and vice) being called into play. He dropped much of the theological material – having been advised by friends that it contained unorthodox opinions which would reduce the appeal of the book – and distributed the rest throughout the body of the work. Whether this represented a change of belief on these matters or merely a prudential move is still a matter of debate among scholars. Further editions appeared in subsequent years, in which he explicitly accepted ideas about the purpose of life on earth that he had rejected in the *First Essay*, while attempting to disguise his change of position.[77] In 1830 Malthus wrote a summary of his theory. Having married in 1804 he was appointed professor at the East India College in Hertford, which later moved to Haileybury. Here he remained until his death, writing on questions of political economy and population.

Malthus's population theory has been much misunderstood or distorted. Karl Marx, that master of malicious misrepresentation, suggested (by placing it in quotation-marks) that the following was the view of 'Parson Malthus': 'Since population is constantly tending to overtake the means of subsistence, charity is folly, a public encouragement of poverty. The state can therefore do nothing but leave the poor to their fate and, at the most, make death easy for them.'[78] As will become evident, Malthus in fact defended positive state action to relieve hardship and stimulate economic growth in certain circumstances. Nevertheless he asserted a tendency for population to grow – if unchecked – faster than food production, the former increasing in geometrical progression, (1,2,4,8...) while the most that can be hoped for is a growth in food production by arithmetical progression (1,2,3,4...). This would bring into operation the painful sanction of famine. Malthus saw this doubling of population taking place in 25-year cycles. He believed that desire for sexual intercourse and the degree of human fertility are fairly constant through time and geographical location, leading, if unregulated, to a growth in population, which would outstrip the means of sustenance.

Malthus began his *First Essay* with a 'disarming' tribute to the utopian vision of William Godwin, later referring to it as 'without doubt by far the most beautiful and engaging of any that has yet appeared.'[79] He went on to demonstrate how a system which abolishes private property and the family will soon result in declining production and lead to a population explosion, with a consequent fall in the standard of living of the poorer classes; famine and disorder would ensue. Malthus distinguished two types of check on population: preventive and positive. The former refers to methods of restricting the birth-rate, while the latter comprises factors which lower life expectancy (such as famine, disease and war). All these checks, he asserted in this early essay, are due to either vice or misery. He does, however, make the suggestion that 'reason' is able to prevent abuses of sexual pleasure by calculating their consequences and that intellectual exertions tend to 'diminish the empire of this passion over man'. Nevertheless he doubted whether 'the lower classes of people in any country' would develop the 'high degree of intellectual improvement' necessary.[80]

In subsequent editions of the *Essay*, Malthus introduced a third check on population, which he called moral restraint, making explicit some of these latter suggestions. By this he meant simply the postponement or renunciation of marriage, with abstinence from all extra-marital sexual relationships. This apparent modification of his theory led him to 'soften some of the harshest conclusions' of the *First Essay*. Later marriages would mean smaller families, and would thus contain population expansion within the bounds prescribed by possible growth in food production, without bringing into play the vicious and miserable alternatives.[81] Malthus believed that education could play an important role in encouraging moral restraint. He considered artificial means of contraception principally in the context of extra-marital intercourse – 'improper arts to prevent the consequences of irregular connections'. Malthus objected to these arts on two grounds: their immorality, which he did not elaborate upon, and 'their tendency to remove a necessary stimulus to industry'.[82]

Indolence, inequality and economic development

This latter point raises a much larger aspect of the Malthusian theory. 'If it were possible,' he wrote, 'for each married couple to limit by a wish the number of their children, there is certainly reason to fear that the indolence of the human race would be greatly increased'.[83] He believed that humans are naturally lazy and need stimulation to activity. The pleasures of sexual intercourse, together with the responsibility of maintaining a family which normally accompanies them, are incentives for working hard and saving, so as to be able to provide for the family. To facilitate intercourse without the risk of procreation might reduce incentives to accumulate. Malthus, however, perceived a much more significant and dangerous policy which would have a similar effect. This was the egalitarian doctrine proclaimed by Godwin, Condorcet and other radical writers of the time.

It is perhaps worth remarking at this point that the widely accepted view that Malthus's primary concern was to limit population, thereby averting the threat of over-population, is erroneous. In the first place over-population, in Malthusian theory, is impossible as a chronic situation. Furthermore, humans have a religious duty to 'replenish the earth'. He actually lamented 'the present scanty population of the earth' and blamed inadequate human institutions for this:

> There are few large countries, however advanced in improvement, the population of which might not have been doubled or tripled, and there are many which might be ten, or even a hundred, times as populous, and yet all the inhabitants be as well provided for as they are now, if the institutions of society, and the moral habits of the people, had been for some hundred years the most favourable to the increase of capital, and the demand for produce and labour.[84]

One purpose of publishing his *Principles of Political Economy* was to refute mistaken economic policies which had the effect of halting population growth short of its 'full complement'.[85] In his *First Essay* Malthus had pointed to rapid growth in population as a sign of prosperity. 'There is not a truer criterion of the happiness and innocence of a people', he maintained, 'than the rapidity of their increase.'[86]

What, then, was the principal aim of Malthus? His own claim was that 'the practical design uppermost in the mind of the writer ... is to improve the condition and increase the happiness of the lower classes of society'.[87] This, however, is not evident from the *First Essay*, where he adopted the generally pessimistic position that 'to prevent the recurrence of misery, is, alas! beyond the power of man' and where he showed little apparent sympathy for 'the unhappy persons who, in the great lottery of life, have drawn a blank'.[88] In the second edition of the *Essay*, Malthus maintained that a poor person whose labour is not required by 'society' 'has no claim of right to the smallest portion of food, and in fact has no business to be where he is. At nature's mighty feast there is no vacant cover for him'.[89] Malthus's primary concern was surely to supply an ideology for the emergence of a 'civilised' state from a 'savage' state by isolating the conditions necessary for social and economic development.

Indispensable conditions for such a development are the security of private property and the existence of a degree of inequality, providing an incentive for men and women to work and save:

> A state in which an inequality of conditions offers the natural rewards of good conduct, and inspires widely and generally the hopes of rising and the fears of falling in society is unquestionably the best calculated to develope the energies and faculties of man, and the best suited to the exercise and improvement of human virtue.[90]

Nevertheless major inequalities are harmful, and Malthus denounced 'the present great inequality of property' as an evil. The division of large estates would increase effective demand and stimulate economic development.[91] While in the abstract it would thus be good to reduce the number of very rich and very poor, there is a limit to the benefits that such a policy would bring, for 'the extreme parts could not be diminished beyond a certain degree without lessening that animated exertion throughout the middle parts'. Furthermore, he doubted whether it is a proper role of government to take positive and direct action to limit large fortunes and to alleviate poverty.[92]

The role of the state

We are thus brought to consider the analogy between the role of the state, and the government of God in their respective spheres. With his eighteenth-century precursors, Malthus clearly believed that human communities are governed by laws ultimately set by 'that Being who first arranged the system of the universe, and for the advantage of his creatures, still executes, according to fixed laws, all its various operations'. It is to the constancy of these laws that we must ascribe the stability of the social and economic system: the industry of the husbandman, the skill of the craftsman, the researches of the physician and the physicist. Without the predictability these laws afford, humankind would lapse into a condition of sloth.[93] How, then, did he see the role of civil institutions, particularly the state, in the workings of the social and economic system?

While it is proper for governments to regulate in a number of ways, they should not attempt to change, the fixed laws of human nature any more than God can be expected to modify the laws of the physical universe. The state cannot supersede the checks on population referred to above, but can direct them 'in such a way as to be the least prejudicial to the virtue and happiness of society'.[94] Malthus was therefore prepared to support Robert Owen's attempts to enact legal regulation of the use of child labour in the cotton industry. The Malthusian position with respect to the role of the state was thus by no means dogmatically *laissez-faire*, and his concern for economic development led him to defend taxation and government borrowing as means to stimulate demand and regenerate the economy. In times of depression he advocated 'public works of all descriptions, the making and repairing of roads, bridges, railways, canals etc.'. No wonder Keynes spoke well of him![95]

Despite this recognition of a positive role for government in the economy, Malthus was frequently critical of state intervention. Ideally the system of free trade was best, and it should be the aim of governments to achieve it so far as is consistent with the general welfare.[96] He criticised British intervention in the Irish economy for being calculated to promote peculiarly English interests. He was against public subsidising of wages, on the grounds that this prevents the population from adjusting itself to a country's diminished resources. By encouraging a higher birth-rate such action harms working people by increasing the supply of labour and thereby reducing wage levels; this was, in his view, precisely the effect of the poor law. While he thus allowed for temporary government action to stimulate growth, he maintained that only those plans which 'co-operate with the lessons of Nature and Providence . . . to encourage and promote habits of prudence and foresight' will offer permanent solutions. He believed that savings banks make an important contribution to this end, 'by giving to each individual the full and entire benefit of his own industry and prudence'.[97]

The Poor Law

The Elizabethan Poor Law, ensuring an institutionalised support for the poor by local authorities, was a particular object of Mathusian censure. Such laws created a permanently dependent class of paupers, deprived people of the incentive to work and save, encouraged a high birth-rate and led to the emergence of an arrogant and tyrannical caste of justices, churchwardens and overseers. The system, moreover, resulted in the persecution of men whose families were likely to become chargeable. The birth-rate was, Malthus thought, determined in the long run and under normal circumstances by the demand for labour,[98] but if it is artificially boosted by a regular system of parish bounties it will lower the level of wages. He asserted the 'absolute impossibility that all the different classes of society should be both well paid and fully employed, if the supply of labour on the whole exceed the demand'.[99] He recognised that the birth-rate commonly takes time to respond to changing economic conditions and that temporary relief might be needed, including emigration, and financial aid. He in fact praised efforts made to relieve distress in the post-1815 years: 'they have not only fulfilled the great moral duty of assisting our fellow-creatures in distress; but they have in point of fact done a great good, or at least prevented great evil'.[100] Thus while he was prepared, particularly in his later writings, to welcome occasional acts of charitable relief or other forms of positive action, by public or private bodies, he believed that any attempt to institutionalise these and to substitute the principle of benevolence for that of self-love would be a disaster.

Malthus thus saw the problem of poverty as structural and not to be cured by individual acts of charity. 'No possible sacrifices by the rich', he declared, 'particularly in money, could for any time prevent the recurrence of distress among the lower members of society.'[101] There is no 'right to subsistence' when a person's labour will not purchase it. He thus saw the poor laws as a prime example of the attempt by governments to contradict the fixed laws of human nature and of the economic system. 'Canute, when he commanded the waves not to wet his princely foot, did not assume a greater power over the laws of nature.'[102] Rather, laws must provide a framework within which the propensities of human nature work to increase the general happiness and particularly the welfare of the poorest, without destroying those challenges which have led to the development of civilisation.

Providence and Process

As the state ought to operate within the constraints of social laws, so God invariably acts in harmony with the general laws of the universe he has created. If he were to act arbitrarily, 'a general and fatal torpor of the human faculties would probably ensue'.[103]

In the *First Essay*, Malthus rejected as inadequate the generally accepted eighteenth-century notion of this life as a time of trial and testing in preparation for a future life. He proposed, in contrast, a position, more consistent with our knowledge of the natural world and our belief in 'the power, goodness and foreknowledge of the Deity'. He criticised prevalent theodicies as raising hypothetical questions about possible worlds rather than attempting to derive a knowledge of God from the created world as we actually know it. We must, he insisted, 'reason from nature up to nature's God and not presume to reason from God to nature'. The 'book of nature' points to 'a long and sometimes painful process in the world'.[104]

In his critique of Godwin, Malthus attempted to refute the philosopher on his own naturalistic assumptions rather than by appealing to supernatural revelation. Whether he himself accepted this quasi-deist position or was simply arguing *ad hominem* is not entirely clear. He insisted, however, that crude and puerile ideas of God's omnipotence had led theologians to 'exalt the power of God at the expense of his goodness' by failing to recognise that 'even to the great Creator, almighty as he is, a certain process may be necessary, a certain time (or at least what appears to us as time) may be requisite, in order to form beings with those exalted qualities of mind which will fit them for his high purposes'.[105]

God cannot do the impossible; neither God nor the civil government can play Canute. They must both observe the laws of the realm they govern. Human maturity *logically* requires a process of maturing. It is impossible – even for God – to create a mature person ready-made. John Pullen accuses Malthus of incoherence, when – discussing divine omnipotence – he declared that God could have created an oak tree ready-made.[106] Malthus would undoubtedly have replied that humans are different from trees, inasmuch as their maturity is achieved by making free responses to the challenges which face them in life. God might be able to create beings *like* humans in a form *as if* they had come to be what they are by having freely responded to challenges, but could not (logically) create – ready made – beings who had *actually* achieved maturity by making free choices.

Malthus went on to outline a 'process theology' in terms similar to that developed by some followers of Whitehead. 'I should be inclined,' Malthus declared,

> to consider the world and this life as the mighty process of God, not for the trial, but for the creation and formation of mind, a process necessary to awaken inert, chaotic matter into spirit, to sublimate the dust of the earth into soul, to elicit an ethereal spark from the clod of clay. And in this view of the subject, the various impressions and excitements which man receives through life may be considered as the forming hand of his Creator, acting by general laws, and awakening his sluggish existence, by the animating touches of the Divinity, into a capacity of superior enjoyment. The original sin of man is the torpor and corruption of the chaotic matter in which he may be said to be born.[107]

Malthus went on to consider how this formative process depends on the existence of stimulants, usually of a painful kind. Mental development requires exertion; pain and evil are necessary to stimulate exertion. In order to produce food in sufficient quantities, for example, it is necessary for people to clear ground, to plough and to plant. This toil should be seen not as assisting God in his creation, but rather as an essential condition of a happy life, 'in order to rouse man into action, and form his mind to reason'. 'It seems highly probable', he continued, 'that moral evil is absolutely necessary to the production of moral excellence.'[108] Malthus developed this theodicy by pointing out that human sorrows and sufferings are factors that encourage in people sympathy and the virtues of Christian charity. Uninterrupted prosperity tends to degrade and harden the human character. 'The heart that has never known sorrow itself will seldom be feelingly alive to the pains and pleasures, the wants and wishes of its fellow beings.'

31

Brotherly love and other amiable affections are developed through the experience of pain.[109]

Divine benevolence

The Malthusian principle – according to which population tends to increase faster than food – is to be seen as urging people 'to further the gracious designs of Providence by the full cultivation of the earth', which in turn will enable it to support 'a more extended population'. The author frankly admitted that this tendency produces much partial evil, but insisted that it is greatly overbalanced by the good. Had the contrary principle obtained, with population and food production increasing at the same rate, 'man might never have emerged from the savage state'.[110] Thus as the state intervenes only rarely to mitigate the harsh effects of economic laws by temporary expedients, being incapable of modifying these laws in any significant way, so God accepts the limitations that the nature of his universe imposes.

Curiously Malthus seems, in his *First Essay*, to have allowed less scope for divine intervention than for that of human government. We have noted how he spoke of God 'always' acting according to general laws.[111] He combined a 'process' understanding of God with a kind of deism, in somewhat the same way as may be found in the early writings of White-head, before he introduced his notion of the 'consequent' nature of God.

Chapter 18 of the *First Essay* met with criticism from contemporary theologians, and Malthus omitted much of this material from later editions. His rejection of eternal punishment and his substitution of the idea that vessels which emerge from the furnace of life 'in wrong shapes' will be 'broken and thrown aside as useless', or 'perish and be condemned to mix again with their original clay',[112] were regarded as unorthodox. So far as theological issues are raised at all in his later writings they are diffused throughout the text. As Pullen notes, there are four things he dropped completely: the explicit rejection of the idea of life as a state of trial and probation, the apparent limitation on divine omnipotence, his idea of original sin, and his belief in conditional immortality.[113] With respect to the first issue, indeed, he wrote in 1816: 'I have always considered the principle of population as a law peculiarly suited to a state of discipline and trial.'[114] Nevertheless a colleague at the East India College, William Empson, declared of his early theological views: 'they contain . . . the principle of the answer which he continued to give, as often as he was applied to for a philosophical solution to the problem of human life'.[115]

Convinced that his own conception was quite consistent with belief in a benevolent God, Malthus denounced the suggestion that 'a large proportion of the human race was doomed by the inscrutable ordinations of Providence to a premature death in large towns'.[116] There is no indication, however, that he would in later life have rejected the principle that 'evil exists in the world not to create despair but activity'.[117]

Whether Malthus's doctrine of God in the *First Essay* can rightly be called Manichaean is doubtful,[118] but there need be little hesitation in calling his theology, from first to last, Pelagian. His praise of such virtues as acquisitiveness and 'prudence' sound rather strange from the pen of a follower of one who taught that his disciples should 'take no thought for the morrow' and should not lay up treasures on earth, but he was by no means alone in this.

The development of Malthus's ideas on population occurred in an intellectual context which had been profoundly influenced by the teachings of Adam Smith.

PROVIDENCE AND THE INVISIBLE HAND: ADAM SMITH

'The *Wealth of Nations*', it has been said, 'is a stupendous palace erected upon the granite of self-interest.'[119] The precise nature of the building and its relationship to a possible foundation in Smith's earlier writings on moral sentiments remain a matter of some controversy. Most recent critics recognise no fundamental conflict between the teachings contained in his two principal works. In this chapter I shall be concerned less with an alleged contradiction between Smith's supposedly egoistic assumptions in the *Wealth of Nations* (1776) and the altruism implied in his *Theory of Moral Sentiments* (1759), than with the analogy to be found in his works between divine providence and state action. The role played by God in the affairs of the universe may be seen as supplying a model for that which should be assumed by the government as regulator of economic and political life. I shall suggest that the key concepts are those of *system* or *machine*, for systems, he believed, in many respects resemble machines, and 'a machine is a little system'.[120] As God is creator and administrator of the system of the universe – which is pictured as a huge machine – so the government operates and manages the machine of state. Here Smith closely followed Isaac Newton, whose system, the economist declared, 'now prevails over all opposition, and has advanced to the acquisition of the most universal empire that was ever established in philosophy'.[121] His own attempts to discover the general laws of the economy were, it has been asserted, inspired by Newton's success in discovering the laws of motion.[122] How these laws operate in relation to celestial and civil government is clearly a question that is central to the theme of this book.

Smith's recent commentators insist that he must be understood principally in the context of the eighteenth-century Scottish Enlightenment, rather than in terms of nineteenth-century liberalism. His spirited assault on mercantilism, with its official monopolies and state bounties, should not be seen as an unqualified approval of what nineteenth-century liberals called *laissez-faire*.[123] Indeed, he recognised a positive, if limited, role for state enterprise and government regulation. Although Smith may properly be seen as an economist who contributed in a major way to the theory of the discipline, he saw political economy as a branch of statecraft, or what we would today call politics. This has sometimes led to incredulity on the part of modern economists.[124] In the view of two recent critics, Smith's principal concern in the *Wealth of Nations* was to outline the conditions of a just economic order in which the majority of labouring people might enjoy abundance. No community, according to him, can be happy if 'the far greater part of the members are poor and miserable'.[125]

Smith's theology

Smith's lectures, while he was professor of Moral Philosophy at Glasgow, began – we are told by his friend John Millar[126] – with a section on natural theology. These have not been discovered, but from what he has written elsewhere it is possible to reconstruct the outlines of his theology. The religious ideas of Adam Smith bear the clear mark of eighteenth-century rationalism and at times of deism. In his later, published work, Smith made little explicit reference to God, but there is no reason to believe that he gave up the theological positions stated in his *Theory of Moral Sentiments*. Although he made some modifications to later editions of the *Theory*, he made no significant changes in what he said about God.

For Smith, God is first and foremost 'the Author of Nature', who wills the happiness of mankind.[127] He is also called the 'Director' of nature, who has 'adjusted with the nicest artifice' each part of the universe to the end for which it was created. God's role is compared to that of the watchmaker, an analogy later made famous in the writings of William Paley.[128] Smith often spoke of the universe as 'an immense machine', created by 'that great, benevolent, and all-wise Being, who directs the movements of nature, and who is determined, by his own unalterable perfections, to maintain in it at all times the greatest possible quantity of happiness'.[129] The wise and virtuous man will recognise that there is on occasion a conflict between his own private interests and those of 'that great society of all sensible and intelligent beings'. As a benevolent and all-wise being 'can admit into the system of his government no partial evil which is not necessary for the universal good', we should not merely accept personal afflictions with resignation, but – seeing them as necessary conditions for the attainment of the general interest – welcome them. Such wise and virtuous persons are compared to faithful soldiers who are prepared, at great risk, to march into battle under a trusted general for the greater good of the whole army and 'cheerfully sacrifice their own little systems to the prosperity of the greater system'. But no military leader can merit such trust more than God, 'the great Conductor of the universe'.[130]

The harmony of nature is an important theme in Smith's moral theory and reflects the influence of Stoic thinkers.[131] Human interposition by rational calculation can have some influence on the course of things, but the scope for such effective action is limited. Humans should 'co-operate with the Deity' in forwarding the happiness of rational creatures – the end for which the universe was created; he suggested that the best way for them to do so in the economic sphere is, typically, by pursuing their own interests in an enlightened manner. This is because God has created a world in which there is a general coincidence between individual interests (reinforced by passions) and the general welfare. By pursuing his own interests the individual 'frequently promotes that of the society more effectually than when he really intends to promote it. I have never', he added drily, 'known much good done by those who affected to trade for the publick good'.[132] While he recognised the utility of self-interest, he by no means admired all its manifestations. Despising the search for trivial material possessions – 'baubles and trinkets' – he nevertheless recognised that the demand for luxuries often stimulates economic development. For his own part, however, he admired the 'sublime' doctrine of the Stoics where true happiness is largely independent of fortune.[133]

There are, however, occasions when rules which are generally benevolent will have unfortunate consequences. Human initiative may then be appropriate, though it is rarely rewarded with total success. Only in the context of an afterlife will the divine plan be completed and all injustices be removed. Our earthly happiness will, therefore, depend on an appeal to 'the all-seeing Judge of the world, whose eye can never be deceived, and whose judgments can never be perverted' and on a 'humble hope and expectation of a life to come'.[134] That the rules of morality are to be seen as 'the commands and laws of the Deity' gives them increased legitimacy and supplies a further incentive for obeying them.[135]

God has thus created a universe where the rational and calculated actions of humans play a relatively small part. The idea of 'contrivance', later taken up by Chalmers, is crucial. 'The economy of nature' reflects a harmony between means and ends. Its author has not left it to human reason to discover the best means of securing 'the welfare and preservation of society', but has endowed human beings with 'an immediate and instinctive approbation' of those things that realise this end.[136] Thus humans have an appetite not only for the end, but also for the means of attaining that end, which are not entrusted to 'the slow and uncertain determinations of our reason'.[137] This is evident in the relationship between parents and children, where Smith sees God's providential hand at work. As the future of the human race depends more upon parents caring for their children than upon children caring for their parents, so parental tenderness is a much stronger sentiment than filial piety. Moralists need generally not to encourage

35

parents to protect and forward the interests of their children, but rather to restrain their fondness.[138]

Again, as 'beneficence is less essential to the existence of society than justice' – which is 'the main pillar that upholds the whole edifice' – so nature has implanted in the human breast a powerful consciousness of injustice and a terror of merited punishment which leads people to protect the weak, restrain the violent and punish the guilty.[139] Thus, although we may properly speak of Smith's theology as reflecting an eighteenth-century rationalism, he fully recognised the role that non-rational factors do actually play in human affairs. In this respect he shares a great deal with such early twentieth-century theorists as Graham Wallas and L. T. Hobhouse.[140]

This is the context in which Smith's celebrated notion of the 'invisible hand' is to be read. D. D. Raphael pronounces that Smith's image of the invisible hand 'is not a piece of theology'.[141] Certainly Smith did not assume the notion of a God who 'pulls the strings all the time', arbitrarily intervening in the world. This would have had effects similar to a polytheism he rejected – 'the invisible hand of Jupiter'.[142] Nevertheless, the metaphor of the invisible hand, as found in Smith's two principal works, is manifestly related to the rational theology that he espoused. Smith's whole doctrine of unintended consequences does not indeed imply a 'god of the gaps' who acts arbitrarily in particularly cases to bring good out of evil by a special providence, but an Author of nature who sets up a system in which social welfare is realised in general by each pursuing his or her own interests. 'Private interests and passions of individuals', he wrote, 'naturally dispose them to turn their stock towards the employments which in ordinary cases are most advantageous to society.'[143] He applied this idea to political economy, recognising a general (though not invariable) coincidence between self-interest and social welfare, consequently warning against excessive governmental regulation.

Many recent commentators on Adam Smith seem set on denying, explicitly or by omission, the importance of these theological foundations of his system. Donald Winch, in a book on *Adam Smith's Politics* makes almost no reference to his ideas about God, while John Dunn, in properly contrasting his position with that of Locke, actually asserts that he was a 'practical atheist'.[144]

Cosmic and social harmony

In his early lectures on the history of physics and astronomy Smith, following Newton again, related the development of the natural sciences to the abandoning of polytheism and to the adoption of monotheistic beliefs. Only when the universe was seen as a single system could a science seeking general laws, and a religion recognising a single rational creator, be developed. Polytheism ascribes 'all the irregular events of nature to the favour

or displeasure of intelligent, though invisible, beings'. The regular occur-
rences in nature are not ascribed to 'the invisible hand of Jupiter', but only
the unusual and the unpredictable: thunder and lightning, storms and
sunshine.[145] In the distant past, the apparent incoherence of the universe
led people to ascribe 'almost every unexpected event, to the arbitrary will
of some designing, though invisible beings, who produced it for some
private and particular purpose'. They had no idea of a universal God who
created and governs the whole according to general laws. But 'as soon as
the Universe was regarded as a complete machine, as a coherent system,
governed by general laws, and directed to general ends' it came to be seen
as the work of a supreme being. 'As ignorance begot superstition, science
gave birth to the first theism that arose among those nations, who were not
enlightened by divine Revelation.'[146]

Yet Smith did not give an unqualified approval to the Stoic belief that all
events, including 'the vices and follies of mankind', are to be seen as
necessary parts of one great system.[147] He claimed that speculations of this
kind fail to diminish our natural abhorrence of vice, the immediate and
harmful consequences of which must outweigh any remote benefits which
might result.[148] It is therefore somewhat misleading of Donald Winch to
speak of his 'Mandevillian cynicism'. Bernard Mandeville had taught that
the public interest may be served by private vices, and this teaching Smith
quite explicitly rejected.[149] He understood Mandeville to abolish the distinction between virtue and vice and to maintain that all preference of
public to private interest is nothing more than the indulgence of vanity.
While admitting for the sake of argument that 'the most generous and
public spirited actions may . . . in some sense be regarded as proceeding
from self-love', he went on to insist that 'self-love may frequently be a
virtuous motive for action'.[150] He is here, of course, following the main-
stream of British eighteenth-century moral theology, as exemplified in
Joseph Butler's notion of 'cool self love' as an acceptable motive for virtuous
action.[151] Smith distinguished between a proper desire to do what is honourable, thereby rendering ourselves legitimate objects of esteem and
approbation, and vanity, which is the desiring of praise for qualities which
are not praiseworthy:

> There is an affinity between vanity and the love of true glory, as both
> these two passions aim at acquiring esteem and approbation. But they
> are different in this, that the one is a just, reasonable and equitable
> passion, while the other is unjust, absurd and ridiculous.[152]

In common with most eighteenth-century British moralists, Smith taught
that self-love is not necessarily vicious and that the universe was created
by a benign author who has generally arranged things so that the common
interest is likely to be forwarded by people pursuing their own interests
and following their sentiments in an enlightened way. He taught that

human instincts which lead to a particular affection for those close to us are also providentially designed to forward the general interest. 'That wisdom which contrived the system of human affections, as well as every other part of nature', he maintained,

> seems to have judged that the interest of the great society of mankind would be best promoted by directing the principal attention of each individual to that particular portion of it which was most within the sphere both of his abilities and of his understanding.[153]

We shall shortly see how Smith applied these ideas to the historical development of states and to the running of a national economy.

The machine of state

There is thus a natural order in the universe as a whole that is replicated at a lower organic level in 'the mechanism of a plant' and at the political level 'in the great system of government.'[154] While he recognised that government is but 'an imperfect remedy' for the deficiency of wisdom and virtue, Smith spoke of the political order as a machine whose end, like that of the universe, is general happiness. Insofar as it fails to attain this end, the cause is a failure to take sufficient account of the effects of human wickedness.[155] Nevertheless, from a philosophical standpoint, 'Human society . . . appears like a great, an immense machine, whose regular and harmonious movements produce a thousand agreeable effects.' It is, moreover, a 'beautiful and noble machine'.[156] He believed that the appeal to human imagination and aesthetic sensibility is more likely to encourage respect for the public interest than are arguments based on material considerations: it will often be to no purpose to tell a person

> what superior advantages the subjects of a well-governed state enjoy; that they are better lodged, that they are better clothed, that they are better fed. These considerations will commonly make no great impression. You will be more likely to persuade, if you describe the great system of public police which procures these advantages, – if you explain the connections and dependencies of its several parts, their mutual subordination to one another, and their general subserviency to the happiness of the society; if you shew how this system might be introduced into his own country, what it is that hinders it from taking place there at present, how those obstructions might be removed and all the several wheels of the machine of government be made to move with more harmony and smoothness, without grating upon one another, or mutually retarding one another's motions.

A person hearing this will feel a desire to put into motion 'so beautiful and so orderly a machine'.[157]

This aesthetic admiration for system and order is characteristic of Smith's cosmology as well as of his political economy. In his essay 'Of the Imitative Arts', Smith compared the pleasure of contemplating an ordered system with that of hearing 'a well-composed concerto of instrumental Music':

> In the contemplation of that immense variety of agreeable and melo-
> dious sounds, arranged and digested, both in their coincidence and
> in their succession, into so complete and regular a system, the mind
> in reality enjoys not only a very great sensual, but a very high
> intellectual, pleasure, not unlike that which is derived from the con-
> templation of a great system in any other science.[158]

Jacob Viner's comment that there is 'a wide divergence between the perfectly harmonious, completely beneficent natural order of *The Theory of
Moral Sentiments* and the partial and limited harmony in the economic order
of the *Wealth of Nations*' is misleading. The cosmic harmony is not complete
and the general rules of the universe allow injustice, oppression and wrong;
all is not well in a fallen world inhabited by beings in a 'depraved' condition.[159] As we have seen, partial evil may in some circumstances be a
condition of universal good, but it is only in a life beyond this world that
true harmony will exist. Thus in the 'economy of nature' as well as in the
civil economy an incomplete order and harmony are to be found. But what
are the nature and limits of the political and economic order?

Social order and class distinction

Smith saw a kind of order in human communities and related this to their
economic base. He outlined four 'periods of society', based successively on
hunting, sheep-rearing, agriculture and, finally, commerce. In this historical process, he acknowledged a principle which, as we have seen, operates
at other levels: the providential role of unintended consequences. In the
agricultural period, for example, the increased production of manufactured
goods encouraged new wants. The great barons and the higher clergy
started spending the whole of their revenue; the only way to increase
revenue was to grant leases to tenants, who thereby acquired a significant
degree of independence. Thus the vanity and excessive desire for opulence
on the part of the landowning classes led to the strengthening of tenants'
rights, to the demand for greater liberty and 'the regular execution of
justice'.[160]

Later social formations are characterised by a hierarchy of orders, ranks
and classes. Smith was ambivalent about the sentiments that produce this
structure; these include an obsequiousness to our superiors, arising largely
from our admiration for the advantages of their situation. He pointed to the
human disposition almost to worship the rich and powerful and despise
the poor, which is a principal cause of the erosion of moral sentiments.[161]

It is partly for this reason, as we shall see, that Smith viewed the development of a commercial system as something of a mixed blessing. He nevertheless insisted on the importance of such divisions. 'Every independent state', he asserted, 'is divided into many different orders and societies. Upon the ability of each particular order or society to maintain its own powers, privileges, and immunities, against the encroachments of every other, depends the stability of that particular constitution.'[162]

With respect to these social divisions Smith made two points which reflect his doctrine of providence and the invisible hand. In the first place the 'distinction of ranks', upon which depends social peace, is founded not on 'the often uncertain difference of wisdom and virtue', but on the more palpable difference of birth and fortune, which provides a firmer footing for affective ties.[163] Second the partiality which individuals have for the groups to which they belong, 'though it may sometimes be unjust, may not upon that account be useless':

> It checks the spirit of innovation. It tends to preserve whatever is the established balance among the different orders and societies into which the state is divided; and while it sometimes appears to obstruct some alterations of government which may be fashionable and popular at the time, it contributes in reality to the stability and permanency of the whole system.[164]

This takes up a point made earlier about how general welfare is typically forwarded by persons pursuing their own interests and responding to the limited responsibilities of their station, though he also insisted that good citizenship implies a wish to promote 'the welfare of the whole society'. Particular loyalties and appetites must therefore be held in check.[165] A good ruler, he declared in Burkean style, will accommodate as well as he can to the prejudices and habits of the people and 'will content himself with moderating, what he cannot annihilate without great violence'.[166]

The foundation of government

Following David Hume, Smith rejected any idea that social order or civil authority can be founded in a social contract and he exposed the fallacy of 'tacit consent'.[167] In *The Theory of Moral Sentiments* he argued that 'society' is held together and subsists 'as among different merchants, from a sense of utility, without any mutual love or affection; and though no man in it should owe any obligation, or be bound in gratitude to any other, it may still be upheld by a mercenary exchange of good offices according to an agreed valuation'.[168] Government also is generally based on 'the principle of utility' in combination with 'the principle of authority'. While republican and democratic governments are based predominantly on the former, monarchies rely greatly on a general respect for authority. This is often reinforced by the divine analogy; the king stands to his realm as God stands to the universe, and disobedience to civil government is understood as 'a sort of sinfulness or impiety'.[169]

Governments, in fact, came into being for the protection of property. A nation of hunters has almost no private property, 'but when flocks and herds come to be reared property then becomes of a very considerable extent'.[170] It is at this stage that governments evolve, for they exist to protect the rich from the poor. In his lectures he is reported as saying:

Laws and government may be considered . . . as a combination of the rich to oppress the poor, and preserve to themselves the inequality of the goods which would otherwise be soon destroyed by the attacks of the poor, who if not hindered by the government would soon reduce the others to an equality with themselves by open violence.[171]

Among the generally beneficial effects of manufacturing and commerce was the introduction of order and good government 'and with them, the liberty and security of individuals'.[172]

In properly ordered states, the government has a threefold duty of protecting the nation from external threats, of protecting each individual from injustice or oppression from fellow citizens – by establishing 'an exact administration of justice' – and, finally, 'of erecting and maintaining certain public works and certain public institutions'.[173] These include especially institutions which 'facilitate the commerce of the society' and which promote education.[174] Smith clearly acknowledged that there were certain enterprises and establishments of public benefit, but which 'it can never be for the interest of any individual, or small number of individuals, to erect and maintain'. He recognised, furthermore, the right of governments to raise revenue by taxation and also to use taxation as an instrument of social policy to deter foolish or anti-social practices.[175] Earlier he had put the position more positively when he argued that the civil magistrate is properly concerned with 'promoting the prosperity of the commonwealth, by establishing good discipline, and by discouraging every sort of vice and impropriety'; to achieve this he may not only prohibit mutual injury among citizens but also 'command mutual good offices to a certain degree'.[176]

Having said this, Smith saw the basic role of government as the regulating and maintaining of the conditions for the smooth running of the social system. 'The natural effort', he wrote,

of every individual to better his own condition, when suffered to exert itself with freedom and security, is so powerful a principle, that it is alone, and without any assistance, not only capable of carrying on the society to wealth and prosperity, but of surmounting a hundred impertinent obstructions with which the folly of human laws too often incumbers its operations.[177]

41

By the regulation of commerce Smith did not mean the introduction of protection or bounties or the establishment of government subsidies for certain products. These are almost always urged by tradesmen whose interests are different from those of the public and 'who have generally an interest to deceive and even to oppress the public'.[178] In a celebrated passage he denounced the 'sneaking arts of underling tradesmen' which are 'erected into political maxims for the conduct of a great empire'. Under the influence of such maxims it becomes the object of each nation to beggar their neighbours and 'commerce, which ought naturally to be, among nations, as among individuals, a bond of union and friendship, has become the most fertile source of discord and animosity'.[179]

Governments should thus provide a structure within which individuals and groups can pursue 'their own interest in their own way'. But, as in a game, the competitor must abide by the rules:

> In the race for wealth, and honours, and preferments, he may run as hard as he can, and strain every nerve and every muscle, in order to outstrip all his competitors. But if he should justle, or throw down any of them, the indulgence of the spectators is entirely at an end.[180]

Honest competition in the marketplace is, he insisted 'advantageous to the great body of the people', who profit greatly by it.[181] Each competitor is thinking primarily of his own interest, and the general interest is forwarded. It is not, he observed in a celebrated dictum, 'from the benevolence of the butcher, the brewer, or the baker, that we expect our dinner, but from their regard to their own interests'. The capitalist who invests in local industry and uses his influence to increase its efficiency does not intend to promote the public interest, but is 'led by an invisible hand to promote an end which was not part of his intention'.[182] The invisible hand is also at work in the distribution of goods. A rich person, despite his vain and insatiable desires, is able actually to consume little more than the poor person. The prosperity of the rich in a community benefits the poor, by what is sometimes called a 'trickle-down effect'. The rich, then,

> are led by an invisible hand to make nearly the same distribution of the necessaries of life which would have been made had the earth been divided into equal portions among all its inhabitants; and thus without intending it, without knowing it, advance the interest of the society and afford means to the multiplication of the species.[183]

This generally optimistic view of political economy is, as I have suggested, part of a picture of the state as a machine and is in turn closely related – univocally and analogically – to an understanding of the universe as a huge system or machine constructed and operated by a benevolent and rational being. It is in this theological context that the social theory of Adam Smith is best understood and on these foundations that the stupendous palace he erected stands – or falls.

3

UNITARIAN RADICALS AND ORTHODOX ANGLICANS

The century following the restoration of the monarchy in 1660, saw a growth in England of different varieties of antitrinitarian theology. As is well known, John Locke and Isaac Newton, like John Milton, were critical of Trinitarian formulae, and their Christology has been described as Arian. Both were circumspect in their expression of these views. The less cautious William Whiston (1667–1752), Newton's successor as Lucasian Professor of Mathematics at Cambridge and a priest, lost his job in 1710, owing to Arian beliefs. These men were members of the Church of England, as was Samuel Clarke (1675–1729), rector of St James's Church, Piccadilly, who published in 1712 his *Scripture Doctrine of the Trinity*. This was denounced as Arian, though the 'high' Arianism of Clarke and other Newtonians was not far from certain forms of Trinitarianism, found particularly among the Fathers of the Eastern Church. What Clarke disavowed was the notion of a deity composed of three equal and practically identical units. Like many of the early fathers of the church, he believed in a kind of priority of the Father, as source and fount of godhead.

Other forms of anti-trinitarianism, inspired by continental Socinianism, were more radical in their implications. While Arians believed that Jesus was the incarnation of a pre-existing divine being (though distinct from and inferior to the deity), Socinians insisted he was a human being chosen and raised by God to be his unique witness on earth. They both tended to be rather 'fundamentalist' in their interpretation of Scripture and accepted most of the New Testament miracles, including the resurrection of Christ. Socinians, however, rejected ideas of satisfaction and atonement, which, they claimed, call into question the unity of the deity.[1] As Albrecht Ritschl pointed out, Socinus and his followers pictured God as an absolute monarch who could forgive sins by his own arbitrary decree, without any need for 'satisfaction'.[2] Sin was seen as disobedience to the personal commands of a ruler rather than the breaking of some eternal law. The more radical Socinians had views similar to those of deists, like Charles Blount (1648–1708), Matthew Tindal (1655–1733) and John Toland (1670–1722), who believed that all the fundamental truths of religion can in principle be

44

derived from human reason, and that revelation adds nothing new to our knowledge of God.

Richard Price and Joseph Priestley were Dissenting ministers of Unitarian persuasion, uninhibited by formal links to the Established Church. They recognised a close relationship between their political and religious beliefs. Furthermore their emphasis upon a monolithic God finds a striking analogy in their belief in a single political will. These concepts and images, indeed, suggest links more fundamental than those which they themselves acknowledged. William Paley's insistence on the' greatest happiness' principle constitutes a significant link between his understanding of human government and divine, while important aspects of the analogical reasoning that characterised Joseph Butler's discussion of the relationship of the natural to the supernatural government of the universe were incorporated into his understanding of civil government. These two divines strove to rehabilitate orthodox theology by rebutting deist and secularising tendencies of their day. Between them they dominated the religious ideas of early nineteenth-century England.

PRIESTLEY AND PRICE

Though Priestley and Price were friends and colleagues, renouncing Trinitarian theology and generally having common political convictions on the major events of their day, they differed in certain fundamental philosophical and religious beliefs. They nevertheless suffer the fate of other 'twins' in the history of political thought, like Fourier and Saint-Simon, Maistre and Bonald, Mably and Morelly. Having once been linked on some particular issue, usually by a hostile critic, they remain – in the popular mind – for ever one. As we shall see, however, Price was an Arian while Priestley was a Socinian; Price believed in free will and self-determination while Priestley was a materialist and a 'necessarian'; Price was a critic of the utilitarianism professed by Priestley; Price believed in a Cartesian duality of body and soul while Priestley believed that, in the case of humans at least, the material body was suffused by spirit. Priestley's materialism is indebted to Hobbes, Hartley and Collins,[3] while Price's idealism drew inspiration from Platonism. They both maintained that providence works through history and that human progress in some way contributes to the coming millennium, when God's kingdom will be established 'on earth as it is in heaven'.[4]

In politics, Price and Priestley might crudely be called 'bourgeois radicals'. They defended the American colonists and the French revolutionaries against their British critics. They were indeed among the leading 'political theologians and theological politicians', who were the object of Edmund Burke's wrath. They were spokesmen of a rising commercial class, arguing for *laissez-faire* and a minimal state, and above all were fervent defenders of 'liberty', religious, civil and social. They protested against Dissenters being deprived of full civil rights and attacked the idea of established churches, believing that the state should be concerned with maintaining order and protecting rights rather than with questions of 'truth'. They saw in the newly founded United States the embodiment of many of the principles they advocated. Priestley went so far as to postulate anarchy as an ideal. 'It would be happy', he wrote, 'if mankind could do without any forms of government, civil or ecclesiastical'.[5]

Though they inherited much from the earlier 'Commonwealth men' and from a radical tradition going back to the Civil War, they were not hostile to monarchy as such. They had little time for dogmas of equality and accepted a rather hierarchical social order, urging a paternalistic concern for the poor on the part of the rich.[6] Yet they were constant and outspoken in their belief in 'the people'. Priestley in particular asserted that there may be only 'one will' in a political community and that must be the will of the people. I shall suggest that this aspect of their thought is closely related to their monolithic view of God. As one commentator points out, Priestley assailed a 'tritheism of political orthodoxy in England', where the ideal of a mixed constitution embodying monarchy, aristocracy and democracy operated under king, lords and commons.[7]

Two political preachers

Richard Price (1723–91) was a Welshman, son of a strictly Calvinist Dissenting minister. He studied for the Dissenting ministry in London, where he came under the influence of John Eames, a disciple and friend of Isaac Newton. By this time, affected by the more optimistic ideas of the day, he had renounced the strict Calvinism of his father. The principal intellectual influences on Price were the Cambridge Platonists, Newton, Samuel Clarke and Bishop Joseph Butler. Of the latter's *Analogy*, Price wrote: 'I reckon it happy for me that this book was one of the first that fell into my hands.'[8] In 1758 Price published a major contribution to eighteenth-century moral philosophy, *A Review of the Principal Questions (and Difficulties) in Morals*, where he defended a basically intuitionist theory, asserting that moral judgments are made in the context of a goodness and 'rectitude' which are given in the nature of the created order.[9] As a member of the 'Honest Whigs', a group which met regularly in the City, he joined Benjamin Franklin, Priestley and a number of – mainly Dissenting – clergy to discuss issues of the day over 'Welsh rabbits and apple puffs, porter and beer'.[10] His friendship with Franklin went back further; the American was, indeed, one of Price's sponsors for the fellowship of the Royal Society, largely on the basis of his work on probability. He was an expert in actuarial problems.[11] However, Price became increasingly involved in the controversies of his day. 'The study of Politics,' he told Lord Monboddo in 1780, has been a late deviation into which I have been drawn by the circumstances of the times and the critical situation of our public affairs. Of this study I am now almost sick; and I am continually resolving to confine my attention for the future to moral, metaphysical, mathematical, and theological subjects.[12]

This was not to be. His concern with America was followed by controversy over the French Revolution, with his November 1789 address to the Revolution Society on the love of our country. He died two years later.

Joseph Priestley (1733–1804) was ten years his junior. They first met in 1766, when Price took him as a guest to the Royal Society, of which he later became a fellow. Priestley made important contributions to the study of chemistry and also to the understanding of electricity. Much of his life was spent as a Unitarian minister and tutor in the north and midlands, among the manufacturing and commercial classes of Leeds, Warrington and Birmingham. In 1791 his home, laboratory and library in Birmingham were sacked by a 'church and king' mob, and he moved to London, succeeding Price as a minister in Hackney. His radical reputation at this time, not entirely deserved, was partly due to a daring analogy he employed in a sermon on 5 November 1785. 'We are,' he declared, 'as it were, laying gunpowder, grain by grain, under the old building of error and superstition, which a single spark may hereafter inflame, so as to produce an instantaneous explosion.'[13] As panic spread among English people, surveying events over the Channel, opposition to radicals became more strident:

> Sedition is their creed;
> Feigned sheep but wolves indeed,
> How can we trust?
> Gunpowder Priestley would
> Deluge the throne with blood,
> And lay the great and good,
> Low in the dust.[14]

Priestley was honoured with French citizenship and was a candidate for the Constitutional Convention in 1792, but withdrew in the face of opposition from Marat and Robespierre. In 1794 Priestley emigrated to the calmer and more congenial climate of the United States, where he died in 1804.

An undifferentiated God

Price believed that Christ, the Son of God, can properly be honoured as saviour and redeemer of a fallen world, but that worship, strictly speaking, should be offered to God alone – 'that one, undivided and self-existent Being and cause of all causes who sent Christ into the world'.[15] Following Samuel Clarke, he maintained that the necessary being of God implies his unity: 'It is contingent existence alone that admits of diversity and multiplicity. Simplicity and unity are included in the idea of necessity.'[16]

Priestley, adhering to the Socinian tradition, denounced ideas of a pre-existent Son. In his 'Forms of Prayer and Other Offices', he frequently addressed God as 'maker and governor of the world' or 'thou great governor of the universe', whose rule contrasts with 'the weak and ambitious lords of this world'. One such prayer went on to urge God to 'shew thyself indeed the King of kings and Lord of lords'.[17] God is the 'the great and only potentate . . . sovereign disposer of all affairs, and of all events'.[18] In these prayers he quoted several times a verse from the Book of Daniel: 'thou dost whatsoever thou pleasest in the armies of heaven, and among the inhabitants of the earth'.[19]

God is seen as omnipotent ruler but also as father. Humans are not only the 'subjects of thy government', but also 'objects of thy care'.[20] The image of God's fatherhood – his parental care for his children – is often employed, and leads to a belief that 'all men are brethren' and to 'a sense of common interest'.[21] Indeed, our intercourse with God is 'founded on the analogy between our relation to him, and that to our earthly parents', and a well-founded patriotism is, Priestley asserted, also grounded on this belief in the fatherhood of God.[22]

The image of God's fatherhood, however, so far from legitimating a belief in God's continual 'paternalistic' intervention in the affairs of the universe – a God of 'caring and concern' – provides rather the justification for a *laissez-faire* position:

> Now it has pleased our universal parent to trust the whole human race as we, if we act wisely, treat children, i.e. leave them as much as they safely may be to themselves, interposing only to prevent some great and fatal evil, of which it was impossible that they should be sufficiently apprized themselves.[23]

This divine restraint provides a model for limited civil government. Addressing Frenchmen in 1793 on the subject of church and state, he wrote:

> If I were to address you as *politicians* on the subject of *religion*, it would be in the language of the French merchants to your famous *Colbert* when he asked them what the government could do in favour of trade, *Laissez nous faire*, let us alone.[24]

Priestley often employed managerial concepts in discussing the work of God, who was pictured as overseeing and administering the affairs of the universe, which he created to run according to pre-established laws.[25] In his relations with humans God is also 'the inspector and judge'.[26] If the images used by Priestley imply a somewhat despotic and managerial figure, it ought also to be recorded that God was seen as wholly benevolent: 'To a mind not warped by theological and metaphysical subtilties', he wrote in 1771, 'the Divine Being appears to be actuated by no other views than the noblest we can conceive, the happiness of his creatures.' He added that justice, veracity and other virtues have 'nothing intrinsically excellent in them, separate from their relation to the happiness of mankind'.[27] This utilitarian assertion represents a bold renunciation of the position maintained by such theologians as Joseph Butler, and not least to the theory of Richard Price.

Price's understanding of God differed in its emphasis from that of his younger colleague in significant ways. In his *Review* Price was insistent that the principles of rectitude are prior to the will of God; the goodness and badness of actions are rooted in the nature of things and apprehended by the conscience. Moral obligation is not created by the will and command of God and 'nothing could ever be commanded by the Deity, was there no reason for commanding it'.[28] His whole treatise represents a sustained attack on moral positivism. The deity is indeed the 'fountain of all power and jurisdiction, the cause of all causes, the disposer of the lots of all beings, the life and informing principle of all nature', but he is a just and good God, whose nature is identical with eternal truth and reason.[29] Rectitude is a universal law which regulates the whole creation; 'it is the source and guide of all the actions of the Deity himself, and on it his throne and government are founded'.[30] In an address to the meeting-house in the Old Jewry, on the text 'Thy Kingdom come', he declared:

> It is evident that by the kingdom . . . is meant, not the absolute dominion of the Deity by which he does *whatever he pleases in the Armies of Heaven and among the inhabitants of the earth,* but that moral kingdom which consists in the voluntary obedience of reasonable beings to his laws.[31]

Here, in contrast to an earlier reference to this military analogy[32] (which Priestley, as we have seen, also employed), the speaker seems critical of the positivism implied in the analogy.

Price's critique of divine positivism was to some degree replicated in his discussion of the role of will and rectitude in politics. As D. O. Thomas observes, 'it is not to be supposed that he rejected the theological version of that doctrine only to surrender himself to a secular form of it'.[33] He opposed 'a government by will' to 'a government by laws made with common consent', which he called a free government.[34] It is to this idea of a free government that we must now turn, in relation to Price's dubious concept of 'the will of the people'.

Free government and popular sovereignty

Freedom, for Price, means self-direction or self-government, with respect to God, the individual and the state. Only in the first is this perfectly realised. The individual and the state can enjoy only a restricted freedom in this life. Borrowing from Locke, he saw 'free government' as a 'trust', administered on behalf of 'the people'.[35] All civil government which can claim to be free is 'the creature of the people'. 'In every free state', he went on,

> every man is his own Legislator. All taxes are free-gifts for public services. All laws are particular provisions or regulations established by common consent for gaining protection and safety. All magistrates are trustees or deputies for carrying these regulations into execution.[36]

However, as J. S. Mill pointed out in his famous essay *On Liberty*, there is a great difference between the government of each man by himself, and the government of each by all the rest. In his 'Fast Sermon' of 1781 Price returned to this theme. A free government is 'the dominion of men over themselves in opposition to the dominion of men over other men, or a government by laws made with common consent, in opposition to a government by will'.[37] Only if the consent is an explicit consent given by all the participants can this case be defended, and this is not practically possible in a civil state. Only by introducing the idea of a social contract and of tacit consent, or by the Rousseauan myth of a general will can Price's position be defended, and it is not clear that he is prepared to go very far down either path. What he seems to do is to opt for as much freedom as possible, with few laws in a minimal state. This world in its present sinful state 'is by no means fitted to be the seat of complete happiness or of a perfect government'.[38] Human hope rests in the fact that this earth is a temporary resting-place and that we look forward to another kingdom not made with hands.

Although Price repudiated the notion of original sin as a fault in individuals passed down from Adam which totally corrupts them, depriving them of freedom, he recognised the fact of a corporate sin in which humans were caught up:

> Those powers which were destined to govern are made to serve, and those powers which were destined to serve are allowed to govern. Passion guides human life and most men make no other use of their reason than to justify whatever their interest or their inclinations determine them to do.[39]

We are, he lamented in his Fast Sermon, 'too corrupt to deserve the favour of Providence'. 'We find ourselves frail, degenerate, guilty and mortal beings', he told his congregation. 'The causes under the Divine government which brought us into this state lie far out of our sight . . . We should learn to take our state as we find it.'[40] With this profound sense of human sin it is not surprising he saw that 'the tendency of every government is to despotism'.[41] Government involves putting power into the hands of a few, and 'nothing corrupts more than power', which needs continual vigilance and must be restrained.[42] Divine government is perfect but all human government falls short:

> such are the principles that govern human nature, such the weakness and folly of men, such their love of domination, selfishness and depravity, that none of them can be raised to an elevation above others without the utmost danger. The constant experience of the world has verified this and proved that nothing intoxicates the human mind so much as power.[43]

Even with respect to God, Price attacked the Hobbist idea that 'unlimited power confers an unlimited right', insisting that God's 'sovereign authority' derives not merely from his power, but from 'the infinite excellences of his nature'.[44]

Belief in the corrupting tendency of power led Price to advocate restricted government within the context of a balanced constitution. Despite his belief in the sovereignty of the people, to which we shall return, Price preferred a 'mixed' form of government to democracy. Nor was he a republican: 'so far am I from preferring a government purely republican, that I look upon our own constitution of government as better adapted than any other to this country, and in theory excellent'.[45] He nevertheless told Benjamin Franklin that he rejoiced to see a federal constitution adopted in the United States.[46] The constitution enshrined the principle of limited government, securing liberty both to the states and to their individual members.

Price reserved particular condemnation for colonial government, or what he called 'provincial government', when colonial residents are unrepresented in the metropolitan legislature: 'The history of mankind proves these to be the worst of all governments and that no oppression is equal to that which one people are capable of practising towards another.' Colonial domination is rapacious and oppressive, and with David Hume he asserted that 'free governments' were worse than despotic governments in this respect.[47] Priestley in turn believed that American independence heralded the end of colonial domination. 'No part of *America, Africa, or Asia,*' he told Edmund Burke, 'will be held in subjection to any part of *Europe*'.[48]

One will

In his *Observations on the Nature of Civil Liberty*, first published in 1776, Price practically defined government in terms of will. It 'is, or ought to be, nothing but an institution for collecting and carrying into execution the will of the people'.[49] While he was keen to reject ideas of parliamentary sovereignty or omnipotence, he appears at times to have granted these attributes to 'the people'. Of the people he wrote: 'theirs is the only real omnipo-

51

tence'.[50] A conservative Anglican critic of contemporary radicalism denounced the setting up of 'the majesty of the people' as the origin of legitimate government.[51] A free state, Price insisted, is one guided by its own will, or '(which comes to the same) by the will of an assembly of representatives appointed by itself and accountable to itself', yet even here he was willing to add to this the possibility of an hereditary council and a supreme executive magistrate as 'useful checks'.[52] In a free state all parts must be represented (here he is thinking of the lack of representation of the American colonies). Also representatives must be freely chosen, act independently when elected and, being chosen for a short term, be 'accountable to their constituents'.[53] He referred to the 'will of the state', which must govern in all free states; it is said to be the 'will of the whole'.

As Price's admirer and biographer admits, 'to conceive of the function of government under the category of will is fraught with danger'. But he goes on to assert that so far from freeing political power from moral restraint, the Welsh preacher 'invested the people with ultimate authority precisely because he believed that they would prove to be the best custodians of moral values and natural rights'.[54] If by 'the people' he meant the masses, then clearly this is not so, as his colleague Priestley discovered to his cost in 1791. As Thomas points out, Price's defence of the French National Assembly rested on its right to suspend the balanced constitution to make urgent reforms: 'it was to be hoped that when they had achieved these reforms the representatives of the people would restore the balanced constitution'.[55] This distinction between constitutional government and revolutionary politics is very close to the doctrine of Robespierre, outlined in Chapter 4 below.

As we might expect from his understanding of divine authority, Priestley was much less ambiguous about the role of will in politics, and appears to have been unconcerned by the dangers of ascribing sovereignty to the people. Just as there is '*one will* in the whole universe', which 'disposes of all things, even to their minutest circumstances',[56] it is, he insisted in Rousseauan mode, 'a manifest absurdity' to have more than one will in the state. 'In every state,' he pronounced, 'as in every person, there ought to be but one will.'[57] To create another will is to create another state. This monolithic conception of the state is thus strikingly analogous to Priestley's monolithic theology. A philosophical monotheism is thus projected on to the state in terms of a single general will. But this does not imply a belief that this sovereign will can fully be represented in political institutions. Priestley in fact rejected the idea of parliamentary omnipotence, the 'preposterous and slavish maxim, that whatever is enacted by that body of men, in whom the supreme power of the state is vested, must, in all cases, be implicitly obeyed'.[58]

Progress and the millennium

Price and Priestley undoubtedly shared, though in different degrees, the eighteenth-century belief in human progress. 'It seems to be the intention of Divine Providence', wrote Priestley, 'to lead mankind to happiness in a progressive, which is the surest, though the slowest, method. Evil always leads to good, and imperfect to perfect.'[59] While by no means denying such a providential movement towards perfection, Price seems more aware of the obstacles to progress. With his colleague he believed that 'the government of the Deity proceeds gradually and slowly', but also spoke of 'a succession of dark preparatory dispensations' prior to the birth of Christ. Before reaching maturity the human race must pass through the instruction and discipline of infancy.[60] Man has risen from a low animal condition to his current state, but

> his progress has been irregular and various. Ages of improvement have been followed by ages of barbarism . . . Yet what has been lost in one place, or at one time, has been gained in another, and an age of darkness and barbarism has been succeeded by ages of improvement more rapid than any that preceded them.[61]

The world has gradually been improving, the human race was being set free from superstition and tyranny and 'such are the natures of things, that this progress must continue'. He saw in the American Revolution and later in the French a proof of this movement.[62]

Priestley taught that 'the great instrument in the hand of Divine Providence of this progress of the species towards perfection, is *society*, and, consequently, *government*'.[63] Government should adopt that authoritarian and managerial model which he ascribed to divine government; but, as with God, it was to be severely limited in its scope, allowing its subjects to learn by their mistakes. This life is a training-ground for the next. Anticipating Robert Malthus, he saw the economic and commercial rigours of a capitalist state leading to the development of human character and to social progress. The present life is providentially designed to be 'a theatre of constant exercise and discipline' in which we may advance in knowledge and virtue.[64] It is God's intention that humans should be largely 'self-taught' and attain truth and progress by experience and observation.[65] Divine government is thus conducted largely on the basis of *laissez-faire*.

The development of a commercial ethos was to be encouraged by reforms in education. Drawing on his own teaching experience at the Warrington Dissenting Academy – where he had taught from 1761 to 1767 – Priestley advocated more emphasis on teaching the supposedly practical use of history, together with the principles of commerce, constitutional law and political science, foreign languages and 'practical mathematics'. Current forms of education in grammar schools and at university were remote from the business of life. Those destined to become merchants would benefit from courses of lectures and discussion in which the principles of commerce were 'discussed in a scientific and connected manner, as they deserve'.[66] Priestley, of course, saw no contradiction between the principles of true religion and those of commerce, but believed that medieval ideas retained their influence in eighteenth-century England. Of St Francis of Assisi, he remarked: 'he discovered a turn of mind so religious, and so unfit for business, that his father was much displeased'.[67] He called for the recognition of a change in ethos and institutions which was taking place in Europe. In his preface to a course of lectures published in 1777, Priestley wrote:

> The rights of hereditary monarchs, and of an hereditary nobility, which grew up with the feudal system, must finally fall with the other parts of the same system, before that prevailing spirit of industry and commerce to which it was ever hostile, and before that diffusion of knowledge on the subject of government . . . which has burst out in the last half-century.[68]

In his prayer for the poor, Priestley addressed the Almighty:

> May the poor have a spirit of industry and frugality. May they have full employment, and be satisfied with bread, through the increase of our manufactures and commerce. May they ever be disposed to submit to salutary laws, and to just though strict government; but may they never want a proper sense of their natural and civil rights or the courage to assert them.[69]

GOD AND THE STATE: WILLIAM PALEY

If Price and Priestley were detested and feared by the governing classes of the day, William Paley (1743–1805) was regarded by them rather with unease and suspicion. Although he generally defended the established order, the implications of his system were not entirely clear to those in authority. Hence he never received, in his lifetime, that preferment which many believed was his due. The religious and intellectual framework within which Malthus and his fellow ecclesiastical economists wrote, and the assumptions about God and the world which they made, were formulated in their most concise and trenchant manner by William Paley, archdeacon of Carlisle. Today Paley is little read and is best known for having set forth a supposedly 'discredited' argument for the existence of God based on elements of design found in the natural world. He also gained some notoriety for having written on the miraculous evidences for the truth of Christianity, which led Coleridge to declare he was 'weary of evidences'. In textbooks on the history of political thought he is also credited with having, in some unspecified way, anticipated the utilitarian philosophy of the Benthamites.

Whether and in what way Charles Darwin's theories on natural selection have undermined all arguments from design is disputed, but what is certain is the admiration expressed by Darwin himself for Paley's writings and lectures. The eminent scientist claimed that the logic of Paley's arguments had given him great delight, as an undergraduate, affirming that Paley's philosophy was the only part of the Cambridge course which was 'of the least use to me in the education of my mind'.[70] Paley's *Natural Theology*, published in 1802, became a set book in Cambridge, and many generations of undergraduates were obliged to study it; the generally unsympathetic Leslie Stephen wrote that it was 'a marvel of skilful exposition'.[71]. His influence was not restricted to this country. Harriet Beecher Stowe recalled how at the tender age of nine she 'listened with eager ears . . . to recitations in such works as Paley's "Moral Philosophy".'[72]

Paley's life and work

Paley taught that in his government of the universe God is guided, as human rulers should be, by the principle of the general happiness; the natural laws by which the universe is ordered have happiness as their end, and all other moral rules are subsumed under the principle of the general happiness. 'Whatever is expedient is right.'[73] In both divine and civil realms, subjects are under a similar kind of obligation to obey the commands of their superiors, and this obligation stems from fear of punishment and hope of reward. These commands are known both by explicit declaration of the sovereign and by a consideration of the tendency of an action to produce happiness. The inequalities existing in the natural world provide an analogy for the inevitable inequalities in the social world. Nevertheless there is an important difference between divine and human laws in the way they operate. The former may be concise and simple, being the commands of an omniscient being, and designed to form human character; the latter are the necessarily complex attempts of fallible civil governors to regulate human actions.

We shall observe how Paley frequently illustrated theological propositions by appealing to a political analogy. The compatibility of divine grace with human freedom he demonstrated with reference to a generous offer which a prince might make to his subjects on condition that they make a specified response. The coherence and efficacy of prayer were defended on the analogy with a civil petition, and charges of divine arbitrariness were refuted by appeal to political models. The cosmic, the natural and the social orders thus operate according to analogous principles, which find their source in the will of a supreme but rational being.

The governing analogy in Paley's work, used to illustrate the relationship between God and the universe is, however, a non-political one. God is seen, first and foremost as the great architect, the celestial designer, the supreme contriver. God's activity is manifest not primarily by direct intervention in terrestrial affairs, but by his having set up a system of rules and principles according to which the life of the universe, animate and inanimate, proceeds.

The general happiness

Paley was a utilitarian. He repudiated popular notions of a 'moral sense' which is able to adjudicate on questions of right and wrong. He believed that right and wrong, good and bad, are determined by their consequences; actions likely to maximise happiness are good, those which increase the sum of unhappiness are bad:

> Self love and Reason to one end aspire,
> Pain their aversion, Pleasure their desire.

Paley moreover provided a theological basis for his hedonistic system. The world was created by a benevolent God in such a manner that the natural end or purpose of sentient beings is related to their happiness. What promotes the general happiness is 'agreeable to the fitness of things, to nature, to reason, and to truth'.[74] In his *Natural Theology* the author rhapsodises on the happiness of the bees in springtime and on the evident pleasure which shrimps find in life. 'It is a happy world after all. The air, the earth, the water, teem with delighted existence. In a spring noon or a summer evening, on whichever side I turn my eyes, myriads of happy beings crowd upon my view'.[75]

Paley furthermore equated happiness with pleasure, and unhappiness with pain, in a way many of his contemporaries would have rejected. 'In strictness, any condition may be denominated happy', he declared, 'in which the amount or aggregate of pleasure exceeds that of pain; and the degree of happiness depends upon the quantity of this excess.' Pleasures, he insisted – siding with Bentham against the position later articulated by J. S. Mill – 'differ in nothing, but in continuance and intensity'.[76] He nevertheless warned that the pleasures of the senses are of short duration compared with the exercise of social affections, the development of our faculties and 'the prudent constitution of the habits'.[77]

The utilitarian principle found manifest application in the civil sphere. 'The final view of all rational politics is', he asserted, 'to produce the greatest quantity of happiness in a given tract of country.'[78] The honour or glory of a nation is of value only insofar as it contributes to the happiness of individual citizens, for they are the sole beings that really exist and feel. National interest, rather than national honour, should thus be the end that politicians should seek to attain.

While the general happiness can indeed be increased in a given community by enlarging the happiness of a constant number of members, the easiest way to increase the sum of human happiness is by a growth in population, so long as it can be achieved without significantly increasing the amount of pain. 'The decay of population,' he wrote, 'is the greatest evil that a state can suffer; and the improvement of it the object which ought, in all countries, to be aimed at in preference of every other political purpose whatever.'[79] In his *Moral and Political Philosophy*, Paley was generally hopeful that the two factors determining population – the fecundity of the species and the capacity of the soil to support mankind – were such that in most countries an increase in population, together with the means to support it, was perfectly feasible. In his later work, under the influence of Malthus, he adopted a somewhat more pessimistic position. The latter, in fact, claimed Paley and Pitt as his two most important converts.

Habits, precedents and rules

In determining the rightness and wrongness of actions it is necessary to consider not just their immediate and particular, but also their remote and general, consequences. Although the particular consequences of assassinating a rich villain may be an increase in the general happiness, the effect of approving or permitting such action would be to 'allow every man to kill anyone he meets, whom he thinks noxious or useless'. The necessity of general rules in human government is apparent, but Paley went on to ask whether the same applies to divine government, and concluded that 'general rules are necessary to every moral government'. Whatever reason there is to expect rewards and punishment by God, 'there is the same reason to believe, that he will proceed in the distribution of it by general rules'.[80] Paley's 'rule utilitarianism' thus requires that we 'refer actions to rules, and rules to public happiness'.[81] Yet rules are not to be seen as inflexible, for there may be extraordinary cases where 'the remote mischief resulting from the violation of the general rule, is overbalanced by the immediate advantage'.[82]

The emphasis upon general rules in Paley's system is due to his belief that 'Mankind act more from habit than reflection' and that 'man is a bundle of habits'.[83] He followed Joseph Butler[84] in teaching that in ethics it is not the status of individual acts, but the development of character that is of fundamental importance. In estimating the value of a moral rule we must judge not merely what it directs us to do in the specific case, but 'the character which a compliance with its direction is likely to form in us'. The injunctions of Jesus in the gospels, such as 'Whoever shall compel thee to go a mile, go with him twain', are designed less to enjoin particular acts than to encourage a certain disposition and character.[85] In his Assize Sermon of 1795 the archdeacon reminded his learned congregation that the use of scriptural precepts 'is not so much to prescribe actions, as to generate some certain turn and habit of thinking' and thus to form in Christians such a temper that 'our first impressions and first impulses' will tend to be virtuous; 'and that we feel likewise an almost irresistible inclination to be governed by them'.[86] In his *Moral and Political Philosophy* Paley illustrated this point with reference to the question of charitable relief. A beggar appeals to us for charity and we may well think that he has brought his condition on himself and that to accede to his request would encourage idleness and vagrancy, or that the money could better be spent, or that the man's condition is not as bad as it appears.

> When these considerations are put together, it may appear very doubtful, whether we ought or ought not to give any thing. But when we reflect, that the misery before our eyes excites our pity, whether we will or not; that it is of the utmost consequence to us to cultivate this tenderness of mind; that it is a quality, cherished by indulgence and soon stifled by opposition; when this, I say, is considered, a wise man will do that for his own sake, which he would have hesitated to do for the petitioner's; he will give way to his compassion, rather than offer violence to a habit of so much general use.[87]

We see here how Paley moves from act utilitarianism to rule utilitarianism and ultimately to a notion of habitual virtue.

God: the omnipotent designer

Paley pictured God as a great designer of stupendous power. He has set up a system that operates according to laws which do not determine events in a crudely mechanical manner, being mysteriously superintended by God in their operation as well as in their origin. These laws he saw as 'disposed and controlled by that Providence which conducts the affairs of the universe, though by an influence inscrutable and generally undistinguished by us'.[88] In his 'Observations upon the Character and Example of Christ', Paley wrote of the Biblical God as

> one, wise, powerful, spiritual, and omnipresent; as placable and impartial, as abounding in affection toward his creatures, overruling by his providence the concerns of mankind in this world, and designing to compensate their sufferings, reward their merit, and punish their crimes in another.[89]

Yet this omnipotent being 'has been pleased to prescribe limits to his own power' and has established general laws by which to govern his realm.[90]

In his so-called 'design argument' for the existence of God, Paley did not suggest that God has directly and immediately intervened in the universe to mould and perfect each biological organ for its specific purpose. The human eye, for example, was not created immediately *ex nihilo* by some act of direct divine intervention. Paley fully recognised the importance of 'secondary causes' by the operation of which the eye came into existence, and would not have asserted (as Richard Dawkins maintains) 'that living watches were literally designed and built by a master watchmaker'.[91] Paley maintained that the many cases of 'contrivance' which he indicated point to the existence of an intelligent and purposeful creator, who established laws by the operation of which such wonders have come into being. He explicitly allowed for the 'many courses of second causes, one behind another, between what we observe of nature, and the Deity'.[92] Yet he insisted that 'a chain, composed of an infinite number of links, can no more support itself, than a chain composed of a finite number of links'.[93] In using this illustration he seems to have suggested a rather different conception of God's relation to the universe than that implied by the image of designer or architect. God is the one who maintains in being or 'supports' the whole process of existence.

Paley could not accept, however, the idea that the universe as we know it could have come to be by the operation of a purely natural series of laws. Indeed the archdeacon explicitly rejected

> the supposition of the present world being the remains of an indefinite variety of existences. . . . The hypothesis teaches, that every possible variety of being hath, at one time or other, found its way into existence . . . and that those which were badly formed, perished.[94]

Such a supposition, he argued, is incompatible with the fact that animals and plants are 'cast into regular classes'.

Few people today would think of the examples of 'contrivance' or design cited by Paley as a 'proof' for the existence of a divine architect. Nevertheless many, not least in the natural sciences, are led to meditate on the wonder and the mystery of the universe and thereby to the creator who maintains all things in being. Furthermore, biologists find it difficult to avoid language about purpose in discussing aspects of their subject, though this may be no more than a convenient short-hand mode of expression (as when computer operators ascribe intentional behaviour to their machines – 'It's trying to print because it thinks the printer is switched on').

For Paley one consequence of an exalted view of the deity, as the omnipotent designer, is that 'from painful abstraction the thoughts seek relief in sensible images'.[95] He thus laid considerable emphasis on 'just conceptions of the Divine Attributes', and on the way popular notions of God are based upon the images used in public worship. False pictures of God lead to 'depravation of public manners'.[96]

Being liberal by political conviction, Paley was keen to avoid any suggestion of tyrannical power in God. He is the author of the contrivance and design to be found in the universe, and stands in relation to us as a maker does to the thing made.[97] Although virtue consists in following God's commands, these commands are directed to benevolent ends. Particularly in his sermons Paley emphasised the justice of God as rewarding the good, punishing the bad and compensating the unfortunate. Yet the purpose of God's punishments and rewards is, like that of the civil law, to create the obligation to act virtuously.

Moral obligation is for Paley no mystery. A man is obliged to do something when 'he is urged by a violent motive resulting from the command of another'. In the case of civil law it is temporal punishment or honour prescribed by the legislator; in the case of divine law it is principally eternal punishment and reward prescribed by the command of God. It follows that 'we can be obliged to nothing, but what we ourselves are to gain or lose something by: for nothing else can be a "violent motive" to us'.[98] We are obliged to pursue a course of action likely to maximise happiness because God has commanded us to do so and has provided the incentives and sanctions – temporal and eternal – as motives for our doing so. Absent is the unearthly altruism of Kantian morality! Gone even the modest requirement of Hutcheson that a necessary condition of moral obligation is approval by our moral sense. Obligation to obey is derived from the command of one who can supply the necessary inducements.

There is, however, an important difference between the punishment administered by God and that which civil laws prescribe. God, who knows the inmost thoughts, is able to arrange that 'every crime shall finally receive a punishment proportioned to the guilt which it contains', and to conduct 'the moral government of his creation' on principles of retributive justice. Human governments, by contrast, are limited in knowledge and power and therefore should ensure merely that crimes are punished 'in proportion to the difficulty and the necessity of preventing them'. 'The proper end of human punishment is not the satisfaction of justice,' he asserted, 'but the prevention of crime'.[99] Paley here took up a distinction made by Joseph Butler when he pointed to the difference between divine and civil laws – the latter being designed solely to ensure conformity, while the former are concerned with motive and character. It is important to note the limited nature of the state's proper sphere assumed by these eighteenth-century writers, in contrast to the high claims made for the state by such mid-nineteenth-century theorists as Mill and Green.

Contract

Paley renounced ideas of social contract as a basis for political obligation. While he followed Hobbes by insisting that 'civil authority is founded in opinion',[100] he was equally clear that governments should be obeyed only so long as they pursue the general happiness. The idea that citizens are obliged to obey governments because of some supposed promise which they have made, explicitly or tacitly, is false and dangerous. No original compact was ever in fact agreed to, nor does it make sense to regard the compact as a fiction, for no rights or duties could be derived from such a fiction. Civil society is not an association entered into freely. Paley, though he recognised a validity to the notion of a tacit promise,[101] attacked the suggestion that a person's residing in a particular country, or holding property there, constitutes such a tacit promise to obey the government. Ideas of social contract may lead, on the one hand, to unjustified claims to legitimacy by despotic governments and, on the other, to 'a dangerous pretence for disputing the authority of the laws' by those arguing that a government has broken its side of the contract and thereby released its subjects from all obligation to obey.[102] Paley proceeded to outline a utilitarian theory of political obligation on the basis of the principle that 'the justice of every particular case of resistance is reduced to a computation of the quantity of the danger and grievance on the one side, and of the probability and expense of redressing it on the other'.[103]

And who, asked the archdeacon, are to be judges in this matter? 'Every man for himself' was the reply. Each individual must judge on the expediency of resistance or civil disobedience, bearing in mind the likely consequences of such action with respect to the general happiness. The oath of allegiance to the monarch by no means excludes the right to resist illegal or unjust actions, for the members of the Convention Parliament, which formulated the oath in its current form, were the very persons who had taken part in the 'Glorious Revolution' against James II.[104] The only obligation to obey a government is grounded on its power to punish offenders and on the divine command that humans should act to promote the general happiness, a command which is itself sanctioned by eternal rewards and punishments. Force, not will, is the basis of the state.

As God's providential government proceeds according to fixed laws, so civil governments should act according to general principles and refrain from arbitrary interference in the life of the community. A principal object of government is, according to Paley, protection of property. Although, abstractly speaking, the great inequalities in property which existed in most countries of Europe were evil, and public laws should be framed so as to favour as far as possible its diffusion, yet inequality is a necessary consequence of generally beneficent laws which incite men to industry and prosperity.[105] The laws which facilitate accumulation are the same laws as protect the poor man in his property. As in the theory of John Rawls:

> The laws which accidentally cast enormous estates into one great man's possession, are, after all, the self-same laws which protect and guard the poor man. Fixed rules of property are established for one as well as another, without knowing beforehand, whom they may affect.[106]

Any significant inequalities, however, which cannot be justified on the grounds that they are consequences of rules which bring general benefit, particularly to the poor, should be corrected. Paley suggested that the poor should stand up for the laws more stoutly than the rich, for 'it is the law which defends the weak against the strong, the humble against the powerful, the little against the great'.[107] (This is in rather stark contrast to the cynical observation of Adam Smith that government and law are the result of a combination of the rich to oppress the poor and maintain their privileged position.)[108] As there is no evidence that the rich are happier than the poor, it is best to leave the inequalities in fortune (as the word itself suggests) to chance – to inheritance, which from the point of view of the heir, is like 'the drawing of a ticket in a lottery'.[109] In the civil sphere he thus affirmed what the poet saw in the natural:

> All Nature is but Art, unknown to thee;
> All Chance, Direction, which thou canst not see;
> All Discord, Harmony, not understood;
> All partial Evil, universal Good:
> And, spite of Pride, in erring Reason's spite,
> One truth is clear, 'Whatever is, is RIGHT'.[110]

Providence and prayer

The fact that human and divine government normally proceed according to fixed general laws does not, however, exclude the possibility of particular intervention in special cases. But how, asked Paley, can prayer affect the course of events? If God is good and powerful, he will surely give what is best in each situation without being asked. If he is consistent in his benevolence, how can he grant something to one person who prays for it while denying it to a person in similar circumstances who does not pray? Paley appealed to the political analogy:

> Suppose there existed a prince who was known by his subjects to act, of his own accord, always and invariably for the best; the situation of a petitioner, who solicited a favour or pardon from such a prince, would sufficiently resemble ours: and the question with him, as with us, would be, whether the character of the prince being considered, there remained any chance that he should obtain from him by prayer, what he would not have received without it. I do not conceive that the character of such a prince would necessarily exclude the effect of his subject's prayers.[111]

He might grant a pardon or favour to this man – who by his very supplication had put himself in a frame of mind such that he could benefit from the gift – which he did not grant to another 'who was too proud, too lazy, or

62

too busy, too indifferent whether he received it or not, or too insensible of the sovereign's absolute power to give or to withhold it, ever to ask for it'. The objection to this kind of particular response by government (divine and civil) unjustifiably assumes its power to be 'inexorable'.[112] But wisdom and benevolence by no means require such inexorability.

DIVINE GOVERNMENT: BUTLER'S ANALOGIES

Bishop Joseph Butler (1692–1752) is important not only for the way his writings reflect the social and intellectual assumptions of his day, but for his influence on Christian thinking well into the following century.[113] If Paley provided a classical formulation of Christian apologetic for nineteenth-century Cambridge men, Butler's *Analogy* was, in the words of Goldwin Smith, 'the Oxford Koran . . . a universal solvent of the theological difficulties'.[114] His insistence on the close relationship between theological truth and the practice of 'external religion' influenced the young Newman at a crucial period of his development,[115] while the bishop's claim that certitude (and not a merely *practical* certitude) could be established on the basis of an assemblage of probable arguments provided the framework within which Newman later elaborated his *Grammar of Assent*. Gladstone recommended Butler to his son as a guide for life. 'I place him before any other author,' he went on. 'The spirit of wisdom is in every line'.[116] Lord Acton believed that his doctrine of conscience had been a milestone in the history of moral philosophy and had been an important influence on Kant.[117] Although Butler's *Analogy* ceased to be a textbook in Oxford during the 1860s, his works were 'read alongside Locke, Hume and Kant', and were recommended reading in Cambridge and Dublin.[118]

The man and his teaching

Butler's writings constitute a defence of orthodox Christianity against what he saw to be the increasingly irreligious spirit of his day and against a particular formulation of this spirit found in writings of deists like Matthew Tindal, whose *Christianity as Old as the Creation* had appeared just six years before the *Analogy*. Butler was not, however, attempting to offer demonstrative proof of religious truth. In an early correspondence with the celebrated Newtonian Samuel Clarke, he had already expressed doubts about the validity of such attempts. His purpose was rather to provide persuasive evidence for the truth of natural religion and to show that objections made against revealed religion 'are no other than what may be alleged with like justness' against natural.[119] His saying 'probability is the very guide of life'[120] became a slogan of nineteenth-century apologetics.

Butler's *Fifteen Sermons* were designed to show how moral obligation relates to the divinely constituted structure of the created order.[121] His basing of moral theology on the supposed facts of human nature is said to have carried the empirical method of Newton into the science of morals.[122] Many regard these sermons as having more lasting influence than the *Analogy*, which was hardly designed to answer the objections which nineteenth-century agnostics, like James Mill and Leslie Stephen, raised against religious belief. Butler's *Analogy*, his fifteen sermons preached at the Rolls Chapel together with six sermons preached on public occasions, a 'charge' and a few letters are all that remain of his writings. It was indeed his expressed wish, stated in his will, that 'all my sermons, letters and papers . . . be burnt without being read by any one, as soon as may be after my decease'.[123] Butler's support for the moderately repressive government in London was reflected in his conception of divine government. Neither government acted arbitrarily; both operated according to a system of laws. The role of the subject in both cases is one of humble submission to authority in this life with the hope of happiness hereafter.

Butler was something of a recluse and appears to have played only a modest role in political and public life; his association with Queen Caroline was due more to her interest in philosophy than to his concern with politics. Butler's six sermons suggest, indeed, an interest in political and social issues, but his contribution in this sphere generally reflected current opinion among moderate churchmen. Central to Butler's argument in the *Analogy* is, however, the notion of God's *government* of the universe; the analogy with forms of social and political domination is quite explicitly drawn. God exercises government, he pronounced, 'of the very same kind with that, which a master exercises over his servants, or a civil magistrate over his subjects'.[124] But what is the nature of this government? Does Butler's understanding of political authority shed light on his conception of God's rule? Are the theological assumptions that he made important in determining his beliefs about the proper role of civil government? Unlike writers of the previous century, the political images that Butler most frequently employed in his theological discourse were 'government', 'constitution' and 'administration' rather than 'kingship'. Under the Hanoverians the role of the king had become less dominant than under the Stuarts, and government was becoming more explicitly a matter of accommodation rather than command. Butler did, however, occasionally speak of the 'monarchy of the universe' and also employed economic analogies, referring to God as 'proprietor'. Considering the prominent role played in Butler's writings by such political and social concepts, it is surprising that his many commentators and critics have effectively ignored the significance of these political concepts in understanding Butler and the religion of his day.[125]

God is the 'author of nature', the creator, who has so ordered the universe that it operates according to certain general laws which are, in turn, part of a single system of government, natural and moral. God does not govern by a succession of disconnected acts.[126] The general plan of our constitution is seen as 'sacred'; reasonable people will 'content themselves with calmly doing what their station requires'.[127] On the basis of a political analogy, Butler asserted that there are limits to what humans can reasonably expect to find out for themselves, 'since the monarchy of the universe is a dominion unlimited in extent and everlasting in duration; the general system of it must necessarily be quite beyond our comprehension'.[128] He went on to argue that, as the universe constitutes a single 'administration or government', we cannot have a thorough knowledge of any part, without a knowledge of the whole. Since, then, the constitution of nature and the government of it are beyond our comprehension, 'We should acquiesce in, and rest satisfied with, our ignorance, turn our thoughts from that which is above and beyond us, and apply ourselves to that which is our real business and concern'.[129] As the poet put it a decade later:

> Know then thyself, presume not God to scan,
> The proper study of mankind is man.[130]

'The fear of the Lord and to depart from evil' is the only wisdom we should seek'.[131]

This world is a place of temporary abode, where we are tested and disciplined for a future life. Human nature, though fallen from its original perfection, is such that with prudence we may live virtuous and happy lives here and be rewarded with eternal bliss hereafter. God's government is not harsh, his burden is light. Virtuous actions are not difficult to perform, for they are in line with authentic human nature. The self-love which is a universal characteristic is not in itself an evil and may be pursued in a manner consistent with the general good and with the happiness of others. This apparent optimism is, however, mitigated by an acute appreciation of evil resulting from the Fall. In fact many commentators have noted the melancholy tenor of his writings, a disposition which is reflected in contemporary portraits of the bishop.

God is the author of nature, and humans are 'under his government, in the same sense, as we are under the government of civil magistrates'.[132] As the world is in a fallen state, God's government, like that of the civil magistrate, consists in making laws and annexing certain sanctions to the transgression of these, so that people tempted by unruly passions to act in vicious ways may be restrained by the prospect of punishment. Rewards and punishments, particularly the latter, play, indeed, a crucial part in his understanding of government.[133] The annexing of pleasure and pain to certain forms of activity, and the publication of advanced notice of these sanctions, 'is the proper formal notion of government'.[134] There is in the constitution and course of nature evidence for a moral government of the universe, with natural tendencies (and only *artificial* hindrances) to the rewarding of virtue and the punishing of vice. God has, however, by no means left his universe to evolve according to its prescribed laws, as contemporary deists taught, but he 'interposes' from time to time, by revelation, to assist humankind to its appointed end, just as civil government must reserve to itself the right to make particular decrees when necessary. Revealed religion reaffirms and supplements the conclusions of natural religion. Butler's notion of God's active government contrasts markedly with the deist notion of God, which supplied – by contrast – the analogy for a more thoroughgoing *laissez-faire* conception of the state.

God and the natural world

God, the supreme being, has designed the creation in such a way that the subordinate beings within it have a particular end or purpose, which is their good. Butler's moral philosophy thus assumed an Aristotelian, teleological understanding of the world, in its relationship to God; he firmly rejected any idea that good and evil are established by divine command. The moral fitness and unfitness of actions is 'prior to all will whatever', he insisted.[135] Rational beings are free to pursue this natural end or – tempted by the prospects of immediate gratification – to stray from it, neglecting the duties they owe to their fellows and denying their own true interests. Thus people may frequently become 'the authors and instruments of their own misery and ruin'.[136] Butler insisted that 'cool or settled selfishness' – that is, attention to one's true interest and happiness – is perfectly consistent with benevolence; most malicious actions are pursued at the cost of one's own interests and thus are often quite 'altruistic' in their nature.[137] While self-love and benevolence are conceptually distinct, one pursuing the happiness of self and the other pursuing the general happiness, the ends ultimately coincide. Moreover, 'self-love is one chief security of our right behaviour towards society'.[138]

> Thus God and Nature link'd the gen'ral frame,
> And bade self-love and social be the same.[139]

'Duty and interest are perfectly coincident', declared the preacher, 'for the most part in this world, but entirely and in every instance if we take in the future, and the whole'.[140] Is Butler, then, saying, as Paley later said, that all actions must proceed from a selfish motive? No, for a person may act benevolently – intending to forward the general good – by following the rule of veracity, justice and charity; true virtue consists in so acting. As C. D. Broad has pointed out, Butler explicitly and conclusively refuted the theory of psychological egoistic hedonism – the idea that all human actions stem from a selfish motive which consists in a desire for our own pleasure, and that disinterested behaviour is impossible.[141] Egoists confuse the pursuit of certain ends, the achievement of which leads to a state of pleasure, with a pursuit of a state of pleasure. People should act benevolently not because it is in their interest to do so; rather, having determined that duty demands a certain course of action, they may be sure that this is in their true interest. Here Butler differs from Paley. Humans should not act in a manner which they conceive to promote 'happiness of mankind in the present state', for there are occasions where vicious acts may have the appearance of producing an overbalance of happiness (he cannot bring himself to admit that this would be more than appearance). 'The happiness of the world', he observed, 'is the concern of him, who is the Lord and the Proprietor of it.'[142] The safest course is for us to pursue veracity and justice guided by the conscience, which enables us to distinguish between right and wrong. Conscience is the 'moral faculty' which 'magisterially exerts itself', determining some actions to be 'in themselves just, right, good', and others to be inherently evil.[143] Human nature is constituted in such a way that we instinctively condemn falsehood, without any consciousness of its tendency to result in unhappiness.[144] Virtue, then, consists in pursuing what is right and good as such, but when we sit down in a cool moment 'we can neither justify to ourselves this or any other pursuit, till we are convinced that it will be for our happiness, or at least not contrary to it'. This is because happiness and misery are 'of all our ideas the nearest and most important to us'.[145]

This general coincidence between interests and morality is in no way adventitious, but follows from the belief in a rational creator. 'Veracity justice and charity, regard to God's authority, and to our own chief interest, are not only all three coincident; but each of them is, in itself, a just and natural motive or principle of action.'[146] It was widely accepted by divines of this period that the creator has ordained 'a perpetual agreement between the faculties of moral perfection, the powers of fancy, and the organs of bodily sensation', as one contemporary put it.[147] It was Bernard Mandeville's denial of this principle that so scandalised his contemporaries. He asserted that Christian morality is radically ascetic, entailing a way of life which runs counter to our inclinations and natural desires.[148] There is little place in Butler's system for the kind of altruism which requires people to act with no concern for their own interests.

While accepting a Whig distinction between crime and sin, Butler went on to observe that 'though civil government be supposed to take cognizance of actions in no other view than as prejudicial to society, without respect to the immorality of them', their perceived immorality greatly contributes to the likelihood of their perpetrators being brought to justice.[149]

Divine government

Butler distinguished God's natural government from his moral government. The temporal consequences of vicious acts, like the sickness that follows intemperance, would be a case of the former, while the eternal punishments affixed to immoral acts would be an example of the latter. The occurrence of temporal punishments may, indeed, be seen as evidence of 'an expectation, that a method of government already begun, shall be carried on', after this life, by a rule which we call distributive justice.[150] He repudiated the utilitarian assumption that a good God's character is constituted solely of benevolence, with the simple object of maximising happiness in this world. The notion of a righteous moral government implies, rather, that happiness is made conditional on good behaviour, so that virtue will be encouraged and vice deterred.

The laws by which God governs the natural world are fixed and of general application, rewarding virtue and punishing vice. God has also endued human beings with the capacity to reflect on the constitution of things and to foresee the good and bad consequences of their actions. The fact that God, as author of nature, conducts his government uniformly and consistently, according to established laws, should not lead people to deny his active government. Echoing Leibniz in his controversy with Samuel Clarke, Butler observed: 'They must not deny that he does things at all, because he does them constantly.' If civil governors were able to ensure that after they had enacted laws the sanctions were applied automatically without further action on their part, we would manifestly be under their government as we are now, and 'in a much higher degree and more perfect manner'.[151] In nature, however, as in the case of civil government, there are always exceptions – the general rule is never adequate to cover all eventualities. Sometimes the wicked prosper and the righteous suffer; even worse, vicious actions appear to be rewarded and virtuous ones punished. But this cannot 'drown the voice of nature in the conduct of Providence'. Such acts are seen to result from the *perverted use* of a natural passion implanted in us for other and good purposes.[152]

Butler accepted the theoretical possibility of particular divine intervention within the natural order to prevent irregularities, but observed that such particular interventions would necessarily have consequences additional to that of preventing the specified irregularity. Being (at least from the human standpoint) arbitrary and not according to established and known laws, they would deter human forethought, encouraging idleness and negligence. We have, therefore, no grounds for believing that all irregularities – the occasional unfortunate consequences of generally benevolent laws – could be prevented by particular interpositions by the divine governor. Often the harm resulting from such a special divine intervention might be greater, in its distant effects, than the immediate good achieved or the evil prevented by such action. It may in fact be the case in the divine government of the universe that a total absence of irregularities is impossible in the nature of things, 'as we see it is absolutely impossible in civil government'.[153] 'Perfection of justice', Butler maintained, 'cannot in any sort take place in this world, even under the very best governments'.[154]

Such a judgment would appear to apply in the case of divine as well as civil government. Thus, in refraining from frequent arbitrary interpositions, God is in truth acting for the best and reasserting the rule of law.[155]

Not only is the universe governed by laws, but we have good reason for believing that these laws form part of a 'scheme, system or constitution, whose parts correspond to each other, and to a whole; as really as any work of art, or as any particular model of a civil constitution or government'.[156] In one of his Rolls sermons[157] Butler had elaborated on the notion of a civil constitution, as involving a structure, a hierarchy and a supreme authority. As in the political and social order 'subordination' is central, so it is in God's administration of the cosmos. Yet with respect to God's natural as well as his moral government, we understand only a part. In the natural order we are incapable of giving an exhaustive account of any single event or action – its causes, ends and necessary adjuncts – 'any one thing whatever may, for ought we know to the contrary, be a necessary condition to any other'. If our understanding of causality be so incomplete in the natural world, is it surprising, asked Butler, that human understanding of God's moral administration is also incomplete?[158]

In his theodicy Butler clearly followed Leibniz closely. His reluctance to recognise particular divine interventions in the natural sphere, echoes those criticisms made of Newtonian theory by the German philosopher in his letter to Queen Caroline, which initiated his celebrated correspondence with Samuel Clarke.[159] While denying arbitrary interpositions by God in the natural order, Butler did, with Leibniz, allow for direct divine action in the sphere of revelation and grace. With respect to the divine analogy, therefore, Butler adhered firmly to a Whig position, where a constitutional monarch follows established laws, intervening by prerogative only in exceptional circumstances. He thus condemned the deist *laissez-faire* understanding of divine government. It is in his discussion of revealed religion that this particular action of the divine ruler is considered more fully.

Revealed religion

In the context of the Christian revelation and the redemption of the world by Christ, Butler does acknowledge a divine interposition to rescue human beings from darkness and from the just punishment of their wickedness. In scripture we are informed of a particular providence supplementary to the system of general rules by which God governs. 'It relates that God has, by revelation, instructed men in things concerning his government which they could not otherwise have known; and reminded them of things, which they might: and attested the truth of the whole, by miracles.'[160] It is at this point that Butler clearly repudiated the deist position.[161] Yet Butler, with Charles Leslie and other defenders of orthodoxy, insisted that revelation cannot conflict with reason; if the apparent meaning of scripture is contrary to natural religion, 'we may most certainly conclude, such seeming meaning not to be the real one'.[162] Furthermore it is reason that 'is indeed the only faculty wherewith we have to judge concerning any thing, even revelation itself'.[163]

. Humankind is in need not only of enlightenment, but also of salvation. We have done evil, and 'it is clearly contrary to all our notions of government . . . that doing well for the future should, in all cases, prevent all the judicial bad consequences of having done evil, or all the punishment annext to disobedience'.[164] Repentance and amendment do not mitigate punishment justly imposed for offences committed. Yet our experience teaches us 'that the moral government of the universe was not so rigid, but that there was room for an interposition, to avert the fatal consequences of vice'. Christ interposed 'in such a manner, as was necessary and effectual to prevent that execution of justice upon sinners, which God had appointed should otherwise have been executed upon them'.[165] Butler is here confronting the strong deist and Socinian attack upon any kind of objective theory of the atonement. He responds that even this interposition by Christ, who died that we might be forgiven, is not entirely without analogy in the natural world, where many instances are found of one person suffering as a result of the sins of others and in order to mitigate the effects of these sins. 'Vicarious punishment' is 'a providential appointment of everyday experience'.[166] As it is impossible for us fully to understand the logic of God's general laws, so we cannot know his special dispensations unless they be revealed. Butler believed that a failure to understand analogies in the natural world, together with a refusal to acknowledge human limitations, led opponents of orthodox Christianity to assume that any connection between the sufferings of Christ and the redemption of the world could only be 'by arbitrary and tyrannical appointment – and hence to reject it'.[167]

Eighteenth-century England was in certain respects a constitutional state, but remained a monarchy; though operating according to general laws, there was still the power of royal prerogative. Butler illustrated the theological argument by supposing 'a prince to govern his dominions in the wisest manner possible, by common known laws; and that upon some exigencies he should suspend these laws, and govern, in several instances, in a different manner'. If it were the case that one of his subjects was incompetent to judge of the ordinary laws, is it likely that he would be able to understand or judge in these special situations?[168] His conclusion is that we are not in a position to judge what God might or might not do in his special revelation. As the laws governing the natural world turn out to be very different from what people might imagine by a priori reasoning, and can be appreciated only by experience and analogy, so speculations about the antecedent probability of God's acting in particular ways must be regarded with caution. Although the whole plan of God, natural and revealed, indeed forms part of 'a scheme or system which is properly one', we cannot make conclusive judgments about it on the basis of the small parts of it which we see in this present life.[169] This became a basic plank of much nineteenth-century apologetic with such theologians as J. H. Newman and H. L. Mansel. Yet, as we have noted, for Butler reason is ultimately the faculty by which we must judge even revelation itself, that is, whether an alleged revelation is what it claims to be.

The analogy between God and the state, like all analogies, has its limits. In answer to the objection that a prince, in sending directions to a servant, would make his orders quite explicit and accompany them with a sure mark that they came from him, he maintained that a prince is concerned simply with outward conformity, while God's concern embraces the whole action including inward dispositions.[170] This difference between human and divine law, it will be recalled, is later to be found in Paley. Newman too insisted that reasonable belief, being founded on probabilities rather than on incontrovertible proof, calls into action the faculties of will and moral choice. 'A good man and a bad man will think very different things probable', he declared in his *Oxford University Sermons*.[171] If religious belief could be *proved* there would be 'no merit in assenting to it'.[172]

Civil government

Butler saw civil government not only as providing an analogy for divine government, but as constituting a part of God's realm. 'Civil government', he told the House of Lords, 'is that part of God's government over the world, which he exercises by the instrumentality of men'.[173] As we cannot live out of 'society,' and society cannot exist without government, the latter may be seen as part of the natural order and thus exists by divine appointment.[174] The limited purpose of civil government is to instruct citizens in 'fidelity, justice and regard to common good, and to enforce the practice of these virtues, without which there could be no peace or quiet amongst mankind'. Such a structure of order also points towards a God with authority over us and provides a model for understanding that authority.[175] In divine moral government, as in civil government, it is a principle that the subjects, living under a rule of law, are nevertheless at liberty to ignore or break the law and accept the consequences. The light of reason, he observed, does not, any more than that of revelation, force men to submit to its authority.

The theology of Joseph Butler contributed to and at the same time reflected the growing stability which was a feature of eighteenth-century England. The universe, like the state, is an ordered hierarchy, governed by laws, with only occasional governmental intervention. The duty of citizens is that of humble submission and acceptance. Pain and suffering are to be seen as part of God's larger plan, which includes our being tested and disciplined for an eternal end; they should therefore be accepted with 'passive submission or resignation to his will'.[176] Butler claimed that 'the whole of piety' consists in resignation to the will of God, so that 'our will is lost and resolved up into his'. Such an attitude Butler describes in terms of the political analogy: 'A loyalty of heart to the Governor of the universe.'[177] In the political realm the citizens of England should accept those inequalities which are inseparable from a stable and prosperous social order and recognise 'the danger of parting with those securities of liberty, which arise from regulations of long prescription and ancient usage'. Reasonable people, he continued, will therefore,

> look upon the general plan of our constitution, transmitted down to us by our ancestors, as sacred; and content themselves with calmly doing what their station requires, towards rectifying the particular things which they think amiss, and supplying the particular things which they think deficient in it, so far as is practicable without endangering the whole.[178]

Like Coleridge after him,[179] Butler envisaged a social order in which each class would have a natural want of and respect for the other. The resulting interrelationships involving superiority and dependence are no accident, but 'arise necessarily from a settled providential disposition of things, for the common good'.[180]

Yet Butler's vision was not of a *static* order. In a sermon preached in the City of London, before the mayor and corporation, he celebrated the growth of a middle class relatively free from the vices of the upper and lower classes.[181] Together with the upper classes, they should set an example to the poor of 'dutiful submission to authority, human and divine'.[182] Butler acknowledged that the kind of mutual responsibility he envisaged was more evident and understandable in an earlier age, when members of different social classes met face to face in a domestic context of master and servant. With the growth of large agricultural enterprises and of manufacturing industry, where products 'pass through a multitude of unknown poor hands successively, and are by them prepared, at a distance, for the use of the rich', the responsibility of the rich for the poor is not always readily acknowledged. In these situations, where the division of labour has modified social relationships, the bishop attempted to maintain the idea of mutual responsibility among unequal classes. He actively supported the Bristol Infirmary and laid the foundation stone for the Newcastle Infirmary. Preaching before the governors of the London Infirmary, he emphasised the duty of charitable support for hospitals. His sermons were designed to encourage among the rich the recognition of a continued responsibility for the well-being of the poor.[183]

The development of charity schools, by such organisations as the Society for Promoting Christian Knowledge, was a notable feature of the early eighteenth century. Butler defended these schools, reassuring critics like

Bernard Mandeville that 'their design was not in any sort to remove poor children out of the rank in which they were born, but keeping them in it, to give them the assistance which their circumstances plainly called for'.[184] There is no more reason to think that the poor will pervert the use of such education than to believe that the children of the rich will misuse the wealth and power they enjoy, 'though the danger of perverting these advantages is surely as great, and the perversion itself of much greater and worse consequence'.[185] The bishop's defence of charity schools was that they would foster among the poor an acceptance of the hierarchical social order. He defended their education when conducted 'in such a manner, as has a tendency to make them good, and useful, and contented, whatever their particular station might be'. Care should be taken to provide an education 'which does not set them above their rank'.[186]

With respect to Christian duties towards the poor, Butler asserted that this applies not only to the so-called 'deserving poor', but to those whose distress has been brought on them by their own fault.[187] Despite his somewhat condescending attitude to the poor (shared by most of his wealthy contemporaries), Butler reminded his comfortable congregation that 'it is not a matter of arbitrary choice, which has no rule, but a matter of real equity, to be considered as in the presence of God, what provision shall be made for the poor'.[188] Following a long Christian tradition, going back through John Donne to St Ambrose and the early Church Fathers, Butler here implied that the poor even have a just *claim* upon the wealth of the rich.

Butler, then, adopted the generally optimistic outlook typical of British eighteenth-century writers, but only when divine initiative and the rewards and punishments of a future life are taken into account. He recognised that this is a fallen world and by no means shared the secular optimism of writers like Hartley, and Adam Smith.[189] The dispensation within which human beings live is a vast system, of which they can only know a small portion, and that imperfectly. The evidence we have is of a limited righteousness in the divine government, but this is 'enough to give us the apprehension that it shall be completed, or carried on to that degree of perfection which religion teaches us it shall'. It is only when a fuller picture of 'the divine administration' is seen that this perfection of divine justice will be apprehended.[190] It is therefore only by analogy from our knowledge and experience of this portion that we can understand anything which lies beyond.

Butler suggested that our knowledge of civil government provides something of an analogy for our appreciation of God's rule, with respect both to the law of nature and to the sphere of divine revelation. Our understanding of these in turn reinforces the legitimacy of the civil government, considered both as a part of the divine realm and as playing an analogical role to God's dominion over the whole created order. Like Hegel, Butler believed that an understanding of things being as they must be leads to a contented resignation:

> The consideration, that the course of things is unalterable, hath a tendency to quiet the mind under it, to beget a submission of temper to it. But when we can add that this unalterable course is appointed and continued by infinite wisdom and goodness; how absolute should be our submission, how entire our trust and dependence![191]

Butler therefore moved from analogy to a univocal argument in his defence of the *status quo*. Not only does civil government operate along lines parallel to divine government, but a recognition of civil as part of divine government leads to a celebration of submission and deference in political and social as it does in personal and devotional life. 'Religion', he insisted, 'consists in submission and resignation to the divine will.'[192] While he was thus critical of any utopian attempts to change the social structure – of 'setting things afloat' – he left room for minor adjustments in the system by occasional interventions from government on the basis of piecemeal reform. His writings can therefore be said to have strengthened the ideological supports for the moderately reforming Whig oligarchy which dominated the political stage in his day. In the House of Lords, we are told, he attended regularly and invariably voted with the government.[193]

As argued earlier, Butler's *Analogy* was not designed to answer the naturalism of nineteenth-century agnostics. Nevertheless naturalism has itself declined as a fashion in secular thinking and it may be that Butler's way of arguing in the *Analogy* has more *rapport* with the late twentieth century than with the mid-nineteenth. He used persuasion rather than proofs, considerations rather than demonstrations. Though the particular arguments employed may not convince in the present day, his attempt to give 'a reason for the hope within' (or, expressed in the inelegant idiom of modern trans-Atlantic philosophy, his 'argumentative redemption of normative validity claims')[194] may have more in common with certain recent trends in secular thinking than do the methods of Mill and Stephen. His emphasis on the 'ignorance of man' and his acute awareness of the limits of human understanding, could hardly be expected to appeal to humanists in an age of optimism, when they could cry:

> Glory to man in the highest,
> For man is the master of things.[195]

Paley and Butler both believed that natural theology is central to a Christian world-view. God governs the universe according to fixed rules. Nevertheless this does not exclude, in their view, particular interpositions by God in the realms of grace and revelation. These, while not conflicting with human reason, may well go beyond what reason can demonstrate.

Both thinkers regarded human government, by analogy, as maintaining the social order within a framework of law. Butler, the more conservative, was suspicious of reform, while Paley allowed limited government action to rectify injustice according to utilitarian criteria.

Price and Priestley might be expected to be nearer to deism than Butler and Paley. But their emphasis on 'one will' led, particularly in the case of Priestley, to a positivism similar to that found among many Socinians. While there is no inevitable link between a Unitarian theology and a sovereign and centralised state, an emphasis on an undifferentiated unity with respect to the godhead disposes a thinker to value unity above diversity. This tendency found practical expression in the activities of Robespierre and the Jacobins, and theoretical articulation in the writings of Jean-Jacques Rousseau.

4

REVOLUTIONARY POLITICS AND CONSTITUTIONAL GOVERNMENT

The French Revolution, observed Alexis de Tocqueville, though political, 'had every peculiar and characteristic feature of a religious movement'. It was a missionary crusade making universal claims.[1] As in the English Revolution of the seventeenth century, religion played a major and explicit role. Principal actors in both movements were inspired, in part at least, by religious ideals and beliefs. Equally important was the fact that the language of politics was often drawn from religious discourse. For the monarchists, the king's majesty was 'sacred', while for the revolutionaries the rights of 'the people' and the sovereign rights of the nation enjoyed this sacred status. As J. McManners has pointed out, the right of the National Assembly to determine the 'Civil Constitution of the Church' in 1790 was justified on the ground that 'sovereign' monarchs had wielded similar powers over the church in the past.[2] Religious concepts and images employed by the monarchists were occasionally questioned, but more often were transferred intact to the Assembly or to some other less tangible entity. Richard Price, the Welsh radical supporter of the French Revolution, wrote of the king: 'His authority is the authority of the community; and the term MAJESTY, which it is usual to apply to him, is by no means *his own* majesty, but the MAJESTY OF THE PEOPLE.'[3] Ways of thinking about and representing the state were intimately related to ideas and conceptions of God, the supreme being.

The religious nature of the movement is graphically illustrated in the liturgy and ceremonial associated with the Revolution. The leaders realised that appeals to reason are insufficient as a basis for political legitimacy. There must be appeals to popular imagination and feeling. The older court pageants, as well as the ceremonies of the Catholic church were modified and related to the new spirit and to beliefs in popular sovereignty; festivals were held throughout the country in which symbols of authority and of the *ancien régime* were destroyed and maypoles or liberty trees were planted on the village green. The first organised national celebration was the festival of the federation, which was invented by the authorities partly to take the steam out of the popular festivals, which seemed to be getting out of hand.

Later, festivals of abundance – of dairy products, fruit and bread – were organised. Seasonal flowers were to be carried and thrown in bunches to the heavens in honour of the Great Orderer. The celebrations were held in the open air, symbolising a new-found freedom. In a remarkable instance, peasants in a village of the Périgord insisted that the doors of the tabernacle, in which the sacrament was kept, should remain open 'for they wanted their good God to be free'.[4] 'The dome of heaven was clearly a theocentric space ordered by the radiating gaze of an architect God.'[5] The image of God as architect is, of course, closely related to masonic ritual, as many other symbols in the revolutionary festivals were.[6]

In the countries of Western Europe, the eighteenth century witnessed a gradual crumbling of medieval institutions and a growing centralisation of power. France, which had subsisted as 'a mosaic of small *pays*', experienced a gradual breaking-down of provincial barriers, and mercantilist policies led to a transfer of economic power from region and local community to the centre.[7] Economic policies designed to protect national markets were administered by a centralised bureaucracy. Customs, excise and other forms of taxation became general. That 'set of administrative, policing and military organizations headed, and more or less well coordinated by, an executive authority' – which we today call 'the state'[8] – was born. Comparing France favourably with England, one French writer claimed: 'here reforms can be accomplished which will change the whole condition of the country in a moment'.[9] The centralising tendency was reinforced by the Revolution and its aftermath. Many believed that this new order needed some kind of supernatural legitimation. As the heavenly monarch had provided a model for the *ancien régime*, the divine legislator – the God of reason, nature and providence – became the pattern for republican government. Nowhere is this theologising tendency more apparent than in the thinking of Maximilien Robespierre. His speeches and writings continually return to the theme of sovereignty, and even when discussing manifestly secular matters his discourse is frequently religious in form. Robespierre claimed to be a disciple of Jean-Jacques Rousseau and was reacting in certain ways to the ideas of the so-called *philosophes*. In the second part of this chapter I shall discuss the theological politics of the Genevan prophet and some of his French contemporaries, finding in them the roots of Robespierre's political theology.

ROBESPIERRE

In this section I shall examine Robespierre's understanding of God and attempt to assess its significance in relation to his political beliefs and actions. French historians, writing either from liberal secular assumptions or coming from a conservative Catholic background have found it difficult to appreciate and assess the significance of religion in Robespierre's thinking. In his classical *Histoire de la révolution française*, Jules Michelet had little sympathy with 'le prêtre Robespierre'; he was pictured as 'le mauvais génie de la Révolution', while Aulard denounced him as 'bigot monomane'.[10] Orthodox Catholics for their part regarded him as little more than a terrorist whose purpose was the destruction of the church and a reconstitution of the state on democratic principles. For the liberal Catholic historian Lord Acton, he was 'the most hateful character in the forefront of history since Machiavelli reduced to a code the wickedness of public men'.[11] Socialist historians, on the other hand, who admire his radicalism, are able to make little sense of his religious obsessions.

Robespierre pictured God as the ultimate cause of all things, fountain of justice and law, whose general providence watches over the course of the whole universe, but he also saw him as a living supernatural being with a special love and concern for the French nation and its Revolution, responding to the prayers of those who call on him. The basic distinction in his political thought between revolutionary politics and constitutional government plays an analogous role. God's general providence is reflected in the ideal of a limited constitutional government, acting through established laws to preserve order and liberty. God's special providence works itself out in a revolutionary politics, where toleration is extended only to those who are with the Revolution; where normal constitutional safeguards are suspended and opponents are eliminated by the ruthless action of a strong centralised government.

Robespierre's life and works

Throughout his life Maximilien Robespierre (1758–93) had a deep and passionate belief in divine providence – in the existence of a supreme being watching over and guiding his own life and that of the French nation. 'Ever since his Arras days', observes Norman Hampson, 'he had felt himself to be in emotional communion with some superhuman force.'[12] Maximilien's mother had died when he was only six, and his father effectively abandoned the family. The children were brought up by relations, and Maximilien attended the local church school. In 1769 he was awarded a scholarship at the Collège Louis-le-Grand in Paris. He was a good student and ironically it was he who was chosen, in 1775, to make the Latin speech of welcome to King Louis XVI and Marie-Antoinette. Later accounts of his character as a student are conflicting and tend to be determined largely by the hostility or affection of his several biographers towards the mature Robespierre.[13] During his time at college he became alienated from organised religion, but retained a powerful belief in a providential deity. Though he later referred to himself as a very bad Catholic from his college days,[14] he did not, even in his youth, totally reject religion.

After studying law in Paris, the young Maximilien returned to practise at the Arras bar and became a familiar figure in the social and intellectual circles of the town. In the spring of 1789 he was elected a representative of the third estate (Commons) of Artois in the National Assembly, becoming the generally acknowledged leader of the Artois deputies. Inspired by a Rousseauite belief in *la volonté générale*, the young radical lawyer became an active participant in the affairs of the Assembly, and a member of the 'Club Breton', later to become the 'Société des Jacobins' (named after the Dominican convent in the rue Saint-Honoré, where the club met); he was full of patriotic and reforming zeal. Though Robespierre followed Rousseau in many ways, he firmly believed (in contradiction to the Genevan's radical rejection of representation in his *Du Contrat social*) that the sovereign will of the people was represented by the Assembly – at least when it adopted his own policies. On occasions, however, he was prepared to make a direct appeal to the people. Soon Robespierre became a power in the land, though his position was often challenged or rejected both in the Assembly and among the Jacobins; he did not always get his own way but his words could never be ignored. He was, for example, unsuccessful in opposing a suspensive veto for the king and the introduction of an income qualification for voting (the celebrated *marc d'argent*); he rejected the consequent and generally accepted distinction between active and passive citizens. His emphasis on *citoyens* rather than *sujets* implies that people should participate actively in 'sovereign' power.[15]

Though Robespierre was, with his fellow radicals, critical of the power of the clergy and insistent on a change in the role of the national church, he was never an extreme anticlerical and, furthermore, became a fierce critic of the later anti-Christian campaigns and of the propagation of atheism.[16] While his own religion was far from orthodox Catholicism, he respected the right of Christians to worship in their traditional ways. This was for him a necessary consequence of that freedom of expression for which he had contended in his early years in politics. In 1791 he had spoken powerfully in favour of the freedom of the press and, in arguing for extending political rights to the free coloured people of the colonies, had claimed *liberté* as his *idole*.[17] With the flight and apparent treason of the king in June 1791, Robespierre with Saint-Just and other radicals opposed the idea of a judicial trial, arguing that the Assembly should decide his fate. The former king was in the event tried, found guilty and executed on 21 January 1793.

In the following months Robespierre endeavoured to steer a course between the more conservative Girondins (led by Brissot) and the extreme radicals, whose strength lay in many of the Paris 'sections' – the so-called *enragés* led by former priest Jacques Roux and later by the *hébertistes*. In July 1793 he became a member of *le Comité de Salut Public*, which had been set up early in April; in this role he was able to dominate political developments in France until his death by the guillotine on 28 July 1794 (10 thermidor in the revolutionary calendar) in company with over one hundred of his disciples.

Robespierre's religion

Robespierre thus retained throughout his short life a deep conviction that a supreme being, who is good and just, watches over human affairs. He is 'the all-powerful being who presides over the destiny of empires'. In this early letter, he urged the king to

> re-forge the immortal chain that must bind man to God and to his fellow-men, by destroying all the forces of oppression and tyranny which fill the earth with fear, suspicion, pride, baseness, egoism, hatred, greed and all the vices that draw men far from the goals assigned to society by the eternal legislator'.[18]

He went on to insist that this idea of God, which had too often been employed by those who wished to reinforce the power of civil rulers, should be seen also as a basis for human rights: 'It is time to recognise that the same divine authority which orders kings to be just, forbids peoples to be slaves.'[19] Belief in a supreme being gives legitimacy to moral and civil laws, supplementing the insufficiency of human authority by imprinting in the soul the belief in a sanction given to moral precepts by 'a power superior to man'.[20]

In a debate at the Jacobins in March 1792, Robespierre referred, almost incidentally, to the death of the Austrian emperor Leopold as being due to a 'providence, which always watches over us better than our own wisdom'. One member objected that this idea of providence would undo the revolutionary work of liberation and bring people back under the yoke of superstition. Robespierre returned to the rostrum denying that using the name of the deity implies superstition. Despite commotion in the meeting he continued:

> Yes, to invoke the name of Providence and to express an idea of the eternal being who intimately affects the destiny of nations, who seems to me personally to watch over in a very special way the French revolution, is not an idea too outrageous, but a heartfelt belief indispensable to me.[21]

The society, remarked J. M. Thompson, was 'suddenly embarrassed by the most shocking thing that can happen in a political debate – profession of religious faith'.[22] Robespierre's religion was, thus, very different from the cold rationalism of much eighteenth-century deism. There was a warm and intimate aspect to his understanding of and relationship to the supreme being, who sees into the very depths of the human heart and receives prayers even from the most miserable and guilty. Indeed, he used this belief as an analogical defence of the right of all citizens to present petitions, when Le Chapelier proposed a prohibition of petitions from 'passive' citizens (the poor).[23]

Robespierre's theology was – like that of Rousseau – always a political theology. 'The two men', concluded Masson, 'walked the same path.'[24] God is the one who upholds justice, inspiring citizens to a life of *vertu*. 'My God', Robespierre wrote in his newspaper, 'is he who created all men for equality and for happiness, who protects the oppressed and exterminates tyrants; my worship is that of justice and humanity.' He went on to denounce priestly power as one of humanity's invisible fetters, but one which reason alone can break. The lawmaker can assist reason in this work but not replace it. Superstition and priestcraft had, he claimed, already declined and what remained were those 'imposing dogmas which lend support to moral ideas, and the sublime and moving doctrine of virtue and equality which the son of Mary taught'.[25] In his celebrated speech, presenting a report on national festivals, in the name of the Committee of Public Safety, he declared that priests had made God in their own image and had used religion for their own ends. They had portrayed God as cruel, arbitrary and jealous; they had relegated him to the heavens as to a palace, and had called upon him only to increase their wealth and power. 'The true priest of the supreme being', he went on,

> is Nature, his temple, the universe, his worship, virtue, his festivals, the joy of a great people assembled before him to bind tighter the sweet bonds of universal brotherhood, and to present him with the homage of pure and sensitive hearts.[26]

Atheism, civil religion and patriotism

Robespierre was an outspoken opponent of atheism and of the anti-Christian campaigns which were being waged in many parts of France, late in 1793. What right have these men to seek a false popularity by attacking the religion of others? Causing discord, they thereby strengthen the royalist party.[27] 'By what right', he demanded, 'do they come to disturb the freedom of worship in the name of liberty, and attack fanaticism by a new fanaticism?' He castigated those who 'under the pretext of destroying superstition would make a sort of religion out of atheism itself'. Atheism is aristocratic and is but a development of that rational deism which Robespierre so detested, associating it with Voltaire and the *philosophes*. He saw atheism as an arid doctrine. The belief that a blind force presides over the universe, recognising no distinction between crime and virtue, provides no support or inspiration for patriotism.[28] The attacks on religion had, however, made little impression on the poor and seem to have prospered only among the middle and upper classes.[29]

81

On the practical question of toleration for atheists Robespierre referred to Rousseau's dictum that they should be banished from the state. There are, however, some truths, he told his fellow Jacobins, which are best left in books; only atheists who conspire against liberty should be punished.[30] Although individuals should be allowed, as private citizens, to practise the religion they believe in, legislators must ensure that the supreme being is acknowledged as the foundation of justice, the protector of public order and of private virtue. The Convention was not, indeed, an author of metaphysical systems, but its duty was to respect the character as well as the rights of the people.[31] Robespierre replied indignantly to the accusation, formulated by Pitt on behalf of the European powers, that the revolutionaries had 'declared war on the divinity itself'. Quite the reverse, it was, he insisted, 'under the auspices of the Great Being that we have proclaimed the immutable principles of every society'.[32]

A number of religious cults developed among the revolutionaries, including a cult of the martyrs and a worship of Reason. Celebrations were held with processions, hymns and discourses on the virtues of republicanism, pronounced sometimes by children of twelve or thirteen years.[33] Notre-Dame cathedral in Paris was taken over by the goddess of Reason. Maximilien, however, remained dissatisfied and set about organising – in implicit opposition to these movements – a cult of the supreme being.[34] In April 1794 Couthon, acting undoubtedly at his behest, announced that the fêtes décadaires (held every ten days under the new calendar) would be in honour of the supreme being; Robespierre wanted the nation to maintain a regular devotion to its civic god. This provision, however, proved too rigorous, so a national festival in honour of the supreme being was decreed for 20 prairial (8 June) 1794.

In Paris, Robespierre, as president of the Assembly, decked in official costume and carrying an enormous bouquet, led the celebration. It was in his view the greatest day since the creation of the universe. The festival began with the solemn cremation of an effigy of atheism. In a hymn to the supreme being, references to Catholicism were avoided, though 'the Children of Israel' feature and God is identified with 'the God of Abraham, Isaac and Jacob'.[35] There is, indeed, something of a Hebrew flavour to Robespierre's belief in God as the tutelary spirit who has a special relationship with the French nation and in particular guides the course of the Revolution. The celebrations in honour of the supreme being were not, however, clearly distinguished from, even less opposed to, the cult of Reason. Many of the same symbols and hymns were employed. The supreme being was the god of reason, nature and liberty(as contrasted with the cloistered god of the clergy), the great architect and orderer of the universe – a god of the open air – not entombed in gothic cathedrals.

Robespierre's speeches contain many outbursts of patriotic fervour in which he invoked a divine providence:

O my country! If destiny had decreed that I should have been born in a distant foreign land I should have addressed continual prayers to heaven for your prosperity . . . O sublime people, receive the sacrifice of my entire being; happy the one who is born in the midst of you! More happy he who can die for your happiness.[36]

The foundation of the French Republic could not, in Robespierre's opinion, be seen as a matter of chance, but was the work of a guiding providence – the same power and wisdom as presided over the creation of the universe.[37] It was, indeed, a divine guardian who had protected the Revolution from the bottomless pit dug by her enemies.[38] In his dispute with Brissot over war policy he nevertheless pointed to a common standpoint: 'Let our union rest upon the holy basis of patriotism and virtue.'[39]

Patriotism had become a kind of religion. Patriotic altars were erected in country houses, 'adorned with Roman axes and fasces, a pike crowned with the cap of liberty, a shield with a portrait of Lafayette and panels engraved with verses from Voltaire'. The radical Jacobins were by no means unique in this quasi-religious devotion to la patrie.[40] The imagery, however, came more from classical paganism than from Christianity, which – as Rousseau had already pointed out – was quite unsuitable as a foundation for civil religion.[41]

Providence and piety

The roots of Robespierre's belief in a supreme being, as source of personal consolation and as inspirer of civic virtue can, as we shall see, be found in the religion of Jean-Jacques Rousseau. His celebrated profession of faith of the Savoyard Vicar and his chapter on civil religion in Le Contrat social are the classic locations of these different (though not incompatible) conceptions of the deity. For Robespierre and Rousseau, religion was not only political expediency, but a vital aspect of civic and personal life.[42] In a paper read to the Arras Academy in 1786 the young lawyer had referred to religion – in almost Marxian terms – as a consolation to the suffering: 'Philosophy is alien to the people; religion alone can protect it against its wretchedness and its passions and restrain it amidst the shadows.'[43] Elisabeth Duplay, whose family home in the rue Saint-Honoré Maximilien shared for the final years of his life, later recalled how often he had reproached her for having too weak a faith in the supreme being, who is our only consolation on earth.[44]

Nor was Robespierre alone among the revolutionaries in his belief in the supreme being. His former colleague and later rival Jean-Pierre Brissot shared this passionate religion – 'emotional Deism', as I. Babbitt has described Rousseau's faith.[45] 'I am happy', Brissot declared,

when I feel myself under the eye of a Supreme Being, when I think I see him smile at my feeble efforts and encourage them. I am happy when I invoke him . . . he is my master, I report to him, we converse, and I draw renewed force, greater energy from that conversation and from the hope that he gives me.[46]

This religion owes a great deal, of course, to the Savoyard Vicar. Billaud-Varenne too admired the 'fine thoughts of Rousseau, who describes so well the power of the Supreme Being.'[47]

It was, however, the *public* role of religion that received more emphasis in Robespierre's writings and speeches. Faith in a supreme being, as we have noted, gives support to social justice and civic virtue, while belief in immortality reinforces moral principles by the notion of eternal rewards and punishments. The 'materialism' he ascribed to the *secte* of the *encyclopédistes* – which he said included many 'ambitious charlatans' – is directly linked to a false conception of the state. They turned egoism into a system and saw social relations as a cynical struggle for supremacy, where success is the measure of justice, and probity is a matter of taste.[48] Saint-Just similarly attacked the idea that the general good in some way will emerge out of each person pursuing his or her own particular interests. Only indirectly can particular and general interests be reconciled, in the sense that individuals – at least ordinary citizens – will realise that it is in their interest, in an act of solidarity, to accept the common interest. 'Your interest commands you to remain united . . . Your interest commands you to forget your own interest; you can be saved only by the public good.'[49]

This is one of the reasons why *vertu* is so important for these Jacobin writers. Unlike some of the eighteenth-century deists, Robespierre and Saint-Just rejected belief in a sovereign providence who has set up things in such a way that private vices will lead to public benefits. They carried further the ideas of those English writers, like Butler, Smith and Paley, who insisted that religion, education, and government action are necessary to ensure a coincidence between the pursuit of enlightened private interest and the realisation of the general good.

Revolutionary politics and constitutional government

There appears to be a contradiction at the very basis of Robespierre's political thought. Particularly in his early writings and speeches, there is a strong libertarian trend. He fully identified with the revolutionary slogan of *liberté*, as the first priority in the new order, symbolised by the liberty trees planted throughout the country. The practical steps which he supported and advocated were calculated to increase human liberty, even in the common-sense 'negative' understanding, the removing of hindrances to human action and individual choice. This went together with a defence of the rule of law, a suspicion of central government, and a belief in the rights of individuals and associations. Later on, however, when he enjoyed a substantial degree of political power Robespierre justified all kinds of repression, terror and strong centralised government. This he did with the help of a crucial distinction between constitutional government and a revolutionary politics. The latter is appropriate in emergency conditions following a revolution, when a strong government must maintain the gains made and suppress all counter-revolutionary movements. The situation is similar to the Marxist idea of the dictatorship of the proletariat, as developed by Lenin. Here there is no possibility of neutrality; everything is drawn into the arena of politics. In the menacing words of Saint-Just:

> You have to punish not only traitors, but even the indifferent; you have to punish whoever is passive in the republic and does nothing for it. Because after the French people has manifested its will everyone who opposes it is outside the sovereign; everyone who is outside the sovereign is an enemy.[50]

The distinction between friend and enemy is crucial and was taken up by Robespierre in a report to the Convention a few weeks later.[51] A revolutionary government owes protection to the good citizen, but to the enemies of the people only death.[52] The first maxim of politics must be 'to conduct the people by reason and the enemies of the people by terror'.[53] The friend/enemy dichotomy was later employed by Carl Schmitt in his notorious defence of an authoritarian populism, quite similar in many ways to Jacobinism.[54] Robespierre denied that a democratic regime should tolerate those who are dedicated to the destruction of democracy. A church cannot be expected to give asylum to atheists. Liberals are in general agreement on this issue and would extend democratic rights only to those groups which accept liberal democratic rules.[55]

The theory of revolutionary government allowed for a considerable degree of arbitrary rule on the part of the representatives of the people, who were not to be bound by narrow conceptions of legality. Responding to Girondin criticisms that the Jacobins were attempting to introduce a dictatorship and were acting illegally, Robespierre declared that the whole revolutionary process – the overthrow of the monarchy, the storming of the Bastille, indeed liberty itself – was 'illegal'. 'Citizens', he cried, 'do you want a revolution without revolution?'[56] Critics of the revolutionary regime cannot claim the same rights as may be granted them in a settled constitutional regime. 'How does a revolutionary government make such claims?' he asked. Because it is at war. In reply to the question 'How long?' Saint-Just declared: 'Jusqu'à la paix.'[57]

The sole justification for a revolutionary politics is that it is temporary; it is seen as appropriate for the *founding* of a new order, which will be continued on quite different principles. Like the dictatorship of the proletariat in Marx and Engels, it will be succeeded by a condition of liberty where the government of men is replaced by the administration of things.

Government and groups

Robespierre and Saint-Just had a considerable suspicion of 'government'. 'The first objective of the law is the defence of public and individual liberty against the abuse of authority by those who govern', Robespierre declared in April 1793, and one month later he charged the Convention to 'shun the former mania of governments to want to govern too much'. He urged them to leave things to individuals, families and communes where possible.[58] Though he opposed the doctrine of the separation of powers (as supposedly practised in England, where it constituted a 'conspiracy' against the people) he favoured radical decentralisation of executive powers. Saint-Just was equally vociferous in his attacks on 'government', which he regarded as the most dangerous enemy of the people.[59] Tyrants had divided the people in order to reign, power must be divided if liberty was to reign.[60] 'Anarchy', he declared, 'is the last hope for an oppressed people.'[61] He believed that liberty comes through 'une salutaire anarchie', just as slavery is often introduced through an exaggerated respect for order.[62] All the arts have produced their marvels; the art of government has produced only monsters.[63] He also warned against the danger of a directly elected executive, claiming that this would give too much power to the government over against the legislature.

On the critical issue of the place played by groups and associations, however, there was some ambiguity. They generally agreed with l'abbé Sieyès that, while individual interests pose no serious threat to the common good, group interests lead to conspiracy and collusion. 'Social order', he had declared, 'inflexibly requires that no citizens must be allowed to organize themselves in *guilds*.'[64] All 'faction', for these men, is criminal because it tends to divide the people. Under the old regime, groups acted as some kind of a check on despotism but with republican government, factions merely inhibit the sovereignty of the people.[65] But what was the Jacobin club itself, if not a faction? It would meet prior to the Convention to discuss a common policy in precisely the way Rousseau had censured. This, however, was not how they saw things. The club was the authentic voice of the people. Although, as we have noted, Saint-Just was critical of government, this did not imply the recognition of significant semi-autonomous associations. The people must be seen as belonging to one integrated nation, through their membership of the *communes*, which is where the sovereignty of the nation resides. He repudiated the idea of the *départements*, as constituting semi-autonomous territorially-based centres of local government. The necessary division of the country for purposes of administration and representation should be guided by the ultimate end of national unity in a single republic with one general will. The founding fathers of the United States, he claimed in prophetic words, had not created a true republic, but left behind a 'principle of dissolution' which would lead to civil war.[66]

Robespierre in 1790 had defended a degree of devolution in decision-making, with local communal goverments regulating their own affairs (making loans, organising elections, supervising public entertainment, controlling the police) without interference from central government. On the other hand he appears to have done nothing to oppose the infamous June 1790 law of Le Chapelier outlawing associations of working men.[67] As Norman Hampson has argued, 'he opposed the survival of any corporate bodies that could interpose their sectional interests between the citizen and the state'.[68] Bodies which many other political theorists have seen as legitimate he – following Rousseau – condemned.

Virtue and popular sovereignty

Returning to the relation between revolutionary politics and constitutional government, we may say that for Robespierre the end of both is the creation of a race 'renewed, strong, hardworking, organised and disciplined'.[69] In a speech on education he called for an 'entire regeneration' and the creation of 'a new people'.[70] This call for renewal is essentially religious and is a characteristic feature of Christianity from St Paul to Paul Tillich. It appears in secularised form in much modern revolutionary rhetoric, notably in the works of Che Guevara.[71] Despite this missionary concern to change human nature, Robespierre was a realistic politician, fully aware of the danger of perfectionism and willing to settle for the best in the circumstances. 'An idea of absolute perfection', he proclaimed in an early essay, 'can only be a source of error in politics.'[72]

Under a constitutional form of government the principal means of instilling and encouraging *vertu* is education. Under a revolutionary government, however, education must be accompanied by terror, defined as 'justice, prompt, severe, inflexible'.[73] In a speech of 1784 he had agreed with Montesquieu that 'le ressort essentiel des républiques est la vertu' – a political virtue consisting of love for the laws and a willingness to sacrifice particular interest for the common good – the 'magnanimous devotion that sinks all private interests in the general interest'.[74] Individual moral reformation was indispensable for the republic's survival. The essential conditions of representative government include not only an honest electoral system, but incorruptibility of the representatives.[75] He opposed the eligibility of deputies for re-election, arguing that this would encourage corruption and excessive personal ambition.

The war between the French Republic and its European enemies was seen as a battle between vice and virtue – the simple, modest, sometimes ignorant or crude, virtue of the poor. Robespierre passionately believed that republicans must substitute 'morality for egoism, probity for honour, principle for custom, duties for proprieties, the empire of reason for the tyranny of fashion'. These were the characteristics of the *vertu* he proclaimed.[76] Like the prophet Jeremiah, he looked forward to a new dispensation, when the laws of eternal justice would be written not on stone, but in the human heart. It was in truth a moral revolution that Robespierre had in mind and he tied this to a rejection of atheism. Denouncing Danton for laughing cynically at the words virtue, glory and posterity, he associated him with Hébert, Vergniaud and other anticlericals. The moral revolution, he contended, demands respect for the supreme being and belief in a just reward for the good, and punishment for the bad.[77]

A revolutionary government needs power centralised in its hands, so that its actions may be free and rapid. But this requires it to be controlled by virtuous and sincere men. If it were to fall into the hands of the impure and perfidious, freedom would be lost. In placing 'toute sa puissance dans vos mains', the 'Incorruptible' told the Convention, the French people expected it to act with benevolence towards patriots and to crush the enemies of France.[78] In a revolutionary situation the people themselves, though the ultimate seat of sovereignty (the very name of *le peuple* is *sacré*),[79] are 'incapable of self-government'.[80] With Saint-Just, Robespierre opposed submitting the fate of the king to a referendum; the Assembly must decide. It is sometimes argued that the Jacobins here departed from the democratic ideas of their Genevan mentor. But Rousseau did not believe that the whole people could normally govern the state; executive power should be in the hands of magistrates. A democratic executive is suitable only for a race of gods.[81] The sovereign people's competence is limited to promulgating general laws (and even then they need the guidance of a legislator); particular decisions must be made by the government.

Under a constitutional government there must exist for every nation the means of reclaiming and reasserting 'its supreme will'.[82] The authority of princes or assemblies must be seen as 'a portion of the sovereignty of the people deposited in their hands'.[83] In the following year Robespierre referred to the Assembly as 'the depository of sovereign power'; the scope of its authority is determined by 'the imprescriptible rights of the sovereign'.

Robespierre, like Rousseau, recognised a paradox in the establishment of a constitutional government: 'To form our political institutions, it is necessary to assume those mores which only these institutions can give us.'[84] How could the vicious circle be broken? Saint-Just particularly was concerned with the absence of republican institutions. In a monarchy there is only the government, but in a true republic there must be civic institutions to maintain moral standards and prevent corruption. In a report to the Convention of February 1794 he declared that France had a government and a system of public administration, but 'institutions, which are the soul of the republic, we lack'.[85] These institutions would form the basis of a constitutional republic, where governmental powers would be restricted and social life regulated by the rule of law. A single general will would operate through laws rather than by decree, property rights (which Robespierre always claimed to be 'sacred') would be respected and the death penalty abolished. It was to be a government of laws, not of men. The ideal social order was a property-owning democracy; no attempt should be made to impose an absolute equality in wealth or income. He envisaged, in the words of Georges Lefebvre, 'une société de petits producteurs chacun possédant une terre, un petit atelier, une boutique' – in a word, a nation of shopkeepers![86] But all this could be achieved, and the vicious circle broken, only by a period of remorseless revolutionary government.

So we return to the special providence of God as the pattern for revolutionary politics, just as the general providence of the supreme being – the basis of law, order and justice – is the inspiration and model for the constitutional government which is to follow. In Robespierre, as in Saint-Just, we find that fatal 'passion for unity' which Albert Camus perceived.[87] There was no place for diversity in God – he was conceived as a monolithic being with a single and undifferentiated will. So in the unified central state for which the Jacobins fought 'there must be one will. One.'[88] It was this 'adherence to a kind of political monotheism'[89] that turned political rivalries into religious wars and ended with the guillotine. It is perhaps significant that it was among English Unitarians, like Joseph Priestley and Richard Price, that the French Revolution received the warmest support. It was pre-eminently Jean-Jacques Rousseau who carried the banner of political monotheism in eighteenth-century Europe, and it is to his work we now turn.

JEAN-JACQUES ROUSSEAU

Robespierre, Saint-Just and other leaders of the French Revolution were children of the eighteenth century, inevitably influenced by the intellectual currents of that time. They reacted strongly against the scepticism of Voltaire and the *philosophes*, looking rather to Rousseau for inspiration and liberation. Many characteristically Jacobin ideas find their roots in the Genevan's writings: their populism and ideas of sovereignty, their notions of law and of a constitutional state, the conceptions of civil religion and divine providence, the appeals to nature, and the vision of a property-owning democracy.

Interpreting Rousseau

Rousseau is surely one of the most complex and subtle writers of the modern world and perhaps the most difficult of all to interpret in a consistent and coherent way. The reader is continually delighted by some penetrating idea, some elegant expression, some devastatingly effective argument. But where did Rousseau stand on the fundamental questions about life? He published a great deal, most of it within a compass of twenty years from 1750 to 1770. In addition to social and philosophical treatises, controversial tracts, novels and his remarkable *Confessions*, Rousseau conducted a voluminous correspondence. His style is rhetorical, having the object of persuading the reader, rather than setting forth some abstract thesis. Even his *Du Contrat social* and his discourses continually return to the controversial issues of his day.

Rousseau sometimes made statements which are, on the face of it, flatly contradictory. This did not worry him, for he was arguing against different opponents on diverse occasions. His discourse must always be understood in the context of the particular argument he was conducting at the time. Furthermore it is by no means clear that his own views were identical with those expressed by the Savoyard Vicar, for example, or by the characters in *La Nouvelle Héloïse*. To discover what he thought about the proper role of reason in human life, to clarify his conception of nature, to find in his writings a consistent view of Christianity, confront the reader with almost insuperable problems. Rousseau's apologists frequently suggest an underlying consistency in his writings, though they can never quite agree in what this abiding position consists. His apparent inconsistencies, however, so far from having diminished his influence, have extended his sway. People of many disparate persuasions have been able to find in his writings support and inspiration. Here I shall principally be concerned with Rousseau's ideas about God, and their relationship to his political theories.

Rousseau's conception of the state – sovereign, monolithic, self-sufficient, total in its concerns – mirrors the sovereignty of the divine legislator. His radical individualism conflicts with any real acknowledgment of natural bonds between humans – leading him to a conception of the state as a collection of individuals. Likewise his God is the self-sufficient, truly autonomous individual, and Jesus is his prophet. It is not hard to discover whence Robespierre derived his ideas about authority, human and divine.

Jean-Jacques Rousseau was born in Geneva in 1712. His first published work was a discourse on whether the restoration of the arts and sciences had a purifying effect on human behaviour. His negative answer embodied a theme which was to run through much of his writing: a worship of nature and a suspicion of sophistication and civilisation. He developed some of these themes in his *Discours sur l'inégalité* appearing in 1755.

Nature and reason

The worship of 'nature' (though not always used in precisely the same sense) was, of course, a familiar theme in the eighteenth century. Baron d'Holbach's atheism consisted in seeing nature as the true deity, while for Denis Diderot 'God and nature had become . . . interchangeable terms'.[90] For the *philosophes*, the order of nature was indeed a model upon which a proper understanding of both the relationship between God and humans, and that between monarchs and their subjects, should be based.[91]

Rousseau developed his critique of civilisation in his 1758 'Lettre à d'Alembert' and broke with many former friends, including Voltaire and Diderot, d'Holbach and the *abbés de salon*. He was revolted by their supercilious attitude to religion and morality. It pleased him, according to Madame d'Epinay, 'to think that there was a hell for them'.[92] In 1761 he published his long novel *La Nouvelle Héloïse* and a year later *Emile*, which contained his controversial 'Profession de foi du vicaire savoyard'. His most famous essay, *Du Contrat social*, appeared in the same year. He fled religious persecution by coming to Britain, where he visited the homes of many radical intellectuals, including the father of Robert Malthus. He subsequently wrote a number of tracts defending his various publications, and the autobiographical dialogues *Rousseau, juge de Jean-Jacques*. Having spent his declining years suffering from acute depression which approached paranoia, he died in 1778.

Human beings in their natural state were, Rousseau believed, good and peaceable. He rejected the idea of Hobbes and others that human beings, in a state of nature, are at war with one another: 'Man is born free; and everywhere he is in chains' are the opening words of the first chapter of his *Du Contrat social*. In answer to the question 'How did this come about?' Rousseau replied: 'I do not know.' His memory must have been remarkably short; only seven years earlier had he not written on the origins of inequality? Although he expressed doubts in the preface whether a state of nature had ever existed, and claimed that he was concerned not with historical facts, but with 'conditional and hypothetical reasonings',[93] he certainly elaborated his argument in chronological form and appears to have been discussing precisely the *origins* of political domination and economic inequality. Human evil stems from unjust and oppressive institutions, which developed out of the phenomenon of private property.[94] This in turn evolved when humans relinquished their primitive independence:

> from the moment one man needed assistance from another; from the moment it seemed advantageous to any one to have enough provisions for two, equality disappeared, property was introduced, work became indispensable, and vast forests became smiling fields, which had to be watered with the sweat of man's brow, and where slavery and misery were soon seen to germinate and spring up with the harvest.[95]

Barbarous times, he asserted, are to be seen as an age of gold, not because men were united but because they were isolated.[96] In explicit opposition to

Hobbist theories about life in a state of nature, Rousseau maintained that it was 'the new-born state of society', that gave rise to 'the most horrible state of war'.[97]

This idea of nature as pure and good, with corruption stemming from human institutions, underlies many of Rousseau's characteristic beliefs. He regarded reason with suspicion, acknowledging the ambivalent role it has played in human history. 'A thinking man', he proclaimed in a memorable dictum, 'is a depraved animal.'[98] Even in civil society Rousseau recognised a limit to human reason and saw it as the source of much evil. In common with many of the *philosophes*, Rousseau distrusted 'philosophy' – grand schemes of rational construction, like those of Descartes and Leibniz. The best that can be expected of philosophy, he pronounced, is to destroy the evils it has caused.[99] Voltaire and the *philosophes* had looked to the English empiricism of Bacon, Locke and Newton for inspiration, while Rousseau himself admired the approach of the Newtonian Samuel Clarke.[100] Frederick the Great reflected the mood of the time, when he wrote to d'Alembert in 1776: 'man is an animal moved more by feeling than reason'.[101]

Rousseau often opposed reason to conscience or instinct. Discussing the character of 'Maman' (Madame de Warens), he wrote:

> her inclinations were upright and virtuous, her taste was refined; she was born for an elegant way of life which she always loved but never followed, because instead of listening to her heart, which gave her good counsel, she listened to her reason which gave her bad.[102]

Too often, mused the Savoyard Vicar, reason deceives us, but conscience never, for it is to the soul what instinct is to the body.[103] 'All the evil I ever did in my life', Rousseau told a correspondent, 'was the result of reflection; and the little good I have been able to do was the result of impulse.'[104]

It would nevertheless be quite wrong to think of Rousseau as an irrationalist *tout court*. 'The heart deceives us in a thousand ways', warns Julie in *La Nouvelle Héloïse*, 'and ever acts on a suspect principle: but reason has no other end than the good; its rules are sure, clear and easy to apply to the conduct of life'. And, she went on, it misleads only when engaged in useless speculations.[105] Rousseau, indeed, suspected human reasoning and was clear about the limits of the legitimate use of logic. It is reason's misuse he condemned, believing – in common with many of his contemporaries – that metaphysics represents such a misuse. As a guide to action one must frequently turn from reason to nature, 'that is to say the interior feeling which directs my belief independently of my reason'.[106] Yet reason is given by God and has its proper uses; it is, indeed, reason itself that confirms our appeal to feelings. 'I must have reasons for submitting my reason', declared the Vicar.[107] Rousseau has been called by one commentator 'a rationalist aware of the limits of reason'.[108]

Sovereignty, law and the general will

Rousseau was clear that the state of nature, if it ever had existed on earth, had passed irretrievably. Nothing could be done to re-establish the natural order, and attempts to do so were misguided. Having lost their primitive independence, humans have been subjected to all kinds of political domination. As victims of injustice and oppression they are in chains. Many social practices and institutions have reinforced their slavery. It is nonetheless possible to conceive of a state in which they can live in freedom. It was the purpose of his *Du Contrat social* to set forth the conditions under which such freedom is feasible. By voluntarily relinquishing the claim to a natural freedom and submitting to the will of the sovereign body, each would acquire civic freedom – the freedom of the citizen to participate in making laws. Simply to renounce liberty would be to renounce one's humanity and become a slave, but to become a citizen is to share in a social order which is 'a sacred right'.[109] 'Create citizens', he cried, 'and you have everything you need'.[110]

It is the making of law that characterises the sovereign's role. In establishing general laws the earthly state follows the divine pattern and is led 'to imitate here below the unchangeable decrees of the Deity'.[111] As Cassirer points out, Rousseau regarded law not as a restriction on human freedom, but as providing the context within which freedom can exist.[112] 'To the ideas of the welfare state and the power state he opposed the idea of the constitutional state (*Rechtstaat*).'[113] Rousseau is indeed opposed to government by personal whim or by particular decree. Government must be conducted on the basis of general laws which have been settled in advance; only thus is freedom possible. As usual Rousseau exaggerated, claiming that 'it is to law alone that men owe justice and liberty'.[114] Law may, indeed, be a necessary condition of freedom and justice but it is certainly not a sufficient condition, for laws may be intrusive, unjust and oppressive. Rousseau agreed with the physiocrat Mercier de la Rivière that the state 'must govern according to the essential rules of order, and when this is the case it ought to be all-powerful'. These economists, in de Tocqueville's words, 'set no limits to the rights of the state'.[115] It was, Rousseau maintained, by means of laws promulgated by the general will and accepted by the particular wills that humans could 'establish the reign of virtue'.[116] These were words that an 'incorruptible' Jacobin leader could savour.

Submission to the general will of the sovereign must be total and without reserve.[117] Citizens carry with them into civil society no rights from the state of nature (as they do in Locke's theory). Nothing is beyond the scope of the law. The fatherland is to be seen as 'the common mother' (*sic*) of all its citizens. The state, in its educational role, is portrayed as 'the tender mother' who nourishes her children, expecting in return an unhesitating acceptance of the 'will of society'.[118] In one of his later writings, Rousseau advised that each Corsican should take a solemn oath, in the name of God the all-powerful: 'I assign my body, goods, will, and all my power to the Corsican nation.'[119] For these and other reasons, later commentators have claimed to find in Rousseau's writings the origin of totalitarian democracy.[120]

Rousseau's conception of the general will has been the most influential and controversial aspect of his political thought. In his vision of a state of free citizens, each must participate in the deliberations and conclusions of the sovereign. The whole body of citizens must come together as sovereign, under the guidance of a wise legislator, to formulate laws. If they come asking not what is good for themselves as individuals, but what is best for the whole, then, Rousseau believed, they will – if in possession of all the facts and properly guided – come infallibly to a right conclusion. 'The general will is always right, but the judgment which guides it is not always enlightened.'[121]

Rousseau evidently supposed that under normal circumstances the decision would be unanimous, though he does allow for the possibility of voting. The decision of the majority binds the rest not because it represents the largest number of voters, but because it is assumed to be the way of finding out what is best for the whole and of discerning the real will of each citizen. There is a remarkable example of the influence of Rousseauite thinking in the modern world in Hans Küng's discussion of voting in a general council of the church:

> this voting . . . is only a means for achieving unanimity; by means of a majority the true mind and direction of the Church as such is determined so that perhaps those few who had not yet perceived it could now – after it had been interpreted and determined – recognize it as a law binding upon all. Hence a council is not the sum total of the individual votes, but the totality of the consciousness of the Church.[122]

This idea led Rousseau to his most daring claim: 'whoever refuses to obey the general will shall be compelled to do so by the whole body: this means nothing other than that he will be forced to be free'. Obedience to a law which one has prescribed to oneself is true freedom, and each citizen has consented, in advance, to be bound by the general will.[123]

Unity and plurality in the state

One necessary condition for the general will to operate is that citizens should come together as isolated individuals, rather than as members of groups. Like Hobbes, Rousseau opposed 'particular interests' and 'sectional societies', on the ground that they would challenge the absolute power of the sovereign and obstruct the process of discovering the common good. This passion for unity, and hostility towards natural groupings was shared by many other thinkers of the time, including l'abbé Sieyès, as we have seen. If there must be partial associations, however, it is best that there be many rather than few. Numerous small groups are safer than a few powerful ones.[124]

Rousseau's political theory represents the apotheosis of individualism. Humans, for him, are essentially isolated beings. They are truly themselves when alone. 'The first idea of man', he wrote, 'is to separate himself from everything that is not himself.' 'Recueillez-vous, cherchez la solitude.'[125] One of his reasons for breaking with Diderot was the latter's attack on the man of solitude: 'only the evil man seeks solitude', he had written.[126]

Individualism and 'collectivism' are often contrasted in social and political theory as two opposite poles. In fact they are two sides of the same coin. The only way individualists can avoid social chaos is by bringing these individual units into a collectivity with a strongly centralised and authoritarian government. I have suggested elsewhere that this applies as much in ecclesiastical as in civil politics, as illustrated in the case of John Henry Newman.[127] He asserted that every man 'is as whole and independent a being in himself, as if there were no one else in the whole world but he'.[128] Like Rousseau, he believed that when a man 'is in solitude, that is his real state'. The church is a political organisation, composed of a collection of these disparate individuals, over whom it exercises 'an absolute and almost despotic rule'.[129]

The political entities postulated by individualists like Rousseau, Newman and Hobbes, despite the organic language used, remain artificial collectivities held together by force and fraud. Rousseau wrote of the state as 'an organised, living body, resembling that of a man . . . a moral being, possessed of a will'.[130] It is easy to be deceived by this language into thinking that Rousseau recognised a truly organic bond between persons, but in fact he remained an individualist at heart. It is indeed this that made him so attractive to Kantians, like Ernst Cassirer. Rousseau himself distinguished between an artificial and a natural body,[131] and his use of organic analogies is incidental. His thought must be seen as a variety of eighteenth-century atomism; his state is ultimately a collection of individuals.[132] Alfred Cobban made this point, but mistakenly believed that this absolves Rousseau from the charge made by C. E. Vaughan that his contract theory is 'the porch to a collectivism as absolute as the mind of man has ever conceived'.[133] It is precisely Rousseau's individualism that leads him to deny the existence of natural bonds between humans – bonds which in reality lead to the formation of those groups and associations which he disliked so much and which have provided some kind of a bulwark against the absolute claims of the state.[134] He had in mind, in de Tocqueville's words, a situation with

> no gradations in society, no distinctions of classes, no fixed ranks, – a
> people composed of individuals nearly all alike and entirely equal –

this confused mass being recognized as the only legitimate sovereign, but carefully deprived of all the faculties which could enable it either to direct or even to superintend its own government.[135]

His absolute collectivism is a direct consequence of his radical individualism.

In Rousseau's state, unity is essential. We have seen how he rejected all particular groups and associations as likely to undermine the general will. 'Now in every political state', Rousseau added in his final draft of the *Lettres écrites de la montagne*, 'there must be a supreme power, a centre to which everything is related, a principle from which everything derives, a sovereign who can do everything'.[136] As we shall see, his state replicates on earth the role which God plays in relation to the universe. Social unity, he insisted, is the *sine qua non* of the state. On this ground he attacked those religions, like the Roman Catholic, which divide human loyalties and allow for plurality in the state. We shall return to this issue in due course. Rousseau was clear that force alone is insufficient to maintain this state in being. 'The strongest is never strong enough always to be the master', he proclaimed in a memorable passage, 'unless he transforms his strength into right and obedience into duty.'[137]

Civil religion

In addition to the myth of the contract, Rousseau perceived a need to reinforce political sovereignty with divine authority. *Vox populi* must be seen as *vox dei*.[138] Some ominous words in his *Discours sur l'inégalité* tell the reader that history teaches

> how much human governments have needed a more solid basis than mere reason, and how public order required the divine will to invest the sovereign authority with a sacred and inviolable character, which would deprive subjects of the fatal right of disposing of it. If the world had received no other advantages from religion, this would be enough to impose on men the duty of adopting and cultivating it, abuses and all.[139]

This ideology, and the 'sacred dogmas which give the sanction of divine right to sovereign authority,'[140] were to be institutionalised in the form of a 'civil religion'.

In early times, Rousseau asserted, kings were gods, and gods were kings. Government was theocratic. Each people had its own god, and 'national divisions thus led to polytheism'.[141] All religions were political religions, until Jesus came to found a spiritual kingdom, 'which, by separating the theological from the political system, made the state no longer one, and brought about the internal divisions which have never ceased to trouble

Christian peoples'.[142] Rousseau believed that Christianity has a rather subversive tendency, yet religion is an indispensable foundation of a state. 'Never', he declared, 'has a State been founded without a religious basis.'[143] He distinguished the allegedly 'simple' message of Jesus from the complex dogmas of the institutional church. Both forms of Christianity, however, pose a challenge to the state. The simple gospel message directs people's attention away from earthly conditions, discouraging political participation and favours thereby the rise of tyranny. 'Christianity preaches only servitude and dependence. . . . True Christians are made to be slaves.' This sublime gospel is universal in scope, recognising all as brothers, and therefore is a poor foundation for political unity and patriotism. He went so far as to declare, with respect to this true Christian religion: 'I know of nothing more contrary to the social spirit.'[144]

Second, institutional religion may establish a rival authority to the state and thereby divide allegiance. Rousseau cites Catholic Christianity as an example. This form of religion is evidently bad, for it too destroys social unity. A third form of religion is civil religion. The fatherland becomes the object of religious adoration, devotion to the tutelary god involves respect for civil laws, and to die for one's country is seen as martyrdom. This religion, manifest in the classical world, strengthens the state but is bad insofar as it is founded on lies, turns the worship of God into an empty formality and undermines any moral duties with respect to those outside its borders; nation is set at war with nation. Yet Rousseau, like many of his contemporaries, was greatly influenced by classical models. In their search for a religion to replace Christianity, many eighteenth-century intellectuals turned to classical symbols, myths and heroes.[145] This represented, according to Mona Ozouf, not merely an aesthetic appeal to the past or a need for moral examples, 'it expressed also, and above all, in a world in which Christian values were declining, the need for the sacred'.[146]

Rousseau was thus faced with a problem. Religion is necessary, yet in all three historical forms it has fallen short in some way. In response he turned to the Erastianism of Thomas Hobbes. Among Protestants, he insisted, 'there is no other church than the state, and no other ecclesiastical legislator than the sovereign'.[147] The sovereign must promulgate a civil religion, whose dogmas are few, simple and exactly worded. These comprise belief in a mighty, intelligent, benevolent and omniscient being, life after death, reward for the just, punishment for the wicked, and the sanctity of the social contract and of laws. It would anathematise intolerance. Those not accepting these dogmas would be banished, those betraying them would be killed.[148] In his *Confessions* he justified his return to Protestantism in 1754 on the Erastian ground that the sovereign has the right to settle the form of worship and 'the unintelligible dogmas as well', and that in any case there is no fundamental difference between Christians. This too is the belief of the Savoyard Vicar.[149]

It is not entirely clear whether Rousseau thought that the sovereign can adopt *any* faith as the state religion, even Catholicism (which would involve adopting the second form of religion mentioned above and would undermine the unity of the state), or whether it should adopt the civic religion outlined in *Du Contrat social*, which falls somewhere between liberal Protestantism and deism. In any event citizens would be free to follow the religion of the heart, the simple gospel, which is an internal religion not susceptible (as Hobbes had recognised) to state control.

Rousseau, of course, shared this belief in civil religion with many other writers of his time. Helvétius, for example, though himself a materialist, believed that the legislature should supply the people with a national, patriotic religion based on the worship of nature.[150] Voltaire attacked the 'atheism' of Helvétius but he too believed that there should be 'cérémonies augustes' and a 'culte majestueux' celebrated in national temples.[151] These ideas were taken up in the revolutionary years. Altars of the fatherland were set up on which might be exposed the bread of fraternity. There would be a sacred book, containing the Declaration of Rights, a national catechism, and patriotic anthems. Even a form for civic baptism was proposed. The Revolution had its calendar of saints and martyrs and much of the social and political rhetoric was religious in tone.[152]

Rousseau's God

Rousseau was essentially a moralist,[153] for whom religion – both civil and personal – was judged by its practical effects. God was the ultimate guarantor of both social and individual morality. In this he emulated the rather liberal position held by a number of contemporary Genevan pastors. Influenced by the teaching of Jean-Alphonse Turrettin, they subscribed to a faith which is 'less a doctrine than a rule of life', a religion purged of marvel and mystery.[154] Following Erastian tradition, Rousseau, as we have noted, saw God as a useful and indeed necessary support for the political order. But in addition to civil religion – the religion of the citizen – there is the religion of the heart – the devout belief of the individual man or woman; not needing temples, altars and rites, it is the 'internal cult of the supreme God'.[155] This is quite compatible with civil religion, for it requires no outward forms or institutions. It is the religion of the Savoyard Vicar. Though a Catholic priest, the Vicar's religion was that of liberal Protestantism, with a deist tinge. Why, then, were the Genevan authorities so incensed by *Emile* and particularly by the 'Profession de foi'? It was, suggested Masson, the aggressive tone rather than the content of the book; their hostility was only confirmed by the contentious nature of the *Lettres écrites de la montagne*.

Rousseau conceived of God as the 'sovereign Creator'[156] – the celestial monarch, disposer supreme and judge of the earth. God was the heavenly analogue of that sovereign body which legislates in the earthly state. In a celebrated letter to the archbishop of Paris, the 'citizen of Geneva' affirmed his belief in God as one who unites supreme and unique power with supreme and unique will.[157] God's power logically takes precedence over his goodness, for absolute power involves the power to define goodness and justice. 'La bonté est l'effet nécessaire d'une puissance sans borne et de l'amour de soi.'[158] In his *Rêveries* he asserted that if he himself were invisible and all-powerful, as God is, he too would be 'as benevolent and good as he'. This divine power is intimately related to supreme will in God; in fact Rousseau went as far as to assert that 'his will makes his power'.[159] This Hobbist notion runs through most of Rousseau's political theology and bears a clear analogy to the general will which takes on a divine aura in *Du Contrat social*. Leviathan is indeed 'democratised' but retains its status as the mortal god.

Rousseau's god contrasts rather sharply with the god of cold rational deism imported from England by Voltaire and many *philosophes*. This latter was called 'sovereign' certainly but was limited by the laws of wisdom and justice, which were seen not merely as products of his will. This position is reflected in the *Manuel des souverains*: 'Dieu est un monarque non arbitraire mais un monarque limité par les règles de la sagesse infinie, prescrites à son "pouvoir infinie"'.[160] As Charles Vereker has shown, the political theory of Quesnay, Le Mercier and the physiocrats was characterised by a belief that will must operate according to wisdom and law – with respect both to God and to the civil sovereign. The analogy between God and the state was drawn though – in contrast to Rousseau – with the purpose of *limiting* the sovereign's legitimate authority. The physiocrat Le Mercier de la Rivière, vindicating his belief in constitutional despotism, maintained that the legitimate despot should govern his realm 'as God, of whom he is the image, governs the universe, in which we see all secondary causes subjected *invariably* to laws from which they cannot deviate'.[161] These men may have written of 'the supreme will of the Creator', but in Vereker's words:

> to see the divine will as supreme did not mean to the physiocrats that it was also arbitrary, a view common to much voluntarist thinking. God's judgments were never arbitrary. He was subject, as it were, to his own laws, a constitutional rather than a Hobbesian monarch.[162]

In *La Nouvelle Héloïse* God is pictured as the all-seeing eye, peering into the depths of the heart.[163] He is addressed by Julie as 'Great Being, eternal Being, supreme intelligence, source of life and happiness, creator, preserver, father of men and king of nature'.[164] Most of Rousseau's commentators would agree that the sentiments expressed by the Savoyard Vicar generally represent the ideas of the Genevan moralist himself. He believed that the universe is an ordered and coherent system governed by a powerful and wise being.[165] Rousseau's concern for order is evident in both his theology and his politics. God's goodness is, declared the Vicar, following the teaching of the French philosopher Nicolas Malebranche, manifested in his love of order. It is humans who introduce disorder. In Rousseau's view, God was largely exonerated from the disastrous consequences of the Lisbon earthquake of 1755, which had led so many to question whether the world was indeed the best of all possible worlds. The catastrophe was due largely to human foolishness in constructing huge cities with 20,000 houses of up to seven storeys high. If they had had more respect for the natural order the widespread destruction would have been averted.[166]

Rousseau's God is an entirely independent and self-sufficient being. Autarky is viewed as an aspect of perfection. In *La Nouvelle Héloïse* the paradise of Clarens is an island, 'separated from the rest of the world – a completely self-enclosed community'.[167] The hero, Wolmar the atheist, is also pictured as entirely self-sufficient, a spiritual Robinson Crusoe. Judith Shklar comments: 'The reason Wolmar does not believe in God is that he *is* God to all intents and purposes.'[168] It was in fact Rousseau's own ambition to become 'self-sufficient and to think without the help of others'.[169] In his *Rêveries*, he speculated on the possibility of becoming 'self-sufficient like God',[170] and in his last years Rousseau elaborated on this theme, seeing heaven in terms of himself acquiring that most impressive feature of God's being, self-sufficiency.[171] 'He has ideas of independence', observed James Boswell, 'that are completely visionary and which are unsuitable for a man in his position.'[172] Yet in the last resort, as Ronald Grimsley points out, Rousseau recognised an ultimate dependence of the human individual on God, the creator, who is the only truly autarkic being.[173]

Prayer and petition

This image of God, as sovereign and self-sufficient – a model for the state – is illustrated and confirmed in Rousseau's remarks about prayer. In his *Confessions* he told of how he preferred to pray in the open air, and to contemplate God through his works. His only requests were for a peaceful and innocent life for himself and for his loved ones. 'For the rest my worship consisted rather of wonder and contemplation than of petitionary prayer.'[174] Here and elsewhere he rejected petitionary prayer. We should not ask God for anything, for he is all-powerful and good and will give to us what we need. The Savoyard Vicar contemplates God and addresses him as the source of justice and truth, but pleads for nothing. His whole emphasis is a prayer of acceptance and resignation to the will of the all-powerful God: 'The supreme wish of my heart is that your will be done.'[175] In his *Lettres écrites de la montagne*, Rousseau indignantly repudiated the charge that he rejected prayer, but went on to affirm that the model prayer, the Lord's Prayer, can be summed up in the phrase 'thy will be done', and that the most perfect prayer is 'the entire resignation to the wishes of God'.[176]

In an early prayer these themes of absolute dependence and resignation to the will of God are clearly stated, as is the 'political' role of God, who is addressed as 'votre immense majesté'. He is 'the master and absolute sovereign of all that exists . . . the absolute and independent being, who depends only on himself for existence . . . whose divine providence sustains and governs the whole world.'[177]

Another reason Rousseau disliked petitionary prayer is somewhat in conflict with his emphasis on resignation and acceptance. He maintained that 'the best means of obtaining from the Dispenser of all benefits those benefits that are necessary to us' is to 'deserve them and not ask for them'.[178] This Pelagian tendency runs through all Rousseau's writings. Like Newman, he asserted that the virtuous will believe in God's existence, because they want God to exist. 'Keep your soul in a state of always desiring that there is a God', the Savoyard Vicar advised his disciple, 'and you will never doubt it.'[179] In a letter of 1769 Rousseau declared that we shall be judged not by what we believe, but by what we do. Moreover, we are not pure intelligences, and our beliefs and opinions are influenced by our wills. God has sufficiently revealed himself in nature and in the human heart; if there are any who do not know God it is 'because they do not want to know him, or because they have no need of him'.[180] Virtue is inextricably tied to religious belief. Atheists are not only mistaken but wicked.

Reacting strongly against the notion of a state governed by the will of a despot (however 'enlightened'), Rousseau and the leading French revolutionaries set forth the vision of a *Rechtstaat* – a centralised and rational state governed not by men but by laws. This vision coincided largely with the way things were going. While the seventeenth century in England and in Western Europe had witnessed frenetic attempts (in theory and in practice) to centralise power in the face of disorder and civil war, the eighteenth century was a period, in France and England, of a slow but relentless growth in centralisation. 'The patchwork of regions, though "bristling with exceptions, privileges and constraints", was thus being stitched together.'[181] As trade expanded, control of economic activity was passing from regions, cities and local communities to the state.[182]

Analogous to this image of the state was the picture of a God who governs the universe according to cosmic laws, which can in principle be discovered by scientific investigation. For some French philosophers of the eighteenth century this was all that need be said about God – that he had created (and, some would add, keeps in being) a system which runs according to a set of inflexible laws. This, for the typical deist, constituted God's government of the universe, God's 'general providence', which

101

ensured that all works ultimately for the best. While natural disasters (such as the notorious Lisbon earthquake) led to doubts, this model of God's relationship to the universe was largely maintained. Even the sceptical author of *Candide*, who had earlier adhered to this theodicy himself, did but modify his position, to·eliminate naive optimism and to introduce a measure of mystery into the ways of God:

> Je ne conçois pas plus comment tout serait bien:
> Je suis comme un docteur; hélas! je ne sais rien.[183]

In his *Métaphysique de Newton* (1740) Voltaire had already rejected the Leibnizian idea that God must necessarily have created the best of all possible worlds, agreeing with Samuel Clarke that creation was an act of God's free will.[184]

Voltaire, Rousseau, Robespierre and many of the *philosophes*, found this deism unsatisfactory, and adopted a position which gave God a more active role in the affairs of the universe – a position sometimes called 'theism'. They asserted a 'special providence', according to which God 'intervenes' to give special protection or guidance to his chosen people. There was, indeed, a growing suspicion in eighteenth-century France of the 'spirit of system', associated with the rationalism of Descartes, Leibniz and Spinoza. D'Alembert and his fellows turned increasingly towards the empiricism of Bacon, Newton and Locke, supposedly founded on 'well-established facts'.[185]

5

DIVINE CONSTITUTIONALISM AND POLITICAL ORDER

French enthusiasm for the concept of constitutional government had been fuelled by the success of the American Revolution. Frenchmen had fought alongside the colonists, celebrating with them the victory of natural rights over arbitrary government, and the formulation of the new order embodied in the state constitutions and supremely in the federal constitution of 1787, with a bill of rights constituting the first ten amendments. Nevertheless the social and political situation in America was quite different from that in pre-revolutionary France. The colonies were characterised by a considerable degree of social equality and mobility, in contrast to the rather rigidly stratified social order in France. Another striking difference was the decentralisation of power in America compared with the concentration of power and political decision-making in Paris. Any attempt to impose a new political order from the centre was quite out of the question in the colonies, where there *was* no generally accepted centre. The kind of revolutionary politics espoused by the Jacobins (which temporarily suspended constitutional safeguards) was never a possibility in North America, where the only hope for union was to be found in a search for compromise and consensus, and the establishment of a constitution with an almost divine status.

In this chapter I shall consider the analogy between divine and civil government as developed by the founding fathers[1] and their contemporaries, and by a series of preachers and pastors, whose sermons illustrate graphically the connection they saw between divine constitutionalism and civic order.

THE AMERICAN CONTEXT

The trans-Atlantic situation was thus very different from that in France, as Edmund Burke was keen to remind his readers. While many French revolutionaries, particularly among the Jacobins, were eager to destroy all traces of the previous regime, American theorists continually appealed to British constitutional precedents in their struggle against the governments of

George III. 'It was', wrote Edward Corwin, 'to the British constitution . . . that our forefathers appealed against British tyranny.'[2]

The 'revolutionaries' saw a taxation of the colonies as unprecedented, unconstitutional and against the law of nature. Furthermore, they firmly rejected the claim by Parliament – in the absence of a written constitution – to an absolute sovereignty. The independence constitutions, in their view, embodied and entrenched the natural rights, precedents and assumptions recognised for centuries in the practice of British government but which were being flouted by the current regime. Although most publicists and preachers in the colonies regarded themselves as loyal subjects of the king, the eighteenth century saw a growing hostility to the policies of the British government. This was exacerbated by the well-founded belief that the colonies brought considerable wealth to the metropole. It would not be difficult, declared Jeremiah Dummer in 1721, 'to prove that London has risen out of the Plantations, and not out of England'.[3] Dummer went on to draw an implicit analogy between God and Parliament, adapting words from Genesis (18:25), 'And shall not the judge of all the earth do right?'[4] to suggest limits to the authority of the British legislature. Most colonial opposition to the governments of George III was essentially conservative, with the colonists defending established ways in the face of innovations imposed by Westminster.

Constitutionalism

The new constitutions, then, were designed to embody many of the principles which the founders perceived in the British system of government, in particular the idea of a balanced structure of power. Looking towards the formation of a new constitution, a contemporary hoped it would be 'a perfect *copy* of that *bright original* which is the envy and admiration of the world'.[5]

This view was not, even in pre-revolutionary America, held unanimously, and some writers contrasted in stark terms the British and American forms of government. After independence, radicals like Jonathan Maxcy, writing in 1799, pointed out that the US president is limited by the constitution; the senate is 'chosen by the people in a constitutional mode'. In Britain the king represents power, hereditary, independent and unimpeachable; the upper chamber is composed of peers who hold their seats in virtue of birth or office rather than by the consent of the people. The British House of Commons in turn is unrepresentative. 'Who but a madman, or an enemy to our country', he cried, 'could have the effrontery to assert that our government is formed after the British model?'[6] From a radically different standpoint, Roger North (1653–1734), Tory nonjuror and high churchman, had earlier observed that, although the *word* 'constitution' was innocuous enough, 'it is commonly brought forward with a republican face' and is therefore to be regarded with circumspection.[7]

The idea of a constitution, as a single document, incorporating the basic structural principles of government and prescribing limits to the authority of the various governmental institutions, and having a legal status superior to ordinary legislation, became a sacred symbol in the American Revolution. A constitution derives its authority, as Thomas Paine insisted, not from the government; it is an act of the people 'antecedent to a government'. Rather, a government derives its authority from operating within the framework of a constitution.[8] This position was one which reflected the beliefs of the founders themselves.

In France, with the execution of the king and the abolition of the aristocracy, there was a real rupture in governmental continuity. This had created, in the view of Robespierre, an exceptional situation requiring a revolutionary politics proceeding on principles quite distinct from those of constitutional government. In America, on the other hand, there was a high degree of continuity in governing elites and consequently few demands for the revolutionary politics of the Jacobins. The constitution, reflecting the will of the people, became the basis upon which these governments claimed legitimacy.

The constitution was viewed by many Americans as an earthly reflection of that divine constitution according to which God rules the universe. During the eighteenth century the controlling symbol of God's relationship to the cosmos had changed. In the previous century puritan preachers and writers solved the problem of how to combine a Calvinist view of divine sovereignty with the conception of a God whose actions are not arbitrary but law-like, by appealing to the idea of covenant.[9] The sovereign God limits himself to act in a predictable way, according to laws, by a covenant with his chosen people. Such a covenant, indeed, became for them a model of civil and ecclesiastical government.[10] But things were changing; in a celebrated letter to Hezekiah Niles, in 1818, John Adams claimed that the real revolution was accomplished before the War of Independence began. 'The revolution', he continued, 'was in the minds and hearts of the people; a change *in their religious sentiments*; of their duties and obligations.'[11] The changing conception of God's relationship to the universe, implying a new understanding of authority, was an aspect of this religious revolution highlighted by Adams.

With the growing influence of rational theology, not only among colonial Anglicans but also among Congregationalists and Presbyterians, the paradigm of divine government was thus modified. The universe was represented more and more on a mechanical model, running according to pre-established laws, with (or in the case of many deists, without) occasional interventions by God. The deity acts justly, not simply because of a decision on his part to do so, but because this is in line with his eternal nature, and with the nature of the universe he has created. This notion of God provided the colonists with a model for the proper understanding of human government. 'Nature is orderly in all her works', wrote Paine, but monarchy 'is a mode of government that counteracts nature'. The republican system of representation, on the other hand 'is always parallel with the order and immutable laws of nature, and meets the reason of man in every part'.[12] Nature rather than covenant became the foundation of constitutional government, both human and divine.

Writers and preachers in the American colonies during the eighteenth century increasingly eschewed monarchical images of God (a tendency also present, it must be said, in Britain itself). Throughout his realms the king was increasingly seen in the context of a parliamentary system of government. If things needed doing it was to the legislature or to the king's ministers, rather than to the monarch himself, that people looked. So God was pictured more as ruler, governor, legislator, teacher, orderer, architect and even president, than as king. Increasingly God was seen as ruling by those 'laws which never shall be broken', referred to in the *Foundling Hospital Hymn Book* of 1796. As J. R. Pole has observed, 'The reception of Newtonian celestial mechanics had given political scientists a new and highly satisfying metaphor, which assimilated politics to the fixed and regular laws of the natural order.'[13]

Belief in God's special providence, however, remained and was embraced on the basis of an empiricism inspired by Bacon, Newton and Locke (Thomas Jefferson's three immortals),[14] in contrast to an earlier rationalism associated with Descartes, Spinoza and Leibniz, which found such special providence less easy to accommodate. American preachers saw this providence manifesting itself in God's guiding and protecting the colonies in their social and political life. They were frequently seen as the new Israel.[15] George Washington was, in the words of Ezra Stiles (president of Yale) the 'American Joshua . . . raised up by God and divinely formed by a peculiar influence of the sovereign of the universe'.[16] In his second inaugural address, Jefferson spoke of 'that Being in whose hands we are, who led our forefathers, as Israel of old, from their native land, and planted them in a country flowing with all the necessaries and comforts of life'.[17] The model of the new Israel led to a defence of republicanism.

It is, then, the thesis of this chapter that the growth of constitutionalism in the American colonies was intimately connected to a changing concept of God's relationship to his creation. This change both reflected political and legal developments in Britain and the colonies and also influenced the way these developments were formulated and justified. Certainly the cultural climate in which the constitution was born showed the traces of a puritan past, but this was tempered by rationalist (and, paradoxically, sceptical) influences from the Enlightenment. The philosophy of the Newtonians was influential, as was the political theory of John Locke and of radical English Whigs like Henry Neville, Algernon Sidney and the authors of *Cato's Letters*, Trenchard and Gordon. The writings of the Swiss-born jurist Jean-Jacques Burlamaqui, which popularised some of Locke's ideas, influenced the thought of James Wilson and probably Jefferson.

Henry F. May has distinguished four different 'enlightenments'. First, what he (rather misleadingly) calls the 'rational' – better, perhaps labelled 'empirical' – enlightenment, associated with Locke and Newton; second, the 'sceptical' enlightenment, of Hume and Voltaire; third, the 'revolutionary' enlightenment, with Godwin and Paine; and, finally, the 'didactic' enlightenment, associated with mid-eighteenth-century Scottish thinkers. Each of these movements or currents of thought made its impression on colonial intellectual life.

Although the founding fathers and other writers of the time frequently made reference to the world of classical antiquity to illustrate their arguments, Bernard Bailyn has convincingly maintained that these references, 'are everywhere illustrative, not determinative, of thought. They contribute a vivid vocabulary but not the logic or grammar of thought.'[18] The same might be said of the much-vaunted 'civic humanism', allegedly deriving from Machiavelli and Harrington.[19] Morton White and Bailyn himself have well outlined the philosophical and ideological background and the various currents of thought which influenced the founding fathers.[20] We shall first look at the ideas of the founders themselves, Thomas Jefferson (1743–1826), James Madison (1749–1836), Alexander Hamilton (1757–1804), John Adams (1735–1826) and Benjamin Franklin (1706–90), going on to consider the politico-religious climate in which these men grew up and elaborated their social theories, as reflected in the sermons and pamphlets of the period.

THE FOUNDING FEDERALISTS

The founders of American independence were generally men of the enlightenment. They believed in reason but still manifested in their thinking the profound influence of a puritan past. Most would have accepted the idea of a 'rational Christianity' which was Unitarian and liberal. For them the divine constitution must be reflected in a civil constitution under which governments should rule. Many recognized a divine guidance not only in personal but also in national life.

Divine providence and cosmic order

James Madison, born in Virginia, was raised an Anglican but was influenced at an early age by the formidable Scottish Presbyterian divine John Witherspoon. Although he later moved towards a more flexible theological position, the statesman carried with him through life the influence of orthodox Calvinism.[21] The young Madison had even considered entering the ministry of the Anglican church. Harriet Martineau declared that his 'political religion' was for him a form of personal piety, and that he was inspired by 'the true religion of statesmanship'.[22]

The founders shared the eighteenth-century fascination with the cosmos, seen as a huge and complex machine. In his 'Preliminary Draft of an Essay on Natural Order', of 1791, Madison pointed to the planetary system, 'regulated by fixed laws', as presenting 'most dramatically, a scene of order and proportion'.[23] John Adams, too, wrote of 'the astonishing machine of the world'.[24] A similar theme is present in George Washington's first inaugural address, which Madison wrote. The president made 'fervent supplications to that Almighty Being, who rules over the Universe, who presides in the Council of Nations, and whose providential aids can supply every human defect'. 'No people', he continued, 'can be bound to acknowledge and adore the invisible hand, which conducts the affairs of men more than the People of the United States.'[25]

The image of the divine hand – familiar to the eighteenth century in the writings of Joseph Addison (quoted by Tom Paine), Adam Smith and others – was taken up in the reply to the president from the House of Representatives (also written by Madison). 'We feel with you', declared the legislators, 'the strongest obligations to adore the *invisible hand* which has led the American people through so many difficulties.'[26] Here the idea of the hand represents not only the general providence of God in supervising a universe working according to fixed laws, but a special providence, which guides and protects a chosen people. The same image is present in number 37 of *The Federalist*. In arguing for the acceptance of the federal constitution proposed by the Convention, with its move towards a stronger central government, Madison remarked: 'It is impossible, for the man of pious reflection, not to perceive in it a finger of that Almighty Hand, which has been so frequently and signally extended to our relief in the critical stages of the revolution.'[27] In an earlier paper, John Jay had appealed to 'the design of Providence' in his plea that the newly independent colonies should not 'be split into a number of unsocial, jealous and alien sovereignties'.[28] Madison's concern for constitutional government, a government of laws not men, is reflected in his description of God as 'the supreme lawgiver of the universe'.[29]

Insisting that the grounds upon which independence was achieved were the general principles of Christianity, together with the general principles of liberty, the New Englander John Adams spoke of 'the divine science of politics', and emphasised the stable and unchanging nature of the cosmic and moral orders. He later told Jefferson that 'these general principles of Christianity are as eternal and immutable as the existence and attributes of God; and that those principles of liberty are as unalterable as human nature and our terrestrial, mundane system'.[30] Adams, like Madison, referred to

God as 'the great legislator of the universe'.[31] The second Continental Congress, meeting at Philadelphia in May 1775, certainly assumed the truth of the Christian faith in calling for days of public humiliation, fasting and prayer.[32] Despite all this, Adams saw the need to desacralise politics. He noted how – in the past – religion had given to political arrangements a fraudulent legitimation: 'It was the general opinion of ancient nations', he observed, 'that the Divinity alone was adequate to the important office of giving laws to men. . . . Is it that obedience to the laws can be obtained from mankind in no other manner?'[33] The United States, he affirmed, was perhaps the first example of government being erected on 'the simple principles of nature' rather than on claims to divine origin.[34] He adopted the 'greatest happiness' principle in discussing the criteria for good government.[35]

Thomas Jefferson, in some respects the most radical of the founders of US independence, was, like two-thirds of those who signed the Declaration of Independence, a member of the Episcopal (Anglican) Church. Eighteenth-century Anglicanism in the colonies had been influenced by the liberal and rather moralistic theology taught by the followers of John Locke. Such ecclesiastics as Archbishop John Tillotson and Benjamin Hoadly, the notorious Bishop of Bangor, were frequently quoted in the colonial church. Hoadly is described by Gad Hitchcock, in a sermon of 1774, as 'a writer of the first class on government'.[36] In his later years Jefferson spoke of 'rational Christianity' as his religion, and his Antitrinitarianism led him to sympathise with Quakerism. George Washington (1732–99), so far as he thought about these matters, took a rather similar position. He is described by a recent writer as 'a man of the moderate Enlightenment', a frequent churchgoer who worshipped 'the great disposer of events', 'the father of lights'.[37] While, as we have noted, the young Madison had come more manifestly under Calvinist influence, the founding fathers in general were Unitarians, who insisted firmly on their Christian allegiance, and their belief in the guiding providence of God. Jefferson, especially, denounced Trinitarian doctrines and cherished a particular animosity towards St Paul, for corrupting the simple message of Jesus.[38]

Jefferson's religion became a public issue of some importance in his presidential campaign of 1800, when he was denounced as an atheist by opponents.[39] He was not an atheist and it would even be misleading to describe him or the other founding fathers as deists, as is sometimes loosely done. There was indeed a deist movement in the American colonies, but it involved a very small minority and was, in the words of Perry Miller, 'an exotic plant in America, which never struck roots into the soil'.[40] Jefferson insisted, in a letter of 1803, that he was 'a Christian in the only sense in which he [Jesus] wished anyone to be; sincerely attached to his doctrines, in preference to all others; ascribing to himself every *human* excellence; and believing he never claimed any other'.[41] He admired and claimed to follow the religion and moral principles of Jesus, as he understood them. In his years of retirement at Monticello he produced for private circulation a synopsis of gospel teaching. 'It is', he told his friend Charles Thomson, 'a document in proof that *I am a real Christian*, that is to say a disciple of the doctrines of Jesus.'[42]

Jefferson saw religion as a question of the individual's relationship with God, and generally rejected any idea that respect for civil rights depends on our religious opinions any more than on our opinions in physics or geometry.[43] His campaign for 'a wall of separation' between church and state culminated in the Virginia Act of 1785. With Madison and other founding fathers, he was therefore hostile towards the establishment of religion, or the support of religious groups from public funds. Churches were seen as private and voluntary bodies. The only public importance of religion was in its teaching of a general and particular providence guiding national life, a common belief of Americans 'acknowledging and adoring an overruling Providence, which by all its dispensations proves that it delights in the happiness of man here and his greater happiness hereafter'.[44] Even on this matter, however, it had needed an amendment from Congress to Jefferson's draft of the Declaration of Independence to add reference to 'a firm reliance on the protection of divine providence'.[45]

Constitutionalism and 'The People'

Madison and his collaborators in the defence of constitutionalism drew a clear distinction between 'a constitution established by the people, and unalterable by the government; and a law established by the government, and alterable by the government'.[46] Even Hamilton (one of the more secular-minded of the founding fathers) referred to 'that *sacred reverence*, which ought to be maintained in the breast of rulers towards the constitution of a country'.[47] For Adams the very definition of a republic is 'an empire of laws not of men'.[48] His thinking also shows the continued influence of the covenant idea. 'The body politic is formed,' he wrote in his draft constitution for Massachusetts, 'by a voluntary association of individuals. It is a social compact, by which the whole people covenant with each citizen, and each citizen with the whole people, that all shall be governed by certain laws for the common good.'[49]

Enthusiasm for constitutional republicanism on the part of the founding fathers is partly due to their suspicion of democracy. Their search for checks and balances, was inspired largely by a fear of government falling into the hands of a mass movement, perhaps under the influence of a charismatic leader. John Adams, in a letter to Benjamin Rush, voiced disquiet about the almost sacred status of George Washington: 'I have been distressed to see some of our members disposed to idolize an image which their own hands have molten. I speak of the superstitious veneration which is paid to General Washington.'[50]

While a break with the colonial past became inevitable, these men sought a continuity of institutions where possible: 'I dread the spirit of innovation', confessed Adams to a correspondent.[51] He viewed government as a framework within which a limited end could be pursued.[52] Hamilton, in particular, feared popular participation in government. His opposition to Jefferson as presidential candidate in 1800 was based on his dread of populism, and he advocated the formation of a 'Christian Constitutional Society' to unite people of similar views. Sidney Ahlstrom describes the political conservatism of *The Federalist* and of Adams (related as it was to a particular idea of human nature) as a puritan contribution to Enlightenment political theory.[53] It was this suspicion that led to such institutions as the Electoral College, which was designed to avoid the danger of a plebicitarian president. It was also behind the 'dualist democracy' which, according to Bruce Ackerman, characterises American constitutionalism – a system whereby ordinary legislation (sometimes inspired by the enthusiasms of the moment) is contained within a legal–constitutional framework, which reflects the settled beliefs and convictions of the American people.[54]

There was nevertheless among the founders a deep-seated belief in 'the people' as the fount of authority. Despite their suspicion of the notion of sovereignty, they were prepared to speak of the sovereignty of the people. Adams once wrote: 'It is a maxim, that in every government there must exist somewhere, a supreme, sovereign, absolute, and uncontrollable power; but this power resides always in the body of the people.'[55] Hamilton believed that 'the people' must give their consent to the constitution, and it was, he thought, a weakness of the pre-1787 loose confederation that 'it never had a ratification by *the people*'.[56] The *Federalist* authors reiterated a belief in the people as 'fountain' of authority and legitimate power.[57] Madison saw 'public opinion' embodying this authority of the people and as setting bounds on government; in republics it is 'the real sovereign'.[58] The true effect, however, of the constitutional debates in America was to call into question the whole notion of 'sovereignty' as it had developed in British political theory from the mid-seventeenth century on. The federal constitution ensured that there was in the United States no person or body of persons whose decisions were supreme and unquestionable.[59] John Quincy Adams criticised even the notion of popular sovereignty. 'The principle that a whole nation has the right to do whatever it pleases', he declared, 'cannot in any sense whatever be admitted as true. The eternal and immutable laws of justice and morality are paramount to all human legislation.'[60] Yet the concept of sovereignty has lingered on to confuse political theorists for two centuries, and to obfuscate contemporary debates from the status of the Falkland/Malvenas Islands to Britain's relationship with the European Community.[61]

Human nature and federal power

The founding fathers generally had a 'realistic' view of human nature as containing both good and evil tendencies: 'As there is a degree of depravity in mankind which requires a certain degree of circumspection and distrust: So there are other qualities in human nature which justify a certain portion of esteem and confidence.'[62] Adams, though he doubted the existence of sincerity, honesty or veracity in any sect or party, agreed rather with Bishop Joseph Butler than with Thomas Hobbes in his assessment of human nature.[63] He rejected the idea of total depravity and shared with Jefferson a belief that 'it is a good world on the whole'.[64] Morality for the latter was a question not of education or intelligence, but of a 'moral sense or conscience', which 'is as much a part of man as his leg or his arm'; it is possessed by a ploughman as fully as by a professor.[65] Jefferson clearly aligned himself with the 'moral sense' tradition associated with the names of Francis Hutcheson and later Adam Smith, incorporating a due measure of Humean scepticism. Although reason can play a supporting role in the moral life, God 'has taken care to impress its precepts so indelibly on our hearts that they shall not be effaced by the subtleties of our brain'.[66]

The particular form of constitution which emerged from the debates of the Constitutional Convention in Philadelphia was, of course, federal. It specified certain powers to be exercised by a central government, and was designed to strengthen that government, at the expense of rights previously exercised only by the individual states. The principal danger was seen to be that each state would pursue its own path, thus weakening the whole. This was the message of *The Federalist*, letters written originally to a New York journal by Hamilton, Madison and Jay under the pseudonym 'Publius'. Hamilton had stated his own position in 1780, when he wrote that the danger facing the United States was that 'the common sovereign will not have power sufficient to unite the different members together, and direct the common forces to the interest and happiness of the whole'.[67]

In a remarkable Election Sermon of 1795, Perez Fobes, Congregational minister and professor of Natural Philosophy at Rhode Island College (later Brown University), drew analogies between the federal system and the structure of the cosmos. No longer could we expect the millions of people who populate the North American territories to gravitate around a metropolitan power, a mere pebble in the political cosmos:

> Nature itself revolted. They arose to independence . . . and formed a new solar system; a system complete of *federal democracy*; in which equal power, emanating from each individual, uniting, formed one

112

central luminary. This is retained in its station by a balance of gravi-
tating power, accumulated in separate branches of the same body, as
well as in a number of separate bodies or states.[68]

This analogy between cosmic and terrestrial rule had been elaborated by
Newtonian writers, especially J. T. Desaguliers.[69]

God and the state

Benjamin Franklin (1706–90) was certainly the most whimsical of the founders who, in the words of French prime minister Turgot 'snatched the
lightning shaft from heaven, and the sceptre from tyrants'.[70] Franklin was
highly respected in both France and Britain for his scientific work with
electricity, which gave him access to intellectual circles in both countries.
He lived in London for several years as the agent for the Pennsylvania and
other colonial assemblies and later became ambassador in Paris. He provided the most important intellectual link between Europe and America in
his day.

Born in Boston, Franklin began his career as a printer's apprentice; he
then moved into journalism and popular satirical writing. His knowledge
of the natural sciences, and his political and legal interests, made him
something of a polymath. In religion Franklin's position is not easy to
determine. John Adams wrote: 'The Catholics thought him almost a Catholic. The Church of England claimed him as one of them. The Presbyterians
thought him half a Presbyterian, and the Friends believed him a wet
Quaker'.[71] He was for some time a deist – God was, for him, 'the greatest
mechanic in the universe'[72] – but he became critical of this position, insisting
that 'the deity sometimes interferes by his particular providence, and sets
aside the events which would otherwise have been produced in the course
of nature, or by the free agency of man'.[73] To deny a particular providence
in God is, he asserted, to 'strike at the foundation of all religion': 'For
without the belief of a providence that takes cognizance of, guards and
guides and may favour particular persons, there is no motive to worship a
deity, to fear its displeasure, or to pray for its protection'.[74]

It was, indeed, Franklin who astonished the Constitutional Convention
of 1787, after a week-long impasse, by suggesting prayer. 'The Convention,
except three or four persons', he remarked dryly, 'thought prayers unnecessary.'[75] In later life Franklin was attracted to the Anglican church, largely
owing to the relatively liberal theology which prevailed among Anglicans
at this time. While not himself a regular worshipper, he and his wife were
associated with Christ Church, Philadelphia. He appears to have been a
devout believer in God and urged his daughter to attend public worship.[76]
He was also a close personal friend of the evangelical preacher George

Whitefield, who played a major role in the Great Awakening. In his *Auto-biography*, Franklin listed his beliefs as follows:

> That there is one God who made all things.
> That he governs the world by his providence.
> That he ought to be worshipped by adoration, prayer and
> thanksgiving.
> But that the most acceptable service of God is doing good
> to man.
> That the soul is immortal.
> And that God will certainly reward virtue and punish vice
> either here or hereafter.[77]

He laid considerable emphasis on his belief that virtue leads to happiness, and adopted a generally utilitarian position, for which he has been much criticised.[78] As we have seen, Jefferson wished to be known as a Christian and the same would probably be true with Franklin, at least in later life. A. O. Aldridge, after distinguishing between 'Christian deism' and 'deism', misleadingly goes on to assert: 'it was to the latter religious system that Franklin and Jefferson adhered'.[79] Their position would be more satisfactorily described as Unitarian or 'rational Christianity'.

For the founders, God governs the universe according to laws established in a cosmic constitution. His actions, far from being capricious dictates of a celestial despot, are the reasonable decisions of a universal ruler. Furthermore, the constitution is seen as adopted by the divine architect not as the result of an arbitrary decision, but as a consequence of his rational nature. Thomas Jefferson denounced the God of an earlier Calvinism as 'a false god' and as 'a daemon of malignant spirit'. He believed, rather, on the basis of 'a conviction of design', in the creator of an ordered cosmos, a 'Preserver and Regulator' of the universe, whose providential government was directed to human happiness.[80] In this he spoke for other founders and reflected certain currents in the religious culture of his day. It is to a discussion of the religious climate of the time that we now turn.

POLITICAL PREACHERS

Preaching was, in seventeenth- and eighteenth-century America, a principal means of communication, not only with respect to religious beliefs, but also in political and social matters. Sermons were frequently printed and joined the many tracts adorning colonial bookshelves.[81] As in England, special sermons were preached by celebrated divines on great national occasions, or on the anniversaries of past events. Many of the sermons quoted below were preached on the occasion of the election of colonial (and later state) legislatures. Successful preaching depends more upon the use of lively images than on the precise use of philosophical concepts, and is concerned with moving a congregation to repentance and good works as much as with imparting theological dogmas. Attention to this mode of communication is therefore appropriate in our search for the ways in which people in North America were encouraged to think about God and the state.

The 'Great Awakening' and the 'New Divinity'

The most significant influence on the contours of American religious life in the years preceding the revolution was the so-called Great Awakening, which occurred from around 1740 to 1743. It was associated particularly with the teaching and preaching of Jonathan Edwards (1703–58), who adhered to a basically Calvinist doctrine, restated in terms which might make some appeal to those affected by Enlightenment thinking. He had been influenced by the philosophy of Locke and the cosmology of Newton, though not, it should be added, by the theology of either man. Edwards taught the Anselmian idea of the solidarity of the human race in Adam. The terms he used to state this position are, from our point of view, significant. 'No solid reason can be given,' he wrote, 'why God . . . may not establish a constitution whereby the natural posterity of Adam . . . should be treated as *one* with him'.[82] The idea of a constitution, divine and human, is of course central to the concerns of this chapter.

Converts to the evangelical message were known as 'new lights' in New England, and as 'new side' in the middle colonies; they called for stricter discipline in the congregations and challenged the rather staid Calvinism of the 'old lights' in New England. Ministers and laypeople not manifesting the signs of conversion were openly denounced. This movement caused a good deal of conflict throughout the colonies, particularly within the Congregationalist churches. Massachusetts imposed restrictions on itinerant preachers; separatist churches sprang up everywhere. The revival also drove many into the Anglican and Presbyterian churches, where they were protected from such extreme forms of enthusiasm by a hierarchical organisation or a fixed liturgy. By the late 1740s, however, some accommodation had been reached between the old and the new lights.

Those theologians most influenced by Edwards – Samuel Hopkins (1721–1803), Joseph Bellamy (1719–90) and Nathaniel Emmons (1745–1840) – taught what was known as the 'New Divinity'. It was a Calvinism with some of its sharpest teeth drawn, or at least filed. While following Edwards in certain respects, these men were also influenced by an older rational Calvinism associated with John Witherspoon (1723–94), who had pioneered the way for an incorporation of Scottish common-sense philosophy into American religious thought. We have noted his influence on the young Madison. Witherspoon has been described as 'probably the most influential teacher in the entire history of American education'.[83] There has been some debate about the explicitly political consequences of the religious revival of

the mid-eighteenth century. Some historians see in these religious movements 'the spirit of American democracy' and claim that 'the evangelical
movement laid the groundwork for the revolution'.[84]

The New Divinity laid great emphasis on God as the creator of a rational
universe, close to the God of nature venerated by European Enlightenment
thinkers. He was for Bellamy the moral governor of the cosmos.[85] Bruce
Kuklick contrasts the God of the New Divinity with the God of traditional
New England puritanism: 'The God of the covenant had limited himself,
but he need not have done so. The God of the New Divinity was confined
by his benevolent character. The limitations on his sovereignty were intrin-
sic rather than adventitious.'[86] Kuklick reminds his readers how
Congregationalists in the American colonies had – like English puritans
and, indeed, most seventeenth-century preachers and writers – employed
political images in their talk about God. Republican imagery began, however, to replace royalist rhetoric: 'The New Divinity and the philosophy of
the state shared the vocabulary of republicanism.'[87] The constitutional
republicanism of the founding fathers envisaged a framework within
which various offices of government could be ordered, while 'theologians
believed that God "constituted" the moral universe and the proper life for
man' and that therefore 'the rule of God's conduct could be read from the
nature of the moral universe'.[88] Although the predominant imagery used
about both God and the state changed, it would be misleading to suggest
that the notion of a republican and constitutional deity had entirely eliminated the earlier images of God as sovereign monarch.

Mechanical images and analogies from nature

The political preachers and publicists of the American colonies were, then,
influenced by the liberal religion practised and taught in England by the
followers of Locke. They also reflected the mechanistic view of the universe
associated with the Newtonians (though, like Newton himself, most of
them saw an active role for God, in the realm both of nature and of grace).[89]
Even puritans like Cotton Mather were keen to set their theology in the
context of Newtonian cosmology. William Livingston, later governor of
New Jersey, wrote of the 'immortal Newton; whose illustrious name will
shine on records of eternal fame'.[90] God was seen above all as the creator
and regulator of a cosmic machine:

> His system fix'd on general laws
> Bespeaks a wise creating cause;
> Impartially he rules mankind
> And all that on this globe we find.[91]

Some, like Freneau, adopted a deist position, and portrayed nature as a
goddess of inflexible laws:

116

> Could she descend from that great plan
> To work unusual things for man, .
> To suit the insect of an hour –
> This would betray a want of power.[92]

Significantly, even those who, like Benjamin Franklin, resisted deism, insisting on divine 'intervention', also assumed a mechanical model. Many writers on political matters saw government too, by analogy, as 'a very complicated machine'. Benjamin Rush taught that the education system should, among other things, 'convert men into republican machines. This must be done', he went on, 'if we expect them to perform their parts properly in the great machine of the government of the state.'[93]

If views of nature in general were important influences on the way people thought about government, their ideas about *human* nature were of particular significance. One writer denounced the idea that government was founded on superstition, conquest 'or a pretended compact between rulers and the people; but it was derived from nature, and reason; and is founded in the nature, capacities, and powers, which God hath assigned to the race of men'.[94] Most, however, accepted a roughly Lockean model of civil society resting on some kind of compact or covenant which men agreed when in a state of nature.[95] Government is subsequently set up as a trust (Locke's own view)[96] or by a second compact between rulers and people. Particular views about human nature as at least flawed, and sometimes thoroughly sinful, determined the exact terms of the compacts.

Human nature being imperfect or worse, it was thought dangerous to allow any person or group to enjoy unlimited power. There was a general insistence that power needs to be hedged around in order to limit its inherent dangers. Power, wrote an anonymous contributor to *The Boston Gazette and Country Journal*, in 1763, 'naturally intoxicates the mind. It even alters men's dispositions and inclines them to be masters instead of benefactors of their country.'[97] Power for Samuel Cooper, in a sermon on the occasion of the commencement of the new constitution of Massachusetts, tends to tyranny, such is the nature of man and of power: 'It makes a perpetual effort to enlarge itself, and presses against the bounds that confine it. It loses by degrees all idea of right but its own.'[98] The celebrated and controversial Jonathan Mayhew, in a 'Discourse' entitled 'The Snare Broken', dedicated to William Pitt, maintained that power is 'of a grasping, encroaching nature'; it aims at extending itself, wherever it meets with no balance, check, control or opposition.[99] Addressing the French National Convention in 1792, Joel Barlow warned that political power is a dangerous thing.[100] This Whig suspicion of power is one of the principal reasons for the centrality of constitutionalism in American thought of this period.

Constitutional government

This mechanical view of the universe was embodied in the notion of a divine constitution, which prescribes limits to the paths of the heavenly bodies and to the movements of matter. In his Election Sermon, delivered at Boston in 1768, Daniel Shute took the solar system as a model for a constitutional separation of powers: 'Each keeping a steady and regular course in his own sphere, will dispense a benign influence upon the community, and harmoniously conspire to promote the general good.'[101]

There is some disagreement about the term 'constitution'. Many writers continued to use it in its older and broader sense as referring to the general system or form of government operating in a country. The British constitution for them was to be found in a number of separate statutes, in unwritten precedents and in such documents as Magna Carta, and was more or less equivalent to 'fundamental law'.[102] Some adopted a narrower definition of a constitution as a single written document defining the powers of different branches of government and possessing some kind of entrenched legal status. An anonymous author from Philadelphia, for example, exposed what he believed to be a confusion between a constitution and a form of government. All countries must have the latter, but few if any have a true constitution. 'The English', he maintained, 'have no Constitution', because there are no limits on the powers of the legislature. 'No country can be called *free* which is governed by an absolute power; and it matters not whether it be an absolute royal power or an absolute legislative power.'[103]

A medical doctor from South Carolina criticised Americans for deriving their ideas about government from the British. He called for a written constitution defining the powers and privileges of the legislature, which should be 'fixed as low as is consistent with the public welfare'.[104] A constitution must, like God himself, be eternal and immutable, at least in principle. Making this point, the people of Pittsfield petitioned the provisional government of Massachusetts, demanding a constitution which has 'such a broad basis of civil and religious liberty as no length of time will corrupt and which will endure as long as the Sun and the Moon shall endure'.[105]

Abraham Williams (1727–84) – Harvard graduate and unconventional Congregationalist minister – told the Governor and General Court of Massachusetts: 'Government is a divine Constitution, founded in the nature and relation of things.' He accepted the Lockean idea of a state of nature and a surrender by individuals of certain rights to 'the society', in particular the rights to judge and to punish. God is the 'head of the system, and supreme governor'. As in the realm of nature, so in the civil condition, there are various ranks and orders, with little suggestion of equality. In his description of civil government Williams employed commercial images, referring to the 'business of *Legislation*' and those who 'manage the affairs

118

of government'. He paid tribute to the 'great governor of the world' for 'placing us under a government, so wise and good in its constitution and administration'.[106] Writers and preachers often linked the end of divine government with that of civil government, in terms of human happiness. Daniel Shute told the Governor, Council and House of Representatives of Massachusetts:

> It being so evidently the will of God, from the general constitution of things, that the happiness of his rational creatures should be promoted, all such are under moral obligation in conformity thereto, according to their ability, to promote their own, and the happiness of others.[107]

David Tappan, in an election day sermon to a similar Boston congregation twenty-four years later, made the identical point. Civil government proceeds on the same principles as divine government of the universe; as the former is conducive to social union and happiness, so the latter brings about 'the harmony and welfare of nature'.[108]

The civil constitution is thus conceived both by analogy with, and also as a part of, the divine constitution of things. Rulers, pointed out Samuel Kendal, are dignified with the title of 'gods'; 'realizing that they are subjects of the divine government . . . they will make the divine character, law and government, as far as possible, the model of their own'.[109] From both angles it was seen as guaranteeing a nice balance between the various branches of government, as also between the claims of liberty and order, avoiding 'anarchy' on the one hand and tyranny on the other. Even before independence, most Americans saw themselves living under a constitution (in its broader sense), at local as well as imperial level.[110] All legitimate government is based on consent; all right to rule 'must originate from those they rule over'. Biblical ideas of covenant were combined with Lockean ideas of political obligation. John Tucker pointed to Magna Carta as virtually a compact which limited the scope of royal government. If it is broken by the king, 'the people have a right to resist'.[111] Civil government 'is founded in the nature of man, and in the constitution of things, which are from God', but these are mediated through human consent.[112] Tucker quoted the Spartan ruler who, on being asked who governs Sparta, answered 'the laws, and the magistrates according to these laws'. He went on to outline a conception of fundamental laws of the state which bind both ruler and subject. 'Even the supreme Ruler of the world', he maintained,

> is not a despotic, arbitrary monarch, nor does he require obedience by mere authority. His sacred laws, – all framed agreeable to the perfect rectitude of his nature, and resulting from his infinite goodness, and righteousness, are wisely adapted to the human system, and calculated for its good.

God sees us not as slaves, but as children.[113]

Preaching in Massachusetts in 1774, Nathaniel Niles based the claim to resistance on the idea of a contract, binding on the ruler and his subjects. If the king were to break the contract the people would be released from their obligations, 'for a default of one party in covenant sets the other at liberty'. For anyone to encourage the monarch to break his side of the covenant (as the ministers of George III were seen to do) 'ought to be deemed the most aggravated kind of high treason, because he at once dethrones the King, and subverts the constitution of nature itself'.[114]

We have already noted the decreasing use of monarchical images of God. When they are used, the idea is generally that of a constitutional monarch ruling in the context of a just system of laws. In a sermon of 1730 Benjamin Coleman alluded to God as 'the great king of the world'.[115] In his sermon to the Council, Senate and Representatives of New Hampshire on the inauguration of the new constitution in 1784, Samuel McClintock, however, asserted: 'God is an absolute sovereign. He presides with an uncontrouled sway over the nations of this earth.' Though working through secondary causes, God's hand can be perceived in all events. The preacher called into question the mechanical model of the universe when he argued:

> what is called the course of nature is only the continual operation of God on this visible system of things, producing the events we behold in a uniform manner, according to certain laws which he hath established; so that these common and ordinary events by which he hath blessed or chastised, are in reality as much effects of his power as miracles are.[116]

Here the divine hand plays a much more active role in human affairs than in the thought of the founding fathers themselves.

Despite his theological absolutism, McClintock generally eschewed royalist language about God, who is seen as the 'almighty ruler', the 'sovereign', the 'omnipotent hand'. Significantly he spoke of God as 'presiding' over the nations. He furthermore insisted that God is a holy and righteous sovereign, 'such is the perfection of his nature that he never *can* do any thing but what is fit and right'.[117] Similarly, when Samuel West preached the unlimited submission and obedience due to God – for he alone has 'uncontrollable sovereignty over us' – this is only in the context of a deity 'who cannot make a law contrary to the law of nature without acting contrary to himself'.[118] This is a far cry from the Hobbist notion of sovereignty, human and divine. In 'an Election Sermon' of 1782 Zabdiel Adams found it necessary to explain that in scripture 'the word king signifies any kind of governor' and that in choosing a text about King Solomon he was in no way speaking contrary to 'the genius of our present constitution'.[119]

The constitution as scripture and American civil religion

Among many of these writers the constitution was given a sacred status. For Stanley Griswold, a Congregationalist minister and Jeffersonian, the constitution was 'the palladium of all that we hold dear. Let it be venerated as the sanctuary of our liberties and all our best interests. Let it be kept as the ark of God.'[120] Woodrow Wilson wrote: 'The divine right of kings never ran a more prosperous course than did the unquestioned prerogative of the Constitution to receive universal homage.'[121] Critics of Jeffersonian populism were less confident that the constitution would guarantee against all future problems. 'The political sphere, like the globe we tread upon', wrote Fisher Ames in a notable tract of 1805, 'never stands still, but with a silent swiftness accomplishes the revolutions which, we are too ready to believe, are effected by our wisdom, or might have been controlled by our efforts. There is', he continued in Machiavellian mode, 'a kind of fatality in the affairs of republics, that eludes the foresight of the wise as much as it frustrates the toils and the sacrifices of the patriot and the hero.'[122] The constitution, however, played a peculiar role in the affairs of the republic. 'It has been, virtually from the moment of its ratification', writes Thomas Grey, 'a sacred symbol, the most potent emblem (along with the flag) of the nation itself.'[123]

The sacred status of the constitution has led some contemporary legal theorists to suggest an analogy with scripture. Sanford Levinson[124] suggests that the written constitution, as a text, has played a role similar to that played by scripture in Christianity and Judaism. The reverence paid to the constitution by many Americans bears comparison with the attitudes of some Protestant fundamentalists, or with the veneration paid to the Gospel Book in Catholic and Orthodox liturgical practice. Levinson distinguishes a 'Catholic' from a 'Protestant' understanding of the role of the constitution in the life of the nation. This distinction operates at two levels. The first concerns the relationship of the text to the tradition of the community which regards it as authoritative. The Catholic approach interprets the constitution (and indeed may supplement it) with reference to unwritten tradition, while the Protestant gives an absolute priority to the written text and either denies the need for interpretation or finds the criteria for such interpretation in scripture itself. ('The Bible only is the religion of Protestants.'[125]) The second level concerns the authority for interpreting scripture. The Catholic (so it is asserted) adopts a hierarchical approach, while the Protestant gives ultimate authority to the individual conscience. Those who, at this second level, adopt a Catholic position with respect to the constitution see the role of the Supreme Court as analogous to that of the *magisterium* of the church. This raises the issue of amendments to the constitution. Ought substantive changes in the understanding of the constitution to be reflected in explicit amendments under article 5, or is it legitimate to achieve the same effect by making 'transformative judicial appointments' to the Supreme Court?[126] Franklin D. Roosevelt adopted the latter path with success, and Reagan attempted to move in this direction with the proposal to appoint Robert Bork. It is, indeed, rare for political factors to be entirely excluded in such appointments. Parallel issues are raised with respect to the interpretation of the Bible.

The constitution, it is being suggested by Levinson, is the sacred scripture of an American 'civil religion'. The widespread use of political imagery in the conceptualisation of God not only serves to influence prayer and worship, but also gives a certain supernatural legitimacy to civil institutions, which are seen to be terrestrial analogues of a heavenly model. Such rhetoric provides a degree of endorsement to the particular form of government from which the images are taken. Many Americans (and of course others) both then and now have, indeed, argued that this kind of religious legitimation is necessary for the stability or even for the very existence of government. They agree with Rousseau that some kind of civil religion must be incorporated into every political system. If the state does not patronise an already existing faith, it is necessary to create such a civic religion, with rituals for national occasions and individual 'rites of passage', as happened in Eastern Europe and the Soviet Union.

These apostles of civil religion agree with Locke that a kind of highest common factor religion should have an official status. 'The idea of God', Samuel Kendal claimed,

> and the hopes and fears connected with it, are indispensably necessary to secure the practice of that virtue, which is requisite to the preservation, order and happiness of society. Impress on the public mind a full belief in an all-seeing God, whose law and government are perfect, whose honor is concerned in the obedience of his creatures, and who will render a just recompense to all; and it will be a steady motive to those virtues which are the ornament and life of society, and the glory of man.[127]

Blasphemy, he insisted, is punished by law, not because God cannot vindicate his honour but because it 'weakens the bands of society'.[128] Jonathan Edwards Jr, pastor of a church in New Haven, told the Governor and General Assembly of the state of Connecticut in 1794 that 'since Christianity appears to be necessary to the public good of the state, it ought to be encouraged by magistrates and rulers of every description'.[129]

Though most Americans were opposed to the establishment of particular churches, they seemed to think that the state could patronise a generalised, 'rational' Christianity, which would provide the rock upon which constitutional government could stand secure. The Pennsylvania constitution of 1776, for example, stated that legislators had to declare a belief in 'one God, the creator, and governour of the universe, the rewarder of the good and punisher of the wicked'.[130] Madison and Jefferson in particular struggled against the official establishment of religious bodies but accepted the social and political utility of a liberal form of Christianity. Here they appear to have been influenced by the ideas of the Welsh Unitarian Richard Price: 'All communities have some religion', he declared, ' . . . those who dislike that mode of worship which is prescribed by public authority, ought (if they can find no worship out of the church which they approve) to set up a separate worship for themselves.'[131] In recent years President Dwight Eisenhower reasserted this extraordinary position, which has been discussed in a good deal of contemporary American literature.[132]

Hierarchy and 'the people'

As we have seen, the pluralism that characterises the celestial constitution was seen by some to legitimate a separation of powers in the civil constitution. The distinction of orders and ranks of archangels, angels, dominions, powers, cherubim and seraphim also served to justify social hierarchy for conservative writers. 'Variety of powers, characters and conditions, so obvious in human life, is an illustrious proof of the benignity and wisdom of the supreme governor of the universe,' declared *The Independent Reflector*, edited by William Livingston.[133] Charles Chauncy, a liberal Congregationalist opposed to the enthusiasm of the Great Awakening, and among the most influential clergy of his day, taught that the heavenly hierarchy suggests by analogy that, even if humans had continued in a state of innocence, there would have been 'some sort of civil superiority'. Government is rendered necessary because of human sin, but it does not follow that government is a merely human invention. Rather, it originates in the reason of things and in the will of God, 'for the voice of reason is the voice of God'.[134] Later Samuel Kendal, a remarkable Congregationalist preacher who appealed to many beyond his own tradition, noted that in the world there is neither real nor apparent equality and he defended such an arrangement as 'the work of Providence'. To attempt the reduction of all to a perfect equality would be 'to wage war with Heaven'.[135] Timothy Stone, the Connecticut Congregationalist minister, took up the analogy between heavenly and earthly hierarchy. The several titles of the angelic beings denote 'various stations among those sinless beings, that they are differently employed, in degrees of subordination to each other, in the government of that holy family of which, God, is the father'.[136] The preacher was here reiterating a familiar theme. The same analogy had been employed more than a century earlier by William Hubbard, who defended a hierarchical social order by a heavenly analogue: 'Beauty arises from symmetry; the heavens were disposed in ranks and orders of cherabims, seraphims, archangels and angels.'[137]

Despite their suspicion of equality, many of these preachers and publicists believed firmly in the sovereignty of 'the People': 'The truth is that in our governments, the supreme, absolute and uncontrollable power *remains* in the people', declared James Wilson. 'As our constitutions are superior to our legislatures; so the people are superior to our constitutions.'[138] Political authority 'flows from the people', insisted a Presbyterian minister, preaching at the request of the Tammany Society, 'and is dependent on their sovereign pleasure.'[139]

For some, writing under the influence of Rousseau, the people are indeed sovereign, but only in their capacity as framers of the fundamental laws of the state – as 'parties to the compact of the constitution'. After that the people are either subjects or agents of the constitution; the powers of sovereignty are divided among several agents: legislative, judicial, executive.[140] Like Hamilton, with respect to the pre-1787 confederation, Thomas Tudor Tucker claimed that the constitution of South Carolina was defective; 'it is not founded on proper authority, being only an act of the legislature'. Nevertheless, even though the sovereign 'people' have not ratified it, they have acquiesced in it, giving it a provisional legitimacy.[141]

Conservative writers were unhappy with the concept of the sovereignty of the people, for it seemed to give power into the hands of the mob, or any leader able to sway the populace, 'for with the democrats the people is a sovereign who can do [no] wrong, even when he respects and spares no existing right, and whose voice . . . bears all the sanctity and all the force of a living divinity'.[142] While defending popular participation in government, Theophilus Parsons cautioned against the danger of the slogan *vox populi vox dei*. 'No man', he declared, 'will be so hardy and presumptuous, as to affirm the truth of that proposition in its fullest extent.' He warned against 'the artful demagogue' who might emerge to mislead the people.[143] Although he accepted the term 'sovereignty', Elizur Goodrich told the Governor and General Assembly of Connecticut:

> In causes of a judicial kind, your high character of sovereignty will not excuse an arbitrary decision, or denial of justice. . . . When the most sovereign and uncontroulable court on earth, gives an unrighteous sentence, and wickedly perverts judgment, there is immediately entered in the high court of heaven, an appeal, which, in the great day of general assise, will be called, and must be answered.

He admonished the legislators not to allow the notion of omnipotence to insinuate itself into their deliberations: the arbitrary actions of a popular assembly are no different from those of a single despot. Though they act 'in the character of gods, on earth', they will be called to account in heaven.[144] David Tappan likewise referred to the sovereignty of God, but immediately added: 'he cannot govern upon any other plan than that of inviolable truth, justice and goodness'. Civil rulers should copy this original:

No idea therefore of omnipotence or uncontrolled sovereignty, will be permitted to infect their deliberations and decisions; but their whole conduct, as it respects particular citizens, the commonwealth in general, and the great American republic, will, we trust, exhibit a fair picture of honest, enlarged and federal policy.[145]

Patriotic republicanism

For many, 'republicanism' became something of an ideology, claiming divine authenticity. Samuel Cooper reminded his congregation in 1780 that 'the form of government originally established in the Hebrew nation by a charter from heaven, was that of a free republic, over which God himself, in peculiar favour to that people, was pleased to preside'.[146] His words were echoed by Perez Fobes: the republic was 'the choice and fabric of God himself for his own people'; the principles encompassed by the religion of Jesus are compatible with no other form of government, least of all with 'monarchical principles and the dynasty of kings';[147] as God governs the universe by the general laws, 'analogous to this divine model, all human governments must be constructed and maintained'.[148] Other preachers and writers spoke of the republic as 'sacred'.[149]

In the years following the Peace of Paris (1763) French influence had increased among intellectuals in the American colonies. Rousseau also was popular among students.[150] In Virginia and parts of the South there was a significant pro-French sentiment, allied to a deist approach to religion. Radical republicans supported the revolutionary movement in France. The 'Revolutionary Legions of the Mississippi' wrote in 1794 to the Committee of Public Safety in Paris: 'May you never sheath your swords while there remains within your powerful grasp, one of those curses of mankind called kings.'[151] Most Americans, however, became alarmed by the excesses of the Jacobins. Noah Webster denounced the movement in France for having 'waged an inveterate war with Christianity', and having established 'not deism only, but atheism and materialism'. The conservative reaction was led by Timothy Dwight, president of Yale College.[152]

As in France, republicanism was linked to a patriotic spirit. Many Americans believed, with their puritan forebears, that America was the promised land, and her people new Israel – God's chosen people. For Phillips Payson, providence had conducted his chosen people to 'within sight of the promised land'.[153] Like Israel of old, the colonies had risen from oppression and emerged from the house of bondage.[154] Samuel Langdon from New Hampshire published his sermon on the theme 'The Republic of the Israelites, an Example to the American States' in 1788.

For Benjamin Rush, friend and correspondent of several of the revolutionary leaders, young men – after their duty to God – must have 'a supreme regard to their country'.[155] In an outburst of patriotic fervour Payson anticipated the Jacobins:

> Hail, my happy country, saved of the Lord. Happy land, emerged from the deluges of the Old World, drowned in luxury and lewd excess! Hail happy posterity, that shall reap the peaceful fruits of our suffering, fatigues, and wars! With such prospects, such transporting views, it is difficult to keep the passions or the tongue within the bounds of Christian moderation.[156]

Political images of God

God was pictured as a ruler who behaves according to a set of established laws. His actions are just and in general predictable. He is 'the supreme governour of mankind', or 'supreme governour of the world', whose wisdom and goodness are shown 'in ordaining and establishing a magistracy and government in the world'.[157] In colonial America it was the governor who was ultimately responsible for running the affairs of the territory. God was seen as combining in his person all functions of government: legislative, executive and judicial. He was 'the supreme lawgiver', 'supreme magistrate of the universe', governor and judge.[158] By 1781, God had become president; he is, in the words of Henry Cumings, 'that almighty being, who presides over the world'.[159]

Some preachers and publicists, like many of their English puritan forebears, denied altogether the analogy between God and the state. Nathaniel Niles, writing on the eve of the Revolution, pointed to a possible analogy between prayer and petition, but proceeded to draw a significant distinction between them: 'A thousand things may intercept our petitions on their way to an earthly monarch; but a combination of all our enemies in earth and hell cannot prevent a pious wish in its flight to heaven.'[160] If God is 'the great sovereign of the universe', all men, even rulers, are his subjects. Samuel West denounced rulers in the pagan world who have 'assumed the title of gods, and had divine honors paid them'; this idolatrous reverence leads to tyranny. Even Christian rulers have been given titles which 'strongly savour of blasphemy, and the reverence paid them is really idolatrous'. Terms like 'most sacred majesty' ought to be applied to no human being. West utilised the imagery of the Revelation of St John the Divine in arguing that to pay an unlimited obedience to rulers, as is due to God alone, is to 'worship the dragon'.[161]

I have suggested that the way eighteenth-century Americans thought about God is closely related to their political and social rhetoric and the experience that this rhetoric reflected. The notion of a constitution became central to their thinking. The challenge facing them was that of an arbitrary and supposedly sovereign parliament interfering with their established way of life, without their consent. They saw an appeal to natural law as an appeal not to some vague moral criterion, but to fundamental laws which lie at the very basis of the state's existence. C. H. McIlwain discusses the successive phases of the colonial argument with the metropolis. The first was based on the royal charters; then came a Whig appeal to 'the rights of Englishmen', exemplified in the writings of James Otis; finally, by 1774 colonial spokesmen were fairly unanimous in denying the right of the British Parliament to tax territories outside the realm of England without their consent, pointing to the cases of the Isle of Man, Ireland and the Channel Islands.[162] The Continental Congress of that year was even prepared to accept natural-rights arguments despite conservative opposition. When these arguments were ignored by the British, colonial leaders became more and more convinced of the need for independence with a written constitution determining the civil structure and limiting the various powers and organs of government. This constitution, as we have seen, attained a truly sacred status.

The writing of the late eighteenth-century American constitutions was the culmination of a long politico-theological debate. Ideas of God acting in a law-like and rational manner developed out of the puritan concept of covenant, reinforced by Enlightenment philosophy. Much of this political theology was indebted to British writers of the school of Tillotson and to deists, like Tindal, Tolland and Bolingbroke, for whom a rational and constitutional system in heaven was a pattern for limited government on earth.

6

DEISTS, DISSENTERS AND FREE THINKERS

The early part of the eighteenth century witnessed a growth in what was called 'free thinking' or 'rational religion'. The Glorious Revolution, with the advent of William of Orange, had resulted, among other things, in a growing toleration for Dissenters and for those of unorthodox views within the established church. Some of these men, renouncing Trinitarianism and believing that true religion can be derived from nature and reason, were known as deists or theists. The more radical of them looked back to the ideas of Lord Herbert of Cherbury (1583–1648), whose religious beliefs were pared down to a minimum: the existence of a God who was to be worshipped, principally by living a virtuous life; the duty of repentance for sin; and the reality of rewards and punishment in an afterlife. This, for him, was the sum of religion. Those we shall discuss in this chapter were all influenced in various ways by ideas of 'rational religion', though they represent very different manifestations of this tendency.

RADICAL RELIGION AND POLITICS

In his notorious sermon preached on 5 November 1709, Dr Henry Sacheverell asserted a close relationship between religion and politics:

> whoever presumes to innovate, alter, or misrepresent any point in the articles of faith of our church ought to be arraigned as a traitor to our state; heterodoxy in the doctrines of the one, naturally producing, and almost necessarily inferring rebellion, and high treason in the other, and consequently a crime that concerns the civil magistrate, as much to punish, and restrain, as the ecclesiastical.[1]

Though he was tried and condemned for his assertion of divine right and non-resistance, the opinions he voiced were widely accepted at the time.

There were close links between religious tendencies and political groupings. Many Tories had opposed the 1688 Revolution, and some of these, who were clergy, refused to take the oath of allegiance to William and Mary. These men, led by Sancroft, archbishop of Canterbury, were known as

'Nonjurors'. Most looked to, and some worked for, the restoration of the Stuarts. Very many Tories, however, were prepared to come to terms with the House of Orange. Though they found themselves in opposition, they were later reassured by the moderately high church and Tory views of Queen Anne, who succeeded to the throne in 1702. Whigs, on the other hand, welcomed and enthusiastically defended the 'glorious revolution' of 1688 and the Protestant succession. They were, however, divided into 'court' and 'country' factions. The former, as their name suggests, generally supported the government and looked for positions of privilege and profit under the Crown. The country Whigs often made temporary alliance with Tory squires to oppose the government and denounce corruption. These country Whigs included some who were theologically unorthodox, such as John Toland. It should be emphasised, though, that most Whigs were churchmen, of liberal or moderate theological views, often of an Erastian tendency. With the death of Anne and the succession of the Hanoverian dynasty in 1714, the Whigs resumed their political ascendancy and under Walpole governed the country for several decades.

However, one of the most radical of the deists was a Tory and a biting critic of Walpole's Whig administration. Henry St John, viscount Bolingbroke (1678–1751), after a dramatic rise to political power under Queen Anne, and an unsuccessful bid to return to power, devoted much of his later life to reading and writing on political and religious themes; his religious writings were published posthumously. He claimed to study religion in an inductive and empirical manner, reasoning on the basis of our knowledge of the natural world. Bolingbroke saw himself as a latter-day exponent of Locke's empiricist philosophy, though he frequently maintained extreme positions which his mentor would have rejected. He was particularly hostile to Platonism and was sceptical of the application of metaphysical theories to religion by such writers as Samuel Clarke (1675–1729) and Thomas Woolston (1670–1773); he rejected attempts to defend God against the charge of injustice due to evil and suffering in the world. Clarke, as a close disciple of Isaac Newton, had in fact been instrumental in reducing the influence of Cartesian rationalism in England and had even converted the sceptical Voltaire to his philosophical standpoint. Nevertheless, in Bolingbroke's view Clarke's philosophy retained too much of rationalist metaphysics. Yet these writers agreed in rejecting the image of an arbitrary God, and Bolingbroke frequently drew analogies between divine and civil government, seeing both in the context of constitutional rules which limit the scope of the governor.

Writers like Charles Blount (1654–93) and Anthony Collins (1676–1729) elaborated a deist theology and attacked all forms of institutional religion. Arthur Bury (1624–1713), rector of Exeter College, Oxford, appeared to cast doubt on orthodox understandings of the Trinity in his book *The Naked Gospel*, for which he lost his job in 1694. Other writers attacked the idea of special providence and miracle.[2] It is, however, misleading to assert that they undermined ideas of divine providence *tout court*, for they saw the benign providential rule of God manifesting itself in the working of general laws.[3]

Probably the most influential English deists of this period were Matthew Tindal (1655–1733) and John Toland (1670–1722). These men not only put forward a deist version of Christianity purged of mystery, but were vociferous defenders of the House of Orange (and later of Hanover) and campaigners for religious toleration. Although their names are frequently linked as radical deists, Tindal (in his early writings at least) reasserted a Hobbist positivism, while Toland appears to have become increasingly influenced by elements in the philosophy of Spinoza. Like Bolingbroke, these men also drew analogies between divine and civil rule, seeing 'balance' as a characteristic of both forms of dominion; divine and civil government must be seen as functioning within a structure of law.

These deists looked to the religion of Archbishop John Tillotson (1630–94) for a legitimation of their position. He was, according to Collins, the one 'whom all English free-thinkers own as their head'.[4] Generally acknowledged as the leading 'latitude man', or latitudinarian, of his day, Tillotson was an influential preacher and master of the English language, greatly admired by Dryden and Addison for style. As the man who, in 1689, succeeded Sancroft – the Nonjuring archbishop of Canterbury – Tillotson was naturally a defender of the Glorious Revolution and of the Protestant establishment, attempting to incorporate Trinitarian Dissenters into the established church, to form a broad front against Roman Catholics on the one hand and Unitarians and deists on the other.

Benjamin Hoadly (1676–1761) generally followed the teachings of Tillotson and, although he denounced the deists, appears to have shared many of their assumptions. He adopted Whig political positions and criticised theories of divine right still widely held by Anglicans of the day. Attacking ideas of an apostolic ministry in the church and undermining any idea of the church as a body distinct from the state, he was a principal target for the wrath of nonjurors and high churchmen, like William Law, Daniel Waterland and Charles Leslie. Hoadly was an admirer of Samuel Clarke, editing and publishing his works in 1738. The intellectual background to all this religious ferment is to be found in the enigmatic system of Isaac Newton as developed by Clarke, Bentley and his other disciples, whom we shall consider in the next chapter. Hoadly was less willing to draw analogies between divine and civil government, denying that a celestial autocracy provides a satisfactory model for terrestrial government.

A distinct stream of religious life was represented by Isaac Watts (1674–1748). His ideas may be seen as a development of the seventeenth-century puritanism of Richard Baxter (1615–91), but he was influenced too by the mechanical world-view propagated by Newton's followers. Though he is best known today for his hymns, he was a popular preacher and a theologian of some standing, exemplifying the 'orthodox' (i.e. Trinitarian) Dissenters of the period. He significantly influenced the revivalist preacher George Whitefield. Watts eschewed direct political involvement, but the language and images he used in his prose and poetry betray a set of assumptions about political power which is revealing. His ideas about the necessity of some kind of civil religion were shared with Bolingbroke and with many thinkers of the time.

BOLINGBROKE

'With reverence be it spoken', wrote Viscount Bolingbroke in his celebrated essay on *The Idea of a Patriot King*, 'God is a monarch, yet not an arbitrary but a limited monarch, limited by the *rule* which *infinite wisdom* prescribes to *infinite power*.'[5] In this section I shall trace some of the connections between Bolingbroke's political and religious ideas centred on the notion of a balanced constitution. He saw himself standing in the tradition of British empiricism going back through Locke to Bacon, and he was correspondingly critical of ambitious metaphysical schemes associated with Leibniz but also with some of the German philosopher's Newtonian critics. He assailed theologians like Clarke, who 'presume to push beyond the bounds that God has set to human inquiries' and 'hope that metaphysics can carry them forward when physics cannot'.[6] Bolingbroke was sceptical about the power of reason to penetrate the being and attributes of God; human knowledge of the supreme being, though certain, is severely limited in scope. His political theory, like his religious thought, was inductively based. 'All science', he asserted, 'if it be real, must rise from below, and from our own level. It cannot descend from above, nor from superior systems of being and knowledge.'[7]

It is in this context that he asserted the importance of history in private and in public life. Individual experience has two defects: 'we are born too late to see the beginning, and we die too soon to see the end of many things. History supplies both these defects.'[8] The study of ancient history in particular enables us to trace events, institutions and whole empires from birth to death. We are able to learn how events are likely to develop from a study of the past and in particular from paying attention to 'those combinations of peculiar circumstance, which we commonly call conjunctures'.[9] The past teaches, among other things, that systematic lying has taken place, particularly in religious history. But 'this lying spirit has gone forth from ecclesiastical to other historians'.[10] In attempting to judge the veracity of alleged past facts, of which we have had no experience, we may appeal to an analogy in our own experience, which if found may give an indirect confirmation. This position was later taken up by David Hume in his discussion of miracles and was systematically elaborated by F. H. Bradley in his essay on 'The Presuppositions of Critical History'.[11]

Though he recognised the limits and dangers of using analogy and allegory, Bolingbroke was acutely aware of their importance in popular and in theoretical discourse. Here we shall be particularly concerned with the analogy of divine and human government. He used the conclusions of his philosophical and religious thought about God to legitimate his political theories of limited monarchy and a balanced constitution, while at the same time warning against the perils of deducing the nature of the supreme being from political structures.

Bolingbroke's life and times

Despite the many ambiguities associated with the writings and actions of Bolingbroke, he clearly signifies the acceptance by many Tories of the constitutional consequences of the Glorious Revolution. While some high Tories remained loyal to the Stuarts and retained seventeenth-century ideas of non-resistance and divine right, Bolingbroke's brief encounter with the Pretender had convinced him that Jacobitism was a dead duck; the prospects of a Stuart restoration were dim. The Revolution of 1688 had by no means been the work merely of Whigs; it had had solid support from many Tories offended by the pretensions of James II. A majority of Tories was prepared to accept William and Mary, and the party was indeed favoured by Queen Anne, who acceded to the throne in 1702. After her death in 1714 most Tories eventually came to terms with the Hanoverian succession. These men carefully distinguished their opposition to Robert Walpole's long Whig ministry (1715–42) from an antagonism to the king himself; they were a 'loyal opposition'. Their attacks were, they claimed, provoked by Walpole's contempt for some basic tenets of the British constitution.

The virulent opposition to the regime, orchestrated from 1725 to 1735 by Bolingbroke, was based on the claim that Walpole's policies and strategies involved a fundamental threat to traditional British liberties. In particular the maintenance of a large standing army, and the control which the prime minister exercised over the House of Commons by the widespread use of patronage, represented a serious challenge to the balance of the constitution re-established in 1688. Corruption, consisting of the effective selling of offices and privileges in exchange for political support, particularly in the House of Commons, had taken the place of royal prerogative as the principal challenge to the integrity of the constitution.[12] Whether these doctrines and principles reflected Bolingbroke's sincerely held beliefs has long been a matter of debate. He was manifestly a man of great personal ambition. At times he appears to have adopted *ad hominem* arguments, to beat a Whig government with traditional Whig principles. Nevertheless in adopting these positions Bolingbroke was shrewdly appealing to a fair cross-section of the politically active population. Even if his assault on Walpole was simply an opportunistic struggle for personal advancement, and the principles he propounded nothing more than weapons in this battle, cynically employed, the fact that he chose these particular principles suggests an assessment on his part of issues which concerned the powerful people of his day.[13] Nevertheless as a tactician he was generally out-manoeuvred by those he assailed.

Henry St John entered politics at an early age, and was appointed secretary of state in Harley's ministry from 1710 to 1714.[14] He was raised to the peerage in 1712. Jonathan Swift was much impressed: he was 'the greatest young man I ever knew'.[15] He much enjoyed the power and privileges of office but quarrelled with Harley and both men fell from power shortly after the queen's death in 1714. He fled to France a few months later, where he joined the Pretender as his secretary of state. James, however, dismissed him within a year, but by then he had, in any case, become convinced that, under this Pretender, Jacobitism was a lost cause. Meanwhile in England Bolingbroke was impeached, condemned to death and deprived of his property, his title, and his seat in the House of Lords, but he managed through skilful negotiation to secure the revocation of all but the last penalty and returned to England in 1725 to lead the opposition to Walpole. He retired from politics in 1735, living mostly in France until his death.

As self-appointed spokesman of the 'country' interest, Bolingbroke led a powerful assault on the government, in the columns of his newspaper, *The Craftsman*. With Pope, Swift and others he assailed the dominance of moneyed men, of stockjobbers and of a rising class of financial speculators, whose activities were encouraged by the Walpole administration. In the words of his friend Alexander Pope:

> At length Corruption, like a gen'ral flood,
> (So long by watchful Ministers withstood)
> Shall deluge all; and Av'rice creeping on,
> Spread like a low-born mist, and blot the Sun;
> Statesman and Patriot ply alike the stocks,
> Peeress and Butler share alike the Box,
> And Judges job, and Bishops bite the town,
> And mighty Dukes pack cards for half a crown.
> See Britain sunk in lucre's sordid charms,
> And France reveng'd of Anne's and Edward's arms![16]

Bolingbroke and his fellow critics of Walpole were fervent antagonists of this rising class, which was defended and celebrated by Daniel Defoe:

> Wealth, howsoever got, in England makes
> Lords of merchants, gentlemen of rakes.

133

Antiquities and birth are needless here;
'Tis impudence and money makes a peer.[17]

In Some Reflections on the Present State of the Nation, Bolingbroke denounced usurers and stockjobbers as 'leeches who fill themselves
continually with the blood of the nation, and never cease to suck it', insisting
that 'the landed men are the true owners of our political vessel: the money
men, as such, are no more than passengers in it'.[18] The South Sea Bubble
had burst in 1720, giving a degree of plausibility to the claims of Bolingbroke and his associates. Many looked back to more stable days:

As nature's ties decay,
As duty, love, and honour fail to sway,
Fictitious bonds, the bonds of wealth and law,
Still gather strength, and force unwilling awe.[19]

After ten years of rumbustious opposition to the regime, Bolingbroke left
once more for exile in France, where, among other things, he read, talked
with his friends and wrote long essays in the form of letters addressed to
Alexander Pope on religious and philosophical matters. These recapitu-
lated the long conversations between them reflected in Pope's celebrated
'Essay on Man', dedicated to the politician. Despite an earlier political
identification with the High Church party in the Church of England, and a
close association with such men as Bishop Francis Atterbury and Dean
Swift, his writings contain bitterly anticlerical and, indeed, anti-Christian
passages.

Constitutional government

Many of Bolingbroke's ideas on constitutional government were pilfered
from the Whigs and take up certain themes which were prominent among
Harringtonian radicals.[20] His attempts, when secretary of state, to form a
high Tory administration, his associations with the Pretender, and other
factors have led some critics to regard his theoretical writings as a mere
camouflage for personal advancement. Into this controversy we have no
need to enter. He does at all events present a generally coherent political
and religious position, which he believed, at the very least, would make an
appeal to the intellectual and political classes of his day. In fact some of his
writings did much more than this and became minor classics in the history
of political thought, exercising an influence far beyond these shores. John
Adams told Thomas Jefferson that he had read the works of Bolingbroke
more than five times, and wrote of the *Dissertation upon Parties*: 'This is a
jewel, there is nothing so profound, correct, and perfect on the subject of
government, in the English or any other language.'[21] High praise indeed
from one who was to play a major role in American constitutional devel-

opments. It is likely that Montesquieu derived his (mistaken) ideas about the separation of powers in the British constitution partly from Boling-broke.[22]

The constitution of the universe – the course of nature – is a 'revelation' of God's will and is thus the source of our knowledge of right action; so the constitution of the country is the tree which bears that 'delicious and wholesome fruit' of liberty by which we may live a contented life.[23] Those engaged in public affairs must therefore understand and protect the con-stitution against its assailants. They must be careful to 'fence it in and trench it round, against the beasts of the field, and the insects of the earth'. Bolingbroke maintained that the British constitution – the 'system of gov-ernment suited to the genius of our nation' – had been preserved inviolate over many hundreds of years, and had continually been drawn back to the principles on which it was originally founded.[24] It reached its perfection under Queen Elizabeth, but became distorted under James I and his succes-sor, whose autocratic rule threatened the independence of the landed gentry. Cromwell was indeed a usurper, but the Rebellion was viewed rather sympathetically as the attempt to defend traditional liberties which had been jeopardized. The re-establishment of monarchy was generally welcomed, though degeneration and 'faction' again set in and a balance was reintroduced with the Glorious Revolution. Walpole was once again threatening the balance and stability of the constitution.[25] Bolingbroke thus generally subscribed to what has come to be called a Whig interpretation of history.[26]

Although he used the image of a tree, the dominant constitutional metaphor is drawn from a Newtonian mechanical model, where successful operation requires a certain equilibrium. The essential characteristic of the civil constitution, as indeed of the international order and of the universe itself, is a balance of power: in the former case, balance between the three parts of the legislature, which requires that each enjoys a certain inde-pendence from the other. The democratical element, represented by the House of Commons, is not powerful enough to subordinate the Lords and the Crown, but it is strong enough, if acting in a genuinely independent fashion, to 'counterwork and balance any other power by its own strength'.[27] Most systems have given too much power to governments, and there is a natural tendency for power to grow.[28] In Europe it is the special role of Britain to act as arbitrator of differences, guardian of liberty and 'the preserver of that *Balance*, which has been so much talked of, and is so little understood'.[29] The universe too is an immense machine composed in turn of balanced solar systems, of which our world is but 'a little wheel'.[30] One modern author criticises Bolingbroke for taking his images and analogies of God from physical science (particularly mechanics) rather than from human nature.[31] This author curiously fails to mention the *political* images which continually reappear in his works: God is a monarch who rules the

cosmos according to the laws which he has himself established. Yet Bolingbroke interprets these political images within a mechanical framework. The
cosmos is governed as a machine is governed; the mechanical model
controls both the political and the cosmological spheres.

Bolingbroke placed the constitution above the ordinary legislative functions of Parliament and ventured to disagree with Bacon's dictum that
'there is nothing, which a parliament cannot do'. 'A Parliament', he insisted,
'cannot annul the constitution.'[32] Laws cannot abolish the very fount from
which they flow. He nevertheless asserted: 'There must be an absolute,
unlimited, and uncontrollable power lodged *somewhere* in every government.'[33] This he stated in the context of a distinction between legislative and
monarchical power, which is as necessary to maintain in political as in
cosmic affairs. A monarchy does not require that this supreme power reside
in the monarch alone; not all monarchies are absolute monarchies. Indeed,
it is unreasonable to insist that the monarch alone determines the rule of
his government. Significantly, Bolingbroke failed to say where this supreme
power lies in Britain. It was at this point that he elaborated the divine
analogy noted in the opening paragraph of this chapter.

God governs the universe not by arbitrary will, but by a rule which, as
the creator, he has prescribed to himself. If it is the case that the supreme
ruler of the universe submits to exercising his government according to
rules, argued Bolingbroke, it is perfectly possible to conceive of a limited
monarchy where the king governs according to principles established by
the wisdom of the state and the consent of the people. This he saw embodied
in the British constitution, which limits the power of the monarch, though
not to the point of depriving him of legitimate executive functions and a
role in the legislative process. 'My aim,' he declared, 'is to fix this principle,
that *limitations* on a crown ought to be carried *as far* as it is necessary to
secure the liberties of a people; and that all *such limitations*, may subsist,
without weakening or endangering monarchy'.[34] Bolingbroke cited Louis
XIV's monarchy as an awful example of an institution that ignored these
limitations. The monarch's education was such that it 'trains up kings to be
tyrants, without knowing that they are so', and Louis objected to the word
l'état 'as a kind of indecency to himself'. Such arrogance, however, was
understandable, being unconsciously derived, by analogy, from the generally accepted but false belief that 'the world was made for man, the earth
for him to inhabit, and all the luminous bodies in the immense expanse
around us, for him to gaze at'. With these theological assumptions, is it
surprising that kings see themselves as the end for which human societies
were formed and governments instituted?[35]

> Has God, thou fool! work'd solely for thy good,
> Thy joy, thy pastime, thy attire, thy food? . . .
> While Man exclaims, 'See all things for my use!'

'See man for mine!' replies a pamper'd goose;
And just as short of reason he must fall,
Who thinks all made for one, not one for all.[36]

Monarchs and ministers

Bolingbroke thus traced the partial cause of political tyranny to a false cosmology and theology. Elsewhere he saw the influence flowing the other way and claimed that primitive heathen ideas of a sole supreme being were later corrupted by 'those which they had of human majesty'. While Christians believe that they have direct access to the divine throne, 'the poor heathen, filled with a religious horror, durst not approach the divine monarch except through the mediation of his ministers'.[37] Bolingbroke saw the existence of ministers as representing a tendency not towards limited constitutional monarchy, but towards an autocracy which shrouded a remote potentate in mystery, permitting access to him only through intermediaries. He related the alleged need that God has of 'ministers to attend his throne', with messengers and troops to execute his commands, to the image of the supreme being as arbitrary and remote.[38] 'I am not one of those oriental slaves', he remarked, 'who deem it unlawful presumption to look their kings in the face.'[39] Indeed, it is of great importance to investigate the desires and intentions of princes. Bolingbroke ascribed the widespread attribution of tyrannical powers to God to a determination by those in political power to 'intimidate mankind'.[40] Tyrannical powers are ascribed to the supreme being, and then by analogy claimed by those in political and ecclesiastical office.[41]

Being convinced that the existence and unity of God can be established by human reason, and that this belief was sanctioned by heathen philosophers, Bolingbroke argued that the idea of divine monarchy follows naturally. 'By degrading the pagan gods, they destroyed the aristocracy of heaven', but, having established monotheism, they illegitimately drew on the analogy from human government, creating 'a multitude of inferior beings', who assisted the supreme being in the administration of the world. When people argue from God's works as empirically perceived to God's existence they do well, but when they reason from human economic and political institutions to the nature of divine government they fall into error. Of the heathen philosophers, he wrote:

They imagined a divine monarchy on a human plan, the administration of which was not carried on by the immediate agency of God himself, but mediately, as in terrestrial monarchies, by that of inferior agents, according to the ranks and the provinces allotted to them.[42]

The 'idolatrous' worship offered to these lesser spirits by pagans was, he reminded Alexander Pope, himself a Roman Catholic though of deistic

137

views, no more absurd than the distinction between *latria* (the worship given to God alone) and *dulia* (the honour paid to the saints) which his church accepted. Christians, led by 'crackbrained enthusiasts' like Denys the Areopagite, had distinguished cherubim and seraphim, thrones, dominions, principalities and powers, forming a whole hierarchy of celestial beings.[43]

He rejected the notion of kings as God's viceregents and denounced talk of divine indefeasible right as 'silly cant, which was invented to make the usurpations of prerogative go down the better'.[44] Much of the blame he ascribed to an alliance between ecclesiastical and civil polity in which the clergy were implicated as interested parties.[45] There is, however, a genuine divine right enjoyed by monarchs insofar as they fulfil the purpose for which they exist. 'Good government alone can be in the divine intention.' 'God has made us', he went on, 'to desire happiness; he has made our happiness dependent on society; and the happiness of society dependent on good or bad government. His intention therefore was, that government should be *good*.'[46] All governments to which people have submitted by consent, 'though they are artificial, are however instituted by virtue of the law of our nature, and are, in this sense, of divine appointment'.[47] Government as such, then, is natural, while particular governments are legitimised by the consent of the people. He therefore criticised the contract theories of both Hobbes and Locke, which postulate a state of nature where individuals battle for survival and supremacy.[48]

Attacking unlimited and arbitrary government and critical of undue deference being paid to the king, Bolingbroke nevertheless defended hereditary monarchy against elective, though on pragmatic grounds. On the death of a king the business of electing another is likely to be divisive.[49]

Contract and consent

Bolingbroke, then, censured ideas of a 'divine, indefeasible, hereditary right' of a monarch to govern, a right that is 'independent of the community' and previous 'to any engagement taken on his part towards the people'. Such doctrines of passive obedience and non-resistance, held by High Church clergy, like the celebrated Dr Henry Sacheverell, give tyrannical power to kings. Thanks, however, to the Glorious Revolution,

> A king of Britain is now, strictly and properly, what kings should always be, a member, but the supreme member, or head of a political body . . .. He can move no longer in another orbit from his people, and like some superior planet, attract, repel, influence and direct their motions by his own. He and they are part of the same system, intimately joined and co-operating together, acting and acted upon, limiting and limited, controlling and controlled by one another; and

when he ceases to stand in this relation to them, he ceases to stand in any.[50]

Thus Bolingbroke spoke of government as the consequence of a contract, or 'an engagement', between ruler and ruled: 'The prince and the people take, in effect a sort of engagement with one another; the prince to govern well, and the people to honour and obey him.'[51] He insisted that the rights and powers of a prince must derive from the people.[52] The very constitution of the realm is 'in the strictest sense a bargain, a conditional contract between the prince and the people'.[53] Government by the consent of the people is, he claimed, characteristic of the British experience from earliest times; 'in all these ages Britain hath been the temple, as it were, of liberty'. As far back as we can look a lawless and arbititrary government has never prevailed.[54]

He asserted the right of freemen to complain, represent, petition and in the last resort to 'do more', that is (in words of John Locke) to 'appeal to heaven', or to revolt. If the people have the right of resistance when they are enslaved by their prince – and much of the defence of 1688 depended on this right – they surely have the same right 'when their representatives sell themselves and them'. He went on to take a radically populist position in maintaining that 'the care of the state is the care of the multitudes'.[55] The king's right to govern is the result of 'original contracts' and 'he may forfeit his right to allegiance, as undeniably and effectually, as the subject may forfeit his right to protection'.[56] Consent, he affirmed, is at the basis of all human associations.[57]

God and the philosophers

Though Bolingbroke was confident that the existence of a supreme being can be demonstrated by reasoning from empirical data derived from creation,[58] he continually assailed rational theologians, like Samuel Clarke – the celebrated Newtonian Rector of St James's, Piccadilly – and denounced the 'acute disciples of Leibnitz who dug for gold in the ordure of the schools'.[59] These men impiously set out to elucidate the attributes of God, presumptuously embarking on a defence of God against his critics with their elaborate schemes of theodicy:

· They presume to enter into his councils, and to account for the whole divine economy, as confidently as they would for any of their own paltry affairs. This they call theology. They build intellectual and material worlds on the hypothetical suggestions of imagination. This they call philosophy.[60]

Divines, whose only claim to distinction is 'that which the tailor gives them by making gowns for them, and coats for everyone else', are in danger of losing that awful respect due to the supreme being.[61] Bolingbroke was critical of the idea that there is 'an uninterrupted scale of intelligence from man up to God', and of the assurance with which theologians spoke of divine qualities and attributes, as though ideas like justice and goodness can be ascribed univocally to both God and humanity. There is an infinite distance between them; 'Let us not therefore humanise him.'[62] 'God', he insisted, 'is hid from us in the majesty of his nature, and the little we discover of him, must be discovered by the light that is reflected from his works.'[63] This explains the significance of the qualification 'with reverence be it spoken', quoted earlier.[64] Having assailed rational theologians and philosophers for presumptuously elaborating on God's nature, he recognised the need to apologise in advance for doing so himself.

> Know then thyself, presume not God to scan;
> The proper study of mankind is man.[65]

Bolingbroke located the source of these mistaken beliefs about God and the world in the philosophy of Plato and his many followers. These, by their doctrine of universal ideas, have undermined the transcendence of God and devalued that empirical method which alone is the proper foundation of human knowledge.

Attempts to defend God against accusations made by atheists are, he argued, misconceived and do more harm than good to the cause of true religion. The ideas of the Manichaeans, with their belief in an ultimate duality between good and evil powers, were more rational than those who postulate a devil, inferior to God yet able to deface his creation. He illustrated his point by appeal to the political analogy, arguing that

> it is no disgrace to a prince to reign acccording to the constitution of his country jointly with another, as the ephori reigned in Sparta, and the consuls governed at Rome, and that the ill government of his partner reflects no dishonor on him. But that to say of a monarch, in the true sense of the word, who is invested with absolute power, that he suffers one of his subjects to abuse the rest without control, and to draw them into crimes and revolts, for which he punishes them afterwards, is the most injurious accusation which can be brought.[66]

Rational theologians, like Clarke, so far from vindicating the providence of God, have brought him to trial at the bar of human reason:

> the self-existent being, the first cause of all things that are, the creator, the preserver, the governor of the universe, in whom we live, and move, and have our beings, has been tried, convicted and condemned, for his government of the world, on the general principles of human justice; like the governor of a province, or any other inferior magistrate.[67]

140

God's ways are not our ways, and there are limits to what we can know about God. The evidence from the natural world suggests that it is designed and created by an infinitely wise being. Who, he demanded, would presume to judge some particular actions of a prince who had by long experience deservedly acquired a reputation for wisdom in this way, when they 'saw the measures imperfectly and because the ends were unknown to them'?[68] If God is pictured as a *constitutional* monarch, however, this ultimate submission to the rule of law is precisely what one would expect; the possibility of impeachment must always be on the agenda!

Considering how little, according to Bolingbroke, it is possible to know about the supreme being, the reader is sometimes surprised how much he is prepared to say about God in the course of his writing: eternal truths, for example, are said to emanate from divine nature and not from divine will; the universe was created not for the sake of humans, though it is God's will that they should achieve happiness;[69] God is good and wise and all-powerful.[70] For though he professed a sceptical position on many occasions, Bolingbroke shared that optimistic eighteenth-century belief in individual human reason. This is particularly evident in his letter to Lord Bathurst, where he declared that every opinion which a person 'has not himself either framed, or examined strictly, and then adopted will pass for nothing more than what it really is, the opinion of other men, which may be true or false for aught he knows'. 'Every man's reason is every man's oracle.' Furthermore this oracle is best consulted 'in the silence of retirement'. Those who follow this path in the search for truth will, when the time of accounting comes, be vindicated rather than 'he who has resigned himself . . . to any authority on earth'.[71]

In a letter to Pope, Bolingbroke called for a recognition of the distinction between revealed and natural religion, between faith and reason, 'divines and philosophers should keep in their distinct provinces'.[72] Those who try to mix these two disciplines will find that the God of natural theology is very different from the God of Moses. So long, however, as the theologian bases his assertions on revelation, as found for example in scripture, and does not wander into the realm of natural theology, he can safely ignore the assaults of philosophical critics and wait for the last day, when all things will be openly revealed. 'In the mean while a sort of truce should take place between the divine and the philosopher.'[73]

Prerogative, providence and nature

God is revealed through his works. Bolingbroke did not, however, reject the possibility of further revelation, so long as it is consistent with and based on this 'original and universal revelation'. Yet even this latter is an object of 'belief' rather than 'knowledge'. For the sake of argument he allowed that, though God knows everything from eternity, he might decide 'to deal

141

out his revelations by parcels, as legislators are forced to make new laws, and new rules of government that are adapted to circumstances unforeseen by them'. Yet these later revelations must be consistent with the fundamental revelation.[74] 'Every instituted religion is dependent on natural religion, and should be made subservient to it.'[75] The analogy with human legislation, however, falls down on the issue of foreknowledge.

Bolingbroke's God is the author of a general providence; he created a world that should run according to laws, such that the best situation would be realised. Like most deists, Bolingbroke was critical of alleged special providence and miracle. He told Pope that 'he who made, preserves the world, and governs it on the same principles and according to the same invariable laws which he imposed at the first'.[76] The poet concurred:

> ... the first Almighty Cause
> Acts not by partial but by gen'ral laws.[77]

Rational theologians, who admit that ideas of a general providence fail to reconcile God's power and his goodness, introduce the concept of special providences, rendering their presumptuous theodicies, in Bolingbroke's opinion, even less coherent. Writers like Woolston and Clarke must recognise that

> these particular providences are exercised so rarely, so secretly, or some how or other so ineffectually, that his government continues liable to the same charge of injustice, and cannot be reconciled to his attributes, and to the eternal reason of things

without an unacceptable hypothesis.[78]

A rejection of special providence, however, by no means implies that humanity has ever been without God, for the evident marks of his providence are present in the world. The instances which are affirmed as special providences do not in fact depart from the regular course of events, and this is indeed a good thing, for

> if it was otherwise, if providences were directed according to the different desires, and even wants of men equally well entitled to the divine favor, the whole order of nature, physical and moral, would be subverted, and the affairs of mankind would fall into the utmost confusion.[79]

To admit special providences would be to allege that God governs the world by two distinct and incompatible rules. When, in the years prior to the institution of King Saul in Israel, God ruled directly by particular providences, 'the people were so little satisfied with this system of government, that they deposed the supreme being, and insisted to have another king, and to be governed like their neighbors'.[80]

Nature is pictured as ordered and rational. It contains the secret of divine purpose. From a study of the cosmos we can prove the existence of an all-wise and omnipotent creator. 'Carry a clock to the wild inhabitants of the Cape of Good Hope', Bolingbroke wrote. 'They will soon be convinced intelligence made it.'[81] A study of the natural world is the only satisfactory method for understanding our duties. 'Man is born to contemplate the world and to conform his behaviour to the will of God, that is manifested, relatively to man, in the constitution of it.'[82] Only thus can human beings co-operate with God. The supreme being has blended together duty and interest, but to ignore the law of nature is to renounce duty and propose another interest. This led him into a further attack on Clarke, whose presumptuous theology assumes that we can know God's inner being and attributes, and imitate him. God is beyond all our knowledge, and divines should content themselves 'to know God, as he has thought fit to be known by them', as he has revealed himself in the natural world.[83] The supreme being has thus revealed himself to the human race through his works and by a law of nature which can be discovered by reasoning on the basis of this natural revelation.[84] It is this law of nature that obliges us to obey civil laws. The latter are like the bylaws of cities, which derive their ultimate sanction from the law of the state.[85]

Francis Bacon had claimed that as miracles occurred only rarely in his day, so the king should seldom use his prerogative.[86] Bolingbroke went further and argued from the same analogy that, as miracles never occur, there is no place in constitutional government for the royal prerogative, which the Glorious Revolution had effectively abolished. 'Our constitution', he contended, 'is no longer a mystery; the power of the crown is now exactly limited, the chimera of prerogative removed, and the rights of the subject are no longer problematical.'[87]

Arbitrary government, whether divine or human, which acts against or outside clearly defined laws, was the object of Bolingbroke's continued attack. 'Clearness and precision are two great excellencies of human law', he observed. 'How much more should we expect to find them in the law of God?'[88]

Bolingbroke was manifestly aware of the power of analogy and allegory. It was a graphic and potent rhetorical tool in both religion and politics. He constantly employed these tropes in his assaults on opponents, and defended their use, particularly in *ad hominem* arguments. When employed by theologians and other victims of his satire, however, it becomes 'the refuge of ignorance, the veil of error, and the instrument of metaphysical and theological deception in its abuse'.[89] His striking use of the deist model of a supreme being as acting according to rules prescribed by himself, rather than in a tyrannical and arbitrary manner, provided an effective model for promoting the kind of constitutional government which was in his view appropriate for his time. This is not to say that his concept of God was cynically limned in order to justify a political order of which he approved.

His writings, indeed, suggest that he was at least as interested in cosmology and theology as he was in politics. The image of God as constitutional monarch is, though, abandoned when it suits his purposes and particularly, as we have noted, in his assault on Leibniz and Clarke.

DEISM AND POLITICS

Anglican latitudinarians and high churchmen of the early eighteenth century developed their theological position in a generally hostile dialogue with each other and with the deists and Dissenters of their day. Orthodox Trinitarians, like William Law and Daniel Waterland, attacked Clarke and Hoadly as Arians; the latter were among the most virulent assailants of the Socinians and deists, who in turn were fiercely critical of atheists, rejecting their claim to legal toleration. Yet looking back on the controversies, what seems to us most significant is what the parties shared. Almost all believed in a general harmony in nature; they were optimistic about the possibility of discovering by reason the laws of nature and about the ability of humans to live according to them. They thought of the universe largely in terms of a machine, running according to pre-ordained laws. Apart from the atheists, who were at this time few and far between, they shared an understanding of God as a supreme, autarkic being, punishing in an afterlife the vicious and rewarding the virtuous. They believed in the reality of human sin and the need for forgiveness. There was a loose connection between theology and politics at this time: between theological unorthodoxy and radical politics, between Anglican liberal theology and Whig politics, and between Anglican high church beliefs and sympathy for the Stuarts. It would, however, be easy to find examples of those who fail to conform to these stereotypes.

Deism

The term 'deism' is difficult to clarify. Some definitions centre on the claim to universality made by the deists, with its corollary of a natural religion open for all people at all times to discover for themselves. 'That rule which is necessary to our future happiness, ought to be generally made known to all men', one deist argued. 'But no rule of revealed religion was, or ever could be, made known to all men. Therefore no revealed religion is necessary to future happiness.'[90] A recent scholar also lays emphasis on the deists' 'denial of revealed religion'. Deism, he states, is a belief that 'only natural knowledge was possible and that all true or correct belief had to be based on reasons that were self-evidently true'. He goes on to assert that a rejection of this clear definition of deism, as the denial of revealed religion, has led to 'an unhelpful blurring of distinctions between deists and those who opposed them'.[91]

Some deists, however, appear to have accepted the notion of divine revelation. Matthew Tindal did not rule out revelation as a possible source of knowledge, confirming the conclusions of natural religion. Toland was more specific: 'God is pleased to reveal to us in Scripture', he wrote in his celebrated *Christianity not Mysterious* (1696), 'several wonderful matters of fact, as the creation of the world, the last judgment, and many other important truths, which no man left to himself could ever imagine.'[92] He insisted, of course: 'Whoever reveals anything ... his words must be intelligible, and the matter possible.'[93] But then establishment theologians, like Hoadly and even Butler, also believed that alleged revelations must ultimately be accepted by human reason. Matthew Tindal was not far wrong when he wrote in 1730: 'All divines, I think, now agree in owning that there's a law of reason, antecedent to any external revelation, that God can't dispense, either with his creatures or himself, for not observing.'[94]

It is, of course, possible that these writers were being ironical in their recognition of revelation, or simply practising 'the art of theological lying'.[95] They were not, to be sure, entirely consistent in what they wrote on the subject, and the universality principle (that the necessary means to salvation must be available at all times and in all places) would seem to exclude a revelation of essential truths at a particular time and place. Emerson's proposed definition (which rules out Tindal and Toland from the category of deist) may have the advantage of clarity, but makes nonsense of history![96] Perhaps the distinctions were in reality blurred.

The universality principle of deism entails a rejection of the Old Testament as in any way containing divine revelation; its laws and practices were thought to be manifestly in conflict with the laws of reason and nature. In defence of the Hebrew scriptures, Anglican critics of Tindal proposed a notion of progressive revelation, according to which God reveals himself and his purposes in proportion to the ability of people to receive the truth. God is pictured as an educator, in dialogue with his people. While the revelation of God in Christ was in essence final, some – like William Worthington (1703–78), Edmund Law (1703–87) and Joseph Butler – suggested the possibility of a growth in understanding of Christian doctrine.[97] God's role as educator of the human race was consonant with the promotion by these men of public education in the form of charity schools.

Toland and Tindal

Janus Junius Toland was born in Northern Ireland and brought up a Roman Catholic, educated, in his own words, 'from his cradle in the grossest superstition and idolatry'.[98] In his mid-teens he became a Protestant and changed his Christian name to 'John'. In 1697 he published his best-known work, *Christianity not Mysterious*, in which, without denying revelation, he argued that true religion was understandable by human reason and that mysterious elements had been introduced from heathen sources and by clerical intrigue. As he put it a little later:

> Natural religion was easy first and plain,
> Tales made it Mystery, Offrings made it Gain;
> Sacrifices and Shows were at length prepar'd,
> The Priest ate roast-meat, and the People star'd.[99]

A passage in his *Life of Milton*, published in 1698, appeared to cast doubt on the authenticity of the New Testament, though he later claimed to be referring to apocryphal writings. Toland was a prolific writer and editor of controversial political and religious books and tracts. His defence of the Act of Succession made him popular with the Hanoverian dynasty and led to friendship with German royalty. His *Letters to Serena*, published in 1704, were addressed to Queen Sophie Charlotte of Prussia. Although he attacked Spinoza's philosophy in these letters as 'not only false, but also precarious and without any sort of foundation', his own position appeared remarkably similar and the influence of Giordano Bruno's hermetic beliefs is evident.[100] Toland was probably the first person to use the term 'pantheism'. His assertion that matter inherently involves motion appeared to deny the need for an unmoved mover, and was rejected by Newton and his followers.[101] He edited the works of James Harrington and saw himself as following the tradition of the seventeenth-century 'Commonwealthmen'.

Matthew Tindal was educated in Oxford and became Fellow of All Souls in 1678. For a short period, under James II, he became a Roman Catholic, but soon returned to the Church of England. His 1706 book on *The Rights of the Christian Church* was generally Erastian in tone, attacking any effective claim to the church's supernatural authority; author, publisher and printer were all prosecuted, but this did not prevent him from writing a *Defence* of the book three years later. This in turn was publicly burned by order of the House of Commons.

The rule of law

The deists asserted that God governs the universe by law; Tindal indeed maintained in his celebrated work *Christianity as Old as the Creation* (1730) that the very idea of government *implies* that of law. These laws were instituted for the purpose of human welfare. Just as it would be tyrannical in earthly rulers to exact things from their subjects which did not contribute to the end for which earthly government exists, 'can we suppose', demanded Tindal, 'a governor of infinite wisdom and goodness, who has always in his mind the end for which he governs mankind, will act the tyrant?'.[102] God must not be thought of as an arbitrary being. In divinity as in politics, 'the good of the people is the supreme law', and it is to be achieved by general laws rather than by particular arbitrary decrees.[103]

Tindal and Toland both, then, saw law as the basis of government, cosmic and civil. God's government is impartial and his laws are of universal validity. Tindal criticised the positive aspects of particular religions for implying the rule of an arbitrary god.[104] The universal laws of God are discovered by the use of natural reason, and any alleged revelation is subordinate to this law of reason. Toland also insisted that 'truth is always and everywhere the same'.[105] Nevertheless, there was in the early writings of Tindal a Hobbist positivism, which gives to government arbitrary powers when the common good is thought to be at stake. This was undoubtedly reinforced by a Socinian influence. There had been among the early Socinians a notion of God as supreme monarch, who can issue decrees of forgiveness without the need for any kind of restitution or retribution. Sin was seen more as a private offence against an absolute monarch than a breaking of the law. It was of course this idea of God and sin that led Socinians to reject anything other than an exemplarist view of atonement.[106]

There was, in the eighteenth century, as we have observed, a link between Dissent and radical social and political ideas. Many leading radicals were from Dissenting backgrounds, including Trenchard, Toland, Wilkes, Hazlitt, Godwin, and Coleridge in his early days. Some called themselves 'Commonwealthmen' and were critical of absolute monarchy. Their republican tendencies, however, as Margaret Jacob has observed, 'could sometimes be subdued for a position within the government'.[107] Toland saw himself as maintaining the seventeenth-century republican tradition, with his *Life of Milton* and his edition of the *Works* of Harrington.[108] It should also be noted that at this time the term 'republican' did not necessarily imply that the person so designated was against all forms of monarchy.

It would be quite wrong, however, to think of most Dissenters as wild revolutionaries. Even those who were thought of as radical were supporters of the post-1688 settlement and on speaking-terms with the Whig leaders of their day; they were occasionally given public office under Walpole's administration. Deists, including Tindal, Toland, Collins and a number of freemasons, whose theology was basically deist, would meet in the Grecian coffee-house off the Strand in London to discuss religion and politics. How do we explain the general link between religious Dissent and political radicalism?

In the first place, many of these men, being outside the established church, suffered certain civil disabilities and even mild forms of persecution. Their demands for toleration frequently led to wider claims for civil liberties. But Roman Catholics were also outside the establishment and subject to similar disabilities and there is little indication that they were notable for their social radicalism.[109] It should also not be forgotten that a number of deists – Tindal and Bolingbroke come to mind – were members of the established church, or at least occasional conformists. Were there, then, theological factors leading the theologically unorthodox towards social radicalism? Colin Russell has suggested that there is an analogy between 'Toland's universe free of divine intervention, and a political world that runs itself'.[110] This might help to account for his anti-government stance; though Toland was by no means consistent on this question. His association with the more radical of the Whigs led him to emphasise the aspects of justice and welfare in government – human and divine – in contrast to some of the more conservative churchmen, who saw government rather in terms of order and stability. The maintenance of social and political stability was in fact an obsession with most churchmen of the late seventeenth century.[111] The deists' critique of ecclesiastical hierarchy easily moved into a more general attack on authority, and this is at least one of the links between their politics and their theology.

Toland was an intransigent elitist, who despised the common people as 'downright gross idolaters'. 'We shall', he told his fellow deists, 'be in safety if we separate ourselves from the multitude.'[112] He celebrated the post-1688 'admirable balanced constitution' and praised Queen Anne for keeping 'such an even balance among the several contending parties at home, so that they are not able . . . to devour one another'.[113]

In his *Letters to Serena* Toland had proposed a vitalism which involves belief in matter as not inert but active. He appeared to be postulating a self-sufficient universe, not requiring the hypothesis of a creator to account for its motion. It was pantheism verging on atheism, in the view of his critics, and touched Newtonians on a raw nerve. Newton's notion of gravity had already led his critics to denounce his system for implying that matter possesses 'occult qualities'. In his Boyle Lectures, Clarke defended Newton on this issue and in the Latin edition of the *Opticks*, which appeared in 1706, the master himself stated categorically that matter is inert, endowed only with a *vis inertiae*, – a view which leaves room for God as the author and sustainer of motion.

Tindal attacked 'the wicked priests' for accepting both the God of the Old Testament and the God of the New Testament without attempting to reconcile the two patently incompatible pictures of God. By adopting this position 'they destroyed both, and natural religion too; in supposing things are not good and evil in themselves; but that all depends on the will of an arbitrary being, which might endlessly change'.[114] He criticised those divines who justified the slaughter of the Canaanites on the grounds that it was a positive command of God. Only if this can be supposed to be consistent with the law of nature is it acceptable, otherwise 'all would depend on an uncertain, fluctuating and arbitrary will'.[115] For Tindal, worship is offered to God wholly for its effects on us, and we pray not in the hope of changing the course of events, but because it 'serves to keep up a constant sense of our dependence on him'.[116] A similar position was maintained in the nineteenth century by Schleiermacher.

Despite their attacks on 'arbitrary government' and 'tyranny', the whole tendency of deist radical thought was to the dissolution of all societies and groups apart from the state. The church was a particular object of their attack. It should operate as nothing more than a department of state, to maintain a minimal civil religion, in a manner made notorious in Hobbes's *Leviathan* and later in *Du Contrat social* of Rousseau. All deny, wrote Tindal, that

> any society can subsist without some notions of religion or the ac-
> knowledging of invisible powers. Therefore the magistrate is obliged
> to punish those who deny the existence of a god, or that he concerns
> himself with human affairs.[117]

He therefore agreed with John Locke and the general opinion of his day that toleration should not be accorded to the atheist, who is an 'enemy of mankind'.[118] With Hoadly, he denied any notion of the church as a body distinct from the state; hence his fierce attacks on priestcraft and hierarchy. Isaac Watts adopted a similar position with respect to the idea of a civil religion.

Consent and the common good

In his early writings Matthew Tindal adopted a largely Hobbist model of the state. To be a member of civil society and to be under government are the same thing. In an attack on Jacobites and Nonjurors, he defended a theory of obedience to the *de facto* government, for: 'None can pretend to be, or claim any civil rights as a member of a society, without owning the actual government which makes it a society.'[119] Tindal maintained that those who 'disown' the government make themselves outlaws and have 'reduced themselves to a state of nature'.[120] Although God is the author of government in general, no particular form of government can claim divine right, – apart, that is, from government 'by consent'. This is the only valid form of human government – or, indeed, of divine government, for when God became the king of his chosen people 'he first required their consent; and a contract between God and the people . . . was the foundation of the theocracy'.[121] Consent is of course interpreted loosely, as in all contract theories of political obligation. 'Though their consent was obtained by forcible means, yet that would not destroy the validity of it.' Though forcible means were used people were not forced to promise, because it was still in their power to avoid promising. Protection is the essence of govern- ment and merely to accept protection is to give tacit consent.[122] In this case, were not the people of England obliged to obey King James II in 1688? They were indeed, but only so long as that ruler was willing and able to offer them protection; when this ceased, obligation departed with it.[123]

Tindal, however, was a kind of utilitarian, insisting that the laws of God always forward welfare. He several times reiterated his belief that the government of God is conducted for 'the good of his creatures', a position which, as we have seen, was later rejected as anthropocentric by Bolingbroke and Pope.[124] All valid laws are designed to this end. In theology as in politics, 'the good of the people is the supreme law'. When human rulers act for the common good they govern by the same rule as God adopts and 'they concur in the same design with him'.[125] Tindal here echoes the views of Charles Blount that 'the good of the community' is the principal end of government.[126] The more radical deists went further: not only is the *welfare* of the people the supreme end, but *'the voice of the people is the voice of God'*.[127]

Tindal's doctrine of *salus populi suprema lex* ('the welfare of the people is the supreme law') leads to an alarming sequel. As laws can never be framed to cover all eventualities, it is 'necessary that a power to dispense with the penalties of the laws should be lodged with the king, *whose power can't be too large if he uses it for the public good'*.[128] The public good is the foundation of both human and divine laws. Once something is thought to be in the common interest it becomes obligatory. To kill an innocent person, if for the public good, is not merely permissible but a duty, for 'the only thing which government looks after in punishing, is the common good'.[129] Tindal's criticism of arbitrary government looks unimpressive in the light of this theory. Not only laws, but customs also, are to be seen in the context of the ruler's power and will. 'In a civil society', he declared, 'customs grow into laws, because 'tis the will of the supreme power they should. Customs are their presumed or unwritten will, which they by their express will may alter as they please.'[130]

The role played by will in the area of law and custom, and the power of the ruler to dispense with the penalties of the law, are replicated at the theological level in God. One of the principal targets in orthodox theology selected by the deists was the doctrine of atonement. While properly denying that God acts vindictively as an injured party when faced by human sin, Tindal insisted that as judge and legislator, 'whether he punishes, or rewards, he acts alike for our good'.[131] God is 'a merciful and benign being', wrote Stephen Nye; a sinner who repents is on the way to reformation, and it is 'not justice but rage, to punish when the person is already mended'.[132] Punishment is purged of all retributive elements, and becomes a question of promoting the common good. Punishing and pardoning are acts of God's will rather than 'properties of his nature'. In this respect the English deists inherited the image of God as an arbitrary monarch dispensing forgiveness at will and with whom justice is subordinated to mercy, an image which we find in earlier Socinian writers. Here, however, Tindal is not entirely consistent. As we have noted, he denounced ideas of God as an arbitrary being.

LATITUDE MEN

Margaret Jacob has shown how the political theology of the Newtonian churchmen, as proclaimed, for example, by successive Boyle lecturers, portrayed religion as a bulwark of order. 'The design and harmony in the material order, imposed by spiritual forces provided a model or guide to show how social and political relations should work if Christians were to fulfill the providential plan and still compete with one another. Without religion', she went on, 'it was believed, the hierarchical structure of society would crumble and with it property rights.'[133]

The other principal office of religion, in the view of latitudinarian church-men, was to encourage people to act in their true self-interest, for without such motivations the market society could not operate in a stable manner. With Joseph Butler, self-interest as such was not seen as evil; rather, its pursuit is perfectly legitimate if done in a responsible manner. Isaac Barrow spoke of profit as that 'great mistress' who provides the impetus for human action.[134] Yet self-interest results in the common good only when long-term interests together with the rewards and punishments of a future life are taken into account. If people act to secure their immediate material interests to the neglect of other considerations no ordered human community can exist. This is why Mandeville's cynical position was the object of such bitter attacks. His critics saw in *The Fable of the Bees* a republication of Hobbist ideas, which they believed to be dangerous for social stability. A system of unrestricted competition, with each person pursuing his own immediate gratification, would spell the downfall of that oligarchy, in which they occupied secure positions near the top. Religion was promoted as 'the cement of society'.[135]

If they had paid more attention to what Mandeville actually wrote they would have seen that he by no means believed that an unregulated free-for-all in which each pursues in a reckless manner his own interests will result in the common good of the whole. It is only 'by the dextrous management of a skilful politician' that private vices may be turned into public benefits.[136] In any case what Mandeville called vice was often regarded as the pursuit of legitimate self-interest, or cool self-love, by less puritanical moralists.

It was the object of churchmen not so much to 'curb' self-interest as to point out to their listeners what their true interests are. Virtuous action will be rewarded in a future life, not just beyond the grave, but in that millen-nium in which many of these men believed. Preachers reminded the rich of their responsibility for the poor, and of the consequent need for charity. Making provision for the poor, declared Bishop Butler, is a question of justice and not mere choice.[137] These churchmen can therefore be seen by no means as apologists of unrestricted competition, but as men who, with remarkable foresight, were able to see the dangers to social stability which uncontrolled capitalism would bring in its wake. They might even be portrayed in a curious way as forerunners of a welfare state.

Benjamin Hoadly exemplifies the alliance between liberal theology and Whig politics in the Hanoverian era. Like his mentor Tillotson, Hoadly stressed the rational foundation of Christianity. 'Natural religion', the archbishop had declared, 'is the foundation of all instituted and revealed religion'.[138] By natural religion he meant obedience to the natural law, and the performance of those duties made clear by natural light, aside from all supernatural revelation. God too was governed by the law of his nature, so that

> it would be little less than a horrid and dreadful blasphemy, to say that God can, out of his sovereign will and pleasure, do anything that contradicts the nature of God, and the essential perfections of the Deity; or to imagine that the pleasure and will of the holy, and just, and good God, is not always regulated and determined by the essential and indispensable laws of goodness, and holiness and righteousness.[139]

Heavenly government provided for the archbishop a model of how earthly government should proceed.

Hoadly generally avoided monarchical language in his references to God. Even in his sermon preached on the anniversary of the restoration of the monarchy under Charles II, God is seen as the 'governor', whose 'management' and 'superintendency' of the universe are celebrated. Though he occasionally spoke of God as 'king', God – like Queen Anne – ruled under 'that envied constitution, in which the commands of the prince, and the obedience of the subjects, are equally regulated by law'.[140]

Hoadly, however, recognised that there is too much in scripture and tradition to suggest a hierarchical order in the heavens, presided over by an absolute monarch, to make it safe for a Whig to argue from the divine analogue. To base civil government on this foundation would be to offer hostages to fortune. 'It is the weakest thing in the world', he maintained, 'to argue from *almighty God's absolute monarchy*, or from imaginary monarchies amongst the good angels, to the necessity of the same amongst mortal men.'[141] Hoadly spent more energy refuting the legitimacy of the analogy between heavenly and earthly government than in challenging the mode of the heavenly, as Tillotson did. In *The Original and Institution of Civil Government Discussed*, published in 1710, Hoadly asserted that God has not revealed the principles of celestial government, and that in any case a system of absolute government that may be appropriate to beings who are perfect in wisdom, knowledge and goodness is unlikely to be safe in 'the hands of weak men'. God cannot possibly require 'the same subjection to a weak and passionate man, as he may perhaps to an exalted angel':[142] a position also maintained by Joseph Addison. Hoadly accepted a kind of sovereignty in God, who 'presides over the whole world', that nothing comes to pass without his will, his decree or his permission' and that he 'holds the sceptre of the universe', but he questioned the appropriateness of this absolute sovereignty to earthly government:

> But if it be said that in all government there must be a last resort, and this must be absolute in all cases, I desire to know why. . . . Is it not sufficient for the ends of government that it be absolute in carrying forward those ends?[143]

To be supreme in one respect is not to be supreme in all, and there is no reason to think that a ruler's authority extends beyond the legitimate ends of his office.

In rebutting patriarchal arguments, which retained their influence into the eighteenth century, Hoadly asserted that paternal and civil authority are quite different and that there is no analogy between them. The bishop of Exeter had argued that as a mayor, though elected by the corporation, holds a commission from the queen and is therefore responsible to her and not punishable by the corporation, so the queen is God's minister, holding God's commission and not responsible to the people or to Parliament. Hoadly replied that if the mayor exceeded the terms of his royal commission he might be opposed by any freeman; so if the monarch exceeded the terms of her divine commission she too could be opposed by her subjects.[144] He furthermore reminded patriarchalists that no contemporary monarch could claim direct descent from the seventy kings constituted by God after the generation of Noah. Possession and prescription have been substituted, so that divine right is claimed for the grandson of 'a robber and usurper, who by violence or fraud first obtained it'.[145]

Rejecting patriarchalism with theories of divine right and passive obedience, Hoadly based legitimate civil authority on consent. The consent and approbation of the people is 'the most secure, as well as the most glorious foundation upon which the throne of any earthly prince can be established'.[146] In his defence of contract theory Hoadly appealed, significantly, to Richard Hooker, rather than to John Locke, whose theological credentials were not entirely sound. It is not hard to see why Hoadly was regarded with great respect in the American colonies, where 'he was widely held to be one of the notable figures in the history of political thought'.[147]

ISAAC WATTS

Born in 1674, Isaac Watts was a contemporary of Hoadly and Bolingbroke, but with a very different conception of God. His God is a fierce king, who 'puts on vengeance like a robe', and reduces earthly monarchs to nought.[148] An absolute and to all appearances an arbitrary ruler, God effects his judgments by a mere nod or frown, like an eastern potentate. Although earthly monarchs are called gods, they are ultimately subjects of the divine monarch and submit to his judgment. Watts did not, however, restrict himself to monarchical images, but, responding to the dominant idiom of his day, also wrote of God in commercial and managerial images and even employed the recently coined term 'prime minister' in his discussion of the Trinity. Though he was very much the child of late seventeenth-century puritanism, in the school of Richard Baxter, Watts was influenced to a considerable degree by the mechanical world-view current in the later part of that century. He believed religion to be not merely of individual, but of social and political, significance. The believer was assuredly the subject of God's particular providence, but so was the British nation, which he sometimes identified with Israel of the Old Testament. In common with Bolingbroke and with other writers of the period, he saw religion as a principal bulwark of civil government.

His life and ministry

Isaac Watts came from Dissenting and Huguenot stock. In 1702 he was appointed pastor of an independent congregation in London, but owing to chronic ill health became tutor and private chaplain to a rich London merchant. He is principally known today as a hymn-writer of great distinction, author of such popular hymns as 'When I survey the wondrous cross' and 'O God our help in ages past'. Watts opposed attempts to impose Trinitarian formulae on Dissenting ministers, and it is sometimes suggested that he adopted Unitarian views. Evidence on this matter is conflicting. Like the Fathers of the early church, he sometimes used concepts and illustrations in his discussion of the Trinity that had unorthodox implications, but he defended Trinitarian beliefs in his essay on 'The Doctrine of the Trinity and the Use of It':

> There is, and there must be, some real union and communion in godhead between the sacred Three, the Father, the Son, and the Holy Spirit, to answer and support the divine names, titles and attributes, &c, which are ascribed to them all: And there is, and there must be, some sufficient distinction between them, to sustain these distinct personal characters and office, and to answer to these distinct representations of scripture.[149]

Jesus is both 'our kinsman and our God'. Watts several times used the phrase 'Jesus the God'.[150] In the economy of salvation the Father is sovereign, the Son redeemer and reconciler, the Holy Spirit the sanctifier.[151] The Father has committed to the Son the reins of government in heaven and on earth, and princes rule under him 'according to his pleasure'.[152] Thus the Son is pictured on the one hand as sharing the royal power of the Father, and worshipped together with him, and on the other as representing and leading humans in their prayers and worship directed to the Father.

Prime ministers and kings

In an age when a constitutional monarch acted on the advice of his principal ministers, the role of 'prime minister' was of growing importance. It was during the long ministry of Robert Walpole that the term gained currency. Watts was not slow to apply it to divine government. Jesus was portrayed as 'the most perfect image of his Father's love, and the prime minister of his grace'.[153] Elsewhere he spoke of the sun, in the firmament of heaven, as 'God's prime Minister in this wondrous world of beings'. But he went on to ask whether God had delegated all his powers to that 'inanimate and unthinking mass of matter'; was there no 'intellectual prime minister' in God's dominions? 'There is a man,' he continued,

> after God's own heart, the fairest Image of the creator, and nearest akin to him, among all the works of his hands: there is a man and his name is Jesus, who holds most intimate and personal union with the Godhead . . . Is not the government of heaven and earth put into his hands?[154]

In his book *The Christian Doctrine of the Trinity*, however, it is the Holy Spirit who plays the part of prime minister:

> He who, considered as true God, is one with the Father, and hath absolute sovereignty; yet considered in the gospel as a prime minister of the Father's and Son's kingdom, is pleased to represent himself as being sent by the Father and the Son as their chief agent, to fulfil many kind offices for us and in us, in the economy of salvation.[155]

In his consideration of the Trinity, Watts employed also the image of ambassador. St Paul had referred to the apostles as 'ambassadors'; Watts spoke of Jesus himself in these terms. The Son is seen as the ambassador of a king who is sent to a foreign land on a mission. Having accomplished his purpose, he leaves behind a resident minister to represent him:

> Thus we may apprehend how God the Father, the king of heaven, sent down his Son, a distinct person, in whom the same godhead dwells, as an ambassador extraordinary to earth; and the Holy Spirit, a distinct person also, who hath the same godhead, was left here as a resident.

Though he spoke of the Son and the Spirit as, in this context, 'inferior' to the Father, he pictured the soul of the king as so united to that of the ambassador and the resident as 'to animate, actuate and move them, and become, as it were one person with each of them'.[156] Sensing that he was on dangerous ground here, Watts reminded his readers, that such analogies, similes and metaphors, drawn from earthly things, represent very imperfectly things heavenly and divine, 'but perhaps they may serve to strike some little light upon this sacred mystery'.[157]

A celestial monarchy

Many of Watts's hymns were based on the Psalms and reflect royalist images which are prominent in these Hebrew writings. These images stress God's power, and sovereign rule, portraying earthly monarchs as wholly dependent on God for their positions:

> High as the Heaven above the Ground
> Reigns the Creator-God,
> Wide as the whole Creation's Bound
> Extends his awful rod.
> Let Princes of exalted State
> To him ascribe their Crown,
> Render their homage at his Feet,
> And cast their Glories down.[158]

God's orders are firm and are not to be questioned by his subjects.[159] Empires are 'fixed beneath his smiles', and 'totter at his frowns', for like an absolute potentate he 'governs with a nod':

> And with an awful Nod or Frown
> Shakes an aspiring Tyrant down.[160]

James Thomson, from a Scottish Presbyterian background, employed the same image, addressing God:

> O Thou, by whose almighty nod the scale
> Of empire rises, or alternate falls.[161]

Those kingdoms that follow the divine law are seen by Watts as built, like God's own kingdom, on firm foundations, but even they have authority only in earthly affairs and not in spiritual matters:

> Kingdoms on firm Foundations stand
> While virtue finds Reward;
> And Sinners perish from the Land
> By justice and the Sword.
> Let *Caesar's* Due be ever paid
> To *Caesar* and his Throne,
> But consciences and souls were made
> To be the Lord's alone.[162]

No claims to divine right dispense king's from the duty to act justly. In his hymn based on Psalm 75, first published in 1719, Watts made the point forcefully:

> No vain pretence to royal birth
> Shall fix a tyrant on the throne:
> God the great Sovereign of the earth
> Will rise and make his justice known.[163]

The great God of heaven surveys the gods (rulers) on earth and judges them:

> Know that his Kingdom is Supreme
> Your lofty Thoughts are vain;
> He calls you *Gods*, that awful Name,
> But ye must die like Men.[164]

As the dominant image of God, in the writings of Watts, is that of absolute monarch, he saw prayer in terms of petitions of subjects addressed to the Father – or the Son insofar as he shares the Father's throne – thus sustaining 'a royal character in this economy':

> Oh 'tis good
> To wait submissive at thy holy Throne,
> To leave petitions at thy Feet.[165]

Worship was viewed as the joining of earthly prayers with the offerings of the saints, united to the supreme sacrifice of Christ himself:

> Petitions now and Praise may rise,
> And Saints their Offerings bring,
> The Priest with his own Sacrifice
> Presents them to the King.

He sharply distinguished this role of the saints from the doctrine of 'papists', who 'pray to the heavenly host'.[166]

Nature's ruler and manager

Not only is God the ruler of rulers and of their subjects, but he also governs the natural world. The rolling mountains observe his commands, and the rivers flow according to his direct rule.[167] Yet Watts's understanding of the natural order was strongly influenced by the mechanical analogies characteristic of his day. He referred to the universe as a 'moving engine', and he accepted a dualistic model of body and soul, probably reflecting a Cartesian strain in his education. He meditated, in gratitude, on how his soul might well have been sent to inhabit the body of a crippled or diseased child, referring to the body of the sick person as 'that poor disabled machine'.[168] The soul, following Neoplatonic beliefs, is seen as imprisoned in the body:

> Hail, holy Souls, no more confin'd
> To Limbs and Bones that clog the Mind,
> Ye have escap'd the Snares, and left the Chains behind.[169]

Related to the mechanical picture of the universe are the managerial and commercial images frequently employed by Watts in his religious writings. God is pictured as riding on the stormy sky and managing the sea. Elsewhere he 'manages our mean Affairs'. He orders his army of angels

> To manage his Affairs of State
> In Works of Vengeance or of Love.[170]

Jesus manages all things in the world of grace, and religion is referred to as our 'best business'. 'Who would venture on a journey', asked Watts, 'without having his soul insured in the hands of Jesus?'[171] The image of Jesus as celestial insurance agent would surely have appealed to Richard Price.[172]

Watts was perfectly at ease with the commercial images of the New Testament. When a merchant lives in a foreign land he appoints a banker to administer his financial affairs at home. It is to him that his servants go to draw the money they need. So God the Father, who is 'too far off for us to converse with him or receive supplies from him in an immediate way', constituted his Son as treasurer of all his blessings. The promises of scripture are 'so many bills of exchange drawn by God the Father in heaven upon his Son Jesus Christ, and payable to every pious believer'.[173] Those who picture God's relationship with his people according to merely political concepts of authority, dominion or government diminish its significance, for God is also 'absolute possessor and proprietor of all his creatures'.[174]

Civil religion and British Israel

From the earliest days of the Christian religion, military images have been used of God. Watts was not embarrassed to speak in the language of battle:

> When God, our leader, shines in arms,
> What mortal heart can bear
> The thunder of his loud alarms?
> The lightning of his Spear?
> He speaks, and at his fierce rebuke
> Whole armies are dismay'd;
> His voice, his frown, his angry look
> Strikes all their courage dead.

It was not, for Watts, a merely general military analogy, but one particularly related to the British nation. God was seen as leader and commander of Britain, as he had been of Israel's children:

> He forms our generals for the field,
> With all their dreadful skill;
> Gives them his awful sword to wield
> And makes their hearts of steel.[175]

God exercises a special providence towards his chosen people:

> He builds and guard the *British* Throne,
> And makes it gracious like his own,
> Makes our successive princes kind,
> And gives our dangers to the Wind.[176]

Watts did not hesitate to apply the blessings of Israel in the Hebrew scriptures, particularly in the Psalms, to the British monarchy:[177]

> His Orders run thro' all their Hosts,
> Legions descend at his Command
> To shield and guard the British coasts
> When Foreign Rage invades our Land.[178]

The contrast with the Wesleys here is striking. The founders of Methodism do not deny God's providential guidance of the British nation. Charles, in fact, applies Abraham's bargaining with God over the future of Sodom to Britain:

> Thou, Lord, in answer to the just,
> Hast long deferr'd *Britannia's* doom.
> And praying on we humbly trust
> The threatened curse shall never come.[179]

Yet the Wesleys generally tended to interpret the great events of the Old Testament in an individualist way. The victorious battles of the Hebrews prefigure the victory of the individual Christian over sin and temptation. The reign of God is first and foremost seen as applying to his reign in the heart of the believer.[180]

Watts believed that civil government exists to protect the persons, properties, liberty and peace of people from their neighbours. Monarchy, aristocracy, democracy and mixed government are alike based on 'a compact or agreement between the governors and the governed, expressed or implied'.[181] What will persuade people to adhere to their side of the bargain and obey governments? He accepted the general belief of his day that every state needs some kind of public or civil religion to bolster its claims to legitimacy. Atheists would have no incentive to obey the laws or adhere to the social compact which is at the basis of all government, apart from the temporal punishments which the civil authorities may inflict, and these are unlikely to prove sufficient. Furthermore it is education, passion, prejudice and stubbornness that influence how people act; good sense and argument have but little effect when in competition with these forces.[182] Religion can maintain and manipulate these non-rational factors in the service of civil order. Though government is concerned only with temporal rights, property and welfare and 'has nothing to do with religion', it needs a spiritual foundation and must be thought of as a 'natural and moral institution of God'.[183]

While Watts defended the notion of a public religion, he rejected the paraphernalia of an established or national church, even when prince and people are all of one faith. A union of church and state leads to a 'loss of all piety and goodness'.[184] The church of Christ, as found in New Testament times, needed no such support from the state. It 'is built on such a foundation, that it wants nothing of civil power to support it, besides the mere protection of the state, which every Christian society may require and expect in common with every other society of men'. Watts repudiated the claim of princes to call or preside over synods or determine forms of worship.[185] He was thus in certain respects a pluralist, arguing that the state should recognise different religious and cultural groups, extending recognition and protection to all of them, so long as they teach obedience to governments, avoid sedition and pray for the public welfare.[186] Churches should be expected to organise 'moral and civil lectures' and join in national days of prayer or of thanksgiving, though each should be free to conduct this worship in its own way.[187]

Watts argued that many non-Christian religions also are socially beneficial. Even idolatrous systems may teach that the gods punish the wicked, and these systems may thus provide a stable basis for civil government. However, 'the common acknowledgement of the one living and true God, both by princes and people, by the governors and the governed, is by far the best and surest bond of government and the common peace'.[188] Basically Watts argued that toleration is a matter not of truth, but of social utility. True religions can claim no more civil rights than false, for until the Last Judgment there is no supreme court to which appeal may be made. He went so far as to maintain that nothing should be imposed by Christian governors on heathen 'which may not also be counted reasonable and lawful for a heathen governor to impose upon Christian; because the religion of Christ makes no change in the nature of civil power'.[189] These advanced views were probably influenced by the ideas of Edmund Calamy (1671–1732).[190]

There was a remarkable consensus among liberal Anglicans, deists and Dissenters on the importance of religion in providing a solid basis for constitutional government and social order. God's government of the universe was a model for a 'balanced' constitutional monarchy. The Newtonian system supplied the general framework within which these men attempted to understand the universe. To a consideration of that system we now turn.

7

LEIBNIZ AND THE NEWTONIANS

When Pierre Simon Laplace (1749–1827), in his celebrated response to Bonaparte's question about the role of God in his system, replied that he found no need for that hypothesis, it was the God of Newton who was dismissed 'with costs' by the French scientist. The arbitrary God – the *Pantocrator* – still, however, played a central role in popular religion, in the preaching of George Whitefield and the poems of Isaac Watts – a God who rules with a nod and a frown; but he had quit the discourse of the natural sciences. In the political sphere, more ominously, the *Pantocrator* was transformed into the world historical leader. 'This morning', wrote Hegel to a friend, 'I saw the Emperor [Napoleon] – this world-soul – ride through the town. . . . It is a marvellous feeling to see such a personality, concentrated in one point, dominating the entire world from horseback.'[1]

In this chapter I shall consider the ascendancy of Newtonianism in the European mind during the eighteenth century, particularly in England and France. I shall then discuss the ideas of one of Newton's principal rivals, Leibniz, contrasting his position with that of Samuel Clarke, probably Newton's most influential and loyal disciple. Newton's own ideas I shall consider later.[2]

THE NEWTONIAN HEGEMONY

'Experiment', wrote Bolingbroke, 'is that pillar of fire, which can alone conduct us to the promised land; and they who lose sight of it, lose themselves in the dark wilds of imagination.' The eighteenth century was in many respects Newton's century. Though the details of his cosmological and mathematical theories needed refining, and his theology fell somewhat into the background, yet his model of the universe and his supposed[3] inductive method reigned supreme for thinkers of the period. Not only had 'our Newton' advanced natural knowledge further than any of his contemporaries, but this knowledge was based 'on the sure foundations of experiment, and geometry'.[4]

161

Nature and Nature's Laws lay hid in Night,
GOD said, *Let Newton be!* and all was light.[5]

Francis Bacon too was serenaded by the poets:

The great deliverer he, who, from the gloom
Of cloister'd monks, and jargon-teaching schools,
Led forth the true Philosophy, there long
Held in the magic chain of words and forms,
And definitions void.[6]

Not only did the empirical method of Newton, Locke and Bacon conquer the scientific mind, but it also determined the categories of discourse in economics, politics and religion.

The Whig oligarchy that ruled Britain from 1688 to the mid-eighteenth century, with only a short interlude during the reign of Queen Anne, was closely associated with liberal (or latitudinarian) clergy, who in turn were strongly influenced by Newtonian ideas. The political opposition, on the other hand, of both the 'left' and the 'right', often had other ecclesiastical links and cosmological ideas. The former were frequently deists, some of whom incorporated elements of Spinoza's philosophy into their religion.[7] The Tory opposition was divided between the Jacobites and those who accepted the Protestant succession. Many of these were high church Anglicans, strongly represented among the parish clergy, some of whom, like George Horne (1730–92), rejected Newtonian theories in favour of the ideas of John Hutchinson (1674–1737).[8] The high church nonjuror George Hickes told Roger North: 'It is their Newtonian philosophy which hath made not only so many Arians but theists.'[9] High Anglican writers were also suspicious of John Locke's philosophy, linking his empiricism with his Unitarian theology and his contractarian political theory.

The Newtonians

'The limited monarchy, whereby our liberties, rights and privileges are so well secured to us', wrote one of Newton's most devoted and imaginative followers, ' . . . seems to be a lively image of our [cosmic] system; and the happiness we enjoy under his present majesty's government, makes us sensible that attraction is now as universal in the political, as the philosophical world.'[10] Whig low churchmen were as keen as Tory high churchmen to maintain the divine analogy and thereby strengthen the Protestant succession. 'The inspired writers', declared William Wake (bishop of Lincoln and future archbishop of Canterbury) in 1715, 'warrant us to say of kings that they are gods: and we may thus far without flattery, ascribe that character to them, that they do not only derive their power from God, but ought to exercise it after the same manner.'[11]

In earlier chapters I have shown how the predominant image of God is closely related to the political and economic assumptions that eighteenth-century thinkers made. The divine architect, having constructed his universe, was – in general – prepared to let it run its course, according to a system of universal laws. God was, however, no absentee landlord. Not only did he actively keep the whole system moving, but he also intervened from time to time in human affairs to set things right; his general providence was supplemented by a special providence – the realm of nature by the ordinances of grace. Newton and his followers, of course, went further and asserted God's direct intervention even in the order of nature, to keep the stars from falling on top of each other. This was, indeed, as we shall see, the burden of Leibniz's criticisms in his celebrated correspondence with Samuel Clarke. In an analogical way, the social order was seen as a generally self-regulating mechanism which nevertheless needed to be kept in being by a strong government, whose principal purpose was the enforcement of the laws, particularly those concerning property. Occasional intervention beyond this was also generally regarded as legitimate in cases of emergency.

The world picture that Malthus and Smith, Paley and Butler inherited derived much of its strength from – and in certain respects reflected – the relatively stable political situation which was a feature of the mid-eighteenth century. It is a picture which is inspired by a number of developments in philosophy and in the natural sciences. The universe was being seen increasingly as a machine, and the mechanical image was transferred to the realm of political economy. Smith believed that the 'connections and dependencies' of the various parts implied a system. It is the object of the wise politician to remove the obstacles to its movement so that 'the several wheels of the machine of government be made to move with more harmony and smoothness, without grating upon one another or retarding one another's motions'.[12]

The popularity in England of the mechanical image of the universe was due largely to the influence of Newton and his followers, and much of this chapter will be concerned with their ideas, enunciated in dialogue with their critics. Robert Boyle (1627–91) had written that the universe is 'like a rare clock . . . where all things are so skilfully contrived, that the engine being once set a-moving, all things proceed according to the artificer's first design'.[13] Nevertheless Boyle, like Newton and his followers, firmly believed in a special providence. Boyle founded a series of lectures which became a principal channel for the propagation of natural theology. A procession of lecturers, beginning with Richard Bentley, master of Trinity College, Cambridge, set out to establish by reason the existence and attributes of God, and to refute atheism in its different forms. In many respects, however, these lectures raised more doubts than they settled, and Anthony

Collins the deist is reported as having stated that nobody doubted the existence of God until the Boyle lecturers set out to prove it.[14]

The Boyle lecturers were carefully chosen from the liberal churchmen of the time. The trustees and those they consulted were Whigs of a low church or latitudinarian persuasion, following closely the philosophy of Newton. They included Thomas Tenison (1636–1715) who succeeded Tillotson as archbishop of Canterbury in 1695, his successor William Wake (1657–1737), and the layman John Evelyn (1620–1706), who had been a close friend of Boyle. It is likely that Newton himself was consulted on the appointment of the early lecturers. The lectures were widely regarded as embodying a classic exposition of the Christian faith and were referred to in this way by writers as diverse as Samuel Johnson, Bolingbroke, Rousseau and d'Holbach. According to Margaret Jacob, the lectures provided justification for 'the pursuit of sober self-interest, for a Christianized capitalist ethic'.[15] Following Bentley, most of these lecturers saw religion as the 'cement of society' and believed that 'no community ever was or can be maintained, but upon the basis of religion'.[16]

The Newtonian system

To attain supremacy, Newton and his followers had to battle with such seventeenth-century philosophical giants as Descartes and Leibniz. The claim of the Newtonians was that while their own system was based on facts, their rivals built metaphysical castles in the air. This battle can be said to have culminated in the Leibniz-Clarke correspondence, which was abruptly terminated in 1716 by the former's death. Clarke, representing the Newtonians, defended a model of the universe as a machine, not only created and kept in being by God's will, but ruled by him – the machine needs occasional adjustment and is kept in motion by divine action. The mechanical analogy was important for these thinkers because it implied a belief in matter as inert and dead, without inherent power of movement. It thus represented a clear rejection of Spinozist pantheism, which was becoming influential in some English circles. The Newtonians, furthermore, believed in a God whose relationship with humankind is that of a king to his subjects or a master to his servants, and not merely of a creator to his creatures. This 'interventionist' God of the gaps was rejected by the German philosopher, in favour of a being who created and conserves a machine which operates according to laws that have been laid down from the beginning. Leibniz accepted the divine analogy in respect of God's relationship to the human race. We are subjects of a celestial prince, who rules according to established laws.

Newtonianism prevailed, but it was in some ways a pyrrhic victory.[17] While the scientific discoveries of Newton provided inspiration for workers in other disciplines, the interventionist God played a smaller and smaller part in the thinking of natural scientists. Newton had shown that beneath the apparently haphazard behaviour of the natural world lay a pattern, a system, of interconnected laws. While Newton's supposed inductive method triumphed, it was Leibniz's God who reigned, not only among deists but also among their orthodox opponents. For although the German polymath rejected the God of the gaps, filling in where science was unable to explain the phenomena of nature, he proclaimed the supernatural involvement of God in the realm of grace.

Voltaire and the *philosophes*

Not only did the Newtonian model dominate British thought, but, partly owing to the efforts of François-Marie Arouet (1694–1778), better known under his assumed name, Voltaire, it was supreme among the intellectuals of France in the second part of the eighteenth century. The Cartesian domination of French intellectual life was brought to an end by the early 1730s, when Leibniz's system became immensely popular.[18] Translations of Alexander Pope appeared from the mid-1730s on, and cosmic optimism became the order of the day. By the middle of the century, however, it was to Newton, Bacon and Locke that French intellectuals looked for inspiration. Voltaire's admiration for England was almost unbounded. He, and later *philosophes*, linked English empiricism with the relative political stability and tolerance of British constitutional monarchy, which they so revered. E. B. de Condillac (1715–80) looked to John Locke, while Jean le Rond d'Alembert (1717–83) in his 'Preliminary Discourse' to Diderot's *Encyclopédie* of 1751, wrote of 'The immortal Chancellor of England, Francis Bacon', whose bold style 'everywhere joined the most sublime images with the most rigorous precision'.[19] But it was Newton who 'appeared at last, and gave philosophy a form which apparently it is to keep', for he banished vague hypotheses and conjectures from physics.[20] These three heroes of the *philosophes* were the same as Thomas Jefferson's 'three immortals'.[21]

Voltaire thought the Leibnizian philosophy ignored evil and human sin and was altogether too optimistic, a fault shared with Bolingbroke, Shaftesbury and Pope.[22] A series of earthquakes, fires and floods reinforced a certain uneasiness among French Enlightenment thinkers, who questioned whether this was indeed the best of all possible worlds.[23] In 1738 Voltaire wrote *Eléments de la philosophie de Newton*, the last chapter of which he published separately in 1740 as an anti-Leibnizian tract (*Métaphysique de Newton*). Voltaire's famous verse on the Lisbon earthquake and his satirical essay *Candide* were, however, less an attack on Leibniz himself than on the alleged systematic formulation of his ideas in the works of Christian Wolff (1679–1754).[24] Voltaire denounced atheists and also rejected the concept of a great chain of being linking the lowest form of creation with God himself.

He saw it as an ideological justification for a hierarchical order in the church. There is, he insisted, an infinity between God and his creatures.[25]

Voltaire's God is the transcendent ruler of Newton, rather than the rational being accepted by many deists. God created the world because he chose to; creation was an act of God's will and not the necessary outcome of his rational nature.[26] A God subject to 'sufficient reason' is no longer self-determined, no longer an agent, no longer God.[27] God is transcendent, and all our language about him is of limited value. To describe the deity as just or unjust is as absurd as to speak of him as blue or square.[28] René Pomeau points out that the deism of Voltaire was by no means a merely negative or critical theology. His attacks on superstition were undertaken in order to protect the transcendence of God, who was not merely the architect of the universe, but a ruler whose subjects we are. He is 'the spirit pure and sovereign, but awfully remote and rather cold'.[29] Voltaire's conception of God, indeed, bears a remarkable similarity to that of Newton. Although God was seen as powerful, he was no cruel tyrant, but a father-figure. In an early poem the Frenchman addressed God: 'On te fait un tyran, en toi je cherche un père' (They make of you a tyran, in you I seek a father).

Voltaire spent many years urging his friends to 'écraser l'infâme' ('wipe out the scandal'). His particular attack was directed against organised religion, particularly in its Catholic form, rather than belief in God. His celebrated line 'Si Dieu n'existait pas, il faudrait inventer' (If God didn't exist, it would be necessary to invent him), was the sentiment by no means of a cynic, but of a believer in God who was convinced that such a belief is necessary for the well-being of the human race. He vehemently attacked the atheism of d'Holbach and pointed to the danger of unbelieving rulers. 'It is', he claimed, 'absolutely necessary for princes and people to have profoundly engraved on their minds the idea of a supreme being, creator, governor, rewarder and avenger.'[30] The existence of God was for Voltaire – as it was for Robespierre, with whom he shared more than is at first apparent – both true and useful. By the language he used it is clear that God is a 'political' figure. 'Voltaire's God', writes Peter Gay, 'was, like Voltaire's ideal king, kind rather than cruel.'[31] But he was also just and powerful.

Though a friend of aristocrats and an *habitué* of large houses, Voltaire was critical of the role of the French nobility, supporting *la thèse royale*, rather than *la thèse nobiliaire*. The kind of tolerance and civilised stability which Voltaire so admired in England would be realised in France only by destroying the feudal power of the nobility and the clergy. Being no democrat, he believed that the best way to bring this about is by the reforming activity of an enlightened but absolute monarch. He believed that 'the happy years of the monarchy were the last years of Henri IV, the years of Louis XIV and Louis XV, when these kings governed by themselves. The prince', he went on, 'must be the absolute master of all ecclesiastical regulations, without restriction.'[32]

Astronomical politics

The most open and undisguised attempt to present the Newtonian system as a political ideology can be found in the extraordinary work of Jean-Théophile Desaguliers (1683–1744), *The Newtonian System of the World the Best Model of Government*. The author was an Anglican priest of Huguenot origins who became in the years after 1717 'the guiding force in British Freemasonry'.[33] 'I have', he wrote in the 'Dedication',

> considered government as a phenomenon and looked upon that form of it to be most perfect, which did most nearly resemble the natural government of our system, according to the laws settled by the all-wise and almighty architect of the universe.[34]

Praising Newton for having presented facts and demonstrations, rather than suppositions, he exclaimed: 'how the mind is charmed with the beauty of the system'.[35] The author claimed to show how successive cosmic theories reflected the political system of their day. Of Pythagoras he wrote:

> What made the planets in such order move,
> He said was harmony and mutual love.
> The music of his spheres did represent
> That ancient harmony of government:
> When kings were not ambitious yet to gain
> Others' dominions, but their own maintain.
> When, to protect, they only bore the sway,
> And love, not fear, taught subjects to obey.[36]

But greed and lust for power reasserted its influence and

> Princes grew fond of arbitrary sway,
> And to each lawless passion giving way,
> Strove not to merit heaven but earth possessed,
> And crushed the people whom they should have blessed.
> Astronomy then took another face.[37]

The Ptolemaic astronomy reflected the political tyranny of the time and misrepresented the cosmic system. Eventually Copernicus restored order and consistency, and 'the sun became once more the central lord'. Only with 'Newton the unparalleled' was the full beauty of the cosmic order revealed, and an evolving system of ministerial government reflected the celestial order. Of the circulation of the planets around the sun Desaguliers wrote:

> Like ministers attending every glance,
> Six worlds sweep round his throne in mystic dance.
> He turns their motion from its devious course,
> And bends their orbits by attractive force.
> His power, coerced by laws, still leaves them free,

Directs but not destroys their liberty . . .
And reigning thus with limited command,
He holds a lasting sceptre in his hand.[38]

Desaguliers clearly believed that false cosmic systems are derived from corrupt political regimes and ideologies. The Newtonian system, by contrast, reflects the true cosmic order, and provides in its turn a pattern for the political order, largely realised in the Hanoverian limited monarchy.

SAMUEL CLARKE

Among the latitudinarian writers and preachers at the turn of the century Samuel Clarke (1675–1729) was outstanding. He was known as a disciple and confidant (so far as he had any) of the great Isaac Newton, who was regarded in early eighteenth-century England as having an all but unchallenged intellectual authority. Unlike his master, Clarke had never experienced the upheavals of the revolutionary years, and he was only thirteen at the time of the Glorious Revolution. Though the emphasis of his theology was rather different from Newton's – more settled and worldly, less apocalyptic – in philosophy and cosmology he was faithful to the Newtonian paradigm. It was Clarke who emerged in 1715 as the *porte-parole* of the Newtonians in the final round of the celebrated battle of giants between Newton and Leibniz.

Clarke was educated at Cambridge, where he fell under the sway of Newton. He wrote widely on issues of natural theology and gave the Boyle Lectures, *A Demonstration of the Being and Attributes of God*,[39] in 1704 and, in the following year, *A Discourse Concerning the Unchangeable Obligations of Natural Religion, and the Truth and Certainty of the Christian Revelation*. In 1709 he became Rector of St James's, Piccadilly, from where he published, in 1712, his controversial *Scripture-Doctrine of the Trinity*. He there set out biblical texts to ratify conclusions, apparently arrived at on the basis of Newtonian philosophy, that were critical of the generally accepted doctrine of the Trinity. He engaged in controversial correspondence with a number of thinkers, the most famous being Leibniz.

Whether Clarke can properly be called an Arian is doubtful. Newtonian Anglicans were eager to maintain the unity of the godhead. Polytheism, the master believed, would make science impossible. Clarke repudiated any notion of the Trinity as three identical units diferentiated only by their relationships. This was a position widely held in the Western church. He insisted that in the dynamic relations of the persons of the Trinity the Father has a certain priority as the source of all being. Clarke saw no reason to deny that

> not withstanding the unity of the divine nature, there may not co-exist
> with the first supreme cause, such excellent emanations from it, as

may themselves be really eternal, infinite and perfect, by a complete communication of the divine attributes in an incomprehensible manner: always excepting self-origination, self-existence, or absolute independency.[40]

In a discussion of the relationship of the Father to the Son, Clarke employed the analogy of the Father as a king, with his son administering the government. Certainly we see here what Leonard Hodgson called a 'relic of subordinationism', the idea of the *principium* of the Father who alone is unbegotten. But this is precisely the element that Hodgson finds in Augustine, Aquinas and Calvin.[41] None of these classic Christian writers would we want to call Arian. Daniel Waterland challenged the analogy on the ground that either the Son is not king, in which case he ought not to be called king, or he is king, in which case there are two kings. Clarke, always a slippery customer in debate, replied that the Son is called king (just as he is called God) in a different sense from the Father. He argued that 'the Father alone is, in the highest strict, proper and absolute sense, supreme over all'.[42] Nevertheless for these Newtonian thinkers Christ indeed rules; Newton used the classical term *Pantocrator* for the office of Christ. It is therefore misleading of Jonathan Clark to suggest that these supposedly Arian writers denied 'that Christ exercised divine authority'.[43]

As Hoadly later pointed out, Descartes was the supreme influence in Cambridge during the last two decades of the seventeenth century, despite the august presence of Newton himself at Trinity College. Clarke had played an important part in undermining the influence of Cartesianism in England. Instead of mounting a direct assault on the French philosopher, Clarke had translated into English the influential work of his disciple Rohault, *Traité de physique*. This he published in 1697, together with a series of annotations, written from a Newtonian standpoint, which effectively undermined the philosophical basis of Rohault's work. Later editions of this translation contained even more outspoken attacks on the Cartesian system.[44] Voltaire described 'the illustrious Dr Clarke' as 'a man of unswerving virtue and a gentle disposition' and included him with Newton, Locke and Leclerc as 'the greatest thinkers and finest writers of their age'; he was 'a real reasoning machine'.[45] On the question of proofs for God's existence, Voltaire told Tournemine that 'reading Dr Clarke's excellent book showed me my error, and I found in his demonstration a clarification I had been unable to obtain elsewhere'.[46]

God, government and gravity

Of Clarke's system of natural theology Leslie Stephen wrote: 'Like the tower of Babel, it was intended to reach heaven from the earth in defiance of any future deluge of infidelity.'[47] Clarke believed that the universe was created by a just and rational being, and that it operated according to general laws set by this being. Yet although God was rational, his creation of the universe must be seen as an act of will. The so-called 'course of nature', he maintained in his Boyle Lectures,

> truly and properly speaking, is nothing else but the will of God producing certain effects in a continued, regular, constant and uniform manner; which course or manner of acting, being in every moment perfectly arbitrary, is as easy to be altered at any time as to be preserved.[48]

In one of his sermons, however, Clarke made it clear that 'arbitrary' should be understood 'not in the sense that the tyrants of this world have occasioned that word to be used'. When applied to God it does not allow the possibility of injustice and unrighteous oppression. On earth, to govern by law and reason is totally opposed to governing according to absolute will or pleasure, 'while in heaven they are nothing but two different *names* of one and the same thing'.[49]

God was to be seen by no means as a remote and disinterested being, but as one intimately involved in the day-to-day government of the universe. Clarke cited the fact of gravitation as a demonstration that the world 'depends every moment on some superior being, for the preservation of its frame'.[50] Richard Bentley had also referred to gravitation in the first series of Boyle Lectures of 1692, and Newton had given guarded approval to the idea that 'the motions which the planets now have could not spring from any natural cause alone, but were impressed by an intelligent agent'.[51] Newton of course firmly rejected any idea that gravity should be seen as 'essential and inherent to matter', and remained agnostic about the cause of gravity. Clarke's position is entirely consistent with the master's own understanding of the way God acts in the world. The Newtonians were particularly sensitive to the accusation that the 'attraction' between bodies, of which Newton wrote, was any kind of occult force, an accusation made by the Cartesian mathematician Saurin among others.[52]

Although in Clarke's view the physical laws of nature can at any moment be altered by God, he does not appear to have held the same view about moral laws. A right action is one taken in agreement with the fitness and proportion of things, and these 'are eternal and in themselves absolutely unalterable'. This, however, is on the supposition that things exist, and exist 'in such a manner as they do', which 'depends entirely on the arbitrary will and good pleasure of God'.[53] Clarke attacked the Hobbist idea that right and wrong are determined simply by the commands of God and that absolute power is the source of legitimate authority. To suggest that good and evil are not prior to positive law is to see no law as better or worse than another and to treat all laws as 'arbitrary and tyrannical or frivolous and needless'.[54] It is noteworthy that by the beginning of the eighteenth century

Clarke was able to appeal to this as a *reductio ad absurdum*. In an earlier century positivists had effectively maintained this position.

Clarke insisted that, as in mathematics the addition of given numbers necessarily produces a certain sum,

> so in moral matters there are certain necessary and unalterable respects or relations of things, which have not their original from arbitrary and positive constitution, but are of eternal necessity in their own nature.

Things are not good because commanded by God; they are commanded by him because they are good. The idea of justice is 'antecedent to will and to all positive appointment'. If this is true on the ontological level, so is it on the epistemological. The best way to find out about the will of God is by deduction from his attributes.[55]

Was Clarke, then, saying that God is in some way constrained by the laws of a pre-existent nature? By no means. For God is the author of nature, and his act of creation was arbitrary and at his own good pleasure. He could have created a different universe but, having created this one, he acts and commands us to act in accordance with the laws which are congruent to its nature. The omnipotent creator and governor of the universe, who is accountable to none, 'thinks it no diminution of his power to make this *reason of things* the unalterable rule and law of all his own actions in the government of the world, and does nothing by his mere will and arbitrariness'.[56] Yet although the laws of God are not positive, they are *posited*. Things which are good are 'declared, confirmed and enforced by penalties', both in the divine and in the earthly dispensation.[57] Here we find Clarke adopting the idea of self-limitation, which was popular among puritans of a previous generation. God, like the sovereign people, is said to limit himself by the acceptance of constitutional limits to his power.

The universe guided and governed by God was, for Clarke, a model for a well-ordered polity. Kings should imitate 'the great King and Sovereign of the universe'.[58] Tyranny and injustice in the state are like

> the sun's forsaking that equal course, which now by diffusing gentle warmth and light cherishes and invigorates everything in a due proportion through the whole system; and on the contrary his burning up, by an irregular and disorderly motion, some of the orbs with insupportable heat, and leaving others to perish in extreme cold and darkness.[59]

Justice requires that virtue is rewarded and that evil is punished. No legitimate lawgiver 'can or ought to see his laws despised and dishonoured, without taking some means to vindicate the honour of them for the support and dignity of his own authority and government'.[60]

It is on this analogy that Clarke saw the sacrifice of Christ as a propitiation for sin. On his death-bed Samuel Johnson recommended the writings of Clarke to his physician on the ground that 'he is fullest on propitiatory sacrifice'.[61] As the civil ruler cannot merely ignore lawbreaking, so 'it becomes the supreme governor of the universe to vindicate the honour and authority of his laws and government, to give some evidences of his hatred and indignation against sin'.[62] God is indeed merciful and wishes to forgive human sin, but not at the cost of humans believing that sin is a trivial matter. His justice must be maintained. It is therefore fitting that God 'should appoint some sacrifice or expiation for sin, at the same time that he forgave the sinner upon his true repentance'.[63] Clarke here rejected the Socinian idea that sin is essentially to be seen as disobedience to the commands of an all-powerful monarch, which could simply be forgiven by his whim. Rather, he accepted the position maintained by Grotius that sin is essentially the breaking of a just law which must be in some way upheld.[64]

God has created a universe where individual interests are interwoven and 'the happiness of every particular person depends upon the welfare of the public'. There is a general harmony of interest. Clarke concluded not that everyone should therefore pursue his or her own interests, but that each might see the reasonableness of 'making it his principal business to do good to others'.[65] Contemporary British government he pictured as a system 'wherein nothing else is designed but the preserving of the public welfare and happiness'.[66]

Clarke was a Whig and like most of the Newtonians supported the Protestant succession and the limited monarchy. Although the good state should run according to a constitution and general laws, this did not mean that extrordinary situations might not demand exceptional action. The Glorious Revolution might be seen as analogical to those direct divine interventions in the universe which keep the system from collapsing. This was the position put forward by Samuel Clarke in his celebrated Boyle Lectures, and the basis from which he was to do battle with Leibniz.

LEIBNIZ

Gottfried Wilhelm Leibniz (1646–1716) was four years junior to Newton and experienced only the final two years of the Thirty Years War. His political and religious thought reflects the somewhat more peaceful and ordered situation which followed. He studied philosophy and law and by the age of twenty had earned his doctorate and written several original articles. He then began a varied career as diplomat, librarian, philosopher and engineer. Leibniz was a mathematician of ability and is now generally recognised as having discovered the differential calculus, somewhat later than, though independently of, Newton. Like the Englishman, he was proud of his nation and eager to maintain its reputation. Yet he had a vision of a federal Europe united under a just system of laws and accepting a common Christian faith. He set forth a pluralist vision where families would join together to make up clans, which in turn would form guilds and cities; 'these would enter into provinces, and all countries finally would stand under the church of God'.[67]

The unity of the Christian churches was for Leibniz an important means to the goal of a federal Europe. He worked for agreement between Reformed and Evangelical churches in Germany, and believed that the Church of England might be something of a bridge between them. He sponsored the publication in Germany of a Latin translation of Gilbert Burnet's *Exposition of the Thirty-Nine Articles*, and wrote a lengthy preface to the projected volume (which never appeared). Leibniz's view, as summarised by Paul Schrecker, was that, from the dogmatic as well as the liturgical point of view, the English church formed the most perfect Christian community, 'that which most closely approached the ideals of reason and justice, in conformity with the divine will'.[68]

Leibniz's thought represents a conscious reaction against the religious, political and legal positivism of the preceding era, exemplified in the writings of René Descartes and, more radically, in those of Thomas Hobbes. No longer was there the same supposed need for a single monolithic authority which could, by its very command, impose order on warring factions. Leibniz, like many English writers of the post-1688 years, can be seen as returning in some significant ways to the paradigm, assumed by medieval writers, of a universe governed by an eternal law according to which God the supreme governor rules. That part of the eternal law applicable to human life is the natural law which can be discovered by reason. Positive human laws are seen as subordinate to this natural law. As God acts in conformity with the eternal laws of justice, so ought the civil ruler to act in accordance with natural justice. 'Sovereigns', Leibniz proclaimed, 'are the images of the Divinity.'[69] True law is not the dictate of the sovereign but is dependent on the nature of things. Thus while Leibniz agreed with Bodin and Hobbes that there is an analogy between God and the king, he firmly rejected their understanding of the 'content' of the analogy. He criticised the positivist conception of sovereignty according to which these rulers – divine and human – were said to govern their respective realms.

God, like the good king, acts in accordance with reason and law, in such a way as to maximise the welfare of his subjects, and has brought into being the best of all possible worlds. Leibniz was constantly concerned to demonstrate the harmony and order which underlie the apparent confusion in the world; and as God is seen as continually bringing good out of evil, so the civil ruler is to conciliate and accommodate the potentially conflicting forces in the national and international sphere. God is the perfect bureaucrat, who foresees all eventualities and arranges things in advance for the best. In his celebrated *Theodicy* Leibniz attempted to show how an all-powerful and all-knowing God can also be thought of as benevolent, in the face of evil and suffering in the world.

Power, reason and law

God always acts according to reason, which requires the establishment of general laws. Even in the case of miracles, God does not act against the general laws of the universe, but 'departs from one law only for another law more applicable'.[70] So central to Leibniz's thought is the concept of law that his theology is a kind of divine jurisprudence.[71] Leibniz assailed Descartes and other positivists for suggesting that the laws of the universe are created simply by God's will and are thereby good. Rather, morality has its basis in nature: *moralitas ex natura est, non ex arbitrio divino.*[72] The works of God, as manifest in the world, he insisted, are really good in themselves, not simply because God has willed and made them. In his *Discourse on Metaphysics* he wrote:

> By saying that things are not good by any rule of goodness but by God's will alone, it seems to me that one unthinkingly destroys all love of God and all his glory. For why praise him for what he has done, if he would be equally praiseworthy in doing just the contrary? Where then will be his justice and his wisdom, if there only remains a certain despotic power, if will takes the place of reason, and if, according to the definition of tyrants, what pleases the most powerful is just by that alone?[73]

He went on to argue against Descartes that the laws of geometry, just like the laws of justice and perfection, are not a creation of God's will but consequences of his understanding.

Leibniz supported Bramhall in his attack on Hobbes's belief that God's absolute power is the source of his authority and the reason for our worship of him and our obligations to obey him. 'This opinion,' he maintained,

> which despoils God of all goodness and of all true justice, which represents him as a tyrant, wielding an absolute power, independent of all right and of all equity, and creating millions of creatures to be eternally unhappy, and this without any other aim than that of displaying his power, this opinion, I say, is capable of rendering men very evil; and if it were accepted no other Devil would be needed in the world.[74]

Drawing on the political analogy, then, Leibniz repudiated the idea that God, the divine ruler, is characterised by an unrestricted will to power – *Machtwille*. Although he denied that God's authority stems from his power, he did believe that God possesses 'infinite power'.[75] Later, in the *Monadologie* he characterised God in terms of power, knowledge and will.[76] He would have had little time for the fashionable twentieth-century idea of a powerless God, insisting that power is, in itself, a good – it is better, *ceteris paribus*, to possess it than not, for without power nothing can be achieved. Power is, however, a hypothetical good, because it is a necessary condition for the translation of intention into reality; it becomes a certain good only when it is united with wisdom and benevolence. Leibniz believed in strong government and claimed that in the dynamic of politics the absence of such government leads to tyranny: 'Nothing is more certain to bring about tyranny than this anarchy', he declared.[77] In the best state the ruler will have sufficient power to put his goodwill into effect.[78] As with God, so with the prince, power is a necessary instrument of action, and it might therefore be said that it all depends upon how that power is used. Yet, in the hands of a fallen race power itself can be dangerous. Anticipating the warnings of Lord Acton, he told Landgraf Ernst:

> As for the conscience of princes themselves, one could say that it is not power, but the bad use of power, which is worthy of blame, though this would not be sufficient. For though a prince be virtuous, he cannot answer for his successor, and one could say that he is wrong to establish or to keep a right which is so subject to corruption in hands other than his own, and which can become pernicious.[79]

In the *Monadologie*, Leibniz envisaged God, both as architect of all that is, and as monarch or prince of that 'city' comprising 'the assemblage of all minds'. God is on the one hand the designer or inventor of the 'machine' of the universe – the kingdom of efficient causes – and on the other, and more importantly, the ruler of the 'city of God', which is a universal monarchy, of final causes, made up of spiritual beings or 'minds'. There is a perfect harmony between the two kingdoms, 'the physical kingdom of nature and the moral kingdom of grace; that is to say between God as architect of the machine of the universe, and God as monarch of the divine city of minds'.[80] This means that things 'conduce to grace by the very ways of nature'.[81] Whereas all sentient beings (at least) have souls which are mirrors reflecting the universe of created things, humans have minds, which are the images of God himself, the author of nature, having a capacity to know the system of the universe and to imitate its divinely established patterns. Each mind is indeed 'a little divinity in its own department'.[82] Hence human minds are able to enter into 'a kind of society with God', who is related to them not only as a maker to his machine but also as 'a prince to his subject'.[83]

Leibniz wished to draw a clear distinction between the realms of nature and of grace, though he saw the former as operating in a way which harmonises with the requirements of the latter, so that 'sins carry their punishment with them by the order of nature, and by the mechanical structure of things itself'; the same applies with respect to rewards for virtuous actions.[84] God's justice involves punishment and reward. Leibniz

175

justified this assertion with reference to the political analogy. God must act in this way, 'for in a perfectly governed monarchy or city it is essential that there be no good action, internal or external, which does not have its proportional reward, and no bad one, which does not have its punishment'.[85] In both cases, civil and divine, the laws will be so designed that the appropriate punishment or reward follows automatically.[86] While the infliction of pain for the purpose of deterrence or prevention does not assume responsibility and freedom on the part of the subject, punishment based on 'the fitness of things, which demands a certain satisfaction for the expiation of an evil action' does.[87] This retributive punishment is generally the work of God, though it may be delegated to earthly rulers, so long as they act under the influence of reason and not passion. Leibniz criticised the Socinians for failing to recognise this retributive aspect of punishment and consequently for arguing that God's forgiveness requires no expiatory sacrifice on the part of Christ. Retributory justice gives satisfaction not only to the injured party but also, like a beautiful piece of music, to those who witness it. His appeal here is thus aesthetic more than ethical, like Adam Smith's admiration for the harmony of a well-organised society.[88]

Justice and goodness are determined not by arbitrary commands of superiors, as Hobbes and Pufendorf had contended, but by 'the eternal rules of wisdom and goodness, in men as well as in God'.[89] This latter phrase is significant. Leibniz insisted that the term 'justice' when applied to God is used in the same sense as when we apply it in human affairs. The difference between divine justice and human justice is a matter of degree. As with the truths of mathematics, justice is necessary and eternal.[90] This insistence on univocality lies at the very basis of Leibniz's theodicy. The question of vindicating God's justice is a matter of applying our own idea of justice to God. Leibniz's position on this question was similar to that of John Stuart Mill in his controversy with H. L. Mansel.[91] Yet, Leibniz observed, there may be occasions when we are unable, owing to our ignorance of the facts, to explain God's actions. He accordingly acquitted Calvin of the accusation of having denied the rationality and justice of God's election of the chosen; it is merely that the reasons are unknown to us;[92] and – in answer to Bayle – he stated that 'what appears injustice on the part of God . . . only appears so'.[93] By analogy he argued that the prince may have 'thoughts about which you know nothing'.[94]

In conformity with his principle of sufficient reason – that nothing happens without there being a sufficient reason to explain its occurrence – Leibniz denied that God could act haphazardly. God acts in conformity to his eternal nature, but nevertheless he does act. While the German philosopher attacked what he called the Socinian idea of God 'as a man who takes decisions according to the exigencies' and 'lives only from day to day',[95] he wished to retain some conception of God's will, as distinct from his nature. Like Hegel a century later, Leibniz contended that laws must be *posited*.

176

Indeed, Feuerbach later criticised him for succeeding only in 'restricting the demon of arbitrary will; he does not rid himself entirely of it'.[96]

Does the principle of sufficient reason imply that God is in some way unfree or constrained? Does free will play no part in divine action? Leibniz argued, first that these reasons incline without necessitating and, second, that any sort of necessity there might be is hypothetical. Having chosen to create Adam, God is assuredly bound to accept the consequences implied in the concept of Adam; but he was not obliged to create Adam at all. For Leibniz, the concept of Adam includes everything that can truly be predicated of him.[97] In choosing to create Adam, God chose, at the same time, everything that follows from this decision, in the same way as a wise prince, in choosing a general, realises that he is also choosing those subordinate officers whom he knows that the general will appoint. This destroys neither his power nor his liberty.[98] I shall return to this question of God's will when discussing the controversy with Clarke.

Leibniz, then, rejected any idea of God as 'an absolute prince employing despotic powers', but he was no republican or democrat.[99] He believed that in his day 'there is no prince so bad that it would not be better to live under him than in a democracy'.[100] His model of government is that of 'enlightened despotism', as it has come to be called. Leibniz thought of God as an absolute monarch possessing 'sovereign power' – though it is important to emphasise that he used the term 'sovereign' in a way quite different from Hobbes or, later, Austin, implying a merely relative superiority. The same is true with respect to the earthly monarch. Absolute government is not necessarily arbitrary. If it is absolute we mean that God or the monarch rules as king over his realm, sharing his authority with none and subject to the will of none. Arbitrary rule suggests government unrestricted by law; Leibniz repudiated this with respect to both divine and earthly rule. Arbitrary power, in contempt of law, could, he told Thomas Burnett, be exercised just as much by a popular assembly as by a monarch.[101] Leibniz was, thus, no democrat and rejected all ideas of popular sovereignty; he was in no sense a forerunner of Rousseau.

Welfare and bureaucracy

Though Leibniz doubted that human happiness was the sole aim of God in creating the world and that all else is absolutely to be subordinated to that end, he did maintain that God's principal aim in creating the world was the welfare of intelligent creatures and that it is therefore possible for people to live relatively happy lives here on earth. Furthermore, 'the end of everything is the practice of moral virtues for the public good, or (what is the same thing) for the glory of God'.[102] We ought always, indeed, to do what is right, but this can be made consistent with our happiness. How, he demanded, is disinterested love possible, 'independent of hope, of fear, and of regard for any question of utility?'. His reply was that 'the happiness of those whose happiness pleases us turns into our own happiness, since things which please us are desired for their own sake'.[103] If we love our fellow human beings we shall find our happiness in forwarding theirs. Even if there were no afterlife, men and women would find their true good in that interior harmony and serenity of spirit which come from acting justly. But this spiritual disposition is difficult to achieve, and God has given a motive more within our reach. He has revealed to us through our reason a knowledge of himself as 'the sovereign monarch of the universe whose government is the most perfect state that one can conceive, where nothing is neglected, where every hair on our head is counted, where all right becomes fact' and 'where it must be imprudent not to be just'.[104] We have here a picture of the universe governed by a celestial bureaucrat, whose administrative capabilities reach to the remotest corner of his realm.

God is concerned with the happiness of each individual, but this must not be allowed to disturb the universal harmony.[105] Leibniz's notion of 'compossibility', according to which certain goods are intrinsically incompatible and cannot co-exist in any possible universe, enables him to assert that even in the best of all possible worlds, the complete good of all individuals may be unrealisable.[106]

As J. M. Gabaude has observed, the God of Leibniz seeks to maximise welfare in his realm by obtaining the greatest possible variety, wealth and abundance at the lowest cost.[107] Moreover, the philosopher's belief in maximisation led him, at the cosmic level, to reject any idea of a vacuum existing in the universe. This would imply that God had wasted some of his resources by not using the whole of space. 'The theory of the vacuum', he told Queen Caroline, 'detracts from the perfections of God'.[108] He therefore rejected the Newtonian idea of gravity operating between bodies at a distance and claimed that the whole of space is full. One of the principal objects of civil – as of divine – government is the maximisation of welfare: 'The greatest amount of good and for the greatest possible number.'[109] The poor must be furnished with a means of earning their livelihood, agriculture be developed and vocational training organised. Conscience, duty, honour and interest unite in obliging the ruler to combat poverty in his realm, 'making his subjects happy'.[110]

Jon Elster, who surprisingly makes no reference to the work of Gabaude, has argued that Leibniz's God is modelled on the rational entrepreneur of an emerging capitalism, who aims at maximising net good rather than gross good, by a cost/benefit approach. This, Elster concedes, is an anticipation rather than a reflection of a capitalist system which was only nascent in Germany at this time, and he concedes that Leibniz's own activities and writings in the explicitly economic field are undertaken from a mercantilist viewpoint – static, protectionist and monetarist – rather than from the perspective of a dynamic and expansive capitalism. While also acknowledging that Leibniz's thinking had little if any effect on the development of economic thought, he defends his *lecture économique* of the German philosopher on the grounds that Leibniz himself employed economic analogies in his theological works.[111] Yet, as we have noted, the principal analogies employed by Leibniz were political rather than economic – of God as king or prince rather than entrepreneur or 'director' (a term sometimes used by Adam Smith) – and it is by no means clear that he thought of these monarchs as entrepreneurs. He certainly applied mathematical techniques (such as games theory) to theological problems (as he did to political problems) but he rarely applied explicitly economic techniques. A political reading of Leibniz is therefore more plausible than Elster's economic reading.

Patriotism and pluralism

Although, as we have noted, Leibniz was a patriot, he was nevertheless committed to the ideal of a federal Europe. Unlike England, which constituted a fairly unified political body with a strong central government, the continent of Europe was made up of many polities of differing sizes, as indeed was Germany itself. The only thing that could possibly hold these states together in peace and stability would be some kind of federal system, operating according to generally accepted laws, where authority is shared by the centre and the constituent states and where power is dispersed. He therefore dissented from the views of 'that sharp-witted Englishman Thomas Hobbes'. If we listen to him, Leibniz remarked, 'there will be nothing in our land but out-and-out anarchy'. In the England of the seventeenth century there was, perhaps, some plausibility in Hobbes's thesis, but the continental position was quite different. Any attempt to impose a single sovereign would lead to endless conflict. True, federal systems of government demand complicated legal arrangements, which inhibit efficiency. 'Hobbes's fallacy', he observed, 'lies in this, that he thinks things which can entail inconvenience should not be borne at all – which is foreign to the nature of human affairs'.[112] Many apologists of federal or pluralist political theories have recognised this. 'Where power is dispersed', remarked de Tocqueville, 'action is clearly hindered, but there is strength elsewhere.'[113]

Leibniz disliked the idea of a highly centralised system of government. He believed that the German system, with its many distinct principalities – a government 'by and with estates' – encouraged participation in public affairs more readily than states where there is 'one absolute head . . . by whose grace the rest must live'.[114] Like Hegel, in a later era, he combined respect for local and regional autonomy with a concern for the inability of the empire to defend itself against adversaries at home and from abroad. There were, however, cultural factors binding the German people together: 'The bond of language, customs, yes even that of common name unites men

179

in a very strong, even though invisible, fashion and makes them in a way relatives.'[115]

From what has already been said when discussing Leibniz's use of the analogy between God and the monarch, it will be clear that he opposed any suggestion that the government was above the law. He clearly rejected arbitrary power, that is, power which is directly opposed to the empire of reason. His attitude towards absolute power, that is power, unrestricted by institutional safeguards, is more ambivalent, and he had little sympathy for democracy.

Leibniz's system – physical, moral and political – was based on the ideas of law and of harmony. It was an elaborate attempt to restore something of the medieval synthesis, taking into account the philosophical, scientific and political developments which had occurred since. While it was impossible to go back to pre-Reformation conditions, he believed that Christendom could be reconstructed on the basis of an ecumenical church and a federal Europe. The distinctive features of the Leibnizian system and also those aspects which are shared with the ideas of the Newtonians, emerge vividly in the celebrated correspondence between Leibniz and Clarke.

Leibniz and Clarke

The German philosopher, keen to maintain his influence with his former pupil Caroline, Princess of Wales and wife of the future George II, maintained a correspondence with her on philosophical and theological matters. Caroline's friendship with Leibniz went back to her youth, when she stayed at the court of Frederick I in Berlin, and it continued after her marriage to the electoral prince of Hanover. On arriving in England, Caroline had approached Samuel Clarke asking that he translate Leibniz's *Theodicy* into English. This request was politely refused, as Caroline reported: 'Dr Clarke is too opposed to your opinions to do it.'[116]

In his letter to the princess of the same month Leibniz lamented the decline of natural religion in England and ascribed it partly to the influence of Newtonian ideas. In the first place he attacked Newton's observation that the universe is God's sensorium – that is, his faculty for perceiving things. If this were the case it would undermine the idea that all things are dependent on God. Clarke replied that Newton was here speaking metaphorically, and this particular issue was not pursued at great length. The principal point of conflict centred on the claim that Newton's picture of the universe, in which God must intervene to prevent the stars from falling on top of each other, implies that God is an imperfect workman. 'Nay, the machine of God's making, is so imperfect, according to these gentlemen; that he is obliged to clean it now and then by an extraordinary concourse, and even to mend it, as a clockmaker mends his work.'[117]

In his reply Clarke too lamented the decline in natural religion, but insisted that, so far from Newton's position encouraging this decline, it is the belief in the universe as a machine which continues to work without any support or assistance from outside that is materialistic and fatalistic, undermining natural religion by excluding God from the universe. He illustrated his position with a political analogy:

> If a king had a kingdom, wherein all things would continually go on without his government or interposition, or without his attending to and ordering what is done therein; it would be to him, merely a nominal kingdom; nor would he in reality deserve at all the title of king or governor. And as those men, who pretend that in an earthly government things may go on perfectly well without the king himself ordering or disposing of any thing, may reasonably be suspected that they would like very well to set the king aside: so whosoever contends, that the course of the world can go on without the continual direction of God, the supreme governor; his doctrine does in effect tend to exclude God out of the world.[118]

Atheism and anarchism, alleged Clarke, are the logical consequences of Leibniz's position.

The German philosopher took up the analogy. God sets things up at the beginning so well that further active intervention is unnecessary. He 'has foreseen everything; he has provided a remedy for every thing beforehand':

> God preserves every thing continually, and nothing can subsist without him. His kingdom therefore is not a nominal one. 'Tis just as if one should say that a king, who should originally have taken care to have his subjects so well-educated, and should, by his care in providing for their subsistence, preserve them so well in their fitness for their several stations . . . as that he should have no occasion ever to be amending any thing amongst them; would be only a nominal king.[119]

What had begun as a cosmological debate was thus being fought out in political terms.

Another related issue was raised in the discussion: whether Leibniz's principle of sufficient reason implies that God acts not by an inexplicable and arbitrary will, but according to reason. Clarke, with tongue in cheek, claimed to accept the principle of sufficient reason but went on: 'this sufficient reason is oft-times no other, than the mere will of God'. Leibniz countered with the claim that 'a mere will without any motive is a fiction'.[120] It is interesting to note, however, than in an earlier text Leibniz had held otherwise. In discussing why God created Adam, he replied that he chose to do the most perfect thing. In response to the further question why God chooses the most perfect thing, he replied because he wills to, 'so he wills because he willed to will and so on to infinity'.[121] This is, however, not typical of Leibniz's mature position, which is that stated in the *Theodicy* and in the correspondence with Clarke.

There are significant differences between the positions maintained by Leibniz and by Clarke about God and civil government. Clearly in the thought of the latter there is a stronger positive element, while in the ideas of Leibniz law plays a more prominent part. The moderate positivism of Clarke reflects a strong English tradition, manifest in the writings of Newton himself. Furthermore, Leibniz drew a clear and objective distinction between the realms of nature and of grace, while Clarke insisted that the course of nature is different from the supernatural action of God only from the human standpoint; intrinsically they were both instances of God's will being put into effect. A miracle for Leibniz is conceived as an event 'which can only occur through the power of the Creator, its reason not lying in the nature of created things'.[122] Thus Leibniz did not deny that God acts directly in the universe to bring about events which would not otherwise have occurred, though this miraculous action is in accordance with some divine law which we cannot comprehend. A miracle for Clarke is only such with respect to ourselves; or, to put it in another way, all events are miraculous, resulting from the direct or indirect exercise of the divine will. This, however, raises problems about human freedom which we need not enter here.[123]

Yet the differences between Clarke and Leibniz should not be exaggerated. Both acknowledged that the universe is governed by laws, and both believed that these laws can be discovered by empirical and mathematical techniques. Both, furthermore, opposed deism, asserting that God intervenes from time to time in mundane affairs, though Leibniz restricted these interventions to the realm of grace rather than of nature. Both were critical of the positivism of an earlier era, exemplified in the writings of Hobbes, and agreed that in the moral sphere at least the laws of justice are not the arbitrary dictates of a sovereign, divine or human, but are embedded in the nature of things. Again, Leibniz and Clarke accepted a general coincidence between self-interest and the common good. God has created a universe in which a moderate and enlightened pursuit of self-interest will generally maximise human happiness. Both thinkers were seeking to move away from earlier doctrines which derived law from command and right from will. Looking back on the controversy, as is the case with Butler and the deists, what impresses us is how many assumptions the contestants shared.

These philosophers, then, saw a close analogy between God and the state. If it is the case that God relates to the universe as a good king relates to his realm, which – we may ask – is the side of the analogy which is known, and which side is being illuminated? At times Leibniz says: you know how God governs the universe, this is how a king should rule his realm; at other times: you should 'envisage God as the sovereign monarch of the universe whose government is the most perfect state than one can conceive'. Undoubtedly he would say, as does the writer of the Epistle to the Ephesians with reference to his analogy between the relationship of Christ to the church and that of husband to wife, that each illuminates the other. Leibniz believed that his idea of authority was one which would make possible the kind of Germany and the kind of Europe he wished to see. Nevertheless one of the reasons he wished to see a federal Europe presided over by enlightened princes was that it mirrored a traditional concept of God which he endorsed.

Leibniz and the Newtonians can be seen, then, as reacting against a particular view of authority which may have been appropriate to a previous age, but which they found increasingly irrelevant to theirs.

Steven Shapin has suggested that one explanation for the heated controversy between Leibniz and the Newtonians, culminating in the Leibniz-Clarke correspondence, was that the Newtonians saw Leibniz as the source of radical political and religious ideas propagated in England by deist writers, like John Toland and Anthony Collins, who in turn backed the opposition 'country' Whigs. The Newtonians, who generally supported the 'court' Whigs, thus saw Leibniz's influence as strengthening the opposition party. Their attack on Leibniz is said to have been politically motivated.[124]

Yet there is little in common between the ideas of Leibniz and those of the English deists and radicals. Most deists were determinists, while Leibniz believed in free will. They were critical of orthodox Trinitarianism, he defended it. Most of them assailed ideas of special providence and particular divine 'intervention', while Leibniz allowed for it in the realm of grace. With respect to specifically political ideas, there is little trace of radicalism in Leibniz, who was himself very much a 'court' man. Toland, indeed, met Leibniz, as Shapin himself observes, but the meeting was cool, not to say hostile. Newtonians insisted that matter is inert, while Toland, in one of his works believed in matter as vital, an idea which tends towards atheism or at least pantheism. But this has nothing to do with Leibniz, who denounced the Newtonians for ascribing occult qualities to nature in their doctrines of gravity and the vacuum, a charge which they found offensive and took pains to rebut. Clarke and Leibniz each tried to embarrass the other by suggesting that, by implication or analogy, the position his opponent maintained had unacceptable consequences, but this was all part of the exercise.

Certainly Leibniz would have been glad to become court philosopher of George I and was alarmed at the growing influence of the Newtonians, especially Clarke, on Princess (later Queen) Caroline. The Newtonians for their part disliked Leibniz and were afraid that their own influence at court would decline if he were to come to London. These personal rivalries were indeed a factor in the conflict between Clarke and Leibniz, which must therefore be seen in the context of Hanoverian court politics,[125] but the role of deism and the country Whigs is clearly a red herring.

Margaret Jacob surely overstates the political intentions of the Boyle Lecturers by asserting that the natural religion of the latitudinarians, exemplified in the lectures, 'deals with religion almost solely as a device for curbing self-interest and maintaining social stability – in imitation of the Newtonian model of the universe'.[126] The Boyle Lecturers were interested in religion, natural and revealed, as stating the truth about God and the world, believing that such a truth would guide people towards a virtuous and godly life. The system they set forth did, to be sure, have social and political implications that were of a conservative tendency – though insofar as they promoted a 'Christianized capitalist ethic' their influence was progressive, not to say radical!

These modern critics tend to simplify unduly the complex relationship between political and religious discourse, ascribing to the partially hidden political motives and intentions (which undoubtedly existed) an undue importance, and reducing the explicit subject-matter of the debates to relative insignificance.

8

CONCLUSION

RELIGION AND POLITICS

The connections between politics and religion are many and varied. Religions are frequently manipulated by governments to strengthen their power, at both institutional and ideological levels. Governments attempt to bring churches under their control, in order to stifle criticism and recruit the support of church members. This is perhaps most blatant when there is a single 'established' church, as in England, Scotland or Scandinavian states since the Reformation, and in Tsarist Russia and contemporary Greece. This phenomenon also occurs in those Catholic countries where governments have reached a concordat with the Vatican, which gives certain privileges to the Roman Catholic church in exchange for granting powers to the government in the appointments of bishops and other matters.

If politicians have attempted to manipulate religion to their own advantage, ecclesiastics have been known to exploit political power to forward their peculiar interests. Calvinists in Geneva and in some of the American colonies did this with some success. Catholic 'centre' and Christian Democrat parties have also used political power to achieve religious ends. Many members of the Roman Catholic hierarchy gave support to Franco in Spain and Mussolini in Italy, who in turn exercised significant powers in church administration and appointments; whether government or hierarchy benefited more from these arrangements is hard to say. In the Khomeni regime in Iran the Muslim clergy played a dominant role in national politics and used their power to impose a strict system of Islamic law on the country.

Religious groups have sometimes attempted to exert pressure in the political realm by sponsoring or at least giving explicit support to sectarian political parties. This can be seen in the Roman Catholic church's backing of Christian Democrat parties in post-1945 Western Europe and Latin America; also when elements in the Dutch reformed churches sponsored the Christian Historical Party. Muslim 'fundamentalists' have also promoted particular parties in some North African and Middle Eastern states. These efforts have not been visited with conspicuous success, and their religious sponsors have often been faced with the dilemma of watering down their principles or accepting the role of a permanent opposition.

Religious institutions are frequently associated with ethnic and national movements; these together are able to strengthen national governments, but in other circumstances to challenge alien governments, constituting a centre around which patriotic opposition can gather. This has happened in Poland and Armenia at different periods of their history and also in a number of Slav countries. Muslim 'fundamentalists' and some extreme groups among orthodox Jews make determined efforts to dominate the political arena.[1] The manifest role played by the Jewish faith in the creation of the state of Israel and that played by Islam in the Algerian war of liberation hardly need mentioning.

Ideologies such as the divine right of kings and more generally the presumed duty of Christians to honour kings and governors (1 Peter 2:13–14) and to regard the powers that be as 'ordained by God' (Romans 13:1) – and therefore to be obeyed in all things – have played a significant role in political conflicts from time to time. Other passages from the Hebrew and Christian scriptures have, however, been used to inspire resistance to governments.

The enigmatic injunction of Jesus 'render to Caesar the things that are Caesar's and to God the things that are Gods' (Mark 12:17, and parallels) has sometimes been employed to justify the church's withdrawal from explicit involvement in politics. Yet the gospels are clear that Jesus was himself crucified by the Romans for claiming to be some kind of 'king'. Much of his trial, particularly in St John's account, is taken up with the question of kingship, and Jesus himself claimed that his kingship was not of this order of things (John 18:36). In the fourth gospel this dialogue reaches its climax in the words of the Jewish religious leaders 'We have no king but Caesar' (John 19:15), betraying, in a single phrase, the integrity of their nation's history. It is also significant that practically all Christian martyrs from the days of the apostles, through Thomas Becket and Thomas More, to Archbishops Luwum and Romero were killed not for their religious beliefs, but for their political commitments.

POLITICAL ETHICS

Christian moralists have appealed frequently to scripture to legitimate the particular policies they recommend. Others have purported to draw their political principles or programmes from particular Christian doctrines. For theologians like F. D. Maurice and Charles Gore creation and incarnation were central. Others, like Reinhold Niebuhr, have laid great emphasis on original sin. Communitarians point to the Trinitarian model. Radicals and conservatives alike have appealed to apocalyptic elements in the gospel to justify their own political commitments. Liberation theologians of Latin

America, and Black theologians from the United States, have taken the story of the exodus of the Jews from slavery in Egypt as a symbol of deliverance from oppression. Some have interpreted salvation in a purely political fashion, identifying the kingdom of heaven with national independence or with social revolution. Others have seen a more complex relationship between salvation and social reform or revolution. 'Earthly progress,' declared the Fathers of Vatican II, 'must be carefully distinguished from the growth of Christ's kingdom. Nevertheless, to the extent that the former can contribute to the better ordering of society, it is of vital concern to the kingdom of God.'[2]

Rarely, however, do religious moralists claim to derive the detailed political programmes they advocate *directly* from scripture, dogma or narrative. An influential group of Christians in the 1930s argued that any moral principles that could be deduced from Christian dogma were of a very general kind. They therefore attempted to elaborate 'middle axioms' which would mediate between general principles and detailed policies. Such thinkers as J. H. Oldham, John Bennett and William Temple advocated this method, but the axioms they discovered were not very different from the principles which their left-of-centre secular contemporaries advocated.[3]

The method used by these 'middle-axiom' theorists was essentially flawed. Most of them assumed that if only they could get their theology straight they could deduce true moral principles and with the aid of economists and other technicians develop valid middle axioms which could then be applied to the social and political world. They failed to acknowledge that theology itself develops in a political, economic and cultural context, and that it cannot be seen as a fixed rock upon which the rest of the moral and political structure can be built. Theology is not untainted by political assumptions and judgments; the very terms in which it has been thought out – the concepts and images used in dogma and worship – ineluctably reflect to some degree the social context in which they have developed. Theologians sometimes react against the political and social forces of the day and develop their ideas in a critical mode; but even then the language and images used are inevitably related to those employed in secular discourse. While it would be mistaken to conceive of doctrine and worship as determined by these social factors, the images and concepts employed in secular conversation do influence the formation and formulation of religious beliefs and practices.

CIVIL RELIGION

Some of the thinkers we have been discussing have advocated the creation or support of a 'civic religion' in order to bolster the legitimacy of the state. Notable among these has been Jean-Jacques Rousseau, but we have also come across the idea in Isaac Watts and in some of the Unitarian writers, like Richard Price. The idea of a civil religion also lies behind the thinking of some of the founding fathers of US independence. Certain images and concepts of God would be officially maintained by governments as being favourable to political authority and social stability. The idea of such a civic religion has often been linked to an established church. In other situations – for example the United States, where establishments of this kind are taboo – it has been seen as a detached collection of ceremonies and symbols, where a 'sacred' status is given to such institutions as the constitution or the flag. At times this civic religion is identified with some kind of liberal Protestant version of Christianity, at other times with 'rational religion' – though, as Rousseau realised, Christianity makes a particularly bad civil religion, subverting civic values.

It has recently been argued that the existence of a tolerant, secular, pluralist state may be strengthened by a civil religion or by a public philosophy and that secular humanism provides an inadequate ideological foundation for such a liberal state. Richard Neuhaus has maintained that the refusal to admit religion into 'the public square', undermines the liberal state.[4] This may be so; but that is very different from the acceptance of a civil religion or public philosophy, enjoying some kind of privileged position in the country. Those who advocate civil religion, though – like Rousseau and Thomas Arnold – they pare down religion to a minimum of dogma, are normally intolerant of those who reject it.[5]

While the Christian religion may truly provide a strong theological basis for a secular state, the history of the Christian churches shows quite conclusively that when they are politically powerful they cease to be even tolerant and attempt to use the instruments of the state to forward their own interests. From the time of Constantine onwards, Orthodox, Catholic and Protestant churches have all used political power to suppress rival religious bodies, attempting to impose their own forms of worship and doctrine on the population.

The development of liberty in the modern world occurred not because any religious group believed in liberty, but because rival groups were determined to secure freedom for themselves to assemble and worship. As J. N. Figgis observed, the religious groups which contributed most to the growth of civil liberty, the Jesuits and the Presbyterians, cared little for liberty as a general principle. 'Political liberty', he remarked, 'is the fruit of ecclesiastical animosities.'[6] The kind of Christian church likely to supply effective support for a secular or tolerant state[7] will be one which does not enjoy significant political power and regards itself as a committed minority group alongside many others. This position I have argued elsewhere.[8]

Civil religions and established churches tend to give a sacred status to civil institutions which is unnecessary for the maintenance of a political structure within which individuals and groups are free to pursue life in the way they choose. Such legitimations give to the state the power to dominate and to impose upon people some substantive pattern of life, rather than recognising their right to live their own life. As in Rousseau's political system, civil religion becomes a significant step in the direction of the total state.

TRANSPOSING IMAGES

I have tried in the above chapters to show how, in particular political contexts, these interactions between images of God and of the state have occurred. At times the dynamic role appears to have been played by the political images, which are openly introduced into religious rhetoric, necessarily bringing with them the connotations they have acquired in secular usage. A striking example is found in Isaac Watts's use of the term 'prime minister' to describe the role of the second (and sometimes the third) person of the Trinity. While it indeed carries with it ideas of power and activity, many would have seen in it a kind of subordinationism, which suggests Trinitarian unorthodoxy.

In seventeenth-century England kingship was probably the concept most frequently applied to God. This is not surprising, for it was the most hotly contested concept in political rhetoric. Political controversy centred on monarchy: the divine right of the king, the duty of passive obedience to the king, the prerogative of the king, the limits of royal power, the execution of the king, the restoration of the king and the right to depose the king. The Glorious Revolution, however, set the stage for a somewhat different understanding of government. The king must be seen as operating within a system, playing an important part but limited by generally recognised or legally established constraints. The political system was increasingly seen on the model of the cosmos. Newtonian conceptions of a law-governed universe, with only occasional intervention from God, became – often quite consciously, as in the extraordinary verse of Desaguliers – a paradigm for understanding the social and political order. God was seen increasingly as the governor of the universe, regulating the machine and occasionally putting it right. So the civil administration should see itself as regulating a system which basically runs according to laws. Bolingbroke argued against the use of the royal prerogative on the analogy of the alleged absence of miraculous interventions by God in the affairs of the universe.

While it would be jejune to think of the political as merely reflecting developments at the theologico-cosmological level, it is equally implausible to view theological developments as wholly dependent on changes in the social and political order. Each field of discourse borrowed images from the other. The cosmic order provided a convenient paradigm for the kind of constitutional monarchy which was evolving in England, while the growing stability of the political system gave feasibility to the rational theology of Tillotson and his followers. Progressive thinkers could still speak of God

189

as a king, so long as this meant a constitutional monarch, whose role is (in Hegel's words) to dot the 'i's and cross the 't's. This was the view of deists like Bolingbroke, but was hardly representative of the religious thought of eighteenth-century England. At the theological level, Butler's patient work gradually demolished the deists' system, though his own world-view had a good deal in common with theirs.

Popular religion of the second part of the century laid considerable emphasis on the particular providence of a living and active God. This was the God in whom the political preachers of the American colonies trusted, carrying over the beliefs and images of their puritan forebears into the age of Enlightenment. Robespierre, like Rousseau, rejected the image of God as a retired architect, affirming that the deity was active in the world, not only in the spiritual lives of individuals, but in the great events of human history. The 'interfering old impresario of cosmic conjuring tricks'[9] in whom Isaac Newton had believed retained his role, despite a century of 'rational religion'. Theologians like Clarke, Butler and Paley, coming from this very tradition, had, indeed, secured a modest but important space for his act.

The language used about God in prayer, worship, preaching and theological dialogue, frequently drawn from political discourse, will naturally influence the way people think of God. How they think of the one they worship will in turn affect their values. If they worship a being who is characterised above all by might, majesty, dominion and power, a monarch of unlimited strength governing by 'a nod and a frown', they will tend to admire and esteem these qualities in earthly matters. Such a religion can often unconsciously reinforce authoritarianism in political and domestic life. With respect to the latter, ideas of patriarchy have been powerful both in religion and in politics. I have generally avoided in this work a discussion of the role played by masculine images in these spheres.[10] Clearly the dominant role of the father over the children or the husband over the wife have been used to depict religious and political relationships. Having been imported into politics and religion, they then sustain and legitimate domestic autocracy.

IMAGES: TRUE AND FALSE

This book is concerned primarily with understanding the analogy between religious and political authority. My purpose is to see how images and concepts of God have been related to political rhetoric (and thereby to social structure and dynamics) at specific periods of history and in particular cultural contexts. I have tried to show a significant link between representations of God and of the state, with respect to the predominant images and concepts employed in particular cultural contexts. I have rejected the notion that there is a direct causal connection between religious and political analogies, suggesting a dialectical relationship, in which sometimes the political and sometimes the religious representation take priority.

It must always be remembered that the political and religious discourse current in a given situation is only partly influenced by contemporary experience; it is in large part inherited from the past. This is to say not that religious images and conceptual devices have been handed on within a hermetically sealed tradition uninfected by secular rhetoric, but that the influences and interactions between different modes of discourse – cosmic, constitutional, legal, artistic, architectural, religious, economic and cultural – must be viewed diachronically, and that no single mode always constitutes a base, an uncaused cause, an independent variable which determines the rest.

The enquiry of which this volume is a part is not primarily normative, but descriptive and analytical. Nevertheless normative questions will surely be asked, not only from the religious or theological standpoints, but also from the political: whether certain images of God and the state are true and others false, whether some have pernicious effects in religious or political life. This raises huge philosophical issues which I cannot attempt to deal with here. Many thinkers deny the possibility of anything like an objective truth which transcends the standpoint of the observer. The best we can hope for, it is alleged, is an intersubjective consensus on questions of truth. Some would go so far as to *define* truth in terms of consensus, – not of course an actual consensus but an 'ideal' consensus between rational beings in full possession of the 'facts'. Others again, though not defining truth in this way, would argue that consensus is a criterion of truth. This is not new. Shaftesbury observed how 'some modern zealots appear to have no better knowledge of truth, nor better manner of judging it, than by counting noses'.[11] Either we consult all noses, which has unacceptable consequences, as Bacon remarked,[12] or we count only rational well-shaped noses, which makes the criterion useless as a practical way of judging, for one of the best ways of assessing rationality is with reference to the beliefs people profess. The criterion is then a *petitio principii*. Nicholas Rescher has mounted a convincing argument against the acceptance of consensus as a satisfactory criterion of truth.[13]

It might be argued that although people commonly talk about some kind of objective truth with respect to beliefs (or propositions),[14] the same cannot be claimed in the case of images or metaphors. Perhaps the nearest we can come is to ask whether there is some criterion by which we may declare such images valid or appropriate. If so, what might this criterion be? People have asserted or assumed an analogy between divine and political authority, but is there any legitimate basis for this? Some writers have altogether rejected analogical reasoning in this matter; are they right?

When we speak of God as 'king' or 'governor', or when we address God in these terms, what are we saying? Are we making some kind of assertion about the way things are in reality? Are we making cognitive, 'reality-depicting', statements? Are we describing God, in some kind of indirect way? I have maintained elsewhere[15] that the political images used of God are essentially relational rather than descriptive. They say something about God's relationship to the world, and more specifically to humankind. I would insist that although these images and concepts are not descriptive of God, they do say something about 'what is the case', and are not merely to be thought of as pieces of advice about *how we ought to think* of our relationship with God. They do not merely say 'you should think of your relationship to God as good subjects think of their relationship to their monarch', but you should think in this way because that is in fact one of the ways God can properly be said to relate to his people.

The political analogies we use of God's relationship to the cosmos (like all our images and conceptions of God) are partial, at best, and of limited applicability. They are, furthermore, frequently ambiguous. When we speak of God as king, what kind of king are we thinking of? A good king certainly, but what is a good king like? Would it not, then, be better to translate the images into propositions about God and his relationship to the cosmos? Then we could more easily make judgments about the truth of what is being alleged. Some philosophers have taught and others have assumed that conceptual knowledge is superior to other supposed representations of reality, in the form of stories, myths, art, music, and so on. Some would also claim that the truth contained in these other representations can be expressed propositionally and that in order to judge which stories, myths, pictures, etc., are legitimate, the propositions which they imply or entail must be explicated and then assessed. When we speak of God as 'father' we are asserting a particular kind of relationship which God has with his people: it is a relationship of authority over them, of love for them, a relationship in which they therefore have a duty to obey and a right to trust God, a relationship which implies a mutual love and respect among humans, as is appropriate among brothers and sisters. All these propositions may then be appraised in the light of Christian doctrine, and the image therefore judged to be an appropriate and legitimate one.

This approach, however, is upside-down. Christian revelation is given first of all in non-propositional form. Jesus himself is the content of revelation. Theological propositions are secondary, both historically and logically. The doctrines of Christianity are assessed by their (always limited) success in reflecting in propositional form the meaning of the life, death and glorification of Christ. The story takes precedence over statements about the story. Christians think of Jesus himself as 'the truth' (John 14:6). Doctrinal statements are to be seen as prescribing limits within which the story may be elaborated.

As I have suggested, metaphors and other tropes can sometimes be ambiguous and therefore misleading. To refer to the state as a 'body', adopting an organic image, can suggest a degree of interdependence and integration which is wholly inappropriate to a political entity. It may also imply an equality resulting from this mutual dependence of the parts. The image may suggest to others a hierarchical and authoritarian organisation, with decision-making concentrated in the 'head'. Such images may thus need explication in propositional form or better be complemented by other images which combat the emphasis upon those aspects of the first image which are thought to be inappropriate.

The truth about God can never be fully stated in a set of propositions, nor indeed in images, metaphors and analogies. Theologians have often stressed the importance of balance. We must assert the supremacy of grace, but also the freedom of the person. We must see God as a rock and a shield as well as a friend and partner. It is not always easy to reconcile these propositions and images into a single consistent and coherent whole. But balance is of more importance than consistency. At times our discourse has the appearance of incoherence, particularly when stated in propositional form. Yet it may well be the case that propositions which seem to us incompatible are in fact compatible, though in a way we are unable to specify. This is not surprising when we consider that the subject-matter of theology is ultimately a mystery.

GOD'S REPUBLIC

A recent American writer has advocated replacing the symbol of the kingdom of God in Christian theology with that of God's federal republic. The former suggests a hierarchical and authoritarian system in which a hereditary king rules over his subjects, while the latter indicates a more co-operative arrangement in which men and women work together with each other and with God in the attainment of a just social order. This republican pattern has been increasingly adopted in family and in political life; it is argued that it might appropriately be incorporated into religious symbolism. The author, William Everett, relates his argument to the experience of the American colonial struggle for justice and eventually independence. 'The crucial separation of republicanism from kingship and monarchy was,' he writes, ' . . . based on the rise of a whole mercantile class for whom heredity, social unity, aristocratic honor, and ascribed inequalities clashed with the virtues of advancement according to merit and achievement, pluralism of interests, and systematic savings.'[16]

Although liturgical images of God's kingship may in truth conjure up notions of a medieval feudal court, or pictures of seventeenth-century absolutism, the reality is paradoxically that most kings and queens have today less power than presidents, relying on influence and advice rather than making executive decisions. Everett's suggestion that monarchy extends patriarchy into political life, and that 'kingship has become practically equated with sexism – that is, the exclusion of women from public life',[17] needs questioning. Queens have played a major part in world history. No woman in the United States has played a role as significant as that of Elizabeth I or Victoria in Britain or of Catherine in Russia. Monarchical images of God certainly need questioning, but it is not at all clear that the kingdom of God can adequately be replaced by God's federal republic, for the connotations of the latter are equally ambiguous. As Everett recognises, a reliance on the federal constitution – the new political god – risks falling into a bureaucratic legalism (a government not of men, but of lawyers) quite as unpleasant as monarchical rule.

Scripture and tradition contain many different images of God's relationship to the world and to humanity, but Christians are not restricted to these. It is the role of poets, hymn-writers and preachers to develop new images of God appropriate to the present day. These may be 'tested' in the worshipping life of the church and be subject to criticism from theologians. They may gain legitimacy by a general consensus that they validly represent the Christian faith. Although I have criticised the notion of 'consensus' as a criterion of truth in the world, the situation is different in the case of a specific society united by a common substantive purpose. There it is an indication of the group 'mind', particularly in the case of a body which claims a supernatural guidance – that the Holy Spirit will lead it into all truth.

IDEOLOGY OR UTOPIA

A further question to be considered is the role that images of God and the state play in the arguments of those who use them. When people speak of the state as a cosmos, or of God as a governor, is this in order to reinforce a position adopted on other grounds? Or do these images play a more constructive role, changing the way people think of God or the state and their own relationship with them? There are, I believe, many occasions when such images may play a utopian rather than an ideological role, to adopt Karl Mannheim's dichotomy. Adam Smith's tendency to think and speak of the state as a machine is not to be seen merely as a cynical attempt to justify, and persuade his contemporaries to adopt, political and economic policies of which he approved, but reflects a particular way of conceiving of the world in its relationship to its creator and governor, transferred to the social realm. Smith's beliefs in a general harmony of interest at the social level, with occasional interventions by government to maintain boundaries and facilitate the efficient working of the machine, would seem in part at least to have been influenced by or derived from the cosmic model. In other cases, perhaps that of Bolingbroke, the images seem frequently to have been manipulated as part of a rhetoric designed to strengthen the position of a particular group and to discredit opponents.

In the final part of this triptych I plan to show how tendencies that have emerged in the last three centuries find their roots in seventeenth-century life and thought. In particular I shall suggest that many modern political fallacies can be traced back to radically transcendent concepts of God on the one hand and to radically immanentist views of God on the other, vividly exemplified in the writings of Hobbes and Spinoza respectively. A Trinitarianism which emphasises the immanence of the transcendent God and the transcendence of the immanent God provides, by contrast, the model for a political order where freedom of individuals and groups is combined with active participation by people in social life at many different levels. It is a shame that Professor Leonard Hodgson did not live to extend his study of the Trinity into this important field.

9

THEOLOGICAL POSTSCRIPT

The principal purpose of this book is not prescriptive but descriptive and analytical. I attempt, rather, to shed light on 'what is going on'. There is a significant interrelationship between religion and politics, at the level of the analogy between divine and civil government. To put it another way, religious and theological discourse frequently borrows concepts and images from political rhetoric, while the language of politics contains many religious symbols. By illustrating this theme from different social contexts and historical periods it has, I believe, emerged that the relationship is a complex one and cannot properly be subject to reductionism. Neither political nor religious discourse can be reduced to a mere dependent variable.

One critic of the first volume observed that 'the recommendations for theological method are rather meagre'. In this postscript I try to illustrate how the theme of the book might have theological implications or consequences, in respect of two interconnected religious themes: prayer, and a Trinitarian image of God. To say that proper theological method depends on a dialogue between scripture and tradition on one hand and the contemporary context on the other is a truism. What is emphasised here is that this contemporary context ought to be one not simply of religious and philosophical ideas, but of economic, legal and political discourse, reflecting (more or less adequately) developments in political and, more generally, social dynamics.[1]

Much of the language used about God in the religions of the world is, and has been from early times, drawn from political rhetoric, while politics is frequently discussed in theological terms. At times, as in some theories of divine kingship, an *identity* has been asserted between gods and kings.[2] In Christian tradition, however, the relationship alleged between God and the king has been analogical, or metaphorical.[3] If this is so, it is not surprising to find not only that God is *referred* to in political images, but that he is also *addressed* in this mode. Forms of prayer are thus related to political discourse and thereby to political practice. It will be argued that petitionary prayer and civil petition have often assumed a remarkably similar structure

196

and function. In respect of both form and content, petitions to God and to political authorities have had much in common:

> Thou art coming to a King:
> Large petitions with thee bring;
> For his grace and power are such
> None can ever ask too much.

So runs a verse in the hymn of an eighteenth-century evangelical, John Newton. The practice of prayer is central to most religions and I shall argue that the language of prayer is often closely related to this political analogy.

PRAYER AND PETITION

Considering the major part which prayer plays in the life of most religious groups, Christian and non-Christian, it is surprising how little attention has been paid to the subject by classic writers on the sociology of religion, including Max Weber and Emile Durkheim. Modern sociologists seem to have done little to remedy the situation. In a book purporting to deal with the sociology of English religion, David Martin[4] states that 'faith in prayer is wide and deep even among agnostics', and proceeds to ignore it from then on, presumably on the well-established principle that if you can't count it, it doesn't count. In *A Sociological Yearbook of Religion* (edited successively by David Martin and by Michael Hill) there is not a single article on prayer in the first eight numbers.[5]

After briefly noting how Christian[6] writers have frequently appropriated political rhetoric, I shall look at some of the ways this analogy between God's relationship to the universe and the ruler's relation to his realm has been applied to the language of petitionary prayer.

Religious discourse and political rhetoric

In the Hebrew Psalms, the term 'king' is frequently applied to Yahweh, as it is in many Christian hymns, which picture Jesus as sharing in this kingship. The feast of the Ascension is a particular occasion for emphasising the royal analogy. The collect (set prayer) for the Sunday after Ascension Day in the Church of England's *Book of Common Prayer* (*BCP*) of 1661 begins: 'O God the King of glory, who hast exalted thine only Son Jesus Christ with great triumph unto thy kingdom in heaven.' The feast of Christ the King in the Roman Catholic church, instituted as late as 1925, has often been celebrated in a triumphalist mode. God is king, kings are gods; the civil sovereign is a 'mortal god', and God is an immortal king. Petitionary prayer may properly be directed to both God and the king. 'Because the King is a god upon earth', declared one Member of Parliament in 1610, 'I would answer him as we should answer God in heaven, that is with a prayer.'[7]

The analogy between divine and civil government has had enormous significance, both in the development of liturgical imagery and by providing a vocabulary for political discourse. While, on the one hand, the terms in which divine action has been described have frequently been taken from the rhetoric of politics and civil law, on the other many significant concepts of modern political theory find their primary reference in religion.[8]

The idea of power has played a major role in liturgical representations of God. As we shall see, it is frequently asserted in prayers. The notion of power is closely allied to that of kingship. The connotation of power is primarily social or political, rather than mechanical or cosmic; this is manifestly due to the fact that power is being ascribed to a personal or quasi-personal being.

Thomas Hobbes, whose elaboration of the analogy between God and the civil ruler is well known, was perfectly prepared to speak of praying to the king, accepting the propriety of such prayer when the request is limited to those things which are in the power of the king to grant. 'To pray to a king for such things as he is able to do for us', he wrote,

> though we prostrate ourselves before him, is but civil worship; because we acknowledge no other power in him, but human: but voluntarily to pray unto him for fair weather, or for any thing which God only can do for us, is divine worship, and idolatry.[9]

While exploiting to the full the analogy between God and the king, Hobbes was always quite clear that it is no more than an analogy and that there are vital differences between God and the king when seen univocally. The king, for example, derives his authority from consent, while God's authority is based on his absolute and irresistible power.

The mode of address

Petitionary prayer in its classic form, after addressing God and recalling some of his relevant properties or his gracious actions, goes on to request some benefit for the person petitioning or for a wider constituency. The mode of addressing God in prayer is normally connected to the nature of the request which is to follow. The 'Prayer for the King's Majesty' in the *BCP*, which is today still included in the Church of England liturgy, begins: 'O Lord our heavenly Father, high and mighty, King of kings, Lord of lords, the only Ruler of princes, who dost from thy throne behold all the dwellers upon earth . . .'. It goes on to pray that the current monarch may 'vanquish and overcome all her enemies'. The prayer for the British Empire, introduced in the 1927–8 proposed revision of the *BCP*, starts: 'Almighty God, who rulest in the kingdom of men, and hast given to our Sovereign Lord, King George, a great dominion in all parts of the earth . . .'.

I have already noted how frequently it is God's *power* that is emphasised

198

in these introductory phrases. Many Christian prayers have begun with the words 'Almighty and everlasting God'. Indeed half the 'collects' (prayers for seasons of the year) in the *BCP* address God as 'Almighty', and many of these are taken from the Roman liturgy (*Omnipotens et aeterne deus*). The term 'Almighty God' has, however, become so familiar that it almost seems to be part of God's name, but with modern translations of the liturgy the point is more starkly made. God is addressed in recent Roman Catholic translations as 'All-powerful God' and referred to as 'God of power and might' (in older translations of the *Sanctus* the words 'Lord God of hosts' had become so familiar that they no longer suggested to most worshippers the military analogy from which they were probably derived). Is power an aspect of God on which the church really wishes to lay such an emphasis? Civil petitions similarly make reference to the power of the king or Parliament to effect the desired change.

God is sometimes reminded of his promises and his acts of deliverance in the past, with the suggestion that failure to grant the petition will reflect badly on God's character or reputation! Some of the prayers of Moses recorded in the Hebrew scriptures adopt this tactic. The great leader reminded Yahweh (God) that if the people were allowed to die in the wilderness God's reputation among 'the nations' would suffer (Numbers 14:13–14)! Occasionally the petitioner expresses his unworthiness to ask, reminding us of the fact that in seventeenth-century England not everyone was permitted to make a petition to the Crown or Parliament. In the collect for the Twelfth Sunday after Trinity, God is requested to give us 'those good things which we are not worthy to ask, but through the merits and mediation of Jesus Christ.' In certain periods of history this sense of unworthiness to ask has led, as we shall see, to prayers being channelled through saints rather than being directly addressed to God. So petitions were sometimes presented by nobles and other patrons on behalf of the more humble petitioners.

The ending of collects, even in modern liturgical practice, tends to take a standard form. Of 110 or so collects for Sundays and major festivals in the Church of England Alternative Service Book (*ASB*) of 1980 about eighty end 'through Jesus Christ our Lord'. Of the thirty which vary from this pattern, twenty-six end with reference to Christ as 'reigning'. Only four make no reference to lordship or reigning (and two of these are on days where there is more than one collect). Certainly there is precedent for this emphasis in the New Testament, where *kyrios* is by far the most frequent way of referring to Jesus, but other terms are employed, including saviour (1 John 4:14), shepherd (Hebrews 13:20), high priest (Hebrews 4), lamb (Revelation 1:5), faithful witness (Revelation 1:5), chief cornerstone (Ephesians 2:20), teacher (John 1:49 and 20:16), servant (Philippians 2:7, Luke 22:27) and friend (John 15:15); the way the truth and the life (John 14:6); the light of the world (John 8:12). In the collects 'saviour' is used a few times but normally in conjunction with 'lord', only once on its own. The other terms are not used at all in the endings to *ASB* collects. Similarly formal and standardised endings to civil petitions became normal by the mid seventeenth-century.

Civil petitions in England

From time to time and in different social contexts petitioning has been a conspicuous feature of civic life, while at other times it has played a relatively modest role. 'Petitioning', writes Colin Leys, 'has a notably discontinuous history.' In England petitions to the king or to Parliament were rare before the year 1272. In the 1270s they had largely contained requests for the redress of individual grievances, and a high proportion of them came from great religious houses or from nobles. Gradually, however, the practice spread to the poorer classes. 'It was only in Edward I's reign,' writes John Maddicott,

> that petitions came to be presented in Parliament and that regular Parliaments came to provide regular opportunities for redress. This was a momentous innovation, for it meant that for the first time the voice of the aggrieved and of the socially insignificant could be heard at the centre of government.

By 1280 petitions were being presented in such numbers that they threatened to disrupt the work of king and council.[10]

It is interesting to see how petitions became fixed in liturgical form. Early on there was no set form of petition: in the sixty-one petitions presented in 1278, thirty-six different modes of address were adopted. Soon, however, the form of address became relatively fixed. By 1305, 120 of the 133 petitions presented began with the words 'A nostre seigneur le roy'. Again, in the Middle Ages there was no common ending to petitions, but by the beginning of the seventeenth century petitions normally concluded with the words 'and your petitioners shall (ever) pray' etc. From Richard II's time onwards, however, petitions became more elaborate with adjectives such as 'sage', 'haut', or 'puissant' applied to the persons addressed, and 'humble', 'pover' or 'obeissant' employed with respect to the petitioners themselves.[11] There is a clear parallel here with the way *ex tempore* prayers soon become formalised, if not in writing (as in Catholic forms of worship), then in the stylised rhetoric of evangelical prayer. Also successive revisions of the English *BCP* show increasingly elaborate and long-winded prayers being added to the more economical and concise prayers, which Cranmer frequently adapted from the Latin.

By the beginning of the seventeenth century a distinction had grown up between petitions of grace – requests to the king to exercise his prerogative in a particular way – and petitions of right, which 'told him what he must and must not do to his subjects'.[12] Perhaps the most celebrated petition in

English history was the so-called 'Petition of Right' presented, by the House of Commons to King Charles I. The king had arbitrarily imprisoned five knights for refusing to contribute to a forced loan in 1626–7, and had failed to respond to the writ of *habeas corpus*.[13] Rather than attempting legislative steps to prevent such arbitrary actions, which might well have led to a confrontation with the king, the Commons – on the advice of Sir Edward Coke, the constitutional lawyer – resolved on a petition, which appears to have had the desired effect.[14] Earlier, a 'bill' had been seen as a petition addressed to the monarch by Parliament, but by the seventeenth century bills were commonly distinguished from petitions.[15] Prior to the seventeenth century, petitions to the monarch or to Parliament were typically concerned with requests for the redress of particular grievances. In the period of the Civil War, however, they became increasing political in their demands.[16] As conflict between king and Parliament became more bitter, petitions gave way to 'remonstrances'.

The content of a petition can be offensive to the person or body receiving it, who may, indeed, not always be the one for whose eyes it is truly intended. It can be a way of addressing the general public or some specific sector of it; the petition may, in short, be a form of propaganda. Furthermore the collecting of signatures may be not simply a recording of current discontent, but a stimulation and encouragement of latent dissatisfactions. Radical groups, like the Levellers, were particularly keen on petitioning, not only as a way to air grievances and make demands for political reforms, but also as a method of organising support for their movement. The very process of soliciting signatures led to improved party organisation. The Levellers' petition of 1647 followed up and made more explicit the call for constitutional reform outlined in *A Remonstrance of Many Thousand Citizens* of July 1646. Directing their petition to the 'Supreme Authority' of the Commons, they first praised the House and 'thankfully acknowledged' the reforms which Parliament had already effected, by abolishing the High Commission, the Star Chamber and the Episcopacy. The petition went on to voice complaints and then to make thirteen demands.[17] Some of its organisers were imprisoned, leading to further petitions for their release.

While in the *form* of humble requests for action to be undertaken by a superior, petitions like prayers are often much more than this. They can contain explicit or implied criticisms of administrative incompetence or protests against social injustice and may, indeed, contain thinly veiled threats.[18] It is for this reason that soon after the restoration of the monarchy in 1660 a law was passed to restrict the right of petitioning the king or Parliament. The preamble to this bill ascribed 'the late unhappy wars, confusions and calamities' partly to 'the tumultuous and other disorderly soliciting and procuring of hands by private persons to petitions.' No petition could be signed by more than twenty persons or be presented by more than ten, unless it had approval from notables in the county or from civic officials in London.[19] Prayers too have at times played a subversive role in challenging divine inaction.

One of the most remarkable petitions of the seventeenth century was presented to the king in his chamber by seven bishops in 1687. King James II had issued a Declaration of Indulgence, which had the effect of undermining the power and privileges of the established church; this declaration was required to be read out in churches throughout the realm. The petition was, in effect, a protest, and the bishops were thrown into the Tower of London on the charge of seditious libel. This reaction to the bishops' petition, however, proved to be a nail in the king's coffin. The bishops were acquitted the following year and on the very day of their acquittal the invitation was sent to William of Orange to become king. The Bill of Rights of 1688 had affirmed that 'it is the right of subjects to petition the king and all commitments and prosecutions for such petitioning are illegal;'[20] but regulations were soon made for restricting the numbers allowed to present a petition. Despite the provisions of the Bill of Rights, a petition from the Grand Jury of Kent to the House of Commons in 1701 was deemed a breach of Parliamentary privilege, and those presenting it were imprisoned for the rest of the Parliamentary session.[21]

The petition has been a particularly salient feature of political life in times of rapid social and constitutional change, when well-established institutions have failed adequately to express popular discontents and demands. In the late seventeenth and early eighteenth centuries electoral corruption was widespread and party conflict was intense. Large numbers of petitions were presented protesting against electoral corruption. These were first dealt with by the whole House of Commons, but as party conflicts abated somewhat they were delegated to a committee of fifteen. These petitions were expensive to organise – often costing more than the election campaign itself – and gradually declined in importance during the first half of the eighteenth century.[22] Prayers too become more frequent and more urgent in times of national crisis or personal anxiety.

Petitions in a developing democracy

Petitions which made explicit political demands, however, became more frequent. A Middlesex petition of 1769, for example, requested the king to dissolve Parliament. Erskine May, indeed, traced 'the origin of the modern system of petitioning' to 1779–80.[23] Petitions multiplied until, by 1829, both Houses did little else than debate petitions. In 1831 the Commons took steps to restrict debates on public petitions.[24] Radical members of Parliament were exploiting the right to speak to petitions and could in this way claim more Parliamentary time than their numbers would warrant. In 1832 Sir Robert Peel proposed the setting-up of a select committee to consider the issue; it recommended a standing committee which would receive petitions and report to the Commons their 'general Prayer', together with a statement on the number of signatures.[25] By 1839 petitioners had effectively been gagged in Parliament. Nevertheless petitions continued to be presented, and in even greater numbers. In the five years ending 1831 there were 24,492 petitions to Parliament, while in the five years ending 1841 the figure was 70,369. In 1843 alone there were almost 43,000 petitions received by Parliament.[26] The most famous nineteenth-century petition was the monster petition presented by the Chartist movement in 1848, calling for widespread electoral and constitutional reforms. The Chartists failed, but a populist Tory, Benjamin Disraeli, defended the right to petition: 'I believe that at this moment the right of petition . . . is a more important and efficient right than has ever been enjoyed at any time by the people of England.'[27]

With the development of democracy and representative government in the late nineteenth century, petitions came to play a less important role in government. The extension of the franchise, the growth of the press, and the increasing power of political parties and pressure groups opened other channels for the expression of political discontent or for the airing of specific grievances. Today, however, petitions are still occasionally presented to Parliament by special interests. One and a quarter million signatures were collected in favour of unilateral nuclear disarmament, and over two million for a reduced tax on petrol.[28]

The growth of the modern state has led to an increasing volume of delegated legislation, by which a government minister is enabled under an act of Parliament to make detailed regulations by an Order in Council, which has the force of law. The normal way that members of Parliament are able to control these statutory instruments is by a form of petition to the monarch, known as a 'prayer'. In this motion they 'pray' that an Order in Council be made or, more frequently, that an Order already made by the minister be annulled.[29]

Prior to the Crown Proceedings Act, which came into force in 1948, it was impossible to enforce a contract or make legal claims against the monarch or against a government department. This was due to the doctrine that the king (like God) can do no wrong, and furthermore that he cannot be sued in his own courts. Accordingly it was necessary for the citizen who sought redress to petition for recovery of property or for compensation for breach of contract. Procedure governing this petition had been formulated in the Petitions of Right Act of 1860. It was necessary for the Crown (on advice from the Home Secretary, after receiving opinion from the Attorney General) to affix a *fiat justitia* to the petition. There was no appeal against the refusal of a *fiat*. Thus monarchs could receive a petition and act upon it only if they had already consented to do so, through one of their ministers.[30]

Prayers of the Anglican liturgy

Almost all the prayers in the Anglican *BCP* contain a petitionary element, and the litany includes calls for deliverance and makes specific requests, followed by the refrain 'We beseech thee to hear us, good Lord'. As is the case with civil petitions, many prayers, though formally addressed to God, are really directed to the congregation, reminding them or informing them of events, or reinforcing a certain ideology. Good examples of this are to be found in 'A Form of Prayer with Thanksgiving to be used yearly on the Fifth Day of November', on the anniversary of the Gunpowder Plot of 1605 and of the arrival of the Dutch Prince William of Orange in 1688:

> O Lord, who didst this day discover the snares of death that were laid for us, and didst wonderfully deliver us from the same; be thou still our mighty protector, and scatter our enemies that delight in blood: infatuate and defeat their counsels, abate their pride, assuage their malice and confound their devices. Strengthen the hands of our gracious sovereign King N., and all that are put in authority under him, with judgment and justice to cut off all such workers of iniquity as turn religion into rebellion and faith into faction, that they may never prevail against us, or triumph in the ruin of thy Church among us.

Or again:

> O God whose name is excellent in all the earth, and thy glory above the heavens, who on this day didst miraculously preserve our church and state from the secret contrivance and hellish malice of popish conspirators; and on this day didst begin to give us a mighty deliverance from the open tyranny and oppression of the same cruel and blood-thirsty enemies . . . we humbly pray that the devout sense of this thy repeated mercy may renew and increase in us a spirit of . . . peaceable submission and obedience to our gracious sovereign lord, King N.

These tirades are clearly directed less at God than at the worshippers! This would also be true of the (apocryphal?) Baptist prayer: 'We beseech thee to give us generous hearts so that we may contribute to the expenses of this church by putting our money into the collection box, which – as thou knowest – is at the back of the church on the right-hand side of the main door'!

Many of the Hebrew Psalms contain veiled protests and criticism of God for his inaction: 'How long, O Lord, will you utterly forsake me?', cried the psalmist.[31] 'Bestir yourself, awake to do me right';[32] 'Rouse yourself, O Lord, why do you sleep?'[33] This is the kind of thing that led one royalist, writing in the context of impending civil war, to maintain that just as we should approach God with true humility and with no hint of threat, in the same manner we should approach the king. We do not petition God

> with our hands upon our sword . . . but we go to him with self-deny-ing hearts and words, confessing his goodness and our own unworthiness, entreating him to take advantage of our necessities, to manifest his own free grace, and to cause his own glory to appear, and after such a manner and with such terms must we go unto our king.[34]

Providence and prayer

In answer to the argument that if God is loving and providential then prayer is unnecessary, the late seventeenth-century prelate William Sherlock draw help from domestic and civil analogies:

> If God governs the world with as great liberty and freedom as a wise and good man governs his family, or a prince governs his kingdoms, there is as much reason to pray to God as to offer up our petitions to our parents, or to our prince; for if we must receive all from God, what imaginable reason is there, that we should not ask everything from him?[35]

That God already knows what we want is again no reason for failing to pray, any more than civil petitions are unreasonable in analogous situations.[36] John Pym had already made the point in a Commons debate of 1621: 'Though I know we can propound nothing to His Majesty but that which he already knows, yet it is good sometimes to show a man's own thoughts to himself'.[37]

In order to illustrate the compatibility of divine benevolence and the effectiveness of prayer, the eighteenth-century theologian William Paley drew on the analogy of a civil petition to a benevolent ruler. How, he asked, can prayer affect the course of events? If God is good and powerful he will surely give what is best in each situation without being asked. If he is consistent in his benevolence how can he grant something to one person who prays for it while denying it to a person in similar circumstances who does not pray? Paley appealed to the political analogy. There is no reason to think that a good prince will not respond to the special requests of a subject giving him something which he might not have received if he had not requested it.[38]

The prince may grant a pardon or favour to this man, who by his very supplication had put himself in a frame of mind such that he could benefit from the gift, which he did not grant to another 'who was too proud, too lazy, or too busy, too indifferent whether he received it or not, or too insensible of the sovereign's absolute power to give or to withhold it, ever to ask for it'. Objection to the possibility of this kind of positive response by government (divine and civil) to petitions, Paley went on, unjustifiably assumes its power to be 'inexorable'. But wisdom and benevolence by no means require such inexorability.[39]

Saints and patrons

The conviction on the part of the petitioner that he or she is unworthy even to approach the ruler has led to the channelling of petitions through a more powerful or influential patron. Friedrich Heiler wrote:

> The feeling of the sublimity and majesty of the Supreme God may be so strong that man does not dare to come into direct intercourse with him. As he sometimes turns to his lord and chief not directly, but indirectly, by asking his lord's friends and servants to bring his situation before the throne, so also he addresses his prayer to the God of heaven not personally and directly, but invokes the lower divinities for their intercession.[40]

Peter Brown has shown how the martyr came to be seen in the fourth century as the *patronus* – 'the invisible, heavenly concomitant of the patronage exercised palpably on earth by the bishop'.[41] Brown quotes the prayer of a late fourth-century hymn-writer: 'And give me a companion, O King, a partner, a sacred messenger of sacred power, a messenger of prayer illumined by the divine light, a friend, a dispenser of noble gifts, a guard of my soul, a guard of my life, a guard over prayers, a guard over deeds.'[42] Brown suggests that it is one of the strengths of Christianity that it was able sensitively to replicate in a celestial mode the social experience of the late Roman empire. He warns, however, that this was a complex process; it was not merely a matter of a projection which served as an ideology for defending the *status quo*, but

> it enabled the Christian communities, by projecting a structure of clearly defined relationships onto the unseen world, to ask questions about the quality of relationships in their own society. . . . It was a form of piety exquisitely adapted to enable late-antique men to articulate and render manageable urgent, muffled debates on the nature of power in their own world, and to examine in the searching light of ideal relationships with ideal figures, the relation between power, mercy and justice as practised around them.[43]

Modern anthropologists have pointed to the way that in Catholic countries, like Malta, Spain and Ireland, the power of local patrons is reflected in (and influenced by?) the cult of the saints. 'There are,' writes Jeremy Boissevain,

> striking similarities between the uses of intermediaries in the religious field and the brokerage and patron-client relations which are particu-

larly strong in Catholic countries. The importance of intermediaries, especially in the political field, is summed up neatly in the proverb often quoted by Sicilians and Maltese: 'You can't get to heaven without the help of saints', for political patrons in both cultures are referred to as saints.[44]

In the Reformation and in succeeding centuries Protestants have generally opposed the emphasis on the mediatorial role of saints and have insisted that prayers be addressed to God only, through the one mediator Jesus Christ. This has accompanied the decline of private patronage in most Protestant countries and the centralising and bureaucratising of power in the hands of the state. One way this role was bureaucratised was in the office of colonial agent. The eighteenth-century American colonial assemblies appointed agents in London to represent their interests and to present petitions on their behalf. Such was Benjamin Franklin, whose role was to defend the interests of the Pennsylvania assembly against the position of the colonial governor.

John Donne, seventeenth-century poet and preacher, represented well the mediating position in the English church. While he was critical of the Protestant tendency to 'depopulate' heaven and recognised the ministry of angels and the prayers of the saints, he attacked the contemporary Roman Catholic practice. 'Why' he asked, using the military analogy, 'should I pray to S. George for victory, when I may go to the Lord of Hosts, Almighty God himself: or consult with a sergeant or corporal when I may go to the general?'[45]

Candidates for sainthood in the Roman Catholic church play an important role as channels for petitionary prayer. Their success in this enterprise is, indeed, seen as a consideration relevant to the 'cause' for their canonisation. 'Favours granted' are regularly listed in the newsletter of the Friends of Cardinal Newman, where we may find such 'favours' recorded:

> Thanks to praying to Cardinal Newman I have got a very important promotion in my work against all odds.

> My husband and I . . . took our grandchildren to see their mother in Denver, Colorado and hadn't the money to get back home. Our daughter took us to play Bingo. We said a prayer to Cardinal Newman to get help to return and we won 200 dollars. I am very grateful to Cardinal Newman.[46]

A miracle is, however, normally required to validate a person's claim to canonisation and ten thousand favours don't make a miracle.

War and peace

As we have noted earlier, military language has from time to time appeared in public prayer. Moses and the victorious Hebrews sang: 'The Lord is a man of war: the Lord is his name.'[47] The psalmist addressed Yahweh: 'it was you that delivered us from our enemies: and put our adversaries to confusion. . . . But now you have cast us off and brought us to shame: you go not out with our armies.'[48] In the post-Constantinian period the interests of the institutional church became to a considerable degree coterminous with those of the empire, and Christians sang of the *Vexilla regis* – the imperial standards or banners – going forward in company with the cross. God became the *Deus hostiae*, the Lord God of hosts. Feminine images of God which had featured in some early Syriac prayers and liturgies – particularly with reference to the Holy Spirit – were replaced with images of domination, military and political.[49] Ernst Kantorowicz records a few cases of Christ being pictured in the military uniform of the Roman emperor or in other military or quasi-military dress.[50] Frequently saints were portrayed in military uniform, while St Anthony of Padua (who died in 1231) was, in 1731, appointed admiral in the Spanish navy by Philip V. He also held a commission in the Brazilian army as captain; he was later raised to the rank of major and then lieutenant-colonel, with a monthly salary of 80,000 cruzeiros, which was actually paid to him – or rather to a Franciscan convent in Rio which received it on his behalf – until 1911.[51]

Prayers have, of course, always been made for peace and, when this fails, for victory in battle. One of the versicles for Morning and Evening Prayer of the *BCP*, 'Give peace in our time O Lord', receives the response 'Because there is none other that fighteth for us, but only thou, O God.' This response was changed in the 1927–8 revision, no doubt under the influence of the strongly pacifist and liberal sentiment of the time, to 'Because there is none other that ruleth the world, but only thou O God.' Pacifism did not, however, prevent the introduction of a prayer for victory, with the condition added 'if it be thy will'. One wit reflected on God's dilemma in time of war:

> God heard the embattled nations shout
> '*Gott straf England*' and 'God save the king';
> God this, God that and God the other thing.
> 'Good God,' said God, 'I've got my work cut out'!

Particularly in periods of civil conflict and disorder prayer is made for protection and peace. This is the theme of each of the four collects prescribed for daily use at Morning and Evening Prayer in the *BCP* which are still with us today. The morning prayers include the petition: 'defend us, thy humble servants, in all assaults of our enemies', and go on to beseech God that 'we fall into no sin, neither run into any kind of danger'. In the evening, worshippers pray for 'that peace which the world cannot give' and for protection against the 'perils and dangers of this night'. The post-Reformation conflicts are manifestly reflected in what might appear to us an almost paranoid concern with menacing threats and hazards; they contain not the trace of a concern for justice or liberty.

Function and form of petition

People of sixteenth- and seventeenth-century England looked to God for 'that peace which the world cannot give'. It is often the case that the predominant image of God in a given period of history is related to inadequacies in the contemporary political system. What the state can do only imperfectly God is able flawlessly to accomplish. It is in this context that we can recognise the God of caring and concern of nineteenth- and twentieth-century Western Europe, reflecting as he does the inadequacies of an under-funded welfare state.[52] When clergy and lay people are today given freedom in the liturgy to pray in their own words, we hear interminable lists of deserving cases, the hungry, homeless, depressed, lonely and sick, the oppressed, repressed, persecuted and mentally ill. All of these, we assume, should be relieved by state action but, owing to incompetence and inadequate resources or lack of bureaucratic resolve, actually receive less than their due. I am not for one moment suggesting that it is inappropriate to pray for such people. I merely point out that this predominant concern with welfare in contemporary prayer is not unrelated to perceived failures in the state welfare system and the apparent unwillingness among rich nations to redress the enormous disparities of wealth in the world.

There are thus significant analogies between civil petition and petitionary prayer. While in the form of humble requests, they both frequently contain protests and even threats. They call, indeed, for changes in current arrangements by the person or body thought capable of making such changes, but their mere formulation and presentation effect a modification in the *status quo*. Paley insisted that 'prayer has a natural tendency to amend the petitioner himself',[53] and the simple fact of a civil petition being organised serves to stimulate protest and to galvanise opposition to the powers that be. Other similarities include the inclination in certain social contexts to channel petitions and prayers through influential intermediaries, and the tendency for both prayers and petitions to assume a liturgical structure and form and to become increasingly verbose and obsequious.

Much modern prayer takes the form less of petitions to a king than of the expression of a need to share problems with a therapist, father or friend. Walter Rauschenbusch early this century called for images of God which reflect human co-operation with God in a common enterprise. His book *Prayers of the Social Awakening* includes prayer addressed to God as our 'chief fellow-worker'. In a 'Prayer for Working-men', God is referred to as 'Thou mightiest Worker in the universe, source of all strength and source of all unity'. A prayer for immigrants begins 'O thou great Champion of the outcast and the weak'.[54]

It would thus appear that the form and content of Christian prayer has been moulded to a considerable degree by the dominant images and concepts of civil power which have been entertained in different cultures and at different periods of history. This is, however, only one of the factors which have influenced the pattern of prayer. Traditions handed down from the past (many of which were themselves developed in dialogue with secular rhetoric in their formative years) have played a major part. Religious people are notoriously conservative with respect to their liturgy. I remember attending a large Anglo-Catholic church in Boston for the feast of Christ the King and noting the abundance of royalist imagery; as I remarked to a neighbour, no one would have guessed that the country had renounced monarchy over two centuries ago, or that Boston had played a major role in this transformation. There seemed to be little connection, in her mind, between tea party and last supper!

It would of course be wrong to see the religious rhetoric as being merely a dependent variable. The mode of address and approach to God adopted in prayer appear to have affected the way subjects have attempted to influence their rulers, particularly in the form of petition. Petitionary prayer has in fact been used as a precedent for the right to present civil petitions. This is vividly illustrated in a debate in the French National Assembly in 1791, when Le Chapelier, whose laws of the previous year had already deprived working people of the right of association, proposed that the right of petition should be restricted to 'active' citizens (i.e. property owners). An already disenfranchised class was to be divested of its principal means of peaceful protest. Maximilien Robespierre insisted that 'to present petitions is the imprescriptible right of every Frenchman'. Even in despotic regimes, he continued, this right was recognised, and – drawing on the religious analogy – he declared that even God himself 'listens to the cry of the unfortunate and the sinner'.[55] The relationship between prayer and petition is therefore a dialectical one, and attempts to generalise about determination and cause must be made with caution.

PRAYER AND PARTICIPATION

In the discussion of prayer and petition above I have assumed a particular relationship between ruler and subject, divine being and pray-er. In both cases we have a person or persons addressing petitions to a person or institution seen as over against them, and upon whom they are (at least formally) in an external relationship of dependence. For Christians, however, this is a very partial understanding of prayer. Developing a theme found in Paul's Epistle to the Romans, Christians have seen prayer as being taken up into a 'conversation' between the 'persons' of the Holy Trinity. The Spirit within and among us prays to the Father through the Son and in this way includes us in an ongoing divine process. Thus prayer is to be seen

210

not only as our shouting across an almost unbridgeable gulf to a being on the other side, but as a participation in the divine life.

In an analogous way, various political theorists from early times have seen government not in terms of a strict dichotomy between ruler and ruled, but as involving partnership in a common enterprise. 'Subjects' are replaced by 'citizens', who not only have certain rights which the government must respect, and certain duties owed in return, but actively participate in the process of government. The Greek city state (*polis*) embodied certain of these principles, as did Roman conceptions of government at particular periods. Citizens were indeed a minority of the population (and excluded women, children, slaves and most foreigners), but they were expected to play an active part in the legislative, administrative and judicial life of the state. Thinkers in seventeenth-century Europe developed some of these themes, which have continually surfaced in politics up to our own day. As with the model of prayer as participation, there is an attempt to overcome the alienation inherent in the 'petition' model and to emphasise the possibility of a relationship not only of interdependence but of active participation. Similarly, in place of a legislature composed of elected 'representatives' it is possible to conceive of a body whose members are selected (rather as juries are) by lot. This would encourage a real sense of participation, and there is little evidence to suggest that they would act in a more foolish or irresponsible way than contemporary legislators.

Sharing the Divine nature

God became human, St Athanasius affirmed, in order that humans might become divine. In saying this he was developing certain themes in the New Testament which emphasised the Christian's identification with Christ in his sufferings (2 Corinthians 1:7), death and resurrection (Romans 6:1–8), that they might become 'partakers of the divine nature'(2 Peter 1:4). Certain Protestant writers have viewed this trend with suspicion. Such a participatory emphasis seems to conflict with the Calvinist focus on divine sovereignty and with Lutheran ideas of *simul justus et peccator* (that the believer is justified but at the same time remains a sinner). Other Protestants, however, especially from 'enthusiastic' and radical sects, would seem to share the Catholic and Orthodox perspective on this matter, though they draw somewhat different conclusions.

This sharing in the life of God is seen not only as future hope, but also as present reality, proleptically made concrete in prayer and sacrament. In a celebrated chapter of his Epistle to the Romans, St Paul conceived of prayer in a participatory mode:

> You are not in the flesh, you are in the Spirit, if the Spirit of God really dwells in you . . . . When we cry 'Abba! Father!' it is the Spirit himself

bearing witness with our spirit that we are children of God . . . .
Likewise the Spirit helps us in our weakness; for we do not know how
to pray as we ought, but the Spirit himself intercedes for us with sighs
too deep for words.

(Romans 8:9, 15–16, and 26)

Commenting on this theme, Michael Ramsey wrote that the Holy Spirit
prays within Christians; prayer and worship are like a stream – flowing
from God to humankind and returning through Christ – into which Christians cast themselves.[56] He criticised Heiler's categorising of prayer into
petitionary and mystical, arguing that Christian prayer is essentially *liturgical*, involving believers in the activity and life of the Trinity. Heiler had
referred to 'the free spontaneous petitionary prayer of the natural man' as
exhibiting 'the prototype of all prayer', but, to be fair to him, he insisted in
the 'Preface to the English Edition' of his classical work that prayer 'is not
man's work, or discovery or achievement; but *God's* work in man'.[57] The
language he used, however, suggests that he is more concerned with
avoiding a Lutheran taboo than in affirming a Catholic or Orthodox understanding.

Charles Wesley, with his strong Methodist emphasis on sanctification,
recognised the significance of this aspect of prayer when he wrote:

> Greater than ancient Israel, we
> With open face his glory see,
> and God more intimately nigh
> Doth now our every want supply.
> > The Spirit of his Son imparts,
> > And prays himself in all our hearts.

and again:

> Spirit of interceding grace,
> I know not what or how to pray;
> Assist my utter helplessness,
> The power into my heart convey,
> > That God, acknowledging thy groan,
> > May answer in my prayer his own.[58]

A recent report of the Doctrine Commission of the Church of England,
entitled *We Believe in God*, devotes a chapter to this theme. In prayer we are
'graciously caught up in a divine conversation'.[59]

It should be emphasised that this notion of prayer as participation in the
life of the Holy Trinity sees the individual Christian and the body of
believers not as passive, but as actively joining in a process of transformation. St Paul said that the apostles were 'workers together' with God (2

Corinthians 6:1), and Jesus insisted that his disciples were to see themselves not as servants but as friends (John 15:15).

Political participation

By analogy, political activity has sometimes been seen not in terms of ruler and ruled, but as an enterprise requiring the active participation of citizens in 'the decision-making process'. Democracy has been understood by many writers as implying such mass incorporation into the governmental process. The possibility of such popular involvement in politics was, however, called into question by a series of writers at the end of the nineteenth century. In the large-scale organisation of a modern state, it was alleged, real power will inevitably be concentrated in the hands of a small elite. People may talk of democracy and 'power to the people' but, declared Sir Henry Maine, 'Aristocracy rises on the decay of aristocracy, and the world makes progress by one privileged class pushing another from its seat.'[60] While in one system the elite will be made up of military officers, in another it will be the wealthy who control power. In a democracy, pronounced Sir James Fitzjames Stephen, it will be the party managers and wire-pullers who will constitute the power elite. The result of cutting up political power into little bits 'is simply that the man who can sweep the greatest number of them into one heap will govern the rest'.[61] Arthur Balfour and a number of Italian and German theorists developed these ideas.[62] Some even wrote of an 'iron law of oligarchy'.[63]

Most of these writers were not merely describing the supposed laws of political sociology, but went on to welcome the fact that power is always in the hands of an elite. Stephen told Lady Grant Duff that when she and her husband returned to England they 'will be of the same illiberal creed as I and . . . will perceive that if a great country is delivered over to be governed by mechanics and labourers it will not long continue to be a great country.[64]

Building on these ideas, Joseph Schumpeter urged in 1942 a revision in democratic theory. The 'classical' theory of democracy, which demands extensive popular participation in government, must be replaced by a notion of representative democracy which requires merely that the population (or a good proportion of it) engage periodically in the election of representatives. It will thus have the opportunity to replace them from time to time if they perform badly. This, he asserted, is the only notion of democracy which has any prospects in the modern world.[65] It is a conception of government well summarised by Max Weber:

> In a democracy the people choose a leader in whom they trust. Then the chosen leader says, 'Now shut up and obey me.' People and party are then no longer free to interfere in his business . . .. Later the people

213

can sit in judgment. If the leader has made mistakes – to the gallows with him.[66]

This conception of democracy was modified by later theorists to allow for interest and pressure groups playing an active role in government; they consequently asserted that political power (in a democracy at least) was in the hands of a number of different and often competing elites.[67]

None of these political theorists, in the view of their critics, permitted a genuine participation in politics by the mass of the people. In the early 1970s a large number of books and articles appeared on the subject of political participation, in the wake of the 1968 disturbances in many Western countries which had manifested a popular discontent with the political system, particularly among the young.[68] Even General de Gaulle called for a participatory democracy. Such participation involved a 'sharing in the framing and/or execution of public policies'.[69] But is such participation possible in a large modern state? Do people want it? 'Only a small minority of the population wish to participate', declared the Labour Party revisionist Anthony Crosland. Most people want to enjoy life with their families, watch football and cultivate their gardens. Who wants 'a busy bustling society in which everyone is politically active'?[70]

The analogy between prayer as participation in the life of God, and political participation does not necessarily require active involvement of the whole population in the affairs of the central government. Participation is possible only 'where there is a strong development of local and corporate societies, and real self-government. The mere fact of a system of so-called representatives will not secure freedom.'[71] Significant involvement of workers in the affairs of their industry has normally led to greater commitment to the job and to a greater sense of dignity. 'There is hardly a study in the entire field', writes Paul Blumberg, 'which fails to demonstrate that satisfaction in work is enhanced or that other generally acknowledged beneficial consequences accrue from a genuine increase in workers' decision-making power'.[72] A genuine application of the principle of subsidiarity – according to which action is taken by the smallest unit which can properly perform the task – would lead to a real possibility for participation of people in the decisions which affect them most closely.

A significant difference between the notion of participation in the life of God through prayer or worship and the kind of political (or rather social) participation I have been describing here is, of course, that the former, unlike the latter, must be considered as an end in itself. Social participation in decision-making is, by contrast, valuable because such involvement leads to greater freedom and responsibility, resulting in the development of human character and personality.

A social dynamic in which people seriously participate, at different levels, in making decisions which affect themselves, their families, their workmates and friends is a healthy one, and by no means falls under the legitimate critique of Anthony Crosland, referred to above. Indeed, if the state ceases to pursue some kind of substantive common good, and sees itself as providing a structure within which groups of different kinds can pursue those common ends which their members choose, mass participation at the state level will cease to be of crucial importance. Citizenship will then involve ensuring that the state institutes and preserves a system of laws which equitably maintains in being a structure within which voluntary, local, regional and functional groups may flourish.

St Paul told his readers at Philippi that 'our *politeuma* is in heaven' (Philippians 3:20), and this is normally translated as our 'citizenship' or 'commonwealth'. The Authorised Version, however, uses the term 'conversation'. The participation envisaged, both in prayer and in social life, might indeed be seen as joining a 'conversation', but it is one which is always threatening to become a dispute. This might appear a truism with respect to social and political life in a fallen world. There will be conflicts of interest between the various groups themselves, conflicts between groups and the state, conflicts between individuals and the groups to which they belong. The object of politics should, however, be not the elimination of conflict, but the containing of it. But with respect to the life of the 'persons' of the Trinity, surely there is harmony and perpetual peace, with no place for conflict in the life of the godhead. The question of conflict in theology and in politics will be the subject of our final section.

TRINITY AND CONFLICT[73]

The prophet's condemnation of those who cry 'peace, peace, where there is no peace' (Jeremiah 6:14), might apply to theologians as much as to politicians. With respect to their concept of God, there is a manifest tendency among them to avoid, at all costs, any recognition of conflict. Trinitarian theology – expressing the inexpressible – relies heavily on analogy, metaphor and image. The 'social' image of the Trinity is increasingly popular in contemporary theology, emphasising as it does the distinctness of the three 'persons', to the point, in the view of its critics, of tritheism. We are urged to think of God as a 'society' – but what kind of society or community? A good society, undoubtedly. But what is a good society like? What degree of unity is appropriate to a human social group? Must it have 'a common mind'? How much plurality is permissible? Is harmony a prerequisite? I wish here to suggest that our commonly accepted judgments about the secular order have influenced, and indeed distorted, our Trinitarian theology, by eliminating totally the idea of conflict from the 'internal' life of the godhead.

God is the one we worship, and we rightly resist ascribing to God any imperfection. Secular dislike of change, going back to the Greek philosophers – who appear to have enjoyed a fairly comfortable way of life – led in the early church to a conviction that as change is bad, ideas of God must be purged of any suggestion of change; hence the dogma of divine immutability (and patristic exegetical acrobatics to explain the Hebrew scriptures). Again, perfection was thought to imply self-sufficiency. The good human being is autonomous, the good *polis* is autarkic, so all traces of dependence must be purged from God; hence the dogma of divine impassibility, and the insistence that Christ suffered only in his human nature. In an era of rapid social change, when individuals, groups and nations are recognised as being interdependent, both these dogmas have been widely challenged. Elsewhere I have suggested that this change, pioneered among theologians in the United States, is not unrelated to a long experience of interdependence between the states of the union.[74] The reassessment of change and of dependence in the secular world has thus liberated theologians from inadequate (and actually unscriptural) images of God. But conflict is still seen as unequivocally bad, and a consensus model has dominated Trinitarian thinking.

Political theologians since Eric Peterson[75] have, indeed, pointed out how monotheism may be used as a legitimation for imperialism or even totalitarianism and it is sometimes asserted that Trinitarianism (on the social analogy) is a guarantee of liberalism and democracy. There is, however, in a writer like Jürgen Moltmann, a curious ambivalence here, centred on the notion of democracy. On the one hand he calls for the 'desacralisation' of politics, and on the other spends a good deal of effort beatifying democracy.[76] Leonardo Boff also adopts an idealist model of the relationship between theology and politics, suggesting that political and ecclesiastical authoritarianism 'could be thoroughly corrected by a return to [the image of] the triune God', and that 'dictators and tyrants could never draw arguments to legitimize their absolutism from the God–Trinity'.[77] A military junta might very well do this, or the triumvirate that ruled Venice in the late sixteenth century and constituted, in Lord Acton's words, 'a frightful despotism'.[78] Boff goes on to assert that the divine Trinity 'serves as a model for an integrated society' that is 'without conflicts and that consists of an interplay of relationships in which the common good is placed above individual good'.[79] This model of an integrated society free from conflict might possibly be fitting for a small Franciscan friary, but not for a modern state.

Even the idea of a common good is questionable; it is the role of a government not to seek for some overall substantive common good, but to enable groups and individuals to realise, as far as may be, their own goods. The kind of integration assumed by Boff can result only in totalitarianism. Theology and political theory, however, call for a more articulated model and for a looser unity, with respect both to the Trinity and to the modern state.[80] A real distinction between the persons of the Trinity is, indeed, alleged by these contemporary writers, but there is little room for conflict, which is assumed to be invariably evil.

If God may be thought of as 'a sort of indivisible and continuous community',[81] what more can we say about this community? Many modern theologians insist on a real plurality in God – a community of equal (or at least not unequal) but distinct and different persons; they are said to co-exist, however, in a *totally harmonious* relationship of unity.[82] But the image of an ideal community that these theologians entertain is a static one, strongly influenced by idealist assumptions. There is no place for incoherence. Aristotle, by contrast, allowed for a certain pluralism in even the best *polis*. To attempt to impose on a *polis* the same degree of unity appropriate to an individual or a family would be to misconceive the nature of politics.[83] Contemporary theologians seem excessively worried that the recognition of an element of plurality (not to say conflict) in the different roles of the three persons of the Trinity will threaten not only the unity of the godhead, but the equality of the persons.

Social conflict

While it is understandable and proper that Christians should be sensitive to the dangers and destructive potential of conflict, they should also be aware that conflict may be a necessary and even a beneficent feature of human communities. Not all conflict is ultimately destructive. In a fallen world, confrontation and conflict may be necessary conditions of progress and improvement. Although the violent and destructive conflicts in Northern Ireland or Bosnia appear, indeed, to have no redeeming features, the confrontations and conflicts inspired and initiated by Mahatma Gandhi, Nelson Mandela and Martin Luther King had positive and beneficial results. Christians must not adopt a policy of 'peace at any price', in their theology any more than in their social ethics. Whereas many appeals to revolutionary violence have had unpredictable and unwelcome consequences (not least in giving some kind of 'legitimacy' to violent governmental repression),[84] there may be circumstances where conditions are so intolerable that violent revolt is justified.

'Do not think that I came to send peace on earth', said Jesus. 'I came not to send peace but a sword' (Matthew 10:34). The sword is a symbol not, indeed, of violence, but of division; nevertheless division was brought about by confrontation and conflict, ending in the violence of the cross. It is sometimes said that the Christian gospel can be summarised in one word, 'reconciliation'. Perhaps in one sense it can, but the only people reconciled as a result of Jesus' teaching seem to have been Pilate and Herod (Luke 23:12)! Hymns to harmony are often premature:

> Lastly between cowardice and
> despair valour is engendered;
> and so the discord of extremes
> begets all virtues; but
> of like things there is no issue
> without miracle.[85]

I am suggesting that a degree of conflict may be not only acceptable, but also beneficial in the state. Conflicting claims and counter-claims may provide a healthy dynamism, a stimulus to progress and the elimination of specific evils. It is good that there are groups making radical (and perhaps even unbalanced) demands on behalf of children or the handicapped or the homeless which may appear – and indeed be – incommensurate. Such a state may be better than one where some central authority produces a single coherent five-year plan, or even a 'Citizens' Charter'.

But surely, it will be said, if the plan were really comprehensive and coherent it would be better than a situation of rival and incompatible claims being made by diverse groups. In any case, the situation must, indubitably, be different in the heavenly realm. If God is good, then who will complain if he be a dictator, handing down a single monolithic plan and presenting a united front in the face of claims made by his subjects? This would be so if his subjects were slaves, but 'I have called you friends' (John 15:15). Friends are drawn into the dialectic of incommensurate goods which the Holy Trinity represents, in particular the conflicting claims of justice and mercy.

Justice and mercy

Justice requires that persons be given what they deserve – their due. But this raises as many questions as it solves. What criteria are available for deciding deserts? Do we allocate resources or apply sanctions and rewards on the basis of past performance, or need, or on a basis of an absolute equality? With respect to the distribution of goods it might be claimed that equality is an appropriate criterion, but not surely in matters of punishment, where what is due to a person is at least partially determined by past performance. Within a judicial system we send people to prison for something they have done in the past, rather than for something they might do in the future. We may in some circumstances imprison people for what they might do, but this can be defended on grounds not of justice, but of national expediency, and ought not to operate within the judicial system. We may forcibly detain people in order to reform them, but if there is any defence of such procedures it is not on the basis of justice. Social expediency and social conditioning must be distinguished clearly from questions of justice.

God, who knows all things including the inmost secrets of the heart, is the perfect judge. God is able to give to each what he or she deserves. Among many other images applied to God, that of judge has been prominent. However, a recent report of the Doctrine Commission of the Church of England summarises Jesus' conception of the Father as one who 'loves, cares, gives, listens, welcomes, seeks, accepts, forgives, provides', and goes on to state that 'the concept is positive, and there is little hint of the darker father-image associated with the idea of the angry God'.[86] This is rather typical of liberal theology in its selectivity. Nothing is said of the Matthean passages where the king (representing, by analogy, the Father) punishes the man without a wedding garment: 'bind him hand and foot . . . and cast him into outer darkness' where there is 'weeping and gnashing of teeth' (Matthew 22:13), or where the 'children of the kingdom' receive similar treatment (Matthew 8:12); and what of the fate of 'those on my left hand' (Matthew 25:41), or of the man who hid his talent (Matthew 25:30), or of those who do not forgive their neighbours from their hearts? 'So likewise shall my heavenly Father do to you '(Matthew 18:35).

No doubt 'biblical scholars' will explain that these passages are late interpolations, but even so they represent a legitimate determination on the part of early Christians to insist on the justice of God. These passages are indeed an embarrassment to Western liberal Christianity, but for those thousands of parents in Argentina having children who disappeared and whose mutilated bodies have been found by the roadside or dumped into a pit, and for those who have witnessed the concentration camps of the Second World War, or who have experienced acts of horrendous torture, this idea of a God without teeth is less than comforting. The story is often told of a Sandinista leader who, after the revolution, as minister of the interior, was visiting the prison. He identified two prisoners and went over to confront them: 'You tortured me and I strongly suspect you both tortured my wife. Now you are going to feel the full weight of this revolution. You are free. Go.'[87] If indeed true, the story simply demonstrates the arrogance of the Nicaraguan elite, in resorting to such arbitrary action. The 'politics of forgiveness', if it makes sense at all, does so only in the context of a politics of justice.

We are too easily disconcerted by the 'God to whom vengeance belongs', who will requite the rich and powerful for their acts of injustice and oppression (Psalm 94). The ASB puts in square brackets verses which suggest severe punishment for the wicked and unjust: 'If only you would slay the wicked, O God: if only the men of blood would depart from me' (Psalm 139:19), 'Let no man of evil tongue find footing in the land: the evil, the violent man, let him be hunted to the end' (Psalm 140:11)

What I am arguing, then, is that there must be, within our conception of God, a place for justice, and that traditionally, among Christians, this has been symbolised by the Father. But also God is merciful and forgiving. At the very centre of Christian, Jewish and Muslim understandings of God is a belief in God's mercy. It is in fact *because of* their emphasis on the justice of God that mercy is so important. It is Jesus, the Son of God, who is 'mercy and compassion incarnate'.[88] But mercy and justice are in principle opposed to each other and in conflict. Their claims can be resolved in the concrete case only by an act of practical judgment (*phronesis*). The contradictory nature of the two principles makes it difficult to incorporate them into a monolithic monotheism. If, however, the Son embodies the principle of mercy, we can make sense of the passages in the New Testament where he is pictured as interceding for us with the Father. Paul wrote of the risen Christ as *'interceding* for us' in heaven (Romans 8:34). In the Epistle to the Hebrews Christ is the eternal high priest, representing the redeemed, and 'ever lives to make intercession for them' (Hebrews 7:25). For the Johannine writer, 'we have an advocate with the Father, Jesus Christ the righteous' (1 John 2:1); again, Christ is portrayed as the 'expiation for our sins' (Romans 3:25). What sense can these images make unless they assume that there is within the life of the godhead a conflict between Father and Son, a conflict of principles and interests whose resolution is possible only in the concrete case. The Son, in interceding as our advocate, indeed appeals to, and assumes, an inherent mercy and disposition to forgive in the Father, which is manifested in the Spirit's healing and transforming action.

In the drama of redemption the Son has a role peculiar to himself, not shared by Father or Holy Spirit. As John Donne wrote:

> Christ was sole and alone, no Father, no Holy Ghost trod the wine-press with him . . . so he is *salutificator*, the very author of this salvation, as that when it came to the act he, and not they, died for us; and when it was in council he, as well as they and as soon as they, decreed it for us.[89]

The doctrine of *perichoresis* asserts an 'interpenetration' of the persons of the Trinity and a 'circulation' of the divine life. It should not, however, be employed in such a way as to undermine the peculiar role that each person plays. It is surely indefensible to say with Moltmann: 'The Father suffers the death of the Son.'[90] The only kind of patripassianism[91] which is legitimate sees a suffering of the Father resulting from his love for the world he has created, rather than a suffering which is 'caught' from the Son. Despite the vociferous adoption of a 'social' model of the Trinity, Moltmann's defence of patripassianism suggests a failure to allow for a real distinction of the persons, and a dangerous modalist tendency.

In his book *The Divine Trinity*, David Brown rejects the idea of conflict between Father and Son: 'Two infinite beings in conflict with one another,' he writes, 'would at most produce a stalemate (i.e. with the power of one cancelling out the power of the other so that nothing happens either way at all).'[92] Brown errs in adopting a mechanical model of power, rather than a personal model – a static rather than a dynamic representation of the godhead. In the latter case, conflict can lead to new possibilities opening up and progress occuring. Again, he states that 'even if the three Persons do not always act together in every instance, they do always act with the same objectives in view'.[93] Common objectives, however, do not exclude conflict. Most politicians claim to be pursuing a common end, but they conflict in respect both of their understanding of the end and of the best means of attaining it.

The spirit of love

'God is love.' Justice and mercy are specifications of love. It is all too easy to think that mercy alone is what love requires, but justice is equally important and logically prior. As already suggested, mercy only makes sense in the context of a system of justice. Mercy and forgiveness are applied to those who have been found guilty according to some principle of justice.

And what of the Holy Spirit in this conflict model of the Trinity? She[94] is on the one hand (as love) the source and origin of the principles of justice and mercy, and on the other the one whose concrete action, in the particular case, puts both justice and mercy into practice in a way that transforms and renews. Justice and mercy in themselves look back; the Holy Spirit's creative appropriation of these principles looks forward. She is the spirit of wisdom, not just *sophia* (Ephesians 1:17), but *phronesis* – the practical wisdom and judgment which relate principles to the concrete case, not simply by subsuming the particular under the general, but by transcending the principles and transforming the situation.

So too in human groups, conflict and confrontation may constructively (if only provisionally) be resolved in a given historical context, by a transforming expectation that old categories can be transcended. The art of politics is to be found not in the rigid application of principles, but in the ability to make a practical judgment in the particular case, a judgment which both takes principles into account and transcends them. Henri Bergson spoke, in this context, of 'a rectitude of judgment, which comes from an integrity of the soul'.[95]

While rejecting the notion that conflict is inherently bad, we should avoid the opposite error of seeing conflict as good in itself. It is good insofar as it contributes to constructive change, and makes sense only if we see social relations as dynamic rather than static. As a recent philosopher puts it, 'to look for commensuration rather than simply continued conversation . . . is to attempt escape from humanity'.[96] So it is with conflict as an element of the internal life of the Trinity. The categories and images we apply to God are ineluctably human in their primary reference. To speak of God as dynamic may be unsatisfactory, but to think of God as static is surely worse.

I have pointed out some of the dangers in thinking of the Holy Trinity, and by analogy the modern state, as entirely bereft of conflict and manifesting an excessive coherence 'before the time'. No doubt when the Son hands over the kingdom to the Father conflict will be superseded and God will be all in all (1 Corinthians 15:24–5), but not yet. I have suggested that conflict can be constructive and that, even when we consider the 'internal' life of the godhead, an acceptance of conflict will help us to take seriously the radical counter-claims of justice and mercy and to forestall an image of God in which mercy totally swamps justice.

To assert, with Boff and other recent authors, some kind of necessary, or logical, connection between images of God and of the state is to err. It is perfectly possible to deny the analogy and (with the puritan Parliamentarians of the seventeenth century, or with Karl Barth in the twentieth century) to employ the concept of the sovereignty of an omnipotent God to relativise and challenge all claims by the state. If God is a supreme monarch we are all his subjects, even kings.[97] There is no *necessary* connection between correct theology and good politics. Nevertheless, if God is the one we worship, it is likely that the qualities we ascribe to him will also be applied in human relationships, and that our image of God may serve as a model in social and political life. Authoritarianism in one sphere is liable to spread to others. A highly integrated and conflict-free image of the Trinity will lend support to the kind of social organisation which will leave little room for freedom in the modern world.

NOTES

1 INTRODUCTION

1 'Commonly recognised' that is, presumably, by his theological colleagues and predecessors as they solemnly made their way, napkin in hand, from high table to dessert in the senior common room.

2 Hodgson, *The Doctrine of the Trinity*, p. 119.

3 Hilton, *The Age of Atonement*, p. 297. The words 'with caution' need to be stressed!

4 Ward, *Philosophy of Theism*, II, p.90.

5 See David Nicholls, 'Conscience and Authority in the Thought of W. G. Ward', *Heythrop Journal* Oct. 1985; and 'Christianity and Politics', in Morgan, ed., *The Religion of the Incarnation*, pp. 416ff.

6 Digges, *The Unlawfulnesse of Subjects Taking up Arms against their Sovereigne* p. 61.

7 Anon. (John Hayward), *An Answer to the First Part of a Certain Conference concerning Succession* (London, 1603), sig. B4; (in Schochet, *Patriarchalism in Political Thought*, p. 49). The classic text is, of course, Filmer, *Patriarcha: or, the Natural Powers of the Kings of England Asserted*.

8 King James I, *The Workes of the Most High and Mightie Prince James &c.*, p. 488.

9 See Nicholls, *From Dessalines to Duvalier*, pp. 232–3.

10 Carswell, *From Revolution to Revolution* p. 29.

11 Plumb, *The Growth of Political Stability*, pp. 2–3.

12 *The New Whole Duty of Man*, p. i.

13 From an essay in *Common Sense*, no. 150, 15 Dec. 1739, quoted in Sambrook, *The Eighteenth Century*, p. 182. Kliger traces idealisation of the Goths to the mid-sixteenth century, in *The Goths in England*. For a study of this theme in the seventeenth century, see Pocock, *The Ancient Constitution and the Feudal Law*.

14 'Satire and Economics in the Augustan Age of Satire', in H.K. Miller *et al.*, eds *The Augustan Milieu*, p. 90.

15 I hope to consider these French authoritarian writers elsewhere.

16 See below, pp. 155–6.

17 See Goldsmith, *Private Vices*, p. 120.

18 Quoted in Sambrook, *The Eighteenth Century*, p. 76.

19 Plumb, *Growth*, p. 7.

20 Quoted in Porter, *English Society*, p. 202.

21 Bishop Berkeley, quoted ibid., p. 237.

22 Josiah Tucker, quoted in Shelton, *Dean Tucker*, p. 75. Yet he also spoke of

taxation as checking 'those vicious artificial wants which are prejudicial to a general, lasting and extensive commerce' (quoted ibid., p. 39).

23 N. S. Hetherington, 'Isaac Newton's Influence on Adam Smith's Natural Laws in Economics', *Journal of the History of Ideas*, 44, 1983, p. 497.
24 Mandeville, *The Fable of the Bees*, p. 9.
25 Mandeville, 'A Search into the Nature of Society', ibid., p. 428 (my italics).
26 James, *Varieties of Religious Experience*, p. 494.
27 'A Hymn' (*Thomson's Poetical Works*, p. 166).
28 Josiah Tucker, *Instructions for Travellers*, pp. 31–2 quoted in Shelton, *Dean Tucker*, p. 115.
29 Nicholls, *Deity and Domination*, chapters 2 and 3; see also Nicholls, *The Pluralist State*, and David G. Green *Reinventing Civil Society*.
30 See my discussion of the relationship in 'The Hidden Hand: Providence and the Market', in Heelas and Morris, eds, *The Values of the Enterprise Culture*.
31 On the intellectual roots of Jacobinism, see particularly Hampson, *Will and Circumstance* and see below chapter 4.
32 Lefebvre, *Etudes sur la révolution française*, p. 97
33 *Oeuvres complètes de Maximilien Robespierre*, I, pp. 670 and 673, quoted in Hampson, *Life and Opinions*, p. 31.
34 'Sur les rapports des idées religieuses et morales . . .', mai 1794 *Oeuvres*, X, p. 453.
35 Douglas Hurd, Speech to Church of England General Synod, fringe group, in 1988.
36 See David Nicholls, 'The Invisible Hand: Providence and the Market', in Heelas and Morris, eds, *The Values of the Enterprise Culture*, p. 232. By 'Pelagian' I mean a system that lays emphasis on 'good works' and minimises the role of divine grace.
37 Quoted in Hampson, *Life and Opinions*, p. 88.
38 'Sur les circonstances actuelles', 26 mars 1792 *Oeuvres*, VIII, pp. 230 and 234–5. See below, pp. 80–84.
39 Robespierre, 'Rapport sur les principes', 25 décembre 1793 *Oeuvres*, X, p. 277.
40 'Laws and government may be considered . . . as a combination of the rich to oppress the poor, and preserve to themselves the inequality of the goods which would otherwise be soon destroyed by the attacks of the poor, who if not hindered by the government would soon reduce the others to an equality with themselves by open violence'. Smith, *Lectures on Jurisprudence*, p. 208; see also Smith *An Inquiry into the Nature and Causes of the Wealth of Nations*, pp. 710 and 715.
41 Quoted in Hampson, *Life and Opinions*, p. 176.
42 Gray, *et al., The Moral Foundations of Market Institutions*.
43 Vereker, *Eighteenth Century Optimism*, p. 198.
44 Earl R. Wasserman, 'Nature Moralized: the Divine Analogy in the Eighteenth Century', *ELH*, 20, 1953, 53.
45 David Fordyce, *Dialogues concerning Education*, I, pp. 337–8, quoted in Wasserman, 'Nature Moralized', p. 49.
46 Spitzer, *World Harmony*, p. 119.

2 GOD AND THE MARKET

Abbreviations of works frequently quoted in this chapter (publication details in Bibliography):

First Essay Malthus, *Essay on the Principle of Population, as it Affects the Future Improvement of Society*
EPS   Smith, *Essays on Philosophical Subjects*
LJ   Smith, *Lectures on Jurisprudence*
TMS   Smith, *The Theory of Moral Sentiments*
WN   Smith, *An Inquiry into the Nature and Causes of the Wealth of Nations*

 1 For an excellent exposition and critique of these writers, see Waterman, *Revolution, Economics and Religion, passim*; also an earlier article by the same author, 'The Ideological Alliance of Political Economy and Christian Theology, 1798–1833', *Journal of Ecclesiastical History*, 34:2, 1983, pp. 231ff. In revising these lectures for publication I am much indebted to the work of Anthony Waterman. See also Soloway, *Prelates and People*.
 2 For example, by Norman, *Church and Society in England*, p. 42.
 3 Salim Rachid, 'Richard Whately and Christian Political Economy at Oxford and Dublin', *Journal of the History of Ideas*, 38, 1977, pp. 147ff.
 4 Malthus, *Essay on Population* (5th edn), III, p. 425, cited by Waterman, *Revolution*, p. 130.
 5 Ricardo to Hutches Trower, Jan.1818, (*Works*, VII, p. 248).
 6 Watt, *The Published Writings of Thomas Chalmers*. .
 7 Malthus to Chalmers, 22 July 1822, quoted in Brown, *Thomas Chalmers* , p. 42.
 8 Though the general framework of his theology must be called Calvinist, he adopted a flexible approach which was deplored by his stricter brethren.
 9 Senior to Chalmers, 8 or 28 July 1832, quoted in Brown, *Thomas Chalmers*, p. 199.
10 McCulloch to Napier, 3 Aug. 1832, quoted in Brown, *Thomas Chalmers*, p. 200.
11 Quoted ibid., p. 371.
12 Chalmers, 'The Political Economy of a Famine', *North British Review*, 13, 1847, p. 247.
13 Chalmers, *On the Power, Wisdom and Goodness of God, as Manifested in the Adaption of External Nature to the Moral and Intellectual Constitution of Man*, II, pp. 2, 3, 26.
14 Ibid, II, p. 36.
15 Chalmers, 'The Political Economy of a Famine', p. 252; see also Chalmers, 'The Political Economy of the Bible', *North British Review*, 2, 1844, p. 29.
16 Chalmers, 'Discourses on the Application of Christianity to the Commercial and Ordinary Affairs of Life' (*c*. 1835) (*Works*, VI, p.62).
17 Brown, *Thomas Chalmers*, p. 50.
18 Chalmers, 'The Importance of Civil Government to Society', *Discourses* (*Works*, VI, pp. 253–4).
19 Chalmers, *Discourses* (*Works*, VI, p. 72).
20 Chalmers, *On the Power*, II, p. 121.
21 Ibid., II, p. 34; see also Chalmers, *Discourses*, (*Works*, VI, pp. 62–3).
22 Chalmers, *Discourses* (*Works*, VI, p. 63).
23 Chalmers, *On the Power*, II, p. 47; also II, p. 117
24 Ibid., I, p. 58.
25 Ibid., I, pp. 60–1. 'I have derived greater aid from the views and reasonings of Bishop Butler, than I have been able to find besides, in the whole range of our existent authorship' (ibid., I, p. vi); see also Chalmers 'Prelections on Butler's Analogy' (*Posthumous Works*, IX, pp. 1 ff.).
26 Chalmers, *On the Power*, I, p. 83.
27 Ibid., II, pp. 304 and 269.
28 Chalmers, 'Lectures on Paley's Evidences of Christianity' (*Posthumous Works*, IX, p. 99).
29 Chalmers, *Congregational Sermons* (*Works*, X, p. 370).

30 Chalmers, *On the Power*, II, pp. 61–2.
31 Ibid., II, p. 101.
32 Chalmers, *On the Christian and Economic Polity of a Nation*, (*Works*, XIV, p. 45).
33 Chalmers, *On the Power*, II, pp. 228–30.
34 Ibid., II, p. 2.
35 Ibid., I, pp. 238–9, and II, p.2; also Chalmers, *Discourses* (*Works*, VI, p. 69).
36 Chalmers, *On the Christian and Economic Polity* (*Works*, XV, p. 305).
37 Chalmers, *The Sufficiency of the Parochial System* (*Works*, XXI, p. 208).
38 Brown, *Thomas Chalmers*, p. 147.
39 Chalmers, *On the Christian and Economic Polity* (*Works*, XV, pp. 308–9).
40 Chalmers, 'The Political Economy of the Bible', p. 52.
41 Chalmers, 'The Political Economy of a Famine', pp. 265 and 280.
42 Brown, *Thomas Chalmers*, pp. 367–8. See Chalmers, 'Political Economy of a Famine', pp. 247–90.
43 Hilton, *The Age of Atonement*, pp. 110 and 112. This is a remarkable piece of special pleading. Presumably Chalmers, who had not changed his theology at this time, could not possibly have changed his social theory! There seems no limit to the lengths Hilton is prepared to go in order to instantiate his fragile thesis.
44 Brown, *Thomas Chalmers*, p. 367. It appears that he still had his doubts about Oastler's proposals for factory legislation. See the conversation between the two men quoted in Hilton, *The Age of Atonement*, p. 90.
45 Chalmers, *Enquiry into the Extent and Stability of Natural Resources*, pp. 141–2.
46 See Brown, *Thomas Chalmers*, pp. 149–51.
47 Chalmers, *On Political Economy* (*Works*, XIX, p. 184).
48 Chalmers, 'The Political Economy of the Bible', p.39, and 'The Political Economy of a Famine', p. 247.
49 Copleston, *A Letter to the Rt Hon Robert Peel*, p. 37.
50 Sumner, *A Treatise*, II, p. 52n.
51 Ibid., II, pp. 64–5.
52 Ibid., II, p. 66.
53 Ibid., II, p. 77. This apparent defence of prostitution is remarkable from a future archbishop of Canterbury!
54 Whately, *Introductory Lectures on Political Economy*, pp. 175 and 171.
55 Ibid., p. 97.
56 Sumner, *A Treatise*, II, p. 105.
57 Ibid., II, p. 104.
58 Sumner, *A Series of Sermons on the Christian Faith and Character*, pp. 279–80.
59 Sumner, *A Treatise*, II, pp. 44, 86 and 149.
60 Ibid., II, pp. 105–6 and 259.
61 Ibid., II, p. 84n.
62 Ibid., II, pp. 103–4. This punishment, however, appears to have been normally withheld from the rich, who seem no less thoughtless, and habitually more extravagant, than the poor!
63 Edward Copleston, *A Second Letter*, pp. 32 and 94, cited in Waterman, *Revolution*, pp. 192–3.
64 Copleston, *A Second Letter*, p. 22; and Sumner, *A Treatise*, II, pp. 339 and 341.
65 Sumner, *A Treatise*, II, pp. 290 and 90.
66 Ibid., II, p. 212.
67 Ibid., II, pp 427–8.
68 Whately, *Introductory Lectures*, p. 136.
69 There has been considerable controversy on the extent and nature of Malthus's

influence on Darwin and his followers. See P. Vorzimmer, 'Darwin, Malthus and the Theory of Natural Selection', *Journal of the History of Ideas*, 30, 1969, pp. 527ff; Robert Young, 'Malthus and the Evolutionists: The Common Context of Biological and Social Theory', *Past and Present*, 43, 1969, pp. 105ff; Peter J. Bowler, 'Malthus, Darwin and the Concept of Struggle', *Journal of the History of Ideas*, 37, 1976, pp. 631ff. ; S. Herbert, 'Darwin, Malthus and Selection', *Journal of the History of Biology*, 4, 1971, pp. 209ff.

70 Meek, ed., *Marx and Engels on Malthus*, p. 24.

71 For the intellectual context of Malthus's first edition, see Waterman, *Revolution*, chapter 2.

72 Malthus, *First Essay*, p. 210.

73 Petersen, *Malthus*, p. 20.

74 For biographical details, see James, *Population Malthus* and John M. Pullen, 'Some New Information on the Rev. T. R. Malthus', *History of Political Economy*, 19, 1987, pp. 137ff.

75 'The Crisis, a View of the Present Interesting State of Great Britain, by a Friend to the Constitution', unpublished pamphlet (1796), quoted in James, *Population Malthus*, p. 53. See also McCleary, *The Malthusian Population Theory*.

76 See Meek, ed., *Marx and Engels on Malthus*, p. 123

77 Waterman, *Revolution*, p. 192.

78 *Vorwarts!*, no, 60, (1844), in Marx and Engels, *Collected Works*, III, pp. 1945. The editors of these volumes are clearly unable to trace the source of this alleged quotation from Malthus.

79 *First Essay*, p. 132. See Eltis, *Classical Theory*, p. 119.

80 *First Essay*, pp. 102 and 148–9.

81 In later editions he linked misery and vice: 'the general consequence of vice is misery' and 'this consequence is the precise reason why an action is termed vicious' (cited in E. N. Santurri, 'Theodicy and Social Policy in Malthus' Thought', *Journal of the History of Ideas*, 43, 1982, p. 319).

82 Malthus, 'A Summary View of the Principle of Population' (1830), printed together with *First Essay*, p. 250; and Malthus, *Additions*, p. 292.

83 Malthus, *Additions*, p. 292.

84 'Summary View', in *First Essay*, p. 249.

85 Malthus, *Principles of Political Economy*, p. 158.

86 Malthus, *First Essay*, p. 106.

87 Malthus, *Additions*, p. 327.

88 *First Essay*, pp. 102 and 143.

89 Malthus, *Essay* (1803), pp. 531–2. A recent writer refers with some justification to 'this brutal dismissal of the traditional Christian doctrine of almsgiving'(Waterman, *Revolution*, p. 122). Malthus, while denying the right of the poor, does not explicitly deny the duty of almsgiving.

90 Malthus, *Additions*, p. 43.

91 Ibid., *Additions*, p. 69.

92 Malthus, *First Essay*, pp. 207 and 177

93 Ibid., pp. 70–1 and 205.

94 'Malthus Summary View', in *First Essay*, p. 249.

95 Malthus *Additions*, p. 63. Bowler writes misleadingly of Malthus as 'associated with the *laissez-faire* school of economics' ('Malthus, Darwin and the Concept of Struggle', p. 636). See Keynes, *Essays in Biography*, pp. 81ff.

96 Malthus, *Additions*, pp. 211–12.

97 Ibid., pp. 279ff.

98 Ibid., pp. 63ff.

99 *Additions*, p. 76.

100 Ibid., *Additions*, pp. 59–60.
101 Malthus, *An Essay* (3rd edn), II, p. 152.
102 Ibid., II, pp. 168 and 179. See also *First Essay*, pp. 91, 97–8, 100–1.
103 *First Essay*, p. 205.
104 Ibid., p. 201. See also D. L. LeMahieu, 'Malthus and the Theology of Scarcity', *Journal of the History of Ideas*, 40, 1979, pp. 467ff. ; and S. M. Levin, 'Malthus and the Idea of Progress', *Journal of the History of Ideas*, 27, 1966, pp. 92ff.
105 *First Essay*, pp. 200–1.
106 J. M. Pullen, 'Malthus's Theological Ideas and their Influence on his Principle of Population', *History of Political Economy*, 13:1, 1981, pp. 41–2.
107 *First Essay*, p. 203. Some of these process writers are discussed in David Nicholls, *Deity and Domination*, pp. 138ff.
108 *First Essay*, p. 204 and 210.
109 Ibid., p. 209.
110 Ibid., pp. 205–6.
111 In his *Summary* (pp. 260–1), considering the causes of a decline in the birth-rate in countries where improved conditions have reduced mortality rates, he rejected the suggestion 'that a special providence is called into action to render women less prolific in healthy countries', in favour of the supposition that in healthy and improved countries the prudential restraint is more prevalent.
112 *First Essay*, pp. 160 and 215.
113 Pullen, 'Malthus's Theological Ideas', p. 50.
114 Malthus, *Additions*, p. 325. There is, however, no conflict between the two views; he may well have asserted that life is both a time of trial and also the scene of human formation and development.
115 Pullen, 'Some New Information', p. 139.
116 Malthus, *Additions*, pp. 3223. Weyland was author of *Principles of Population and Production*.
117 Malthus, *Additions*, p. 325, and *First Essay*, p. 217.
118 Some recent critics of Malthus are discussed in David Nicholls, 'Parson Malthus', *Anglican Theological Review* 77:3, 1995. By ' Manichaean' is meant a belief in the eternal status of evil as well as good.
119 G. J. Stigler, 'Smith's Travels on the Ship of State', in Andrew S. Skinner and T. Wilson, eds, *Essays on Adam Smith*, p. 237.
120 *EPS*, p. 66.
121 Ibid., p. 104.
122 N. S. Hetherington, 'Isaac Newton's Influence on Adam Smith's Natural Laws in Economics', *Journal of the History of Ideas*, 44, 1983, p. 497.
123 See Viner, 'Adam Smith and *Laissez-Faire*', in his *The Long View and the Short*.
124 See Blaug, *Economic Theory in Retrospect*, p. 59.
125 *WN* 1:8:36 (p. 96); Hont and Ignatieff, eds, *Wealth and Virtue*, p. 7.
126 Quoted in Dugald Stewart, 'An Account of the Life and Writings of Adam Smith' (*TMS*, p. xvii).
127 *TMS*, p. 235.
128 Ibid., pp. 110 and 126; see also p. 346. On Paley, see below, p. 59 f.
129 *TMS*, p. 345; see also pp. 347 ff.
130 Ibid., p. 347.
131 See Raphael, *Adam Smith*, p. 73.
132 *WN*, p. 456.
133 *TMS*, pp. 397ff.
134 Ibid., pp. 235, 239ff. and 187.
135 Ibid., pp. 232 and 447.
136 Ibid., p. 109.

137 Ibid., p. 110.

138 Ibid., p. 199.

139 Ibid., p. 125

140 See Wallas, *Human Nature in Politics* and many works of Hobhouse. These writers did not, of course, share his theological views.

141 Raphael, *Adam Smith*, p. 72.

142 *EPS*, p. 49.

143 *WN*, p. 630.

144 In Hont and Ignatieff, eds, *Wealth and Virtue*, p. 119.

145 'The History of Astronomy' (*EPS*, pp. 48ff.) See Alec Macfie, 'The Invisible Hand of Jupiter', *Journal of the History of Ideas*, 32, 1971, pp. 595ff. It is particularly in the context of weather forecasting that modern scientists have developed ideas of the so-called 'butterfly effect', according to which the most minute change (which some would say is inherently unpredictable, because in principle unmeasurable) can have huge effects on weather systems. They are less likely to see the universe as a closed system than Smith was, and acknowledge that perhaps, after all, God does play dice. See Polkinghorne, *Science and Providence*.

146 Smith, 'History of Ancient Physics' (*EPS*, pp. 112ff).

147 Macfie suggests that Smith 'seems to accept, and interpret in his own way, the broad outline of the 'ancient stoics'' ('The Invisible Hand', p. 599).

148 *TMS*, p. 47.

149 Winch ascribes a Mandevillian position to Smith, in *Adam Smith's Politics*, pp. 80 and 172. Curiously, however, he fails to note the paragraphs in *TMS* where Smith describes the system of Dr Mandeville as having a tendency which is 'wholly pernicious' (*TMS*, p. 451).

150 *TMS*, p. 452.

151 On Butler's concept of cool self-love, see below, p. 66f.

152 *TMS*, p. 454.

153 Ibid., p. 337.

154 Ibid., pp. 126 and 265.

155 Ibid., p. 269.

156 Ibid., pp. 463–4.

157 Ibid., p. 267.

158 Smith, 'Of the Imitative Arts', in *EPS*, p. 205. He drew attention also to the role of imagination in scientific discovery ('The History of Astronomy', in *EPS*, p. 105).

159 *TMS*, p. 109n.

160 *WN*, pp. 421 and 803.

161 *TMS*, pp. 73 and 84.

162 Ibid., pp. 338–9.

163 Ibid. p. 332.

164 Ibid., p. 339.

165 Ibid., p. 339.

166 Ibid., p. 342.

167 *LJ*, pp. 316–17. See Hume's essay 'Of the Original Contract' (*Essays*, pp. 322ff).

168 *TMS*, p. 124.

169 *LJ*, p. 318.

170 *WN*, pp. 709ff and 'Report of 1762–3' (*LJ*, p. 16).

171 *LJ*, p. 208; also p. 404; and see *WN*, pp. 710 and 715.

172 *WN*, p. 412.

173 Ibid., pp. 687–8.

174 Ibid., p. 723.

175 Ibid., pp. 688 and 831–2.
176 *TMS*, p. 116.
177 *WN*, p. 540.
178 Ibid., p. 267.
179 Ibid., p. 493.
180 *TMS*, p. 120
181 *WN*, p. 494.
182 Ibid., pp. 27 and 456.
183 *TMS*, p. 265.

3 UNITARIANS AND ANGLICANS

Abbreviations:
E˙   Paley, *Evidences of Christianity*
MPP   Paley, *Principles of Moral and Political Philosophy*
NT   Paley, *Natural Theology*
S   Paley, *Sermons and other minor writings*
PW   Price, *Political Writings*

1 Priestley, *Discourses on the Evidence of Revealed Religion* (1794), (*Works*, XV, p. 207).
2 'The peculiar Socinian view of the purpose and of the contents of Christianity is historically conditioned by that mediaeval doctrine which regards God as the absolute Will' (Ritschl, *A Critical History of the Christian Doctrine of Justification and Reconciliation*, p. 298).
3 See Henri Laboucheix, 'Chemistry, Materialism and Theology in the *Works* of Joseph Priestley', *Price–Priestley Newsletter*, 1, 1977, pp. 31ff.
4 On this aspect of their thought, see Jack Fruchtman, 'The Apocalyptic Politics of Richard Price and Joseph Priestley: A Study in Late Eighteenth-Century Republican Millenarianism', *Transactions of the American Philosophical Society*, 73, 1983.
5 Priestley, *Discourses on Various Subjects* (1773) (*Works*, XV, p. 37).
6 See Margaret Canovan, 'Joseph Priestley on Rank and Inequality', *Enlightenment and Dissent*, 2, 1983, pp. 23ff.
7 Lincoln, *Political and Social Ideas*, p 166.
8 Cited in Thomas, *The Honest Mind*, p. 9. For the influence of Newton and Clarke, see Laboucheix, *Richard Price*, pp. 79ff.
9 'My principal design has been to shew that right and wrong are distinctions in the natures of things; and that moral obligations constitute a part of eternal truth and reason' ('A Dissertation on the Being and Attributes of the Deity', Appendix to Price, *A Review of the Principal Questions in Morals*, p. 295).
10 The words are those of James Boswell; see Thomas, *The Honest Mind*, p. 143.
11 On the friendship of Price with Franklin, see Thomas, *The Honest Mind*, pp. 143ff.; on his contributions to the theory and practice of insurance, see ibid., chapter 11.
12 Knight, *Lord Monboddo*, p. 119.
13 Priestley, *Discourses on Various Subjects*, p. 185. This celebrated passage was published as an appendix to his sermon on 5 November 1785. It appears to have been omitted from volume 15 of Rutt, ed., *The Theological and Miscellaneous Works of Joseph Priestley*, in which the sermon itself was reprinted.
14 'Old Mother Church', cited in Lincoln, *Political and Social Ideas*, p. 6.

15 Price, *The Evidence for a Future Period of Improvement in the State of Mankind* (1787) (*PW*, p. 168).
16 Price, *Review*, p. 294.
17 Priestley, 'Forms of Prayer and Other Offices' (*Works*, XXI, pp. 509 and 518).
18 Priestley, 'Forms' (*Works*, XXI, p. 558).
19 Ibid., XXI, pp. 553 and 558.
20 Ibid., XXI, p. 502.
21 Priestley, *Discourses on the Evidence*, p.6 (*Works*, XV, p. 201).
22 Priestley, 'A Vindication of Public Worship' (*Works*, XX, p. 314); and *Discourses on the Evidence*, p. 7 (*Works*, XV, p. 201).
23 Priestley, *Discourses on the Evidence*, pp. 28–9 (*Works*, XV, p. 210).
24 Priestley, 'Letters to the Philosophers and Politicians of France on the Subject of Religion' (*Works*, XXI, p. 105).
25 Priestley, 'The Deity administers *all* the affairs of the world' and 'A Free Discussion' (*Works*, III, p. 451).
26 Priestley, *Discourses on the Evidence*, p. 360 (*Works*, XV, p. 350).
27 Priestley, *An Essay on the First Principles of Government* (1771) (*Works*, XXII, p. 13).
28 Price, *Review*, p. 112.
29 Ibid., pp. 141 and 295
30 Ibid., p. 109.
31 Price, *The Evidence for a Future Period of Improvement in the State of Mankind* (1787) (*PW*, p. 152).
32 Price, *Britain's Happiness and the Proper Improvement of It* (1759) (*PW*, p. 7).
33 Thomas, *The Honest Mind*, p. 331.
34 Price, *A Fast Sermon* (1781) (*PW*, p. 106).
35 Price, *Two Tracts* (1778) (*PW*, p. 28).
36 Ibid., pp. 23–4.
37 Price, *A Fast Sermon* (*PW*, p. 106).
38 Ibid. ; see also D. O. Thomas, 'Neither Republican nor Democrat', *Price-Priestely Newsletter*, 1, 1977, pp. 31ff.
39 Price, *Two Tracts* (*PW*, p. 90). It is misleading for Robert Hole to declare that 'Price denied entirely the doctrines of original sin and the Fall of man' (*Pulpits, Politics and Public Order*, p. 64; see also p. 46).
40 Price, *A Fast Sermon* (*PW*, p. 112), and *Sermons on the Christian Doctrine as Received by the Different Denominations of Christians*, pp. 17–18.
41 Price, *A Discourse on the Love of our Country* (1789) (*PW*, p. 187).
42 Price, *A Fast Sermon* (*PW*, p. 109). See also *Two Tracts*, (*PW*, p. 30). Priestley basically agreed that those with 'unbounded power' will tend to 'pursue their own interest, though it be opposite to the community at large': *Essay on the First Principles* (*Works*, XXII, p. 17).
43 Price, *Two Tracts* (*PW*, p. 83). Priestley, though generally more optimistic about human perfectibility, referred to 'the imperfections of our nature': 'Forms of Prayer' (*Works*, XXI, p. 514).
44 Price, *Review*, pp. 112–13.
45 Price, *The Evidence for a Future Period of Improvement in the State of Mankind* (1787) (*PW*, pp. 164–5).
46 Price to Franklin, 26 Dec. 1788, quoted in Thomas, *The Honest Mind*, p. 283.
47 Price, *Two Tracts* (*PW*, p. 93), and *A Fast Sermon* (*PW*, p. 113).
48 Priestley, 'Letters to the Rt Hon Edmund Burke' (*Works*, XXII, p. 238).
49 Price, *Two Tracts* (*PW*, p. 64).
50 Ibid., p. 29.
51 Daubeny, *Vindiciae ecclesiae Anglicanae*, quoted in Clark, *English Society*, p. 271.

52 Price, *Two Tracts* (*PW*, pp. 26–7).
53 Ibid., pp. 78–9.
54 Thomas, *The Honest Mind*, pp. 330–1.
55 Ibid., p. 333.
56 Priestley, *The Doctrine of Philosophical Necessity*, (*Works*, III, p. 451).
57 Priestley, *Lectures on History and General Policy* (*Works*, XXIV, p. 230); see also *A Political Dialogue* (*Works*, XXV, p. 96).
58 Priestley, *An Essay on the First Principles of Government* (*Works*, XXII, p. 27).
59 Ibid., pp. 123–4.
60 Price, *The Evidence* (*PW*, p. 159).
61 Ibid., p. 157.
62 Price, *Observations on the Importance of the American Revolution* (PW, pp. 118–19).
63 Priestley, *An Essay on the First Principles* (*Works*, XXII, pp. 8–9).
64 Priestley, *Discourses on Various Subjects* (*Works*, XV, p. 71).
65 Priestley, *An Essay on the First Principles* (*Works*, XXII, p. 124).
66 Priestley, *An Essay on the Course of Liberal Education for Civil and Active Life* (1765) (*Works*, XXIV, pp. 7ff).
67 Priestley, *General History of the Christian Church* (1802) (*Works*, IX, p. 417).
68 Priestley, *A Course of Lectures on Oratory and Criticism* (1777) (*Works*, XXV, p. 92); 'before' means here 'in the face of', rather than 'prior to'. See Canovan, 'Joseph Priestley'.
69 Priestley, *Forms of Prayer* (*Works*, XXI, pp. 556–7).
70 *The Life and Letters of Charles Darwin*, I, p. 47.
71 Stephen, *English Thought,*, I, p. 408
72 *The Autobiography of Lyman Beecher*.
73 Paley, *MPP* (*Works*, I, p. 46).
74 Ibid., I, p. 36; see also *E* (*Works*, III, p. 1).
75 *NT* (*Works*, IV, p. 300).
76 *MPP* (*Works*, I, pp. 14–15).
77 Ibid., I, chapter 6; see also *S*, (*Works*, V, p. 8).
78 *MPP* (*Works*, II, p. 50).
79 Ibid., II, p. 52.
80 Ibid., I, pp. 48–9.
81 *E* (*Works*, III, p. 212).
82 *MPP* (*Works*, I, p. 66).
83 Ibid., I, pp. 28 and 30.
84 Butler, *The Analogy of Religion, Natural and Revealed, to the Constitution and Course of Nature*, pp. 81ff. and 99–100 (*Works*, I, pp. 86ff and 107).
85 *E* (*Works*, III, pp. 219 and 227).
86 *S* (*Works*, V, p. 383; see also p. 374). For a recent writer who emphasises the importance of character in Christian ethics, see Hauerwas, *Character and the Christian Life*; *A Community of Character*, and other works.
87 *MPP* (*Works*, I, p. 29).
88 *E* (*Works*, III, p. 408).
89 Paley, 'Observations upon the Character and Example of Christ, and the Morality of the Gospel' (*Works*, V, p. 411).
90 *NT* (*Works*, IV, p. 27).
91 Dawkins, *The Blind Watchmaker*, p. 37; *NT* (*Works*, IV, p. 275).
92 *NT* (*Works*, IV, p. 276).
93 Ibid., IV, p. 9.
94 Ibid., IV, p. 43.
95 Ibid., IV, p. 290.
96 *MPP* (*Works*, I, p. 270).

97 S (*Works*, V, p. 5).
98 *MPP* (*Works*, I, pp. 37ff).
99 Ibid., II, p. 1.
100 Ibid., I, p. 308.
101 Ibid., I, p. 80.
102 Ibid., I, pp. 310ff.
103 Ibid., I, p. 318.
104 Ibid., I, pp. 126ff.
105 Ibid., I, p. 70; and *NT* (*Works*, IV, p. 335).
106 Paley, 'Reasons for Contentment Addressed to the Labouring Part of the British Public' (*Works*, IV, p. 392); cf. Rawls, *A Theory of Justice*, p. 12.
107 Paley, 'Reasons for Contentment', (*Works*, IV, p. 393).
108 See above, p. 41.
109 *NT* (*Works*, IV, p. 341).
110 Pope, 'Essay on Man', *Poetical Works*, p. 249.
111 *MPP* (*Works*, I, p. 251).
112 Paley: *MPP* (*Works*, I, pp. 251ff).
113 See the excellent essay of Jane Garnett, 'Bishop Butler and the *Zeitgeist*', in Cunliffe, ed., *Joseph Butler's Moral and Religious Thought*, pp. 63ff.
114 Goldwin Smith, *Reminiscences*, p. 65, quoted in Newsome, *Two Classes of Men*, p. 73. Smith was a rather hostile critic of Butler.
115 Newman to James Stephen, 16 Mar. 1835 (Cambridge University Library, MSS Add. 7349/15(C), fol. 138).
116 *Correspondence on Church and Religion of W. E. Gladstone*, II, p. 163.
117 *Selections from the Correspondence of the First Lord Acton*, pp. 224ff.
118 Garnett, in Cunliffe, ed., *Butler's Thought*, p. 82.
119 Butler, *Analogy*, p. x (*Works*, I, p. 11).
120 Ibid., p. iii (*Works*, I, p. 3).
121 On Butler's preaching, see Downey, *The Eighteenth Century Pulpit*, chapter 2; for his moral philosophy, see Duncan-Jones, *Butler's Moral Philosophy*.
122 See a view of Matthew Arnold in *Last Essays on Church and Religion*, p. 47, quoted in Garnett, 'Bishop Butler and the *Zeitgeist*'.
123 Bartlett, *Memoirs of Bishop Butler*, pp. 275–6. If only Newman had followed this precedent he might have been canonised years ago!
124 Butler, *Analogy*, p. 44 (*Works*, I, p. 47); see also p. 112 (*Works*, I, p. 120), where he included the rule of a father over his children.
125 See, for example, Cunliffe, ed. *Butler's Thought*, a recent collection which ignores this aspect of his thought.
126 Butler, *Analogy*, p. 121 (*Works*, I, p. 130).
127 Butler, Sermon 3: Preached before the House of Lords, in 'Six Sermons' (*Works*, II, p. 262).
128 Butler, Sermon 15, in 'Fifteen Sermons' (*Works*, II, pp. 200–1).
129 Ibid., II, p. 207.
130 Pope, 'Essay on Man', *Works*, p. 250.
131 Butler, Sermon 15, in 'Fifteen Sermons' (*Works*, II, p. 209).
132 Butler, *Analogy*, p. 35 (*Works*, I, p. 38).
133 Ibid., p. 36 (*Works*, I, pp. 39–40).
134 Ibid., p. 35 (*Works*, I, p. 38).
135 Ibid., p. 285 (*Works*, I, p. 303).
136 Butler, Sermon 1, in 'Fifteen Sermons' (*Works*, II, p. 16).
137 i. e. more concerned with harming others than with one's own pleasure.
138 Butler, 'Preface' (*Works*, II, pp. 3 and 6).
139 Pope, 'Essay on Man', (*Poetical Works*, p. 267).

140 Butler, Sermon 3, in 'Fifteen Sermons' (*Works*, II, p. 37).
141 Broad, *Five Types of Ethical Theory*, chapter 3.
142 Butler, 'Dissertation II', *Analogy*, p. 319 (*Works*, I, p. 338)
143 Butler, Sermon 2, in 'Fifteen Sermons' (*Works*, II, p. 24).
144 Butler, 'Dissertation II', *Analogy*, p. 318 (*Works*, I, p. 337)
145 Butler, Sermon 11, in 'Fifteen Sermons' (*Works*, II, pp. 150–1).
146 Butler, *Analogy*, p. 100 (*Works*, I, p. 107).
147 Gilbert, *The Power of Harmony*, Preface, quoted in E. Wasserman, 'Nature Moralized: The Divine Analogy in the Eighteenth Century', *ELH*, 20, 1953, p. 45.
148 See the words of Cleo, in *An Enquiry into the Origins of Honour*: 'to be acceptable to God, men should . . . make war with themselves, and mortify the flesh', (p. 104).
149 Butler, *Analogy*, p. 54 (*Works*, I, p. 58).
150 Ibid., p. 48 (*Works*, I, p. 52).
151 Ibid., pp. 34–5 (*Works*, I, pp. 37–8).
152 Ibid., p. 57 (*Works*, I, p. 61).
153 Ibid., p. 128 (*Works*, I, p. 137).
154 Butler, Sermon 5, in 'Six Sermons' (*Works*, II, p. 293).
155 Butler, *Analogy*, pp. 128–9 (*Works*, I, pp. 137–8).
156 Ibid., p. 122 (*Works*, I, p. 131).
157 Butler, Sermon 3, in 'Fifteen Sermons' (*Works*, II, p. 30).
158 Butler, *Analogy*, p. 123–4 (*Works*, I, pp. 132–3).
159 See below, pp. 180ff; and David Nicholls 'Images of God and the State: Political Analogy and Religious Discourse', *Theological Studies*, 42, 1981, pp. 195ff.
160 Butler, *Analogy*, p. 171 (*Works*, I, p. 181).
161 As we shall see (below, p. 145), not all deists rejected the idea of divine revelation, though they generally denied that this involved anything more than a reassertion of natural religion.
162 Butler, *Analogy*, p. 160 (*Works*, I, p. 171).
163 Ibid., p. 170 (*Works*, I, p. 180); see also p. 182 (*Works*, I, p. 193).
164 Ibid., p. 200 (*Works*, I, p. 212).
165 Ibid., pp. 201–2 (*Works*, I, pp. 213–14).
166 Ibid., p. 211 (*Works*, I, p. 224); vicarious suffering we can recognise, but vicarious punishment only in the sense in which the term 'punishment' is used by boxing commentators!
167 Butler, *Analogy*, p. 211 (*Works*, I, p. 224).
168 Ibid., pp. 171–2 (*Works*, I, pp. 181–2).
169 Ibid., p. 124 (*Works*, I, p. 133).
170 Ibid., pp. 232–3 (*Works*, I, pp. 246–7).
171 Newman, *Fifteen Sermons Preached before the University of Oxford*, p. 191.
172 Newman, *Discourses addressed to Mixed Congregations*, p. 189. See David Nicholls, 'Individualism and the Appeal to Authority' in Nicholls and Kerr, eds, *John Henry Newman*, pp. 198ff.
173 Butler, Sermon 4, in 'Six Sermons' (*Works*, II, p. 278).
174 Butler, Sermon 3, in 'Six Sermons' (*Works*, II, p. 254).
175 Butler, Sermon 4, in 'Six Sermons' (*Works*, II, p. 278).
176 Butler, *Analogy*, p. 100 (*Works*, I, p. 107).
177 Butler, Sermon 14, in 'Fifteen Sermons', (*Works*, II, pp. 185–7).
178 Butler, Sermon 3, in 'Six Sermons' (*Works*, II, p. 262.)
179 Coleridge, *Essay on the Constitution of Church and State* and *Lay Sermons*.
180 Butler, Sermon 2, in 'Six Sermons' (*Works*, II, p. 236).

181 Ibid., II, p. 235
182 Butler, Sermon 4, in 'Six Sermons' (*Works*, II, p. 281).
183 Butler, Sermons 2 and 6, in 'Six Sermons' (*Works*, II, pp. 239 and 319).
184 Butler, Sermon 4, in 'Six Sermons' (*Works*, II, p. 279). He probably had Mandeville in mind when he observed how 'such as pretend to be distinguished for the love of liberty should be the only persons who plead for keeping down the poor': Sermon 3, in 'Six Sermons' (*Works*, II, p. 250).
185 Butler, Sermon 4, in 'Six Sermons' (*Works*, II, p. 280).
186 Ibid., II, p. 283
187 Butler, Sermon 6, in 'Six Sermons', (*Works*, II, p. 308).
188 Ibid., II, p. 314.
189 Vereker, *Eighteenth Century Optimism*, pp. 73ff. ; for Adam Smith, see above, pp. 34ff.
190 Butler, *Analogy*, p. 46 (*Works*, I, pp. 49–50).
191 Butler, Sermon 14, in 'Fifteen Sermons' (*Works*, II, p. 186). Hegel, 'The German Constitution', (*Political Writings*, pp 144ff.).
192 Butler, Sermon 15, in 'Fifteen Sermons'(*Works*, II, p. 203).
193 Mossner, *Bishop Butler*, p. 11.
194 Bernstein, *Beyond Objectivism and Relativism*, p. 190.
195 Swinburne, 'Hymn of man' (*Songs before Sunrise*, p. 124).

4 REVOLUTIONARY POLITICS

1 Tocqueville, *On the State of Society*, p. 19.
2 McManners, *The French Revolution and the Church*, p. 42.
3 Price, *A Discourse on the Love of our Country*, p. 23. On the general theme of the sovereign people, see Morgan, *Inventing the People*.
4 Vergniaud, cited in Ozouf, *Festivals*, p. 128.
5 Ozouf, *Festivals*, p. 129.
6 M. Vovelle, 'Sociologie et idéologie des fêtes de la révolution', *Annales historiques de la révolution française*, 47, 1975, pp. 408ff.
7 Braudel, *Civilization*, III pp. 315, 320, 287.
8 Skocpol, *States and Social Revolutions*, p. 29.
9 Cited by Tocqueville, *On the State of Society*, p. 297.
10 J. Michelet, *Histoire de la révolution française*, I, p. 290, and A. Aulard in an article of 1885, both quoted in Guilllemin, *Robespierre*, pp. 376n. and 404.
11 Quoted in Thompson, *Robespierre*, p. 620.
12 Hampson, *Life and Opinions*, p. 179.
13 Early biographies included one by his sister and a hostile account of his early life from a former schoolteacher of his. For details of Robespierre's early life, see chapter 1 of Thompson, *Robespierre*.
14 Robespierre, 'Pour la liberté des cultes', 21 novembre 1793, *Oeuvres*, X, p. 197 (*Ecrits*, p. 284).
15 W. H. Sewell, 'Le citoyen/la citoyenne: Activity, Passivity and the Revolutionary Concept of Citizenship', in Lucas, ed., *Political Culture*, pp. 105ff.
16 On the anti-Christian campaigns, see J. de Viguerie, 'L'idéologie antifanatique dans les sections de Paris en l'an II', *Mélanges de science religieuse*, 48:1–2, 1991, pp.51ff.
17 Robespierre, 'Sur la liberté de la presse', 22 août 1791 (*Oeuvres*, VII, pp. 647ff.) and 'Sur les droits politiques des hommes de couleur', 24 septembre 1791, *Oeuvres*, VII, p. 738 (*Ecrits*, pp. 105 and 112).

18 *Oeuvres*, I, pp. 670 and 673, quoted in Hampson, *Life and Opinions*, p. 31.
19 *Oeuvres*, I, p. 677, quoted in Hampson, *Life and Opinions*, p. 32.
20 'Sur les rapports des idées religieuses et morales avec les principes républicains et sur les fêtes nationales', 7 mai 1794, *Oeuvres*, X, p. 453 (*Ecrits*, p. 317).
21 'Sur les circonstances actuelles', 26 mars 1792(*Oeuvres*, VIII, pp. 230 and 234–5).
22 Thompson, *Robespierre*, p. 215.
23 'Sur le droit de pétition', 9 mai 1791, *Oeuvres*, VII, pp. 313ff. (*Ecrits*, p. 107). See David Nicholls, 'Addressing God as Ruler: Prayer and Petition', *The British Journal of Sociology*, 44, 1993, pp. 125ff; and below, pp. 209ff.
24 Masson, *La Religion de Rousseau*, III, p. 233.
25 *Oeuvres*, V, pp. 116–17.
26 'Sur les rapports', 7 mai 1794, *Oeuvres*, X, p. 457 (*Ecrits*, pp. 323–4).
27 'La guerre declarée à la divinité n'est qu'une division en faveur de la royauté', 'Sur les principes de morale politique', 5 février 1794, *Oeuvres*, X, p. 361 (*Ecrits*, p. 303). 'Il s'agit de considérer seulement athéisme comme national, et lié à un système de conspiration contre la République', 'Sur les rapports', 7 mai 1794, *Oeuvres*, X, p. 452 (*Ecrits*, p. 317).
28 'Sur les rapports', 7 mai 1794, *Oeuvres*, X, p. 451 (*Ecrits*, p. 316).
29 'Pour la liberté des cultes', 21 novembre 1793, *Oeuvres*, X, p. 196 (*Ecrits*, p. 283); see also Tocqueville, *On the State of Society*, p. 273.
30 Speech at Jacobin Club, 15 mai 1794, quoted in A. Cobban, *Rousseau and the Modern State*, p. 54.
31 'Pour la liberté des cultes', 21 novembre 1793, *Oeuvres*, X, pp. 194ff. (*Ecrits*, pp. 283–5).
32 Speech on 5 décembre 1793 (*Oeuvres*, X, p. 229).
33 'L'enseignement dispensé a un caractère religieux. Il est destinéà inculquer au peuple et à exalter des idées ou plutôt des mots divinisés', de Viguerie, 'L'idéologie antifanatique', p. 56.
34 On the complex relationship between the cult of reason and the cult of the supreme being, see Michel Vovelle, 'The adventures of Reason: of from Reason to the Supreme Being', in Lucas, ed., *Rewriting the French Revolution*, pp. 132ff.
35 Hampson, *Will and Circumstance*, p. 240; and Guillemin, *Robespierre*, pp. 387ff.
36 Robespierre, 'Sur les rapports', *Oeuvres*, X, p. 445 (*Ecrits*, p. 309).
37 Robespierre, 'Rapport sur les principes', 25 décembre 1793, *Oeuvres*, X, p. 277 (*Ecrits*, p. 291).
38 Robespierre, 'Rapport sur la situation', 18 novembre 1793, *Oeuvres*, X, p. 185 (*Ecrits*, p. 271).
39 Robespierre, in *Courrier*, janvier 1792, quoted by Thompson, *Robespierre*, p. 209.
40 McManners, *The French Revolution*, p. 69.
41 Rousseau, *Du Contrat social*, 4:8 (*Political Writings*, II, pp. 130ff.).
42 See Gustave Laurent, in *Oeuvres de Robespierre*, V, p. 270.
43 Berthe and de Langre, *Maximilien Robespierre*, pp. 55ff., quoted in Hampson, *Life and Opinions*, p. 16.
44 Stéfane-Pol, *Autour de Robespierre*, p. 150, quoted in Hampson, *Life and Opinions*, p. 88, 'as Stéfane-Pol'. 'Stéfane-Pol' was the *nom de plume* of Paul Coutant.
45 Babbitt, *Rousseau and Romanticism*, p. 122, quoted in Cassirer, *Rousseau, Kant and Goethe*, p. 47.
46 J.- P. Brissot, *De la vérité*, p. 212, quoted in Hampson, *Will and Circumstance*, p. 88.
47 Billaud-Varenne, *Le Dernier Coup porté aux préjugés et à la superstition*, pp. 348–9, quoted in Hampson, *Will and Circumstance*, p. 62.
48 'Sur les rapports', 7 mai 1974, *Oeuvres*, X, pp. 454–5 (*Ecrits*, p. 320).
49 Saint-Just, Speech on 28 janvier 1793 (*Oeuvres complètes*, I, p. 409).

50 Saint-Just, 'Rapport à la Convention', 10 octobre 1793 (*Oeuvres*, II, p. 76).
51 'Il faut que les législateurs du peuple français fixent les principes de leur politique envers les amis et les ennemis de la République', 17 novembre 1793, *Oeuvres*, X, p. 168 (*Ecrits*, p. 269).
52 'Sur les principes du gouvernement révolutionnaire', 25 décembre 1793, *Oeuvres*, X, p. 274 (*Ecrits*, p. 288).
53 'Sur les principes de morale politique', 5 février 1794, *Oeuvres*, X, p. 356 (*Ecrits*, p. 300).
54 See Nicholls, *Deity and Domination*, pp. 99ff.
55 See, for example, Popper, *The Open Society*, I, p. 265.
56 'Réponse à l'accusation de J.- B. Louvet', 5 novembre 1792, *Oeuvres*, IX, p. 89 (*Ecrits*, p. 191).
57 Saint-Just, in *Moniteur*, 25 avril 1793 (*Discours et rapports*, p. 131).
58 'Sur la nouvelle Déclaration des Droits', 24 avril 1793, *Oeuvres*, IX, p. 467 (*Ecrits*, p. 249) and 'Discours dur la constitution', 10 mai 1793, *Oeuvres*, IX, p. 501.
59 'Rapport présenté à la Convention', 10 octobre 1793, *Oeuvres*, II, p. 76 (*Discours*, p. 118).
60 'Discours à la Convention', 24 avril 1793, *Oeuvres*, I, p. 426 (*Discours*, p. 102).
61 22 octobre 1792, *Oeuvres*, I, p. 358 (*Discours*, p. 55).
62 'Rapport présenté à la Convention', 10 octobre 1793, *Oeuvres*, II, p. 86 (*Discours*, p. 130).
63 24 avril 1793, *Oeuvres*, I, p. 420 (*Discours*, p. 96).
64 Sieyès, *Qu'est ce que le Tiers Etat* (1789), chapter 6 (*What is the Third Estate?*, p. 159).
65 Saint-Just, 'Rapport à la Convention', 13 mars 1794, *Oeuvres*, II, p. 273 (*Discours*, p. 171).
66 Saint-Just, 'Discours sur la division constitutionnelle du territoire', 15 mai 1793, (*Oeuvres*, I, p. 456).
67 See Jaurès, *Histoire socialiste*, II, p. 267, quoted in Thompson, *Robespierre*, p. 92.
68 Hampson, *Will and Circumstance*, p. 219.
69 'Discours sur le plan de l'éducation nationale', 29 juillet 1793, *Oeuvres*, X, p. 32 (*Ecrits*, p. 264).
70 'Plan de Michel Lepeletier', 13 juillet 1793 (*Ecrits*, p. 256).
71 See Mona Ozouf, 'La révolution française et l'idée de l'homme nouveau', in Lucas, ed., *The Political Culture*, pp. 213ff.
72 Berthe and de Langre, *Maximilien Robespierre*, p. 74.
73 'Sur les principes de morale politique', 5 février 1794, *Oeuvres*, X, p. 357 (*Ecrits*, p. 300).
74 'Discours à l'académie royale d'Arras', *Oeuvres*, I, p. 24 (*Ecrits*, p. 72); and 'Lettres de Maximillien Robespierre à ses commettans', *Oeuvres*, V, p. 17.
75 'Sur la rééligibilité des députés', 18 mai 1791; *Oeuvres*, VII, p. 404 (*Ecrits*, p. 116).
76 'Sur les principes de morale publique', 5 février 1794, *Oeuvres*, X, pp. 250ff. (*Ecrits*, pp. 292 and 298).
77 'Sur les rapports', 7 mai 1794, *Oeuvres*, X, pp. 442ff. (*Ecrits*, p. 322).
78 'Sur les principes du gouvernement révolutionnaire', 25 décembre 1793, *Oeuvres*, X, p. 277 (*Ecrits*, p. 291).
79 'Sur le marc d'argent', avril 1791, *Oeuvres*, VII, p. 165 (*Ecrits*, p. 99).
80 Quoted in Thompson, *Robespierre*, p. 373.
81 'S'il y avait un peuple de Dieux, il se gouvernerait démocratiquement'. Rousseau, *Du Contrat social*, 3:4 (*Political Writings*, II, p. 74).
82 'Adresse de Maximilien Robespierre aux Français' (1791) (*Ecrits*, pp. 126–7).
83 'Sur la pétition du peuple avignonnais', 18 novembre 1790, *Oeuvres*, VI, p. 587 (*Ecrits*, p. 89).

84 3 décembre 1792; *Oeuvres*, IX, p. 123, quoted in Guillemin, *Robespierre*, p. 406.

85 26 février 1794, *Oeuvres*, II, p. 230 (*Discours*, p. 135).

86 '... a society of small producers, each possessing a property, a small workshop, and a boutique', Lefebvre, *Etudes sur la révolution française*, p. 97.

87 Camus, *The Rebel*, p. 95.

88 Robespierre, cited in Hampson, *Will and Circumstance*, p. 254.

89 Hampson, *Will and Circumstance*, p. 226.

90 Frankel, *The Faith of Reason*, p. 70; and Vereker, *Eighteenth Century Optimism*, pp. 178ff. and 184.

91 Frankel, *The Faith of Reason*, p. 107.

92 *Mémoires de Mme d'Epinay*, quoted in Masson, *La Religion*. She may not, however, be an entirely reliable witness!

93 *L'Inégalité*, 'Preface' (*Political Writings*, I, pp. 136 and 141). P.- M. Masson doubts that Rousseau's statements are merely ironical attempts to avoid persecution by police and theologians, as was the case with Buffon, Maupertuis and Diderot (*La Formation religieuse de Rousseau*, I, pp. 214ff).

94 *L'Inégalité*, part 2 (*Political Writings*, I, p. 179).

95 Ibid., I, pp. 175–6.

96 'L'essai sur l'origine des langues', chapter 9; cited in Derathé, *Rousseau et la science politique, p. 176*.

97 *L'Inégalité*, part 2 (*Political Writings*, I, p. 180).

98 'L'homme qui médite est un animal dépravé', *L'Inégalité*, part 1 (*Political Writings*, I, p.146).

99 'Sur le luxe, le commerce et les arts' (*Political Writings*, I, p. 341). Though Rousseau was hostile to Descartes, there is evidence of debt to Malebranche: see Emile Bréhier, 'Les lectures malabranchistes de Jean-Jacques Rousseau', *Revue internationale de philosophie*, octobre 1938, pp. 98–120.

100 Rousseau expressed admiration for Clarke in his letter to M. de Franquières (1769), (*Religious Writings* p. 383) and in 'Profession de foi du vicaire savoyard' (1762) (ibid., p. 124).

101 D'Alembert, *Oeuvres*, XIV, p. 267, quoted in Vereker, *Eighteenth Century Optimism*, pp. 162–3.

102 *Confessions*, book V, p. 190.

103 *Religious Writings*, p. 153.

104 *Correspondance générale de Jean-Jacques Rousseau*, XVII, pp. 2–3, quoted in Cassirer, *Question*, p. 127. It is not clear in which category he would have placed the commital of his five children to the foundling hospital!

105 *La nouvelle Héloïse*, 3:20 (*Oeuvres complètes*, IV, p. 256). We cannot, of course, take the words of characters in Rousseau's novels as always representing his own position; but they represent positions which he has considered and reinforce opinions expressed in his non-fictional works.

106 Letter to a Genevan Minister (1758) (*Religious Writings*, p. 69).

107 'Lettre à d'Alembert sur les spectacles' (1758) (*Religious Writings*, p. 75); 'Profession de foi du vicaire savoyard' (1762) (ibid., pp. 128 and 171).

108 R. Derathé, *Le Rationalisme de Jean-Jacques Rousseau*, p. 176. The same might be said of J. H. Newman; see particularly his *Oxford University Sermons*, and *Grammar of Assent*.

109 *Du Contrat social*, 1:1 (*Political Writings*, II, p. 24).

110 *L'Economie politique* (1755) (*Political Writings*, I, p. 255).

111 Ibid., I, p. 245.

112 Cassirer, *Question*, p. 58.

113 Ibid., p. 70.

114 *L'Economie politique* (*Political Writings*, I, p. 245).

115 Tocqueville, *On the State of Society*, p. 297.
116 *L'Economie politique* (*Political Writings*, I, p. 248).
117 *Du Contrat social*, 1:6 (*Political Writings*, II, p. 33); but he appears to have qualified this in 2:4, where he stated that each alienates only those powers which it is important for the community to control; the sovereign, however, is the sole judge of what is important (*Political Writings*, II, p. 45).
118 *L'Economie politique* (*Political Writings*, I, pp. 254 and 257).
119 'Projet de constitution pour la Corse' (*Political Writings*, II, p. 350).
120 See especially Duguit, *Rousseau, Kant and Hegel*; and Talmon, *Origins*.
121 *Du Contrat social*, 2:6 (*Political Writings*, II, p. 50).
122 Küng, *Structures of the Church*, p. 34.
123 *Du Contrat social*, 1:7 and 1:8 (*Political Writings*, II, pp. 36 and 37).
124 Ibid., 2:3 and 4:1 (*Political Writings*, II, pp. 42–3 and 103). In his essay *De l'économie politique*, however, he does recognise the fact that the state is made up of smaller groups. (*Political Writings*, I, p. 242).
125 '. . . withdraw, search for solitude', 'Lettres morales' (1757–8) (*Religious Writings*, p. 60). Rousseau began his *Rêveries du promeneur solitaire* by characterising himself as one who is 'alone on the earth' (p. 3).
126 See Cassirer, *Rousseau, Kant and Goethe*, p. 8.
127 See David Nicholls, 'Individualism and the Appeal to Authority', in Nicholls and Kerr, eds, *John Henry Newman*, pp. 194–213.
128 Newman, *Parochial Sermons*, I, p. 48 and II, p. 245, and *The Via Media of the Anglican Church*, p. lxxx.
129 The reason why Rousseau, like Newman in the following century, made so much fuss about 'conscience' was his uneasy apprehension that in his political system citizens are tied hand and foot. Rousseau's dangerous myth of a social contract implies that each unit has consented to a political imprisonment, handing over its conscience to the sovereign, whose general will is ultimately infallible. Newman in turn spoke of drinking to conscience first and to the pope afterwards; Lord Acton applauded. But Newman also taught that the well-instructed Catholic conscience must accept the infallible teaching of the pope and, even more generally, 'we must *never* oppose his will, or dispute his word, or criticise his policy, or shrink from his side' (*Sermons Preached on Various Occasions*, p. 286, my italics). Appeals to conscience in the context of these authoritarian political systems turn out to be quite vacuous: see Grave, *Conscience in Newman's Thought*; and David Nicholls, 'Gladstone, Newman and the Politics of Pluralism', in James Bastable, ed., *Newman and Gladstone*, pp. 32ff.
130 *L'Economie politique* (*Political Writings*, I, p. 241).
131 'L'état de guerre' (*Political Writings*, I, p. 298).
132 Derathé, *Rousseau et la science politique*, pp. 410–13. This author follows the argument of A. Merstre, 'La notion de personnalité morale chez Rousseau', *Revue de droit public et de la science politique en France et à l'etranger*, 18, 1902, pp. 447ff.
133 *Political Writings*, I, p. 39. He rightly points out that Rousseau gave a new turn to contract theory and to the relation between the citizen and the state, but this does not amount to a rejection of individualism.
134 See Nicholls, *The Pluralist State, passim*.
135 Tocqueville, *On the State of Society* , pp. 298–9.
136 *Lettres écrites de la montagne* (1764) (*Political Writings*, II, p. 217).
137 *Du Contrat social*, 1:3 (*Political Writings*, II, p. 26).
138 *L'Economie politique* (*Political Writings*, I, p. 243).
139 *L'Inégalité*, part 2 (*Political Writings*, I, p. 189).

140 Ibid., (*Political Writings*, I, p. 196).
141 *Du Contrat social*, 4:8 (*Political Writings*, II, p. 124).
142 Ibid., (*Political Writings*, II, p. 126).
143 Ibid., 4:8, (*Political Writings*, II, p. 129).
144 Ibid., 4:8 (*Political Writings*, II, pp. 131 and 129). In the first of his *Lettresé crites de la montagne*, however, he interpreted this chapter on civil religion in a manner clean contrary to the plain sense of the words: 'je pense avoir dit que l'Evangile est sublime, et le plus fort lien de la société' (*Political Writings*, II, p. 169). This ability to impose a new meaning on a perfectly clear text is also something Newman shared with Rousseau. See Valentine Cunningham, 'Dangerous Conceits or Confirmations Strong?', in Nicholls and Kerr, eds, *John Henry Newman*, pp. 233–52.
145 See Parker, *The Cult of Antiquity*, and Rawson, *The Spartan Tradition*.
146 Ozouf, *Festivals*, p. 276.
147 *Lettres écrites de la montagne*, 5 (*Oeuvres*, p. 110).
148 *Du Contrat social*, 4:8 (*Political Writings*, II, pp. 132ff).
149 *Confessions*, book VIII, p. 365. ; 'Profession de foi' (*Religious Writings*, p. 191).
150 Talmon, *The Origins*, p. 22.
151 Pomeau, *La Religion de Voltaire*, p. 102.
152 Ozouf, *Festivals*, p. 268.
153 See especially Hendel, *Jean-Jacques Rousseau Moralist*.
154 Masson, *La Formation*, I, pp. 198ff.
155 Rousseau, *Du Contrat social*, 4:8 (*Political Writings*, II, p. 128).
156 *De l'Inégalité*, part 2 (*Political Writings*, I, p. 182).
157 'Lettre à M. de Beaumont' (1763) (*Religious Writings*, p. 258).
158 'Goodness is the necessary consequence of a power without limits and love of self', 'Profession de foi' (*Religious Writings*, p. 146).
159 *Rêveries*, 6, p. 84; 'Profession de foi' (*Religious Writings*, p. 151).
160 'God is a monarch, not arbitary but limited by the rules of infinite wisdom enjoyed to his 'infinite power''*Manuel des souverains*, pp. 106–7), cited in Plongeron, *Théologie et politique* , p. 105n.
161 Le Mercier de la Rivière, *L'Ordre naturel et essentiel des sociétés politiques*, I, p. 302, cited in Vereker, *Eighteenth Century Optimism*, p. 204.
162 Vereker, *Eighteenth Century Optimism*, p. 198.
163 Grimsley, *Quest*, p. 108.
164 Rousseau, *Religious Writings*, p. 94.
165 'Profession de foi' (*Religious Writings*, p. 137).
166 Ibid., (*Religious Writings*, pp. 152 and 146); 'Lettre à Voltaire' (1756), (*Religious Writings*, pp. 33–4).
167 Grimsley, *Quest*, p. 118; see also p. 95.
168 Shklar, *Men and Citizens*, p. 136.
169 Cited in Grimsley, *Quest*, p. 12.
170 *Rêveries*, 5, p. 71.
171 Grimsley, *Quest*, p. 34.
172 *Boswell on the Grand Tour*, p. 300, cited in Shklar, *Men and Citizens*, p. 130.
173 Grimsley, *Quest*, p. 107.
174 *Confessions*, book VI, p. 225.
175 'Profession de foi' (*Religious Writings*, pp. 165–6).
176 *Lettres écrites de la montagne* (*Religious Writings*, pp. 371–2). This is the theme of Julie's prayer (ibid., p. 94).
177 The prayer goes on to penitence for past sins and an expression of amendment of life. It concludes, however, with petitions for spiritual blessings

on 'maman' and his other benefactors and friends (*Religious Writings*, pp. 4–7).

178 *Confessions*, book VI, p. 225.

179 'Profession de foi' (*Religious Writings*, p. 196).

180 'Lettre à M. de Franquières' (*Religious Writings*, pp. 384–5). Newman wrote: 'Faith is a moral principle. It is created in the mind, not so much by facts, as by probabilities . . . a good and a bad man will think very different things probable . . . a man *is* responsible for his faith, because he is responsible for his likings and dislikings' (*Fifteen Sermons*, pp. 191–2).

181 Braudel, *Civilization*, III, p. 320.

182 Ibid., III, p. 287; see also Rothkrug, *The Opposition to Louis XIV*, p. 217

183 See Voltaire's *Poèmes sur le désastre de Lisbonne*; also Barber, *Leibniz in France, from Arnaud to Voltaire*, pp. 225ff.

184 See Pomeau, *La Religion de Voltaire*, p. 209.

185 Frankel, *The Faith of Reason*, p. 44.

5 DIVINE CONSTITUTIONALISM

Abbreviations:

APW   Charles S. Hyneman and Donald S. Lutz, eds, *American Political Writing during the Founding Era, 1760–1805*.

PS   Ellis Sandoz, ed., *Political Sermons of the American Founding Era, 1730–1805*.

1 The term has often been used to refer only to those who were present at the Constitutional Convention, but here I adopt a more general usage, referring to all who played a significant part in the process which culminated in the adoption of the constitution.

2 Edward S. Corwin, 'The Worship of the Constitution' (1920) (*Corwin on the Constitution*, p. 49).

3 Dummer, *A Defence of the New England Charters*, p. 64, quoted in Pole, *Gift*, p. 22.

4 See Pole, *Gift*, pp. 22–3.

5 Cited in Bailyn, *Ideological Origins*, pp. 278–9.

6 Jonathan Maxcy, 'An Oration' (1799) (*APW*, II, pp. 1045–6). The Senate was at this time indirectly elected, its members being chosen by state legislatures.

7 North, 'A Discourse on the English Constitution' (Society for the Reformation of Principles, *The Scholar Armed*, I, p. 254).

8 Paine, *The Rights of Man* (1791–2) (*Representative Selections*, p. 91).

9 I shall discuss this in part 3 of this triptych, *Political Rhetoric and Religious Discourse in the Seventeenth Century*.

10 See the classic works of Perry Miller: *The New England Mind: the Seventeenth Century; The New England Mind: From Colony to Province; Errand in the Wilderness*. Also de Jong, *The Covenant Idea*.

11 Cited in Bailyn, *Origins*, p. 160.

12 Paine, *The Rights of Man* (*Representative Selections*, p. 195).

13 Pole, *Gift*, p. 67.

14 See Malone, *Jefferson the Virginian*, p. 101.

15 Cherry, ed., *God's New Israel*; Brock, *Mosaics*.

16 Cited in Cherry, ed., *God's New Israel*, p. 85.

17 Jefferson, 'Second Inaugural Address' (1805), (*Basic Writings*, p. 363).

18 Bailyn, *Origins*, p. 26.

19 Pocock writes: 'the American Revolution and Constitution . . . form the last act of the civic Renaissance' (*The Machiavellian Moment*, p. 462).
20 White, *The Philosophy of the American Revolution*; Bailyn, *Origins*.
21 See R. L. Ketcham, 'James Madison and Religion', *Journal of the Presbyterian Historical Society*, 28, 1969, pp. 65ff. ; and J. H. Smilie, 'Madison and Wither- spoon', *Princeton University Library Chronicle*, 17, 1961, pp. 118ff.
22 Quoted in McCoy, *The Last of the Fathers*, p. 6.
23 *Papers of Madison*, XIV, p. 100.
24 *Works of Adams*, II, p. 15.
25 30 Apr. 1789 (*Papers of Madison*, XII, p. 123).
26 5 May 1789 (*Papers of Madison*, XII, p. 132).
27 Hamilton, Madison and Jay, *The Federalist*, no. 37, p. 181.
28 *The Federalist*, no. 2, p. 6.
29 James Madison, *et al.*, 'Memorial and Remonstrance Against Religious Assess- ments' (1785) (*APW*, I, p. 637).
30 Adams to James Warren, 17 June 1782 (*Works*, IX, p. 512); and Adams to Jefferson, 28 June 1813 (*The Adams–Jefferson Letters*, II, pp. 339–40).
31 Adams, 'Draft Constitution for Massachussets' (*Works*, IV, p. 220).
32 The preamble to such a resolution for a day of prayer in May 1775 began; 'As the great governor of the world, by his supreme and universal providence, not only conducts the course of nature with unerring wisdom and rectitude, but frequently influences the minds of men to service the wise and gracious purposes of his providential government . . .' (Ford, *et al.*, eds, *Journals of the Continental Congress*, II, p. 87).
33 Adams, preface to *A Defence of the Constitution* (1787) (*Works*, IV, p. 291).
34 Ibid., IV, p. 292.
35 'Thoughts on Government' (1776) (*APW*, I, p. 402).
36 'An Election Sermon' (*APW*, I, p. 289). On Hoadly, see below, pp. 152–3.
37 See May, *The Enlightenment*, p. 72.
38 See his letter to Benjamin Waterhouse, 26 June 1822, where he attacked the Trinitarianism of Athanasius and Calvin and declared: 'I trust that there is not a *young man* now living in the United States who will not die a Unitarian' (*Basic Writings*, p. 775).
39 On Jefferson's religion, see William D. Gould, 'The Religious Opinions of Thomas Jefferson', *Mississippi Valley Historical Review*, 20, 1933, pp. 197ff; G. H. Knoles, 'The Religious Ideas of Thomas Jefferson', *Mississippi Valley Historical Review*, 30, 1943, pp. 195ff; also *Thomas Jefferson on Democracy*, p. 121; Foote, *The Religion of Thomas Jefferson*; Sandford, *The Religious Life of Thomas Jefferson*; C. O. Lerch, 'Jefferson and the Election of 1800', *William and Mary Quarterly*, 3rd series 5, 1948, pp. 467ff.
40 Perry Miller, 'From the Covenant to the Revival', in Smith and Jamison, eds, *Religion in American Life*, p. 353; Morais, *Deism*; also Koch, *Republican Religion*.
41 Jefferson to B. Rush, 21 April 1803 (*Basic Writings*, p. 660).
42 Cited in Peterson, *Thomas Jefferson*, p. 960.
43 Jefferson to Mrs S. H. Smith, 6 Aug. 1816 (*Basic Writings*, p. 753); and, 'A Bill for Establishing Religious Freedom' (1779), ibid. p 48.
44 Jefferson, 'First Inaugural Address' (1801) (*Basic Writings*, p. 334).
45 See May, *The Enlightenment*, p. 163.
46 *The Federalist*, no. 53, p. 274. (There is doubt as to whether this was by Madison or Hamilton.)
47 *The Federalist*, no. 25, p. 124; (my italics).
48 'Thoughts on Government' (*Works*, IV, p. 194).
49 Ibid.

50 *The Letters of John Adams*, II, pp. 15–16.
51 Adams to Hitchbourne, 29 May 1776, cited in Colbourne, *The Lamp of Experience*, p. 98.
52 See the discussion in White, *Philosophy*, pp. 192ff.
53 Ahlstrom, *A Religious History*, p. 358.
54 Ackerman, *We the People*.
55 John Adams, 'Proclamation of the Great and General Court' (1775–6) (*Works*, I, p. 193). This notion of sovereignty is based upon Blackstone's *Commentaries*, where it is alleged that this power is located in Parliament, whose actions 'no power of earth can undo'. See Barker, *Essays on Government*, pp. 135ff. On the conception of 'the people', see Morgan, *Inventing the People*.
56 Hamilton, *The Federalist*, no 22, p. 110.
57 *The Federalist*, nos 49 and 51, pp. 257 and 264.
58 'Public Opinion', in *National Gazette*, 19 December 1791 (*Papers of Madison*, XIV, p. 170).
59 See the discussion in Bailyn, *Origins*, pp. 198ff. (esp p. 208). Bailyn unfortunately misrepresents Hobbes in this discussion.
60 Cited in Sandoz, *A Government of Laws*, p. 210.
61 See Nicholls, *The Pluralist State*.
62 Hamilton or Madison, *The Federalist*, no. 55, p. 287.
63 Adams, 'Defence of the Constitutions of Government of the United States of America' (*Works*, IV, p. 406).
64 The words are Jefferson's, 8 Apr. 1816 *Adams–Jefferson Letters*, II, p. 467); see also Adams to Jefferson, 19 Apr. 1817, (ibid., II, p. 509).
65 Jefferson to Peter Carr, 10 Aug. 1787, cited in Koch, *Philosophy*, p. 18.
66 *Writings of Jefferson*, XII, p. 315.
67 Hamilton to James Duane, 3 Sept. 1780 (*Works of Hamilton*, I, p. 207).
68 In *APW*, II, p. 1003.
69 See below, pp. 167–8.
70 Quoted in Clark, *Benjamin Franklin*, p. 84.
71 In *Works of Adams*, II, p. 661.
72 In *Memoires of Benjamin Franklin*, I, p. 448.
73 Franklin, 'On the Providence of God in the Government of the World' (*Papers*, I, p. 268).
74 Franklin, letter to an unknown correspondent (1757) (*Papers*, VII, p. 294).
75 Farrand, ed., *Records of the Federal Convention of 1787*, I, p. 452n.
76 May, *The Enlightenment*, p. 127.
77 *Autobiography of Benjamin Franklin*, p. 162.
78 For a recent defence of Franklin, see Steven Forde, 'Benjamin Franklin's *Autobiography* and the Education of America', *American Political Science Review*, 86, 1992, pp. 357ff.
79 Aldridge, *Benjamin Franklin*, p. 3.
80 Jefferson to Adams, 11 Apr. 1823, cited in George H. Knoles, 'The Religious Ideas of Thomas Jefferson', *Mississippi Valley Historical Review*, 30, 1943, p. 199.
81 Stout, *The New England Soul*.
82 *The Great Doctrine of Original Sin Defended* (1758) (*The Works of President Edwards*, II, pp. 487–91), (quoted in Ahlstrom, *A Religious History*, p. 308).
83 Wills, *Explaining America*, p. 16.
84 Alan Heimert, 'Introduction' in Heimert and Miller, eds, *The Great Awakening*, p. lxi; McLoughlin, *Isaac Backus*, p. 231. Pole questions the evidence for such assertions, in *The Pursuit of Equality in American History*, p. 68, note 18.
85 Ahlstrom, *A Religious History*, p. 407.
86 Kuklick, *Churchmen and Philosophers*, p. 61.

87 Ibid., p. 60. It should be noted that the term 'republican' did not always imply an alternative to monarchy, but was compatible with limited or constitutional monarchy.

88 Ibid., pp. 60–1.

89 It is not entirely accurate to suggest that 'Newtonian cosmic philosophy furnished the deists with their central concept of God as a passive policeman' (Morais, *Deism*, p. 56). It was, indeed, Leibniz's quarrel with Newtonianism that it postulated a God who is always tinkering with things. See below, pp. 180ff.

90 Livingston, *Philosophic Solitude*, p. 39.

91 Freneau, 'On the Universality and other Attributes of the God of Nature' (Cady, ed., *Literature of the Early Republic*, p. 389).

92 Freneau, 'On the Uniformity and Perfection of Nature' (Cady, ed., *Literature of the Early Republic*, p. 390).

93 Robert Coram, 'Political Inquiries' (1791) (*APW*, II, p. 757); Benjamin Rush, 'A Plan for the Establishment of Public Schools and the Diffusion of Knowledge in Pennsylvania; to which are added, Thoughts upon the Mode of Education, Proper in a Republic' (1786) (*APW*, II, p. 687).

94 Samuel Williams, 'The Natural and Civil History of Vermont' (1794) (*APW*, II, pp. 964–5). See also 'Americanus' (Timothy Ford), who insisted that talk of a state of nature is misleading and that God placed humans in a social state. 'The Constitutionalist' (1794) (*APW*, II, pp. 902–3).

95 'All civil communities have their foundation in compacts, by which individuals immerge out of a state of nature, and become one great whole, cemented together by voluntary engagements; covenanting with one another, to observe such regulations, and perform such duties as may tend to mutual advantage': Timothy Stone, 'Election Sermon' (*APW*, II, p. 847).

96 'Rulers are but trustees, and government a trust', Phillips Payson ('A Sermon' (1778) (*APW*, I, p. 532); Locke, *Second Treatise on Civil Government*, §§ 221–2.

97 T. Q. (*APW*, I, p. 21).

98 Samuel Cooper, 'A Sermon' (1780) (*PS*, pp. 639–40).

99 Jonathan Mayhew, 'The Snare Broken' (1766) (*PS*, p. 258). On this theme, see Bailyn, *Ideological Origins*, pp. 58ff.

100 Joel Barlow, 'A Letter to the National Convention of France on the Defects of the Constitution of 1791' (1792) (*APW*, II, p. 826).

101 Daniel Shute, 'An Election Sermon' (*APW*, I, p. 121).

102 See Gough, *Fundamental Law*, and Pocock, *The Ancient Constitution*. See also the writings of C. H. McIlwain on constitutionalism, and Pennock and Chapman, eds, *Constitutionalism*.

103 'Four Letters on Interesting Subjects' (1776) (*APR*, I, p. 385); see also James Kent, 'An Introductory Lecture to a Course of Law Lectures' (1794) (*APW*, II, p.941).

104 'Philodemus' (Thomas Tudor Tucker), 'Conciliatory Hints' (1784) (*APW*, I, pp. 610–11).

105 Petition printed in Handlin and Handlin, eds, *Popular Sources*, pp. 61ff.

106 'An Election Sermon' (1762) (*APW*, I, pp. 6ff).

107 Daniel Shute, 'An Election Sermon' (1768) (*APW*, I, p. 111).

108 David Tappan, 'A Sermon' (1792) (*PS*, p. 1116).

109 Samuel Kendal, 'Religion the Only Sure Basis of Free Government' (1804) (*APW*, II, pp. 1247–8). See also Shute (ibid., I, p. 128).

110 This view would not, of course, be accepted by those who define a constitution in terms of a single written document, like the anonymous Philadelphian quoted above.

111 John Tucker, 'An Election Sermon' (1771) (*APW*, I, pp. 162 and 164).

112 Ibid., I, p. 162.

113 Ibid., I, p. 171.
114 Nathaniel Niles, 'Two Discourses on Liberty' (*APW*, I, p. 268n).
115 Benjamin Coleman, 'Government the Pillar of the Earth' (1730) (*PS*, p. 20). Some royalist imagery is to be found in the tract by Elisha Williams, 'The Essential Rights and Liberties of Protestants' (1744) (*PS*, pp. 55ff.) and in an election sermon, 'On the Right to Rebel against Governors' (1776) (*PS*, p. 431). See also Samuel Langdon (1775), in Thornton, ed., *Pulpit*, pp. 227ff.
116 Reprinted in *PS*, pp. 796–7. He here echoed the ideas of Samuel Clarke: see below p. 170.
117 McClintock (*PS*, p. 804; my italics).
118 Samuel West, 'On the Right to Rebel against Governors' (1776) (*APW*, I, pp. 422 and 414).
119 Zabdiel Adams, 'An Election Sermon' (1782) (*APW*, I, pp. 539–40).
120 'Overcoming Evil with Good' (1801) (*PS*, p. 1549).
121 Wilson, *Congressional Government*, p. 17.
122 Fisher Ames, 'The Dangers of American Liberty' (1805) (*APW*, II, p. 1300).
123 Thomas C. Grey, 'The Constitution as Scripture', *Stanford Law Review*, 37:1, 1984, p. 3. See also Corwin, 'The Worship of the Constitution'.
124 Sanford Levinson, 'The 'Constitution' in American Civil Religion', *Supreme Court Review*, 1979, pp. 123ff. ; and Levinson, *Constitutional Faith*; see also Grey, 'The Constitution as Scripture'.
125 Chillingworth, *The Religion of Protestants* (1638), p. 463.
126 See Ackerman, *We the People*, Part 1, *passim*.
127 Samuel Kendal, 'Religion' (*APW*, II, p. 1247); see also Abraham Williams: 'without social Vertues, Societies can't subsist; and these vertues can't be expected or depended on, without a belief in, and regard to the Supreme Being, and a future World: Consequently a religious Fear and Regard to God, ought to be encouraged in every Society, and with this View, publick social Worship and Instructions in social Virtues, maintained', 'An Election Sermon' (1762) (*APW*, I, p. 8).
128 Kendal, 'Religion' (*APW*, II, p. 1256).
129 Jonathan Edwards, Jr, 'The Necessity of the Belief of Christianity by the Citizens of a State, in Order to our Political Prosperity' (*PS*, p. 1220).
130 Selsam, *The Pennsylvania Constitution of 1776*, cited in May, *The Enlightenment*, p. 199.
131 Richard Price, 'A Discourse on the Love of our Country' (1790) (*PS*, p. 1015).
132 See Herberg, *Protestant, Catholic, Jew*; Bellah, *The Broken Covenant*; Neuhaus, *The Naked Public Square*.
133 Klein, ed., *The Independent Reflector*, p. 359.
134 Charles Chauncy, 'A Sermon' (1747) (*APW*, I, pp. 142–3).
135 Samuel Kendal 'Religion' (*APW*, II, p, 1247).
136 Timothy Stone 'Election Sermon' (1792) (*APW*, II, p. 841).
137 Hubbard, *Happiness*; quoted in Pole, *Gift*, p. 7.
138 James Wilson (Jensen, *Documentary History of Ratification*, II, p. 361), quoted in Morgan, *Inventing*, p. 281.
139 Samuel Miller, 'A Sermon' (1793) (*PS*, p. 1157).
140 Alexander Addison, 'Analysis of the Report of the Committee of the Virginia Assembly (1800) (*APW*, II, p. 1058). Rousseau himself, of course, extended popular sovereignty to the sphere of general legislation.
141 'Philodemus', 'Conciliatory Hints' (1784) (*APW*, I, p. 619).
142 Fisher Ames, 'The Dangers of American Liberty' (1805) (*APW*, II, p. 1301).
143 Theophilus Parsons, 'The Essex Results' (1778) (*APW*, I, p. 490).
144 Elizur Goodrich, 'A Sermon' (1787) (*PS*, pp. 931–2).

145 David Tappan, 'A Sermon' (1792) (*PS*, p. 1121).
146 Samuel Cooper, 'A Sermon preached before his excellency John Hancock Esq . . .' (1780) (*PS*, p. 634).
147 Perez Fobes, 'An Election Sermon' (1795) (*APW*, II, p. 1000).
148 Fobes (*APW*, II, pp. 904–5).
149 For example, Stanley Griswold, 'Overcoming Evil with Good' (1801) (*PS*, p. 1547).
150 Fay, *The Revolutionary Spirit*; May, *The Enlightenment*, pp. 245ff.
151 Cited by May, *The Enlightenment*, p. 248.
152 Noah Webster, 'The Revolution in France, Considered in Respect to its Progress and Effects' (1794) (*PS*, p. 1253). See also works by Timothy Dwight, 'The Duty of Americans, at the Present Crisis' (1798) (*PS*, pp. 1367ff.), *The Nature and Danger of Infidel Philosophy* and *A Discourse on Some Events of the Last Century*.
153 'A Son of Liberty' (Silas Downer), 'A Discourse at the Dedication of the Tree of Liberty' (1768) (*APW*, I, p. 99); Samuel Dunbar, 'The Presence of God with his People' (1760) (*PS* pp. 211ff.); Phillips Payson, 'A Sermon' (*APW*, I, p. 533).
154 Samuel Cooper, 'A Sermon' (*PS* p. 631).
155 'A Plan for the Establishment of Public Schools' (1786) (*APW*, I, p. 684).
156 Phillips Payson, 'A Sermon' (1778) (*APW*, I, p. 536).
157 Israel Evans, 'A Sermon Delivered at Concord' (1791) (*PS*, p. 1064); Benjamin Coleman, 'Government the Pillar of the Earth' (1730) (*PS*, p. 20). See also Joseph Lathrop, 'The Reformer, number II' (1786) (*APW*, I, p. 667).
158 Timothy Stone, 'Election Sermon' (*APW*, II, p. 842); Samuel West, 'On the Right' (*APW*, I, p. 416).
159 Henry Cumings, 'A Sermon Preached at Lexington' (1781) (*PS*, p. 664). God is 'a presiding Deity' for Samuel Kendal, 'Religion' (*APW*, II, p. 1254).
160 Nathaniel Niles, 'Two Discourses on Liberty' (1774) (*APW*, I, p. 273).
161 West, 'On the Right to Rebel Against Governors' (*PS*, pp. 440–5).
162 On this issue, see McIlwain, *The American Revolution*.

6 DEISTS, DISSENTERS AND FREE THINKERS

1 Sacheverell, *The Perils of False Brethren*, p. 12.
2 See, for example, Chubb, *A Short Dissertation on Providence*, and *A Discourse on Miracles*.
3 Clark misleadingly asserts that, as a result of their work, 'Belief in Divine Providence was a major casualty, and rejection of it strengthened with time among Deists' (*English Society*, p.280). Chapter 5 of Clark's book provides, however, an interesting assessment of the political aspects of religious heterodoxy in this period.
4 Collins, *A Discourse of Freethinking* (1713), p. 171, quoted in Stephen, *English Thought*, I, p. 79. The archbishop may have been less happy to own the self-styled freethinkers as his body! The roots of Collins's religion are indeed mainly British: O'Higgins, *Anthony Collins*, pp. 46ff.
5 Bolingbroke, 'On the Idea of a Patriot King', in *Letters on the Spirit of Patriotism: On the Idea of a Patriot King; and On the State of the Parties at the Accession of King George the First*, p. 94, reprinted (with minor changes) in *Works*, II, p. 382.
6 Bolingbroke, 'Letters or Essays Addressed to Alexander Pope, Esq. : Essay 1' (*Works*, III, p. 195).
7 Bolingbroke, 'Letters: Introduction' (*Works*, III, p. 50).
8 Bolingbroke, 'Letters on the Study and Use of History' (*Works*, II, p. 186).

9 Bolingbroke, 'A Dissertation upon Parties' (*Works*, II, p. 49); see also 'The Study and Use of History' (*Works*, II, p. 249).
10 Bolingbroke, 'Study and Use' (*Works*, II, p. 214).
11 Hume, 'Essay on Miracles'; Bradley, 'The Presuppositions of Critical History'; Bradley, *Collected Essays*, I, pp. 1–70.
12 Bolingbroke, 'Dissertation' (*Works*, II, pp. 155 and 166).
13 See Q. Skinner, 'The Principles and Practice of Opposition: the Case of Bolingbroke versus Walpole', in McKendrick, ed., *Historical Perspectives*.
14 For details of his early life, see Dickinson, *Bolingbroke*, chapter 1.
15 Swift, *Journal to Stella*, II, p.401; see also Swift, 'An Enquiry into the Behaviour of the Queen's Last Ministry', (*Political Tracts, 1713–1719*, pp. 134–5).
16 Pope, 'Epistle III, to Allen, Lord Bathurst' (*Poetical Works*, p. 306).
17 Defoe, *The True-born Englishman*, part 1, lines 8–11: startling anticipation of the world of Norman Tebbit, Cecil Parkinson and Nigel Lawson, leading to some of the same reactions from the traditional establishment!
18 Bolingbroke, 'Some Reflections', in *A Letter to Sir William Windham, II: Some Reflections on the Present State of the Nation; III: a Letter to Mr Pope*, pp. 375 and 407 (*Works*, II, p. 451).
19 Goldsmith, *The Deserted Village*, lines 348–52.
20 See Skinner, 'Principles and Practice'.
21 Quoted in Haraszti, *John Adams*, p. 54.
22 R. Shackleton, 'Montesquieu, Bolingbroke and the Separation of Powers', *French Studies*, 3, 1949, pp. 25ff.
23 Bolingbroke, 'Dissertation' (*Works*, II, p. 112), and 'Fragments or Minutes of Essays', (Ibid., IV, p. 154).
24 Bolingbroke, 'Dissertation' (*Works*, II, p. 112).
25 Bolingbroke, 'Study and Use' (*Works*, II, p. 187).
26 J. H. Burns, 'Bolingbroke and the Concept of Constitutional Government', *Political Studies*, 10, 1962, p. 276.
27 Bolingbroke, 'Dissertation', (*Works*, II, p. 148).
28 Ibid., p. 116.
29 Bolingbroke, 'Patriot King', p. 194 (*Works*, II, p. 418).
30 Bolingbroke, 'Fragments' (*Works*, IV, pp. 333 and 336).
31 James, *The Life of Reason*, p. 263.
32 Bolingbroke, 'Dissertation' (*Works*, II, p. 150).
33 Bolingbroke, 'Patriot King', p. 93 (*Works*, II, p. 382).
34 Ibid., p. 97 (*Works*, II, p. 383).
35 Ibid., pp. 101–3 (*Works*, II, pp. 384–5).
36 Pope, 'Essay on Man' (*Poetical Works*, p. 259–60).
37 Bolingbroke, 'Letters: Essay 2' (*Works*, III, pp. 260–1).
38 Ibid., p. 327.
39 Bolingbroke, 'Patriot King', p. 66 (*Works*, II, p. 372).
40 Bolingbroke, 'Fragments' (*Works*, IV, p. 251).
41 Ibid., p. 473.
42 Bolingbroke, 'Letters: Essay 2', (*Works*, III, p. 255; see also p. 225).
43 Ibid., p. 311.
44 Bolingbroke, 'Dissertation' (*Works*, II, p. 144).
45 Bolingbroke, 'Patriot King', p. 79 (*Works*, II, p. 377).
46 Ibid., p. 87 (printed in error as p. 77 in edition I have used) (*Works*, II, pp. 379–80).
47 Bolingbroke, 'Fragments' (*Works*, IV, p. 193).
48 Ibid., pp. 194ff.
49 Bolinbroke, 'Patriot King', pp. 83 and 89ff. (*Works*, II, pp. 378 and 380).
50 Bolingbroke, 'Dissertation' (*Works*, II, p. 85).

51 Bolingbroke, 'Patriot King', p. 106 (*Works*, II, p. 386).
52 Bolingbroke, 'Letters: Essay 4' (*Works*, III, p. 489).
53 Bolingbroke, 'Dissertation' (*Works*, II, p. 117).
54 Ibid., p. 109.
55 Bolingbroke, 'Study and Use' (*Works*, II, p. 237).
56 Bolingbroke, 'Dissertation' (*Works*, II, p. 85).
57 Bolingbroke, 'Fragments' (*Works*, IV, p. 149).
58 Bolingbroke, 'The Substance of Some Letters, Written Originally in French about the year 1720, to M. de Pouilly' (*Works*, II, p. 462).
59 Bolingbroke, 'Letters: Essay I' (*Works*, III, p. 47). Of the German polymath, he arrogantly wrote: 'one of the vainest, and most chimerical men that ever got a name in philosophy' (ibid, p. 52).
60 Bolingbroke, 'Letters: Essay 2' (*Works*, III, p. 209).
61 Bolingbroke, 'Fragments' (*Works*, IV, p. 137).
62 Ibid., pp. 155 and 170; 'Letters: Essay 1' (*Works*, III, p. 204). 'Let them not assume, that the moral attributes are precisely the same in God as they are in our ideas and notions' (ibid, p. 402).
63 Bolingbroke, 'Letters: Essay I' (*Works*, III, p. 52).
64 See above, p. 131.
65 Pope, 'Essay on Man', II.1–2 (*Poetical Works*, p. 250). 'We may be the better contented to confine our inquiries to the limits God has prescribed to them, since we may find within those limits abundant matter of real use and ornament to employ the studious labours of mankind. Experimental knowledge of body and mind is the fund our reason should cultivate and the first is a fund that philosophers will never exhaust', Bolingbroke, 'Letters: Essay 2' (*Works*, III, p. 211).
66 Bolingbroke, 'Letters: Essay 2' (*Works*, III, p. 267).
67 Bolingbroke, 'Fragments' (*Works*, IV, p. 438).
68 Ibid., p. 335.
69 Ibid., pp. 118n and 336; 'Letters: Essay 4' (*Works*, III, p. 397); 'Patriot King', p. 87 (ibid., II, pp. 379–80).
70 Bolingbroke, 'Letters: Essay 2' (*Works*, III, p. 264); see also 'Fragments', (ibid., IV, p.333).
71 Bolingbroke, 'Of the True Use of Retirement and Study' (*Works*, II, pp. 348–9).
72 Bolingbroke, 'Letters: Essay 2 (*Works*, III, p. 328).
73 Ibid., p. 329.
74 Bolingbroke, 'Fragments' (*Works*, IV, pp. 476–7).
75 Ibid., p. 478.
76 Ibid., p. 427.
77 Pope, 'Essay on Man' I. 145–6 (*Poetical Works*, p. 245).
78 Bolingbroke, 'Fragments' (*Works*, IV, pp. 422–3).
79 Ibid, p. 419
80 Ibid., p. 399.
81 Bolingbroke, 'Letters: Essay 3' (*Works*, III, p. 281).
82 Bolingbroke, 'Fragments' (*Works*, IV, p. 154).
83 Ibid., p. 155. This position was asserted by H. L. Mansel in his celebrated Bampton Lectures of 1858, *The Limits of Religious Thought*; it led to the expostulation of J. S. Mill: 'I will call no being good, who is not what I mean when I apply that epithet to my fellow-creatures; and if such a being can sentence me to hell for not so calling him, to hell I will go' (Mill, *An Examination of Sir William Hamilton's Philosophy*, p. 129).
84 Bolingbroke, 'Letters: Essay II' (*Works*, II, p. 253).
85 Bolingbroke, 'Patriot King', pp. 84ff. (*Works*, II, p. 379).

86 Francis Bacon, *Of the Dignity and Advancement of Learning*, quoted in Weston and Greenberg, *Subjects and Sovereigns*, p. 12.

87 Bolingbroke, 'Dissertation' (*Works*, II, pp. 80–1).

88 Bolingbroke, 'Letters: Essay 1' (*Works*, II, p. 59). He here commits precisely the fallacy for which he denounced Clarke and the heathen philosophers, of deducing the attributes and laws of the supreme being, from analogy with human social institutions.

89 Bolingbroke, 'Letters: Essay 2' (*Works*, III, p. 259).

90 A. W., 'To Charles Blount, Esq: of Natural Religion as Opposed to Divine Revelation' (*The Miscellaneous Works of Charles Blount*, p. 198).

91 R. L. Emerson, 'Latitudinarianism and the English Deists', in Lemay, ed. *Deism*, p. 26.

92 Toland, *Christianity not Mysterious*, p. 41.

93 Ibid., p. 42.

94 Tindal, *Christianity*, I, p. 166.

95 David Berman 'Deism, Immortality and the Art of Theological Lying', in Lemay, ed., *Deism*, pp. 61ff.

96 See Byrne, *Natural Religion*, p. 71.

97 R. S. Crane, 'Anglican apologetics and the Idea of Progress, 1699–1745', *Modern Philology*, 31, 1934, pp. 281ff and 352ff; see also Chadwick, *From Bossuet to Newman*, chapter 4.

98 Toland, *Christianity*, preface.

99 Toland, *Letters to Serena*, p. 123.

100 See Rosalie L. Colie, 'Spinoza and the Early English Deists', *Journal of the History of Ideas*, 20, 1959, pp. 43ff.

101 Toland, *Letters to Serena*, pp. 161 and 163ff. More generally see Colie, 'Spinoza and the Early English Deists', pp. 23ff. and 'Spinoza in England, 1665–1730', *Proceedings of the American Philosophical Society*, 107, 1963, pp. 184ff.

102 Tindal, *Christianity*, I, pp. 24–5.

103 Ibid., I, p. 39.

104 Ibid., I, pp. 9, 17 and 26.

105 Toland, *Christianity*, p. xix.

106 Ritschl, *The Christian Doctrine of Justification*, pp. 238ff.

107 Jacob, *The Radical Enlightenment*, p. 151.

108 It is also possible that he was responsible for Edmund Ludlow's *Memoires* and an edition of Algernon Sidney's *Discourses*.

109 The support which many lent to the Jacobite cause meant that they were in a certain sense politically radical; indeed, some were revolutionary. But they were not particularly radical with respect to social relations.

110 Russell, *Science and Social Change*, p. 62.

111 R. Harvey, 'The Problem of Social–Political Obligation for the Church of England in the 17th Century', *Church History*, 39, 1971, pp. 156ff.

112 Toland, *Letters to Serena*, p. 123, and *Pantheisticon*, p. 5. It is therefore curious to find Margaret Jacob writing of Toland's vision of a 'utopian republic . . . where intellectual and political freedom amounted to a loosely defined social equality. All men were equally a part of nature' (*The Newtonians*, p. 248).

113 Toland, *The Art of Governing by Parties*, and *Letters to Serena*, Preface, section 7.

114 Tindal, *Christianity*, I, p. 244.

115 Ibid., I, pp. 245–6.

116 Ibid., I, p. 37.

117 Tindal, *An Essay Concerning the Power of the Magistrate and the Rights of Mankind, in Matters of Religion* (1697), (*Four Discourses*, p. 133).

118 Ibid.

119 Tindal, *Of Obedience to the Supreme Powers* (1694) (*Four Discourses*, pp. 2–3).
120 Ibid., p. 3.
121 Ibid., p. 3.
122 Ibid., pp. 45–6 and 2.
123 Ibid., p. 19.
124 Tindal, *Christianity*, I, pp. 18, 26–9, 34, 36. On Bolingbroke and Pope, see above, p. 136.
125 Tindal, *Christianity*, I, pp. 39 and 252.
126 Blount, *King William and Queen Mary Conquerors*, p. 41, quoted in Clark, *English Society*, p. 294.
127 Toland, *Anglia Libera: or, The Limitation and Succession of the Crown of England Explain'd and Asserted*, quoted in Clark, *English Society*, p. 296.
128 Tindal, *Of Obedience* (*Four Discourses*, p.18, my italics).
129 Ibid., pp. 25 and 27.
130 Tindal, *An Essay concerning the Law of Nations, and the Rights of Sovereigns* (1694), (*Four Discourses*, p. 91).
131 Tindal, *Christianity*, I, p. 34.
132 Nye, *Natural Religion*, pp. 85–6, quoted in Tindal, *Christianity*, I, p. 354.
133 Jacob, *The Newtonians*, pp. 61 and 168.
134 *The Theological Works of Isaac Barrow*, I, pp. 175–7, quoted in Jacob, *The Newtonians*, p. 55
135 *The Works of Richard Bentley*, III, p. 22.
136 Mandeville, 'A Search into the Nature of Society', in *The Fable of the Bees: or, Private Vices, Public Benefits*, p. 428.
137 Butler, 'Sermon preached before the House of Lords' (*Works*, II, p. 293).
138 Tillotson, Sermon CIII (*Works* V, p.241). For a recent comment on Tillotson's theology, see Gerard Reedy SJ, 'Interpreting Tillotson', *Harvard Theological Review*, 86, 1993, pp. 81ff.
139 Tillotson, Sermon CXXXVI (*Works*, VI, p. 368); see also Sermon CLII (ibid., VII, pp. 132ff).
140 Hoadly, Sermon on 29 May 1709 (*Works*, III, pp. 685–6).
141 Hoadly, 'The Happiness of the Present Establishment and the Unhappiness of Absolute Monarchy' (*Works*, II, p. 111).
142 Hoadly, *The Original* (*Works*, II, pp. 189–90).
143 Ibid., II, p. 202.
144 Hoadly, 'Some Considerations Humbly Offered to the Right Reverend the Lord Bishop of Exeter' (1709) (*Several Tracts*, p. 313).
145 Hoadly, *The Original* (*Works*, II, p. 239).
146 Ibid., II, p. 235; see also 'Some Considerations' (*Several Tracts*, pp. 307ff).
147 Bailyn, *Origins*, p. 37. Hoadly influenced Jonathan Mayhew, John Adams and many others: see ibid., p. 38, and Robbins, *The Eighteenth Century Commonwealthmen*, p. 84.
148 Watts, *Hymns and Spiritual Songs* (1707), 2:CXV, p. 289.
149 Watts, 'The Doctrine of the Trinity and the Use of it' (*Works*, I, p. 486).
150 Watts, *Reliquiae Juveniles*, p. 90, and *Hymns*, 2: XLIII, pp. 203–4.
151 Watts, 'The Christian Doctrine of the Trinity' (*Works*, VI, p. 287).
152 Watts, 'Sermon on the Death of George I' (1727) (*Works*, I, p. 614).
153 Watts, 'Discourse XII: the Nature of the Punishments in Hell' (*Works*, II, p. 267).
154 Watts, 'A Meditation for the 1st of May' (*Reliquiae Juveniles*, pp. 34–5). To speak of Jesus as the work of God's hands might seem unorthodox, but Watts is evidently referring to his human nature; it does not therefore have Arian implications.
155 Watts, 'The Christian Doctrine' (*Works*, VI, p. 339; see also p. 349).

156 Ibid., pp. 339–40.
157 Ibid., 340.
158 Watts, *Hymns*, 2: CXV, pp. 288–9.
159 'God is a King of Power unknown
    Firm are the Orders of his Throne;
    If he resolves, who dare oppose,
    Or ask him why, or what he does?'
    (Watts, *Hymns*, 2: CLXX, p. 342)
160 Watts, *Hymns*, 2: CXI, p. 285; 2: XCIX, p. 270; 2: XIII, p. 154.
161 The Seasons: 'Summer', lines 1602–4 (*Thomson's Poetical Works*, p. 85).
162 Watts, *Hymns and Spiritual Songs*, 2: CXLIX, p. 321.
163 Watts, 'The Psalms of David in the Language of the New Testament' (*Works*, IV, p. 182).
164 Watts, 'The Psalms' (*Works*, IV, p. 186), and *Hymns*, 2: CXV, p. 289.
165 Watts, *Reliquiae*, p. 182.
166 Watts, *Hymns*, 2: XXXVII, p. 197.
167 Watts, 'Horae Lyricae: a Song to Creating Wisdom, part 4' (*Works*, IV, p. 436).
168 Watts, *Reliquiae*, p. 23.
169 Ibid., p. 50.
170 Watts, *Hymns*, 2: XXX, p. 189; 2:XLVI, p. 206; 2: CXII, p. 285.
171 Watts, *Reliquiae*, pp. 35 and 234, and 'Sermon' (*Works*, I, p. 608).
172 See above, p. 46. Price pioneered actuarial methods in the insurance business.
173 Watts, 'Bills of Exchange' (1705) (*Works*, IV, p. 654).
174 Watts, 'The Christian Doctrine' (*Works*, VI, pp. 291–2).
175 Watts, 'The Psalms' (*Works*, IV, p. 139).
176 Watts, *Hymns*, 2: I, p. 154.
177 J. F. Maclear, 'Isaac Watts and the Idea of Public Religion', *Journal of the History of Ideas*, 53, 1992, p. 43.
178 Watts, *Hymns*, 2: CXII, p. 285.
179 Wesley, *Short Hymns*, I, p. 21.
180 See, for example, ibid., pp. 120ff. and 269.
181 Watts, 'A New Essay on Civil Power in Things Sacred' (1739) (*Works*, VI, p. 6).
182 Watts, *Reliquiae*, p. 193.
183 Watts, 'A New Essay' (*Works*, VI, pp. 37–8 and 7).
184 Ibid., p. 45.
185 Ibid., 36–7.
186 Ibid., pp. 31f.
187 Ibid., pp. 25 and 33.
188 Ibid., p. 11.
189 Ibid., p. 38.
190 Calamy, *A Defence of Moderate Nonconformity*, Introduction to part 2.

7 LEIBNIZ AND THE NEWTONIANS

A consistent way of listing references to the works of Leibniz is difficult, because there is no complete edition of his works. Where possible I have given references to C. I. Gerhardt, ed., *Die philosophischen Schriften von Gottlieb Wilhelm Leibniz* (referred to as *Phil. Schriften*); I have also made reference to a number of English translations.

1 Hegel to Niethammer, 13 October 1806 (*Briefe I, p. 120*).
2 In part three of this triptych, *Political Rhetoric and Religious Discourse in the Seventeenth Century.*

3 I say 'supposed' because many philosophers would deny that his method was inductive.

4 *Works of Bolingbroke*, III, pp. 88 and 93.

5 Pope, 'Epitaphs' (*Poetical Works*, p. 651).

6 The Seasons: 'Summer', lines 1543ff. (*Thomson's Poetical Works*, p. 83).

7 See above, pp. 145 ff.

8 See C. B. Wilde, 'Hutchinsonianism', *History of Science*, 18, 1980, pp. 1ff. ; and A. J. Kuhn, 'Glory or Gravity: Hutchinson vs Newton', *Journal of the History of Ideas*, 22, 1961, pp. 303ff.

9 Hickes to North, 23 May 1713, quoted in L. Stewart, 'Samuel Clarke, Newtonianism and the Factions of Post-Revolutionary England', *Journal of the History of Ideas*, 42, 1981, p. 65. By 'theists' he, of course, referred to those we would call 'deists'.

10 Desaguliers, *The Newtonian System*, p. v.

11 Wake, *A Sermon Preached before the King*, p. 9, cited in Clark, *English Society*, pp. 176–7.

12 Smith, *The Theory of Moral Sentiments*, p. 267.

13 Robert Boyle, 'A Free Enquiry into the Vulgarly Received Notion of Nature' (*Robert Boyle on Natural Philosophy*, p. 150). Newton, of course, believed that the cosmic system requires occasional direct action by God in order to keep going.

14 Stephen, *English Thought*, I, p. 80.

15 Jacob, *The Newtonians*, p. 160

16 *Works of Bentley*, III, p. 22.

17 See Koyré, *From Closed World to Infinite Universe*, pp. 274ff.

18 See Barber, *Leibniz in France*.

19 D'Alembert, *Preliminary Discourse*, p. 74.

20 Ibid., p. 82.

21 Gay, *Voltaire's Politics*, p. 26.

22 Voltaire, *Philosophical Dictionary*, I, p. 121.

23 See Plongeron, *Théologie et politique*, p. 26.

24 'In the Leibnizian organic universe, the individual was an active collaborator in God's purposes; in Wolff's mechanistic universe, he was a victim of the immutable workings of the divine law': Barber, *Leibniz in France*, p. 235.

25 Voltaire, *Philosophical Dictionary*, I, pp. 103 and 161.

26 See Pomeau, *La Religion*, p. 209.

27 Voltaire to Frederick, 8 Mar. 1738 (*Oeuvres complètes*, XXXIV, p. 433).

28 Voltaire, *Traité de métaphysique*, quoted in Barber, *Leibniz in France*, p. 211.

29 Pomeau, *La Religion*, pp. 218, 220 and 221.

30 Voltaire, *Philosophical Dictionary*, *s. v.* 'Atheist, Atheism', p. 103.

31 Gay, *Voltaire's Politics*, p. 242.

32 Quoted ibid., p. 136.

33 Jacob, *The Radical Enlightenment*, pp. 122–3.

34 Desaguliers, *The Newtonian System*, p. iii-iv.

35 Ibid., p. iv.

36 Ibid., p. 4.

37 Ibid., pp. 4–5

38 Ibid., pp. 22–6.

39 Later editions were entitled, more modestly, *A Discourse concerning the Being and Attributes of God*.

40 Clarke, *Being and Attributes* (3rd edn), proposition VII, p. 51. Clarke omitted this passage from later editions.

41 Hodgson, *The Doctrine of the Trinity*, pp. 156, 158 and 171.

42 Clarke, 'A Modest Plea, or a Brief and Distinct Answer to Dr. Waterland's

Queries' (*Works*, IV, p. 456), and *The Scripture Doctrine of the Trinity* (ibid., IV, p. 123).

43 Clark, *English Society*, p. 281. In discussion of these eighteenth–century theologians it is important to distinguish between 'deity' and 'divinity'.
44 Michael A. Hoskin, 'Mining all Within', *Thomist*, 24, 1961, pp. 357ff.
45 Voltaire, *Letters on England*, p. 42.
46 Cited in Buckley, *At the Origin of Modern Atheism*, p. 171. The book Voltaire referred to was the *Demonstration of the Being and Attributes of God*.
47 Stephen, *English Thought*, I, p. 120.
48 Clarke, *Being and Attributes*, p. 375.
49 Clarke, 'Sermon 9' (*Works*, I, p. 54).
50 Clarke, *A Discourse concerning the Unalterable Obligation of Natural Religion*, p. 14.
51 Newton to Bentley (*Opera*, IV, p. 431).
52 See Fontenelle, 'Eloge de M. Saurin' (*Oeuvres*, VI, p. 338).
53 Clarke, *Being and Attributes*, p. 244.
54 Ibid., pp. 237, 122 and 179.
55 Ibid., pp. 215–6, 114 and 243
56 Ibid., pp. 244 and 185
57 Ibid., pp. 180 and 244.
58 Clarke, 'Sermon 10' (*Works*, I, p. 65).
59 Clarke, *Unalterable Obligation*, ed. Watson, p. 143, quoted in Jacob, *The Newtonians*, p. 190.
60 Clarke, *Being and Attributes*, p. 250.
61 *Boswell's Life of Johnson*, IV, p. 416.
62 Clarke, *Being and Attributes*, p. 328.
63 Ibid., p. 347.
64 The debate on this question is a long and complex one relating doctrines of atonement to theories of punishment. It is discussed in classic form in Ritschl, *Die christlicher Lehre*, and more popularly in Rashdall, *The Idea of Atonement*, and in Aulén, *Christus Victor*.
65 Clarke, 'Sermon 1', in 'Eighteen Sermons on Several Occasions' (*Works*, II, p. 388).
66 Clarke, Sermon 2, in 'Eighteen Sermons' (*Works*, II, p. 409). This was a view questioned by Joseph Butler: see above, p. 67.
67 Leibniz, 'A Classification of Societies or Communities' (*Philosophical Papers*, p. 430). Some of the following paragraphs are based on David Nicholls, 'Images of God and the State: Political Analogy and Religious Discourse', *Theological Studies*, 42, 1981, pp. 203ff.
68 Schrecker, *Leibniz*, p. 23.
69 Leibniz, 'Portrait of the Prince' (*The Political Writings* , p. 88).
70 Leibniz, *Theodicy*, p. 257 (*Phil. Schriften*, VI, p. 241).
71 See, for example, Grua, *Jurisprudence universelle*; also Baruzi, *Leibniz* , p. 20.
72 Leibniz, *Textes inédites*, II, p. 474.
73 Leibniz, *Discourse on Metaphysics* (1686), p. 5 (*Phil. Schriften*, IV, p. 428). Leibniz repeats the same view through many of his published writings and private correspondence. See, for example, Leibniz to G. W. Molanus, octobre 1699 (*Lettres et fragments inédits*, p. 95).
74 Leibniz, *Theodicy*, pp. 402–3 (*Phil. Schriften*, IV, p. 398).
75 Leibniz, 'Dissertatio de Arte Combinatoria' (1666) (*Phil. Schriften*, IV, p. 32).
76 Leibniz, *Monadologie*, section 48 (*Phil. Schriften*, VI, p. 615).
77 Leibniz to Thomas Burnett (*Political Writings*, p. 194).
78 Baruzi, *Leibniz*, , p. 371.

79 Leibniz to Landgraf Ernst of Hesse-Rheinfels (*Political Writings*, p. 187).
80 Leibniz, *Monadologie*, section 87 (*Phil. Schriften*, VI, p. 622).
81 Ibid., section 88 (*Phil. Schriften*, VI, p. 622).
82 Ibid., section 83 (*Phil. Schriften*, VI, p. 621).
83 Ibid., section 84 (*Phil. Schriften*, VI, p. 621). Earlier Leibniz had written of the human relationship to God as 'not that of machines to their artificer (like the rest of the world) but rather that of citizens to their prince': see 'On the Ultimate Origin of Things' (1697) (*Phil. Schriften*, VII, p. 307). He discussed this question in a number of places; see also *Discourse on Metaphysics* (1685–6), section 36, p. 61 (*Phil. Schriften*, IV, pp. 461–2).
84 Leibniz, *Monadologie*, section 88 (*Phil. Schriften*, VI, p. 622).
85 Leibniz, 'Memoire for Enlightened Persons of Good Intention' (mid-1690s) (*Political Writings*, p. 105).
86 'The sovereign wisdom has so well regulated all things that our duty must be our happiness, that all virtue produces its reward, and that all crime punishes itself, sooner or later': 'La Felicité' (1694–8) (*Political Writings*, p. 84).
87 Leibniz, *Theodicy*, p. 161 (*Phil. Schriften*, VI, p. 141).
88 Leibniz referred to the controversy between Grotius and the Socinians: *Theodicy*, p. 162 (*Phil. Schriften*, VI, pp. 141–2). For Smith, see above, p. 38.
89 Leibniz, *Theodicy*, pp. 402–3; (*Phil. Schriften*, VI, p. 398).
90 Leibniz, 'The Common Concept of Justice'(*Political Writings*, p. 49).
91 See Mill, *An Examination of Sir William Hamilton's Philosophy*, p. 129; see above, p. 248, note 83.
92 Leibniz, *Theodicy*, p. 165 (*Phil. Schriften*, VI, p. 145).
93 Ibid., p. 101 (*Phil. Schriften*, VI, p. 78).
94 Leibniz, 'Dialogue entre un habile politique et un ecclésiastique d'une piété reconnue', *Oeuvres*, II, p. 551).
95 *Leibniz-Clarke Correspondence*, p. 19
96 Feuerbach, *Werke*, III, p. 181, cited in Wartofsky, *Feuerbach*, p. 115.
97 On some of the consequences of this principle, see C. D. Broad, 'Leibniz's *Predicate-in-Notion Principle* and some of its Alleged Consequences', in Frankfurt, ed. *Leibniz*, pp. 1ff.
98 Leibniz discussed this question in his correspondence with Arnaud: see, for example, Leibniz to Arnaud, 14 juillet 1686, (Montgomery, ed., *Leibniz*, pp. 119ff.).
99 Leibniz, *Theodicy*, p. 127 (*Phil. Schriften*, VI, p. 106).
100 Leibniz to Landgraf Ernst of Hesse-Rheinfels (*Political Writings*, p. 186).
101 Leibniz to Thomas Burnett (*Political Writings*, p. 193).
102 Leibniz to T. Burnett, 24 août 1697 (*Phil. Schriften*, III, p. 218).
103 Leibniz, 'Codex Iuris Gentium (Praefatio)' (*Political Writings*, p. 171).
104 Leibniz, 'The Common Concept of Justice' (*Political Writings*, p. 58).
105 Leibniz, 'De rerum originatione radicali' (*Phil. Schriften*, VII, pp. 306–7).
106 Leibniz, 'Not all Possibles *per se* Can Exist Along With Others; Otherwise Absurdities Would Follow' (1676) (*Philosophical Papers*, p. 168).
107 J. M. Gabaude, 'Théopolitisme leibnizien', *Annales de l'Université de Toulouse: Homo*, 10, 1971, p. 71.
108 Leibniz to Queen Caroline, 2 June 1716 (*Leibniz–Clarke Correspondence*, p. 195).
109 Leibniz, *A System of Theology*, p. 37.
110 Leibniz, *Theodicy*, p. 165 (*Phil. Schriften*, VI, p. 145).
111 Elster, *Leibniz*, pp. 14, 110, 26, 239 and 27.
112 Leibniz, 'Caesarinus Fürstenerius' (*Political Writings*, pp. 11819).
113 Tocqueville, *Journeys to England and Ireland*, p. 24. See David Nicholls, *The Pluralist State*, chapter 2.

114 Leibniz, 'Ermahnung an die Deutschen', cited in Carl J. Friedrich, 'Philosophical Reflections of Leibniz on Law, Politics and the State', in Frankfurt, ed., *Leibniz*, p. 58.
115 Leibniz, 'Ermahnung an die Deutschen' (*Werke*, 1:6, pp. 188–9).
116 Caroline to Leibniz, 26 Nov. 1715 (*Leibniz–Clarke Correspondence*, p. 190).
117 Ibid., pp. 11–12
118 Ibid., p. 14.
119 Ibid., pp. 18 and 19–20.
120 Ibid., pp. 20 and 36.
121 Leibniz, 'Réflexions sur Bellarmine' (*Textes inédits*, II, p. 302).
122 Leibniz to Conti, 26 Feb. 1716 (*Leibniz-Clarke Correspondence*, p. 187).
123 See John Gay, 'The Idea of Freedom as the Basis of the Thought of Samuel Clarke', Ph. D. thesis, Columbia University, 1958.
124 S. Shapin, 'Of Gods and Kings: Natural Philosophy and Politics in the Leibniz–Clarke Correspondence', *Isis*, 72, 1981, pp. 187ff. The author has many interesting things to say about the relationship between politics, theology and natural science in Leibniz and the Newtonians.
125 See Arnold Thackray, 'The Business of Experimental Philosophy', *Actes du XIIᵉ Congrès International d'Histoire des Sciences*, 38, 1970–1, pp. 55ff.
126 Jacob, *The Newtonians*, p. 142. Geoffrey Holmes, while generally welcoming this book, warns his readers that the author's 'thesis is far less watertight than its apparent boyancy might suggest': 'Science, Reason and Religion in the Age of Newton', *The British Journal for the History of Science*, 11, 1978, p. 170.

8 CONCLUSION

1 There is an interesting comparative study of radical or fundamentalist groups in Christianity, Islam and Judaism in Kepel, *The Revenge of God*.
2 'Gaudium et Spes', section 39, in Abbott, ed., *The Documents of Vatican II*, p. 237.
3 A similar point has forcefully been made by Norman, *Christians and the World Order*. For a critique of certain aspects of this book, see, however, Leech, ed. *Christianity Reinterpreted*?
4 Neuhaus, *The Naked Public Square*. See also works by Robert Bellah. In a recent book, Ian Markham, *Plurality and Christian Ethics*, considers some of these issues; his optimism about the political role of churches is somewhat out of touch with the real world. In asserting that pluralism is an American invention, Neuhaus, Markham and others appear ignorant of the British pluralist writers of the early part of the century.
5 Rousseau would put atheists to death, and Arnold was intolerant of Jews. See David Nicholls, 'The Totalitarianism of Thomas Arnold', *Review of Politics*, 29, 1967, pp. 518ff.
6 Figgis, *Studies of Political Thought*, pp. 118 and 180, and *Churches in the Modern State*, p. 101.
7 A tolerant state is, of course, different from a secular state (which attempts to be indifferent with respect to the truth claims of the religious, and anti-religious, groups within it). Toleration, on the other hand, implies that the state patronises one religious group, while allowing others to live freely.
8 Nicholls, *The Pluralist State*, especially chapter 6.
9 Gellner, *Legitimation of Belief*, p.3.
10 I have avoided this aspect of the subject not because I think it unimportant; indeed, it is a subject about which much has been written and to which I could not do justice in the present work. See, for example, McFague, *Metaphorical*

Theology, chapter 5, and *Models of God*; Eleanor McLaughlin, 'Christ my Mother', *St Luke's Journal of Theology*, 18, 1975; Metz and Schillebeeckx, eds, *God as Father?*, New York, 1981; Wren, *What Language Shall I Borrow?* See also various works by Rosemary Radford Ruether.

11 Shaftesbury, *Characteristics*, I, pp. 147–8.

12 'If the multitude assent and applaud, men ought immediately to examine themselves as to what blunder or fault they may have committed': Francis Bacon, quoting Phocion, *Novum organum*, 1:77, quoted in Rescher, *Pluralism*, p. 29.

13 Rescher, *Pluralism*.

14 Whether there is a distinct 'world' of propositional truths, between the psychological world of true (and false) beliefs on the one hand and the way things are in the world on the other, is a matter of dispute among philosophers. See McTaggart, *The Nature of Existence*, chapter 2; Popper takes an opposing position in *Objective Knowledge*, esp. chapters 3 and 4. He makes no reference to the powerful arguments of McTaggart, who elsewhere he affects to admire (*The Open Society*, II, p. 29).

15 Nicholls, *Deity and Domination*, p. 6.

16 Everett, *God's Federal Republic*, p. 82. Everett quotes Pocock's *Machiavellian Moment* as an authority.

17 Everett, *God's Federal Republic*, p. 104.

9 THEOLOGICAL POSTSCRIPT

1 This first section is based on David Nicholls, 'Addressing God as Ruler', *British Journal of Sociology*, 44, 1993, pp. 125–41, and is also printed in Bax and Koster, eds, *Power and Prayer*, pp. 183ff.

2 Frankfort, *Kingship and the Gods*.

3 David Nicholls, 'Deity and Domination', *New Blackfriars*, nos 775–6, Jan. and Feb. 1985.

4 Martin, *A Sociology of English Religion*, p. 55.

5 A modern selection of Durkheim's writings on religion (W. S. F. Pickering, ed., *Durkheim on Religion*), contains but three references in the index under 'prayer', compared with several dozen citations under 'totem'. In a classic work, Max Weber (*The Sociology of Religion*) has much more about 'orgy' than about 'prayer'. Bryan Wilson, in two of his books on religion from a sociological viewpoint (*Religion in Secular Society* and *Religion in Sociological Perspective*) has no index entry for 'prayer'.

6 Unfortunately I have neither the space nor the competence to discuss the role of petitionary prayer in other religions.

7 Speech by John Hoskyns, in Foster, ed., *Proceedings in Parliament: 1610*, II, p. 89.

8 Schmitt, *Political Theology*, p. 36.

9 Hobbes, *Leviathan*, p. 427.

10 John Maddicott, 'Parliament and the Constituencies, 1272–1377', in Davies and Denton, eds, *The English Parliament* pp. 62–3. See, however, G. L. Haskins, 'The Petitions of Representatives in the Parliaments of Edward I', *English Historical Review*, 53, 1938, pp. 1ff; and part II of Doris Rayner, 'The Forms and Machinery of the 'Commune Petition' in the Fourteenth Century', *English Historical Review*, 56, 1941, pp. 549ff.

11 A. R. Myers, 'Parliamentary Petitions in the Fifteenth Century, I', *English Historical Review*, 52, 1937, p. 387.

12 Morgan, *Inventing the People*, p. 224. This distinction is made, for example, by

Sir Edward Coke in 1624: see Elizabeth Read Foster, 'Petition and the Petition of Right', *Journal of British Studies*, 14, 1974, p. 21.

13 Cust, *The Forced Loan*.

14 J. A. Gray, 'The Origins of the Petition of Right Considered', *The Historical Journal*, 25, 1982, pp. 289ff.

15 Foster, 'Petition', pp. 26 and 35.

16 Taswell-Langmead, *English Constitutional History*, p. 745.

17 Wolfe, *Leveller Manifestos*, pp. 135ff.

18 Petitions played a similar role in the disturbed period of the French Revolution. The revolutionary leader Jean-Pierre Brissot denounced the petitioners from one of the Paris sections for presenting their petition of August 1792 in the form of a threat: Hampson, *Will and Circumstance*, p. 179.

19 13 Car. II, st. 1 c. 5, in Taswell-Langmead, *English Constitutional History*, p. 473.

20 4 Parl. Hist. 1174, in Emden, *The People and the Constitution*, p. 73.

21 Costin and Watson, *Law and the Working of the Constitution*, pp. 192–3.

22 O'Gorman, *Voters, Patrons, and Parties*, p. 164.

23 May, *Constitutional History*, I, p. 350.

24 Peter Fraser, 'Public Petitioning and Parliament before 1832', *History*, 46 (no. 158), 1961, p. 200.

25 *Parliamentary Papers*, 1832, XII, p. 153.

26 Colin Leys, 'Petitioning in the Nineteenth and Twentieth Centuries', *Political Studies*, 3 1955, pp. 47ff.

27 *101 Parliamentary Debates*, 3s: 673.

28 Leys, 'Petitioning', p. 61.

29 See Alan Beith, 'Prayers Unanswererd: a Jaundiced View of the Parliamentary Scrutiny of Statutory Instruments', *Parliamentary Affairs*, 34, 1981, pp. 165ff.

30 Wade and Phillips, *Constitutional Law*, pp. 309–10.

31 Psalm 13:1.

32 Psalm 35:24.

33 Psalm 44:24.

34 Edward Symmons, *A Loyall Subjects Beliefe*, p. 19.

35 Sherlock, *A Discourse concerning the Divine Providence*, p. 379.

36 Ibid., p. 382.

37 Cited in Notestein, *et al.*, eds, *Commons Debates: 1621*, II, p. 463.

38 *Works of Paley*, I, p. 251. See above, p. 62.

39 Ibid., pp. 251ff.

40 Heiler, *Prayer*, p. 52.

41 Brown, *Cult*, p. 38.

42 *The Essays and Hymns of Synesius of Cyrene*, II, p. 386.

43 Brown, *Cult*, p. 63. See also Brown, *The World of Late Antiquity*, p. 37, and J. M. Sallmann, 'Image et fonction du saint dans la région de Naples à la fin du XVIIe et au début du XVIIIe siècle', *Mélange de l'Ecole Français de Rome*, 91, 1979, p. 871.

44 Boissevain, *Friends of Friends*, p. 80; see also Michael Kenny, 'Patterns of Patronage in Spain', *Anthropological Quarterly*, 33, 1960, pp. 14ff; and Mart Bax, 'Patronage Irish Style: Irish Politicians as Brokers', *Sociologische Gids*, 17, 1970, pp. 179ff.

45 Quoted in David Nicholls, 'The Political Theology of John Donne', *Theological Studies*, 49, 1988, p. 62.

46 Friends of Cardinal Newman, *Newsletter*, Summer 1991, p. 8. In the same number a somewhat more sinister favour (though one not entirely out of character) is recorded: 'An elderly priest friend, aged 82, a convert to Catholicism, had to retire from the ministry and went to live with his non-Catholic sister. She forebad all mention of religion and made it nigh on impossible for

him ever to say Mass. I started the novena to Cardinal Newman that he could say his daily Latin Mass. My prayer was heard. The lady had a stroke and was taken to hospital.'

47 Exodus, 15:3.
48 Psalm 44:8 and 10.
49 Brock, *The Holy Spirit*.
50 Kantorowicz, *Selected Studies*, pp. 18ff.
51 Kleinschmidt, *Antonius von Padua*, pp. 358ff.
52 Nicholls, *Deity and Domination*, pp. 31ff.
53 *Works of Paley*, p. 250.
54 Rauschenbusch, *Prayers of the Social Awakening*, pp. 57 and 59.
55 *Oeuvres de Robespierre*, pp. 313–14.
56 Ramsey, *The Gospel and the Catholic Church*, p. 93.
57 Heiler, *Prayer*, pp. 1 and iv.
58 Wesley, *Short Hymns*, I, p. 89, and II, p. 283.
59 Church of England Doctrine Commision, *We Believe in God*, p. 108. This chapter was basically written by Sarah Coakley, who has developed this understanding of prayer in her recent Hulsean Lectures. I am grateful to her for sending me the draft manuscript.
60 Henry Maine, 'Radical Patriarchalism', *St James Gazette*, 18 June 1880, p. 260.
61 Stephen, *Liberty Equality Fraternity*, p. 256.
62 See David Nicholls, 'Few Are Chosen: Some Reflections on the Politics of A. J. Balfour', *Review of Politics*, 30, 1968, pp. 33–42. See also writings of Robert Michels, Vilfredo Pareto and Gaetano Mosca. See chapter 7 of Hughes, *Consciousness and Society*, for a discussion of some of these thinkers; also Bachrach, *The Theory of Democratic Elitism*.
63 Michels, *Political Parties*, pp 365ff.
64 Quoted in Feaver, *From Status to Contract*, p. 227.
65 Schumpeter, *Capitalism, Socialism and Democracy*.
66 Gerth and Mills, eds, *From Max Weber*, p. 42.
67 Writers in this school include David Truman, Robert Dahl, Nelson Polsby. There is a vast literature on the subject, some of which I attempted to summarise in chapter 3 of *Three Varieties of Pluralism*.
68 For example; Pateman, *Participation in Democratic Theory*; Verba and Nie, *Participation in America*; Cook and Morgan, eds, *Participatory Democracy*; Pennock and Chapman, *Participation in Politics*; Benello and Roussopoulos, eds, *The Case for Participatory Democracy*.
69 S. E. Finer, 'Groups and Political Participation', in Parry, ed., *Participation in Politics*, p. 59.
70 Crosland, *A Social Democratic Britain*, pp. 12ff.
71 Figgis, *Churches in the Modern State*, p. 150. See also Nicholls, *The Pluralist State*.
72 Blumberg, *Industrial Democracy*, p. 123. See also the writings of G. D. H. Cole and the guild socialists. There is a useful account of their ideas in Glass, *The Responsible Society*. For a recent application of these ideas, see Hirst, *Associative Democracy*.
73 This section is based on David Nicholls, 'Trinity and Conflict', *Theology*, no. 769, Jan. /Feb. 1993, pp. 19ff.
74 Nicholls, *Deity and Domination*, chapter 5.
75 Eric Peterson, 'Monotheismus als politisches Problem' (1935) (*Theologische Traktate*, pp. 48ff.).
76 For example, Moltmann, *The Crucified God*, pp. 328ff.
77 Boff, *Trinity and Society*, p. 22.
78 Acton, *Essays on Freedom and Power*, p. 101.

79 Boff, *Trinity and Society*, pp. 119 and 130.
80 For a development of these themes, see Nicholls, *The Pluralist State*.
81 Saint Basil of Caesarea, *Letters*, 38:4. quoted in Gunton, *The Promise*, p. 96.
82 Typical would be Gunton, *The Promise*; Moltmann, *The Trinity and the Kingdom of God*; Thomas Parker, 'The Political Meaning of the Doctrine of the Trinity', *Reformed World*, 35, 1978, pp. 126ff.; Gerd Decke, 'Trinity Church and Community', *Lutheran World*, 23, 1976, pp. 48ff.; D. L. Migliore, 'The Trinity and Human Liberty' *Theology Today*, 36, 1980, pp. 497ff.; J. Vives, 'El Dios trinitario y la comunión humana', *Estudios eclesiasticos*, 52, no. 200, 1977, pp. 129ff.
83 Aristotle, *Politics*, II, 13 (p.51).
84 I have criticised Frantz Fanon in this respect in Nicholls, *From Dessalines to Duvalier*, pp. 249ff.
85 John Donne, Paradoxes, no. ix (*Paradoxes and Problems*, p. 21).
86 Church of England Doctrine Commission, *We Believe in God*, pp 82–3.
87 The latest person caught peddling this nonsense is Elliott, *Is there a Liberation Theology for the UK?*, p. 4. The author goes on to say that 'liberation theology is about exactly that'. Is he advocating a similar policy in Britain? Whether the Crown's prerogative of pardon can be justified in the modern world is debatable, but it should surely not be used arbitrarily.
88 Bernard Häring, *The Beatitudes: their Personal and Social Implications*, p. 49. Curiously Häring says little about mercy and forgiveness in his *magnum opus*, *The Law of Christ*.
89 *The Sermons of John Donne*, V, p. 379. See Nicholls, 'The Political Theology of John Donne', pp. 45ff.
90 Moltmann, *The Trinity and the Kingdom of God*, p. 81, but cf. ibid., p. 135.
91 Patripassianism is the belief that God the Father suffers. It was generally asserted in the early church that only the Son suffers, and then only in respect of his human nature. Any further suffering in the godhead was thought to endanger the self-sufficiency of God.
92 Brown, *The Divine Trinity*, p. 295. The significance of 'at most' is not clear.
93 Ibid., p. 298.
94 In Aramaic and Hebrew the noun for 'spirit' is feminine.
95 Henri Bergson, 'Le bon sens et les études classiques' (1895) (*Ecrits et paroles*, I. p. 88). For an illuminating discussion of the role of practical judgment in politics, see Beiner, *Political Judgment*.
96 Rorty, *Philosophy and the Mirror of Nature*, p. 377.
97 See David Nicholls 'Deity and Domination', *New Blackfriars*, no. 775, Jan. 1985, pp. 26ff.

BIBLIOGRAPHY

Abbott, W. M., ed., *The Documents of Vatican II*, New York, 1966
Ackerman, Bruce, *We the People*, Cambridge, Mass., 1993
Acton, J. E. E. D., Lord, *Essays on Freedom and Power*, Boston, Mass., 1956
—— *Selections from the Correspondence of the First Lord Acton*, ed. J. N. Figgis and R. V. Laurence, London, 1917
Adams, John, *The Adams–Jefferson Letters*, ed. L. J. Cappon, Chapel Hill, NC, 1959
—— *The Letters of John Adams*, ed. C. F. Adams, Boston, Mass., 1841
—— *The Works of John Adams*, ed. C. F. Adams, Boston, Mass., 1851–65
Addison, Joseph, *Addison: Selections from Addison's Papers contributed to the Spectator*, ed. Thomas Arnold, London, 1875
Ahlstrom, S., *A Religious History of the American People*, New Haven, Conn., 1972
Aldridge, A. O., *Benjamin Franklin and Nature's God*, Durham, NC, 1967
Aristotle, *Politics*, ed. E. Barker, Oxford, 1946
Arnold, Matthew, *Last Essays on Church and Religion*, London, 1903
Aulén, G., *Christus Victor*, London, 1931
Babbitt, I., *Rousseau and Romanticism*, Boston, Mass., 1919
Bachrach, Peter, *The Theory of Democratic Elitism*, New York, 1967
Bailyn, Bernard, *The Ideological Origins of the American Revolution*, Cambridge, Mass., 1967
Barber, W. H., *Leibniz in France, from Arnaud to Voltaire*, Oxford, 1955
Barker, Ernest, *Essays on Government*, Oxford, 1945
Barrow, Isaac, *The Theological Works of Isaac Barrow*, Cambridge, 1859
Bartlett, Thomas, *Memoires of Bishop Butler*, London, 1839
Baruzi, Jean, *Leibniz et l'organisation religieuse de la terre*, Paris, 1907
Bastable, James, ed., *Newman and Gladstone: Centennial Essays*, Dublin, 1978
Bax, Mart, and Koster, A. eds, *Power and Prayer: Religious and Political Processes in Past and Present*, Amsterdam, 1993
Beecher, Lyman, *The Autobiography of Lyman Beecher*, ed. B. M. Gross, Cambridge, Mass., 1961
Beiner, Ronald, *Political Judgment*, London, 1983
Bellah, Robert, *The Broken Covenant*, Chicago, Ill. 1992
Benello, C. G., and Roussopoulos, D., eds, *The Case for Participatory Democracy*, New York, 1971
Bentley, Richard, *The Works of Richard Bentley*, ed. A. Dyce, London, 1838
Bergson, Henri, *Ecrits et paroles*, Paris, 1957
Bernstein, Richard J., *Beyond Objectivism and Relativism*, Oxford, 1983
Berthe L. N. and de Langre, M., *Maximilien Robespierre: Les Droits et l'état des bâtards; et Lazare Carnot, Le pouvoir de l'habitude*, Arras, 1971

Billaud-Varenne, J. *Le Dernier Coup porté aux préjugés et à la superstition*, London, 1789
Blaug, Marc, *Economic Theory in Retrospect*, London, 1968
Blount, Charles, *King William and Queen Mary Conquerors*, London, 1693
—— *The Miscellaneous Works of Charles Blount*, London, 1695
Blumberg, P., *Industrial Democracy*, New York, 1969
Boff, L., *Trinity and Society*, London, 1988
Boissevain, Jeremy, *Friends of Friends*, Oxford, 1974
Bolingbroke, Henry St John, Viscount, *A Letter to Sir William Windham, II: Some Reflections on the Present State of the Nation; III: A Letter to Mr Pope*, London, 1753
—— *Letters on the Spirit of Patriotism: On the Idea of a Patriot King; and On the State of the Parties at the Accession of King George the First*, London, 1749
—— *The Works of Lord Bolingbroke*, London, 1844
Boswell, James, *Boswell on the Grand Tour: Italy, Corsica and France, 1765–1766*, New York, 1955
—— *Boswell's Life of Johnson*, ed. G. B. Hill, Oxford, 1887
Boyle, Robert, *Robert Boyle on Natural Philosophy*, ed. M. B. Hall, Indianapolis, Ind., 1965
Bradley, F. H., *Collected Essays*, Oxford, 1935
Braudel, Fernand, *Civilization and Capitalism, 15th–18th Century, III: The Perspective of the World*, London, 1984
Brissot, J. P., *De la vérité*, Neuchatel, 1782
Broad, C. D., *Five Types of Ethical Theory*, London, 1930
Brock, Charles, *Mosaics of the American Dream: America as New Israel*, Wheatley (Oxford), 1994
Brock, Sebastian, *The Holy Spirit in the Syriac Baptismal Tradition*, Poona, 1979
Brown, David, *The Divine Trinity*, London, 1985
Brown, Peter, *The Cult of the Saints: Its Rise and Function in Latin Christianity*, Chicago, Ill., 1981
—— *The World of Late Antiquity*, London, 1971
Brown, Stewart J., *Thomas Chalmers and the Godly Commonwealth*, Oxford, 1982
Buckley, Michael J., *At the Origin of Modern Atheism*, New Haven, Conn., 1987
Butler, Joseph, *The Analogy of Religion, Natural and Revealed, to the Constitution and Course of Nature*, Dublin, 1736
—— *The Works of the Right Reverend Father in God Joseph Butler, D. C. L., Late Lord Bishop of Durham*, Oxford, 1874
Byrne, P., *Natural Religion and the Religion of Nature*, London, 1989
Cady, Edwin H., ed., *Literature of the Early Republic*, New York, 1950
Calamy, Edmund, *A Defence of Moderate Nonconformity*, London, 1704
Campbell, R. H., and Skinner, A. S., *Adam Smith*, London, 1982
Camus, Albert, *The Rebel*, trans. Anthony Bower, Harmondsworth, 1971
Carswell, J., *From Revolution to Revolution: England 1688–1776*, London, 1973
Cassirer, Ernst, *The Question of Jean-Jacques Rousseau*, New York, 1954
—— *Rousseau, Kant and Goethe*, Princeton, NJ, 1945
Chadwick, Owen, *From Bossuet to Newman: The Idea of Doctrinal Development*, Cambridge, 1957
Chalmers, T. , *Enquiry into the Extent and Stability of Natural Resources*, Edinburgh, 1808
—— *The Collected Works of Thomas Chalmers*, Glasgow, 1835–42
—— *The Posthumous Works of Thomas Chalmers*, Edinburgh and London, 1849
Cherry, Conrad, ed., *God's New Israel: Religious Interpretations of America's Destiny*, Englewood Cliffs, NJ, 1971
Chillingworth, W., *The Religion of Protestants: A Safe Way to Salvation* (1638), London, 1870

Chubb, Thomas, *A Discourse on Miracles*, London, 1741
—— *A Short Dissertation on Providence*, London, 1738
Church of England Doctrine Commission, *We Believe in God*, London, 1987
Clark, J. C. D., *English Society, 1688–1832*, Cambridge, 1985
Clark, Ronald W., *Benjamin Franklin: A Biography*, London, 1983
Clarke, Samuel, *A Demonstration of the Being and Attributes of God*, London, 1711–28
—— *A Discourse Concerning the Unalterable Obligation of Natural Religion*, London, 1724
—— *The Works of Samuel Clarke DD*, London, 1738
Cobban, A., *Rousseau and the Modern State*, London, 1964
Colbourne, H. T., *The Lamp of Experience*, Chapel Hill, NC, 1965
Coleridge, S. T., *Essay on the Constitution of Church and State*, London, 1839
—— *Lay Sermons*, London, 1852
Cook, T. E., and Morgan, P. M., eds, *Participatory Democracy*, San Francisco, Calif., 1971
Cooper, Anthony Ashley, 3rd Earl of Shaftesbury, *Characteristicks of Men, Manners, Opinions, Times*, London, 1711
Copleston, Edward, *A Letter to the Rt Hon Robert Peel*, Oxford, 1819
—— *A Second Letter to the Rt Hon Robert Peel*, Oxford, 1819
Corwin, *Corwin on the Constitution*, ed. Richard Loss, Ithaca, NY, 1981
Costin, W. C. and Watson, J. S., *Law and the Working of the Constitution*, London, 1952
Crosland, C. A. R., *A Social Democratic Britain*, London, 1970
Cunliffe, Christopher, ed., *Joseph Butler's Moral and Religious Thought*, Oxford, 1992
Cust, R. P., *The Forced Loan and English Politics, 1626–1628*, Oxford, 1987
D'Alembert, J. le R., *Preliminary Discourse to the Encyclopedia of Diderot*, Indianapolis, Ind., 1963
Darwin, Charles, *The Life and Letters of Charles Darwin*, ed. Francis Darwin, London, 1887
Daubeny, Charles, *Vindiciae ecclesiae Anglicanae*, London, 1803
Davies, R. G. and Denton, J. H., eds, *The English Parliament in the Middle Ages*, Manchester, 1981
Dawkins, Richard, *The Blind Watchmaker*, London, 1988
Defoe, Daniel, *The True-born Englishman*, London, 1701
de Jong, P. Y., *The Covenant Idea in New England Theology, 1620–1847*, Grand Rapids, Mich., 1945
Derathé, R., *Le Rationalisme de Jean-Jacques Rousseau*, Paris, 1948
—— *Rousseau et la science politique de son temps*, Paris 1950
Desaguliers, J. T., *The Newtonian System of the World, the Best Model of Government*, London, 1728
Dickinson, H. T., *Bolingbroke*, London, 1970
Digges, Dudley, *The Unlawfulnesse of Subjects Taking up Arms against their Sovereigne, in what Case soever*, Oxford, 1643
Dijksterhuis, E. J., *The Mechanization of the World Picture*, Oxford, 1961
Donne, John, *Paradoxes and Problems*, Oxford, 1980
—— *The Sermons of John Donne*, ed. G. R. Potter and E. M. Simpson, Berkeley, Calif, 1953–62
Downey, James, *The Eighteenth Century Pulpit*, Oxford, 1969
Duguit, L., *Rousseau, Kant and Hegel*, Paris, 1918
Dummer, J., *A Defence of the New England Charters*, London, 1721
Duncan-Jones, Austin, *Butler's Moral Philosophy*, Harmondsworth, 1952
Dwight, Timothy, *A Discourse on Some Events of the Last Century*, New Haven, Conn., 1801
—— *The Nature and Danger of Infidel Philosophy*, New Haven, Conn., 1798

Edwards, Jonathan, *The Works of President Edwards*, New York, 1879

Elliott, Charles, *Is there a Liberation Theology for the UK?*, York, 1985

Elster, Jon, *Leibniz et la formation de l'esprit capitaliste*, Paris, 1975

Eltis, Walter, *The Classical Theory of Economic Growth*, London, 1984

Emden, C. S., *The People and the Constitution*, Oxford, 1956

Everett, W. J., *God's Federal Republic: Reconstructing our Governing Symbol*, New York, 1988

Farrand, Max, ed., *Records of the Federal Convention of 1787*, New Haven, Conn., 1966

Fay, Bernard, *The Revolutionary Spirit in France and America*, New York, 1927

Feaver, G., *From Status to Contract: A Biography of Sir Henry Maine*, London, 1969

Feuerbach, Ludwig, *Werke*, Stuttgart, 1903–10

Figgis, J. N., *Churches in the Modern State*, London, 1913

—— *Studies of Political Thought from Gerson to Grotius, 1414–1625*, Cambridge, 1916

Filmer, R., *Patriarcha: or, the Natural Powers of the Kings of England Asserted*, Oxford, 1949

Fontenelle, B. de, *Oeuvres*, Amsterdam, 1764

Foote, Henry W., *The Religion of Thomas Jefferson*, Boston, Mass., 1960

Ford, Worthington C., et al., eds, *Journals of the Continental Congress*, Washington DC, 1904

Fordyce, David, *Dialogues concerning Education*, Cork, 1755

Foster, Elizabeth R., ed., *Proceedings in Parliament: 1610*, New Haven, Conn., 1966

Frankel, Charles, *The Faith of Reason*, New York, 1948

Frankfort, Henri, *Kingship and the Gods*, Chicago, Ill., 1948

Frankfurt, Harry G., ed., *Leibniz: a Collection of Critical Essays*, Notre Dame, Ind., 1976

Franklin, Benjamin, *The Autobiography of Benjamin Franklin*, ed. L. W. Labaree *et al.*, New Haven, Conn, 1964

—— *The Papers of Benjamin Franklin*, ed. L. W. Labaree and W. J. Bell, New Haven, Conn., 1959

Franklin, W. T. ed., *Memoires of the Life and Writings of Benjamin Franklin*, Boston, Mass., 1892

Gay, Peter, *Voltaire's Politics: the Poet as Realist*, New Haven, Conn., 1988

Gellner, Ernest, *Legitimation of Belief*, Cambridge, 1974

Gerth, H. H. and Mills, C. Wright, eds, *From Max Weber*, London, 1948

Gladstone, W. E., *Correspondence on Church and Religion of W. E. Gladstone*, ed. D. C. Lathbury, London, 1910

Glass, S. T., *The Responsible Society: The Ideas of Guild Socialism*, London, 1966

Goldsmith, M. M., *Private Vices: Public Benefits*, Cambridge, 1985

Goldsmith, Oliver, *The Deserted Village*, London, 1921

Gough, J. W., *Fundamental Law in English Constitutional History*, Oxford, 1955

Grave, S. A., *Conscience in Newman's Though*, Oxford, 1989

Gray, John, *et al*, *The Moral Foundations of Market Institutions*, London, 1992

Green, David G., *Reinventing Civil Society*, London, 1993

Grimsley, Ronald, *Rousseau and the Religious Quest*, Oxford, 1968

Grua, Gaston, *Jurisprudence universelle et théodicée selon Leibniz*, Paris, 1953

Guillemin, Henri, *Robespierre: Politique et mystique*, Paris: 1987

Gunton, Colin, *The Promise of Trinitarian Theology*, Edinburgh, 1991

Hamilton, Alexander,*The Papers of Alexander Hamilton*, ed. H. C. Syrett, New York, 1961–

Hamilton, Alexander, Madison, J., and Jay, J., *The Federalist*, Oxford, 1948

Hampson, Norman, *The Life and Opinions of Maximilien Robespierre*, Oxford, 1988

—— *Will and Circumstance: Montesquieu, Rousseau and the French Revolution*, London, 1983

Handlin, O. and M. eds, *The Popular Sources of Political Authority*, Cambridge, Mass., 1966

Haraszti, Z., *John Adams and the Prophets of Progress*, Cambridge, Mass., 1952

Häring, Bernard, *The Beatitudes: Their Personal and Social Implications*, Slough, 1976

—— *The Law of Christ*, Cork, 1963

Hauerwas, Stanley, *Character and the Christian Life*, San Antonio, 1975

—— *A Community of Character*, Notre Dame, Ind., 1981

Heelas, Paul, and Morris, Paul, eds, *The Values of the Enterprise Culture*, London, 1991

Hegel, G. W. F., *Briefe von und an Hegel*, ed. J. Hoffmeister, Hamburg, 1952–60

—— *Hegel's Political Writings*, trans. T. M. Knox, Oxford, 1964

Heiler, Friedrich, *Prayer: A Study in the History and Psychology of Religion*, London, 1932

Heimert, A., and Miller, Perry, eds, *The Great Awakening: Documents illustrating the Crisis and its Consequences*, Indianapolis, Ind., 1967

Hendel, Charles W., *Jean-Jacques Rousseau Moralist*, London, 1934

Herberg, Will, *Protestant, Catholic, Jew*, New York, 1955

Hilton, Boyd, *The Age of Atonement: The Influence of Evangelicalism on Social and Economic Thought, 1785–1865*, Oxford, 1988

Hirst, Paul Q., *Associative Democracy: New Forms of Economic and Social Governance*, Cambridge, 1994

Hoadly, Benjamin, *Several Tracts*, London, 1715

—— *The Works of Benjamin Hoadly*, ed. John Hoadly, London, 1773

Hobbes, Thomas, *Leviathan: or, the Matter Forme and Power of a Commonwealth Ecclesiastical and Civil*, Oxford, 1946

Hodgson, Leonard, *The Doctrine of the Trinity*, London, 1943

Hole, Robert, *Pulpits, Politics and Public Order in England, 1760–1832*, Cambridge, 1989

Hont, I. and Ignatieff, M., eds, *Wealth and Virtue*, Cambridge, 1983

Hubbard, William, *The Happiness of a People*, Boston, Mass., 1676

Hughes, H. Stuart, *Consciousness and Society*, London, 1967

Hume, David, *Essays*, London, n.d.

Hyneman, Charles S., and Lutz, D. S., eds, *American Political Writing during the Founding Era, 1760–1805*, Indianapolis, Ind., 1983

Jacob, Margaret C., *The Newtonians and the English Revolution, 1689–1720*, Hassocks, 1976

—— *The Radical Enlightenment: Pantheists, Freemasons and Republicans*, London, 1981

James I, *The Workes of the Most High and Mightie Prince James &c.* , London, 1616

James, D. G., *The Life of Reason: Hobbes, Locke, Bolingbroke*, London, 1949

James, Patricia, *Population Malthus: His Life and Times*, London, 1979

James, William, *Varieties of Religious Experience*, London, 1904

Jaurès, Jean, *Histoire socialiste de la révolution française*, Paris, 1922–4

Jefferson, Thomas, *The Basic Writings of Thomas Jefferson*, ed. P. Foner, Garden City, NY, 1950

—— *Thomas Jefferson on Democracy*, ed. Saul K. Padover, New York, 1967

—— *The Writings of Thomas Jefferson*, Washington DC, 1903–4

Kantorowicz, Ernst H., *Selected Studies*, Locust Valley, NY, 1965

Kepel, Gilles, *The Revenge of God*, Cambridge, 1994

Keynes, J. M., *Essays in Biography*, London, 1951

King, Peter, Lord, *The Life and Letters of John Locke*, London, 1864

Klein, Milton M., ed., *The Independent Reflector*, Cambridge, Mass., 1963

Kleinschmidt, Beda, *Antonius von Padua*, Düsseldorf, 1931

Kliger, S. L., *The Goths in England*, Cambridge, Mass., 1952

Knight, W., *Lord Monboddo and Some of his Contemporaries*, London, 1900

Koch, Adrienne, *The Philosophy of Thomas Jefferson*, New York, 1943

Koch, G. Adolf, *Republican Religion: the American Revolution and the Cult of Reason*, New York, 1964

Koyré, Alexandre, *From Closed World to Infinite Universe*, Baltimore, Md, 1968

Kuklick, Bruce, *Churchmen and Philosophers: From Jonathan Edwards to John Dewey*, New Haven, Conn., 1985

Küng, Hans, *Structures of the Church*, New York, 1964

Laboucheix, H., *Richard Price*, Paris, 1970

Le Clerc, Jean, *The Lives of the Primitive Fathers*, London, 1701

Le Mercier de la Rivière, P-. F-. J-. H., *L'ordre naturel et essential des sociétés politiques*, London and Paris, 1767

Lefebvre, Georges, *Etudes sur la révolution française*, Paris, 1954

Leech, K., ed., *Christianity Reinterpreted*? London, 1982

Leibniz, G. W., *The Leibniz – Clarke Correspondence*, ed. H. G. Alexander, Manchester, 1956

—— *Lettres et fragments inédits*, ed. Paul Schrecker, Paris, 1934

—— *Oeuvres de Leibniz*, ed. A. Foucher de Careil, Paris, 1859–75

—— *Philosophical Papers and Letters*, ed. L. Loemker, Dordrecht, 1976

—— *Die philosophischen Schriften von G. W. Leibniz*, ed. C. I. Gerhardt, Hildesheim, 1875–90

—— *The Political Writings of Leibniz* , ed. Patrick Riley, Cambridge, 1972

—— *A System of Theology*, London, 1850

—— *Textes inédits*, ed. G. Grua, Paris, 1948

—— *Die Werke von Leibniz*, ed. O. Klopp, Hanover, 1864–84

Lemay, J. A. Leo, ed., *Deism, Masonry, and the Enlightenment*, Newark, NJ, 1987

Levinson, Sanford, *Constitutional Faith*, Princeton, NJ, 1988

Lincoln, Anthony, *Some Political and Social Ideas of English Dissent, 1763–1800*, Cambridge, 1938

Livingston, W., *Philosophic Solitude*, New York, 1747

Lucas, Colin, ed., *Rewriting the French Revolution*, Oxford, 1991

—— ed., *The Political Culture of the French Revolution*, Oxford, 1988

Mc Cleary, C. F., *The Malthusian Population Theory*, London, 1953

McCoy, Drew R., *The Last of the Fathers*, Cambridge, 1989

Mc Fague, S., *Metaphysical Theology*, London, 1982

—— *Models of God*, London, 1987

McIlwain, C. H., *The American Revolution: A Constitutional Interpretation*, New York, 1924

McKendrick, Neil, ed., *Historical Perspectives: Studies in English Thought and Society*, London, 1974

McLachlan, H., *Sir Isaac Newton: Theological Manuscripts*, Liverpool, 1950

McLoughlin, W. G., *Isaac Backus and the American Pietistic Tradition*, Boston, Mass., 1967

McManners, John, *The French Revolution and the Church*, London, 1969

McTaggart, J. M. E., *The Nature of Existence*, Cambridge, 1921

Madison, James, *The Papers of James Madison*, ed. W. T. Hutchinson *et al.*, Chicago and Charlottesville, 1962

Malone, Dumas, *Jefferson the Virginian*, London, 1948

Malthus, Thomas Robert, *Additions to the Fourth and Former Editions of An Essay on the Principles of Population etc. etc.*, London, 1817

—— *An Essay on the Principle of Population, as it Affects the Future Improvement of Society, with Remarks on the Speculations of Mr. Godwin, M. Condorcet and Other Writers* (1798), ed. Anthony Flew, Harmondsworth, 1982

—— *An Essay on the Principle of Population* (3rd edn), London, 1806

—— *Principles of Political Economy*, London, 1836
Mandeville, Bernard, *An Enquiry into the Origin of Honour*, London, 1732
—— *The Fable of the Bees: or, Private Vices, Public Benefits* (2nd edn), London, 1723
Manuel, Frank, *A Portrait of Isaac Newton*, Cambridge, Mass., 1968
—— *The Religion of Isaac Newton*, Oxford, 1974
Markham, Ian S., *Plurality and Christian Ethics*, Cambridge, 1994
Martin, David, *A Sociology of English Religion*, London, 1967
Marx, Karl and Engels, F., *Collected Works*, Moscow and London, 1975–
Masson, P-. M., *La Formation religieuse de Rousseau*, Paris, 1916
—— *La Religion de Jean-Jacques Rousseau*, Paris, 1916
May, Henry F., *The Enlightenment in America*, New York, 1976
May, Thomas Erskine, *The Constitutional History of England*, London, 1912
Meek, Ronald L., ed, *Marx and Engels on Malthus*, London, 1953
Metz, J. B., and Schillebeeckx, E., *God as Father?*, New York, 1981
Michelet, Jules, *Histoire de la révolution française*, Paris, 1879
Michels, Robert, *Political Parties*, Glencoe, Ill., 1949
Mill, J. S., *An Examination of Sir William Hamilton's Philosophy*, London, 1889
Miller, H. K., et al, eds, *The Augustan Milieu*, Oxford, 1970
Miller, Perry, *Errand into the Wilderness*, Cambridge, Mass., 1956
—— *The New England Mind: From Colony to Province*, Cambridge, Mass., 1953
—— *The New England Mind: The Seventeenth Century*, Cambridge, Mass., 1939
Moltmann, Jürgen, *The Crucified God*, London, 1974
—— *The Trinity and the Kingdom of God*, London, 1981
Montgomery, G. R., ed., *Leibniz*, La Salle, Ill., 1957
Morais, Herbert M., *Deism in Eighteenth Century America*, New York, 1934
Morgan, Edmund S., *Inventing the People*, New York, 1988
Morgan, R., ed., *The Religion of the Incarnation*, Bristol, 1989
Mossner, E. C., *Bishop Butler and the Age of Reason*, New York, 1936
Neuhaus, Richard J., *The Naked Public Square*, Grand Rapids, Mich., 1986
New Whole Duty of Man, The, London, 1747
Newman, J,H., *Discourses Addressed to Mixed Congregations*, London, 1871
—— *Fifteen Sermons Preached before the University of Oxford*, London, 1909
—— *Grammar of Assent*, London, 1870
—— *Parochial Sermons*, New York, 1843
—— *Sermons Preached on Various Occasions*, London. 1891
—— *The Via Media of the Anglican Church*, London, 1899
Newsome, David, *Two Classes of Men*, London, 1974
Newton, Isaac, *Opera quae extant omnia*, London, 1792
—— *Opticks* (2nd edn), London, 1718
Nicholls, David, *Deity and Domination: Images of God and the State in the Nineteenth and Twentieth Centuries*, London, 1989
—— *From Dessalines to Duvalier: Race, Colour and National Independence in Haiti*, Cambridge, 1979
—— *The Pluralist State: The Political Thought of J. N. Figgis and his Contemporaries*, London, 1994
—— *Three Varieties of Pluralism*, London, 1974
Nicholls, David, and Kerr, Fergus, eds, *John Henry Newman: Reason, Rhetoric and Romanticism*, Bristol, 1991
Norman, E. R., *Christianity and the World Order*, Oxford, 1979
—— *Church and Society in England, 1770–1970*, Oxford, 1976
Notestein, Wallace, *et al.*, eds, *Commons Debates: 1621*, New Haven, Conn., 1935
Nye, Stephen, *A Discourse Concerning Natural and Revealed Religion*, London, 1696
O'Gorman, Frank, *Voters, Patrons, and Parties*, Oxford, 1989

O'Higgins, J., *Anthony Collins: The Man and his Works*, The Hague, 1970

Ozouf, Mona, *Festivals and the French Revolution*, Cambridge, Mass., 1988

Paine, Thomas, *Representative Selections*, ed. H. H. Clark, New York 1961

Paley, William, *The Works of William Paley*, ed. Robert Lynam, London, 1825

Parker, H. T., *The Cult of Antiquity and the French Revolutionaries*, Chicago, Ill., 1937

Parry, G., ed., *Participation in Politics*, Manchester, 1972

Pateman, Carole, *Participation in Democratic Theory*, Cambridge, 1970

Pennock, J. R. and Chapman, J. W., eds, *Participation in Politics*, ('Nomos', No. 16), New York, 1975

—— *Constitutionalism* ('Nomos' No. 30), New York, 1979

Petersen, William, *Malthus*, London, 1979

Peterson, E., *Theologische Traktate*, Munich, 1951

Peterson, Merrill D., *Thomas Jefferson and the New Nation*, New York, 1970

Pickering, W. S. F., *Durkheim on Religion*, London, 1975

Plongeron, E., *Théologie et politique au siècle des lumières*, Geneva, 1973

Plumb, J. H., *The Growth of Political Stability in England, 1675–1725*, London, 1967

Pocock, J. G. A., *The Ancient Constitution and the Feudal Law*, Cambridge, 1957

—— *The Machiavellian Moment*, Princeton, NJ, 1975

Pole, J. R., *The Gift of Government*, Athens, Ga, 1983

—— *The Pursuit of Equality in American History*, Berkeley, Calif., 1978

Polkinghorne, John, *Science and Providence: God's Interaction with the World*, London, 1989

Pomeau, René, *La Religion de Voltaire*, Paris, 1969

Pope, Alexander, *Poetical Works*, ed. Herbert Davis, Oxford, 1964

Popper, Karl R., *Objective Knowledge: An Evolutionary Approach*, Oxford, 1972

—— *The Open Society and its Enemies*, London, 1957

Porter, Roy, *English Society in the Eighteenth Century*, Harmondsworth, 1982

Price, Richard, *A Discourse on the Love of our Country*, London, 1789

—— *Political Writings*, ed. D. O. Thomas, Cambridge, 1991

—— *A Review of the Principal Questions in Morals*, ed. D. D. Raphael, Oxford, 1948

—— *Sermons on the Christian Doctrine as Received by the Different Denominations of Christians*, London, 1787

Priestley, Joseph, *Discourses on Various Subjects*, Birmingham, 1787

—— *The Theological and Miscellaneous Works of Joseph Priestley*, ed. J. T. Rutt, London, 1817–31

Rae, John, *The Life of Adam Smith*, ed. J. Viner, New York, 1965

Ramsey, A. M., *The Gospel and the Catholic Church*, London, 1936

Raphael, D. D., *Adam Smith*, Oxford, 1985

Rashdall, Hastings, *The Idea of Atonement in Christian Theology*, London, 1920

Rauschenbusch, Walter, *Prayers of the Social Awakening*, London, 1927

Rawls, J., *Political Liberalism*, New York, 1993

—— *A Theory of Justice*, Oxford, 1973

Rawson, E., *The Spartan Tradition in European Thought*, Oxford, 1969

Rescher, Nicholas, *Pluralism: Against the Demand for Consensus*, Oxford, 1993

Ricardo, David, *The Works and Correspondence of David Ricardo*, ed. P. Sraffa, Cambridge, 1951–73

Ritschl, Albrecht, *The Christian Doctrine of Justification and Reconciliation: The Positive Development of the Doctrine*, Clifton, NJ, 1966

—— *Die christlicher Lehre von der Rechtfertigung und Versönung*, Bonn, 1870–4

—— *A Critical History of the Christian Doctrine of Justification and Reconciliation*, Edinburgh, 1872

Rivers, Isobel, *Reason, Grace and Sentiment*, Cambridge, 1991

Robbins, *The Eighteenth Century Commonwealthmen*, Cambridge, Mass., 1959

Robespierre, Maximilien, *Ecrits*, ed. Claude Mazaurie, Paris, 1989
—— *Oeuvres complètes de Maximilien Robespierre*, Paris, 1910–
Rorty, Richard, *Philosophy and the Mirror of Nature*, Princeton, NJ, 1979
Rothkrug, Lionel, *The Opposition to Louis XIV*, Princeton, NJ, 1965
Rousseau, J-. J., *Correspondance générale de Jean-Jacques Rousseau*, Paris, 1924–34
—— *Oeuvres complètes de Jean-Jacques Rousseau*, ed. Bernard Gagnetin and Marcel Raynaud, Paris, 1959–
—— *The Political Writings of Jean-Jacques Rousseau*, ed. C. E. Vaughan, Oxford: 1962
—— *Religious Writings*, ed. Ronald Grimsley, Oxford, 1970
—— *Rêveries du promeneur solitaire*, ed. H. Roddier, Paris, 1960
Russell, Colin, *Science and Social Change*, London, 1983
Sacheverell, Henry, *The Perils of False Brethren, both in Church and State*, London, 1709
Saint-Just, L. A. L. de, *Oeuvres complètes de Saint-Just*, edited by Charles Vellay, Paris, 1908
Sambrook, James, *The Eighteenth Century*, London, 1986
Sandford, Charles B., *The Religious Life of Thomas Jefferson*, Charlottesville, Va, 1984
Sandoz, Ellis, *A Government of Laws*, Baton Rouge, La, 1990
—— ed., *Political Sermons of the American Founding Era, 1730–1805*, Indianapolis, Ind., 1991
Schmitt, Carl, *Political Theology*, Cambridge, Mass., 1985
Schochet, G. J., *Patriarchalism in Political Thought*, Oxford, 1975
Schrecker, Paul, *Leibniz: Ses idées sur l'organisation des relations internationales*, London, 1937
Schumpeter, Joseph A., *Capitalism, Socialism and Democracy*, New York, 1942
Selsam, J. Paul, *The Pennsylvania Constitution of 1776*, Philadelphia, Pa, 1936
Shelton, G., *Dean Tucker: Eighteenth Century Economic and Political Thought*, London, 1981
Sherlock, William, *A Discourse Concerning the Divine Providence*, London, 1694
Shklar, Judith N., *Men and Citizens: A Study of Rousseau's Social Theory*, Cambridge, 1969
Sieyès, Emmanuel (l'abbé), *What is the Third Estate,?* London, 1963
Skinner, Andrew S., and Wilson,T., *Essays on Adam Smith*, Oxford, 1975
Skocpol, Theda, *States and Social Revolutions*, Cambridge, 1979
Smith, Adam, *An Enquiry into the Nature and Causes of the Wealth of Nations*, Oxford, 1979
—— *Essays on Philosophical Subjects*, Oxford, 1980
—— *Lectures on Jurisprudence*, Oxford, 1978
—— *The Theory of Moral Sentiments*, London, 1853
Smith, Goldwin, *Reminiscences*, London, 1910
Smith, James W., and Jamison, A. L., eds, *Religion in American Life, I:The Shaping of American Religion*, Princeton, NJ, 1961
Society for the Reformation of Principles, *The Scholar Armed Against the Errors of the Time*, London, 1812
Soloway, R. A., *Prelates and People*, London, 1969
Spitzer, Leo, *Classical and Christian Ideas of World Harmony*, Baltimore, Md, 1963
Stéfane-Pol, (Paul Coutant) *Autour de Robespierre: Le conventionnel La Bas*, Paris, 1901
Stephen, J. F., *Liberty Equality Fraternity*, London, 1874
Stephen, Leslie, *English Thought in the Eighteenth Century*, London, 1902
Stout, Harry S., *The New England Soul: Preaching and Religious Culture in Colonial New England*, New York and Oxford, 1986
Sumner, J. B., *A Series of Sermons on the Christian Faith and Character*, London, 1821
—— *A Treatise on the Records of the Creation and on the Moral Attributes of the Creator*, London, 1825

Swift, Jonathan, *Journal to Stella*, Oxford, 1963
—— *Political Tracts, 1713–1719*, Oxford, 1964
Symmons, Edward, *A Loyall Subjects Beliefe expressed in a Letter to Master Stephen Marshall*, Oxford, 1643
Synesius of Cyrene, *The Essays and Hymns of Synesius of Cyrene*, ed. Augustine Fitzgerald, London, 1930
Talmon, J. L., *The Origins of Totalitarian Democracy*, London, 1952
Taswell-Langmead, T. P., *English Constitutional History*, London, 1946
Tawney, R. H., *Religion and the Rise of Capitalism*, Harmondsworth, 1948
Thayer, H. S. ed., *Newton's Philosophy of Nature: Selections from his Writings*, New York, 1960
Thomas, D. O., *The Honest Mind*, Oxford, 1977
Thompson, J. M., *Robespierre*, Oxford, l988
Thomson, James, *Thomson's Poetical Works*, Edinburgh, 1861
Thornton, John W., ed., *The Pulpit of the American Revolution*, Boston, Mass., 1860
Tillotson, John, *The Works of the Most Reverend Dr John Tillotson*, Edinburgh, 1772
Tindal, Matthew, *Christianity as Old as the Creation*, London, 1730
—— *Four Discourses*, London, 1709
Tocqueville, Alexis de, *Journeys to England and Ireland*, London, 1958
—— *On the State of Society in France before the Revolution of 1789*, London, 1856,
Toland, John, *Anglia Libera: or, The Limitation and Succession of the Crown of England Explain'd and Asserted*, London, 1701
—— *The Art of Governing by Parties*, London, 1701
—— *Christianity not Mysterious*, London, 1696
—— *Letters to Serena*, London, 1704
—— *Pantheisticon*, London, 1751
Tucker, Josiah, *Instructions for Travellers*, privately printed, 1757
Verba, Sidney, and Nie, N. H., *Participation in America*, New York, 1972
Vereker, Charles, *Eighteenth Century Optimism*, Liverpool, 1967
Viner, Jacob, *The Long View and the Short: Studies in Economic Theory and Policy*, Glencoe, Ill, 1958
Voltaire (François-Marie Arouet), *Letters on England*, Harmondsworth, 1980
—— *Oeuvres complètes de Voltaire*, Paris, 1877–85
—— *Philosophical Dictionary*, New York, 1962
—— *Poèmes sur le désastre de Lisbonne*, Geneva, 1755
Wade, E. C. S., and Phillips, G. G., *Constitutional Law*, London, 1950
Wake, William, *A Sermon preached before the King*, London, 1715
Ward, W. G., *Essays on the Philosophy of Theism*, London, 1884
Wartofsky, Marx W., *Feuerbach*, Cambridge, 1977
Waterman, A. M. C., *Revolution, Economics and Religion: Christian Political Economy, 1798–1833*, Cambridge, 1991
Watt, H., *The Published Writings of Thomas Chalmers: A Descriptive List*, Edinburgh, 1943
Watts, Isaac, *Hymns and Spiritual Songs*, ed. Selma L. Bishop, London, 1962
—— *Reliquiae Juveniles*, London, 1734
—— *Works of the Reverend and Learned Isaac Watts*, London, 1810
Weber, Max, *The Sociology of Religion*, Boston, Mass., 1964
Weir, D. A., *The Origins of the Federal Theology in Sixteenth-Century Reformation Thought*, Oxford, 1990
Wesley, Charles, *Short Hymns on Select Passages of the Holy Scriptures*, Bristol, 1762
Westfall, R. S., *Never at Rest*, Cambridge, 1980
Weston, C. C. and Greenberg, J. R., *Subjects and Sovereigns*, Cambridge, 1981

Weyland, John, *Principles of Population and Production, as they are Affected by the Progress of Society*, London, 1816

Whately, Richard, *Introductory Lectures on Political Economy*, London, 1831

White, Morton, *The Philosophy of the American Revolution*, New York, 1978

Wills, Garry, *Explaining America: The Federalist*, Harmondsworth, 1981

Wilson, Bryan, *Religion in Secular Society*, London, 1966

—— *Religion in Sociological Perspective*, Oxford, 1982

Wilson, Woodrow, *Congressional Goverment*, New York, 1885

Winch, Donald, *Adam Smith's Politics*, Cambridge, 1978

Wolfe, Don M., *Leveller Manifestos of the Puritan Revolution*, New York, 1944

Wren, Brian, *What Language Shall I Borrow?*, New York, 1993

Yoder, J. H., *The Politics of Jesus*, Grand Rapids, Mich., 1972

INDEX